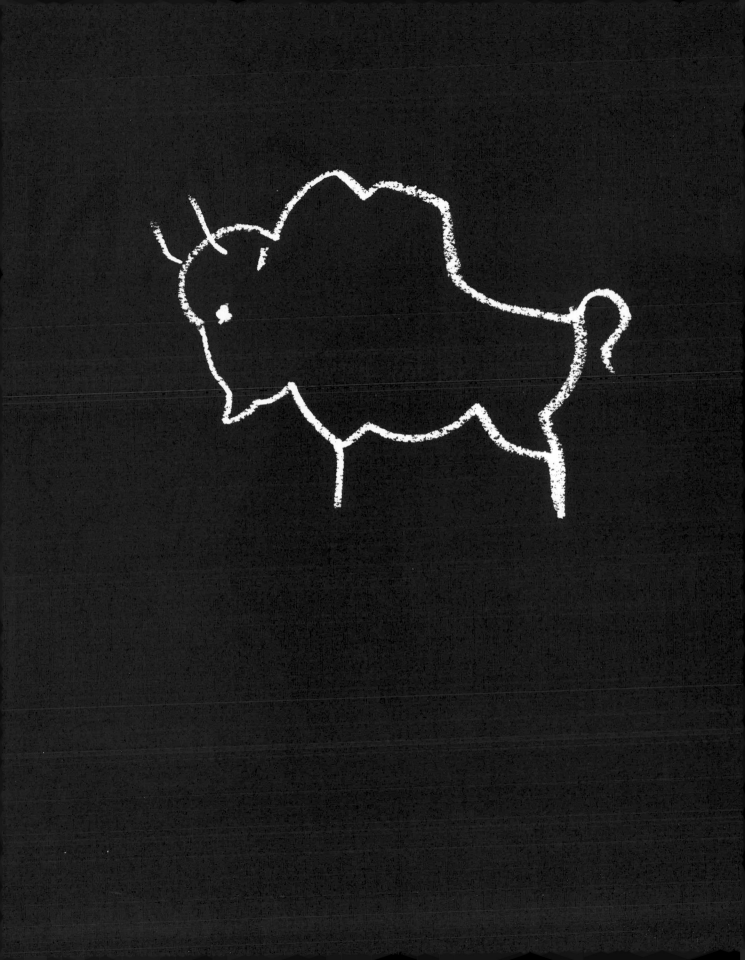

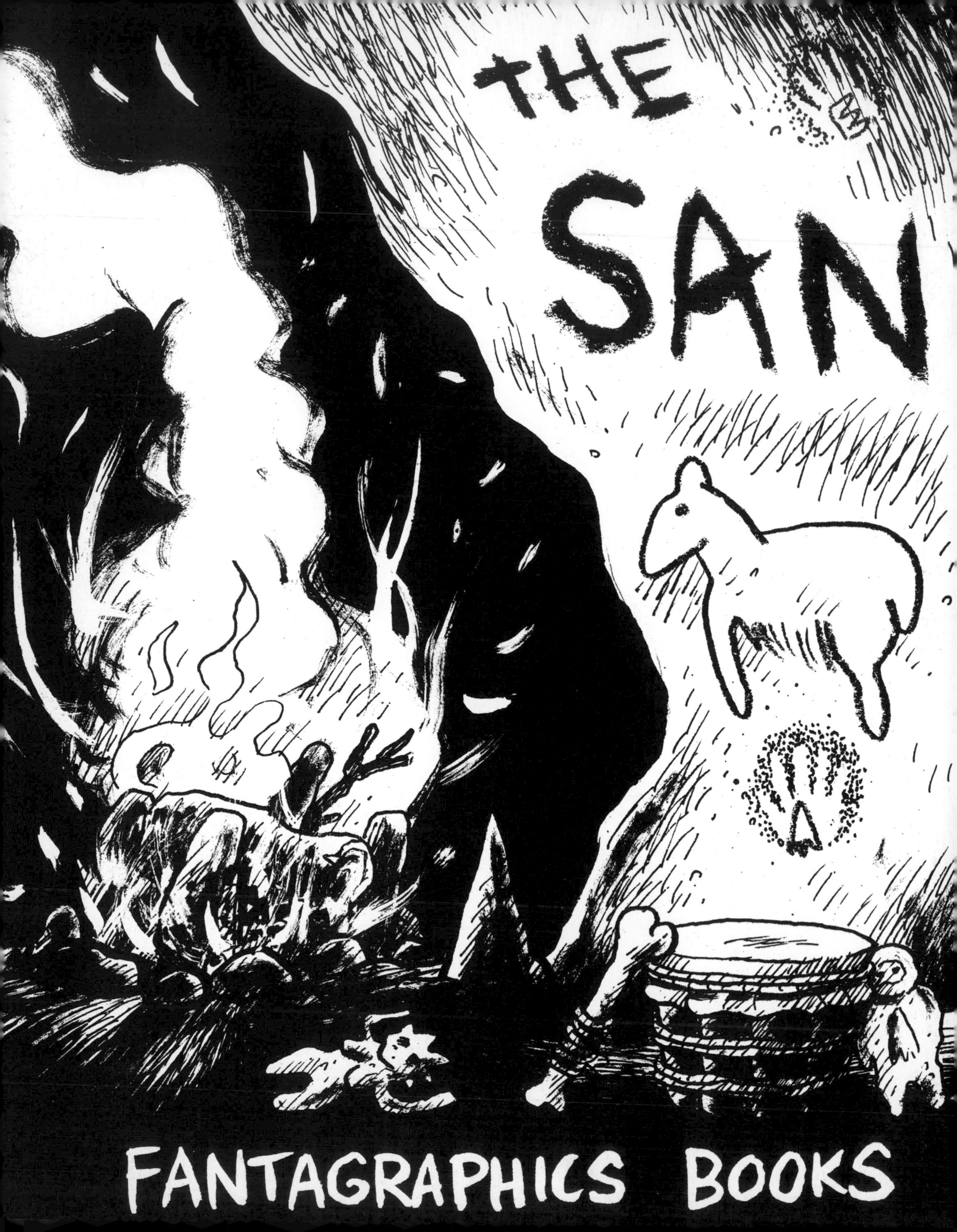
THE
SAN
FANTAGRAPHICS BOOKS

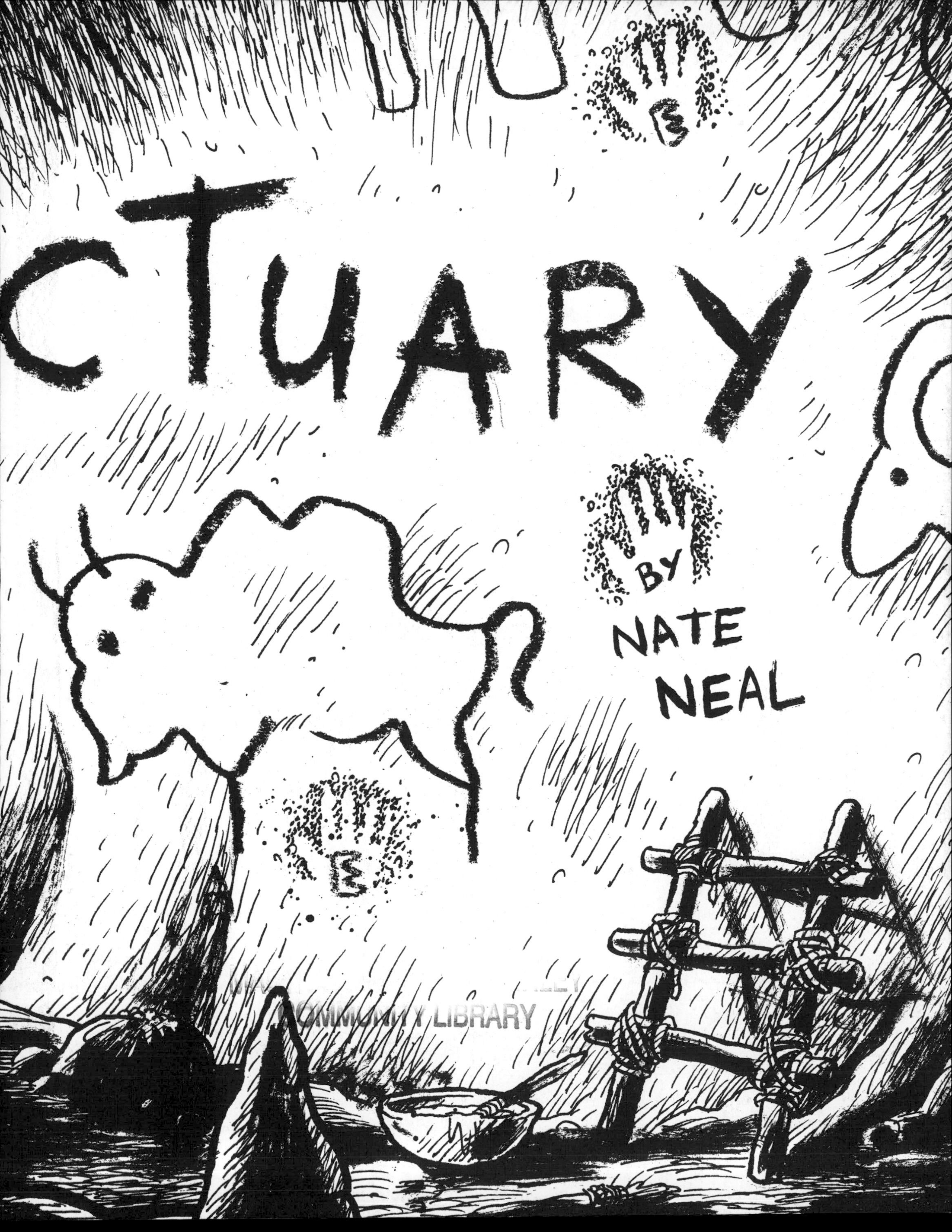
CTUARY
BY
NATE
NEAL

Fantagraphics Books
7563 Lake City Way NE
Seattle, Washington 98115

Publishers: Gary Groth and Kim Thompson
Editorial liaison: Gary Groth
Production: Paul Baresh
Associate Publisher: Eric Reynolds

To receive in the mail and have delivered to your home a free full-color paper
catalog of comics, graphic novels, prose novels, and other fine works of artistry,
call 1-800-657-1100; or visit our website at www.fantagraphics.com. You may
order books at our web site or by phone.

Distributed in the U.S. by W.W. Norton and Company, Inc. (212-354-5500)
Distributed in Canada by the Canadian Manda Group (416-516-0911)
Distributed in the United Kingdom by Turnaround Distribution (108-829-3009)

ISBN: 978-1-60699-388-0

First Fantagraphics printing: October, 2010

Printed in China

INTRODUCTION
BY DAVE SIM

I AM AN UNASHAMED AND UNAPOLOGETIC **CREATIONIST**.

NO, THAT DOESN'T MEAN THAT I BELIEVE THE EARTH IS 4,000 YEARS OLD AND WAS CREATED ON A TUESDAY. IT MEANS THAT I BELIEVE THE FIRST BOOK OF MOSHE— THE FIRST CHAPTER, WITH THE EXCEPTION OF A FEW "SATANIC VERSES" (14 TO 19, TO BE SPECIFIC)— CHRONICLES THE UNIVERSAL **FORM** WHICH CREATION TAKES EVERYWHERE IN THE UNIVERSE. I BELIEVE THE SECOND AND THIRD CHAPTERS DOCU-MENT THE RISE OF THE CURRENT EPOCH ON EARTH STARTED AMID THE RESIDUE OF THE PREVIOUS EPOCH WITH A DAM (HEBREW FOR "THE MAN") AND CHAUAH (LATER COR-RUPTED AS "EVE").

NOW, IF YOU ARE A TYPICAL READER OF BOOKS PUBLISHED BY FANTAGRAPHICS (NOT THAT THERE'S ANYTHING WRONG WITH THAT) YOU AREN'T GOING TO WANT TO HEAR OR READ THAT. BE OF GOOD CHEER, THAT WILL DO IT FOR THE BIBLE TALK.

IT IS PERTINENT BECAUSE THE EXCELLENT (A TERM I DON'T USE LIGHTLY) GRAPHIC NOVEL YOU ARE ABOUT TO READ ORIGINATES IN THE SAME IMPULSE AS MY COMMENTARIES ON THE FIRST BOOK OF MOSHE (ER— ENUN-CIATED BY CEREBUS IN VOLUME 15, **LATTER DAYS**, IF YOU ARE THAT RARE AVIS, AN OPEN-MINDED FANTAGRAPHICS READER). NATE NEAL STARTS WITH THE EVIDENCE AT HAND: THESE CAVE PAINTINGS EXIST. THEY TAKE A SPECIFIC FORM WHICH IS ALMOST ENDLESSLY REITERATED. AND THEN HE ASKS THE MOST PERTINENT QUESTION.

WHY?

AS ANYONE WITH A TWO-YEAR OLD CAN TELL YOU, THAT IS THE CORE QUESTION WHICH INFORMS HUMAN EXISTENCE. AS ANYONE WITH ANY EXPERIENCE WITH **HIGH THEOLOGY** OR **LARGE EXTRAPOLATIONS** ON EINSTEIN'S **THEORY OF RELATIVITY** CAN TELL YOU (BUT DON'T) THERE HAS BEEN MORE ENERGY AND TIME AND BRAIN POWER EXPENDED IN THE HISTORY OF CIVILIZATION THAN— I DARE SAY— IN ANY OTHER FORM OF HUMAN EXERTION IN AVOIDING WHAT IS MOST OFTEN THE ACCURATE THEOLOGICAL AND SCIENTIFIC ANSWER:

WE DON'T KNOW.

THE ACCURATE ANSWER IN VIRTUALLY ALL CASES IS NOT "WE HAVEN'T A **CLUE**" (YOU UNDERSTAND). **CLUES** WE HAVE IN PROFUSION AND ABUNDANCE. WE ARE, METAPHORICALLY, **LOUSY** WITH CLUES. AND "EXPERTS" BOTH IN THE FIELD OF THEOLOGY AND SCIENCE MAKE A VERY GOOD LIVING, AND HAVE FOR CENTURIES, FINDING EVER MORE NEW AND DIFFERENT AND COMPLEX WAYS OF AVOIDING SAYING "WE DON'T KNOW." BOTH ARE HIERARCHICAL SYSTEMS, HAVING MORE IN COMMON WITH PROFESSOR MARVEL PRETENDING TO BE OZ THE GREAT AND POWERFUL THAN THE RE-SPECTIVE BELIEF SYSTEMS CAN COMFORT-ABLY ALLOW.

SO, GIVEN THAT THE ANSWER IS "WE DON'T KNOW" IT MAKES SENSE TO APPLY IMAGI-NATION (A TRAIT UNIVERSALLY LACKING IN HIERARCHICAL SYSTEMS: ALL OF ONE'S TIME AND ENERGY BEING DEVOTED TO MAINTAIN-ING "PLACE"— FIRM GRIP ON ONE'S PARTICU-LAR RUNG OF THE LADDER WHILE TRYING TO FIGURE OUT EVER-MORE-ARTFUL WAYS OF DISLODGING THE OTHER FELLOW ABOVE AND RETARD THE FELLOW BELOW). WHICH NATE NEAL DOES HERE. IN SPADES.

ALL THAT IS REQUIRED TO DO A SUCCESS-FUL STORY ON THOSE UNKNOWN INDIVIDUALS WHO DID THOSE CAVE PAINTINGS IS TO FIT THE FACTS. THIS IS WHAT WE KNOW, THIS IS THE IRREFRTABLE EVIDENCE. STAYING WITHIN THOSE PARAMETERS WHAT COULD THE ANSWER **POSSIBLY** BE?

IF NATE NEAL WAS SEEKING TENURE AS A PROFESSOR OF ARCHEOLOGY AT A MAJOR UNIVERSITY, THAT WOULD NOT BE POSSIBLE. TENURE WOULD DEPEND ON HIS WILLINGNESS TO BEND TO THE PREVAILING ORTHODOXIES BOTH OF THE DISCIPLINE AND THE UNIVERSITY. HERE THAT ISN'T THE CASE. HERE A WORLD OF POSIBILITIES OPENS UP AND THAT WORLD IS LITERALLY NATE NEAL'S OYSTER.

AND THE IDEA OF THE OYSTER IS THE POSSIBILITY OF A PEARL.

AND IT'S ONE HECK OF A PEARL WHEN YOU GET TO IT.

YES, FANTAGRAPHICS READER, YOU HOLD A PEARL IN YOUR HAND.

A JAW-DROPPER. AN "OMG I CAN'T BELIEVE I JUST READ THAT. I'LL NEVER GET THAT OUT OF MY HEAD."

NOT TELLING YOU WHERE IT IS.

NO, A PEARL YOU HAVE TO WORK FOR. HOW MANY OYSTERS DO YOU THINK YOU WOULD HAVE TO OPEN TO FIND A PEARL, ON AVERAGE?

THE SANCTUARY TAKES SOME GETTING USED TO. THE STORY IS TOLD ENTIRELY IN PICTURES AND WITH GIBBERISH PHONET-ICS THAT HEARKEN BACK TO CHESTER BROWN'S **UNDERWATER**. IT'S PRETTY EASY TO PICK UP, BUT— LIKE PROGRAMMING AN iPHONE, IT DOESN'T HAPPEN IMMEDIATELY. YOU'LL HAVE TO "RE-READ" PAGES AT THE BEGINNING UNTIL YOU "GET IT" AND "GET THEM." IF YOU TRY TO SKIM, YOU'LL MISS IT. LIKE THROWING AWAY AN OYSTER YOU KNOW HAS A PEARL INSIDE BECAUSE YOU CAN'T FIGURE OUT— RIGHTAWAYTHISMINUTE— HOW TO GET THE SHELL OPEN.

NOT BRIGHT.

TAKE THE TIME— LOOK AT IT AS BETTER VALUE FOR THE MONEY THAN YOU EXPECTED— AND **THE SANCTUARY** WILL REWARD YOU A THOUSANDFOLD.

I'M VERY PLEASED TO HAVE A PRE-PUBLI-CATION PRINT-OUT WITH COVER NOTE BY NATE— AS WELL AS THE ORIGINAL SELF-PUBLISHED PRINTINGS— HOUSED IN THE **CEREBUS ARCHIVE**. YOU'LL BE GLAD TO HAVE IT IN YOUR LIBRARY TOO.

DAVE SIM
KITCHENER, ONTARIO
26 FEBRUARY 2010

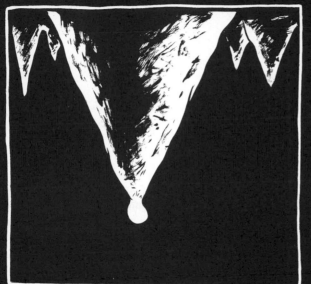
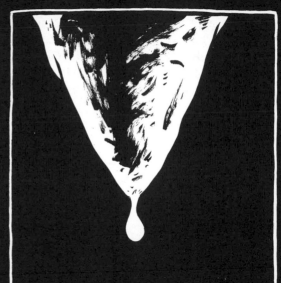

DOYT.

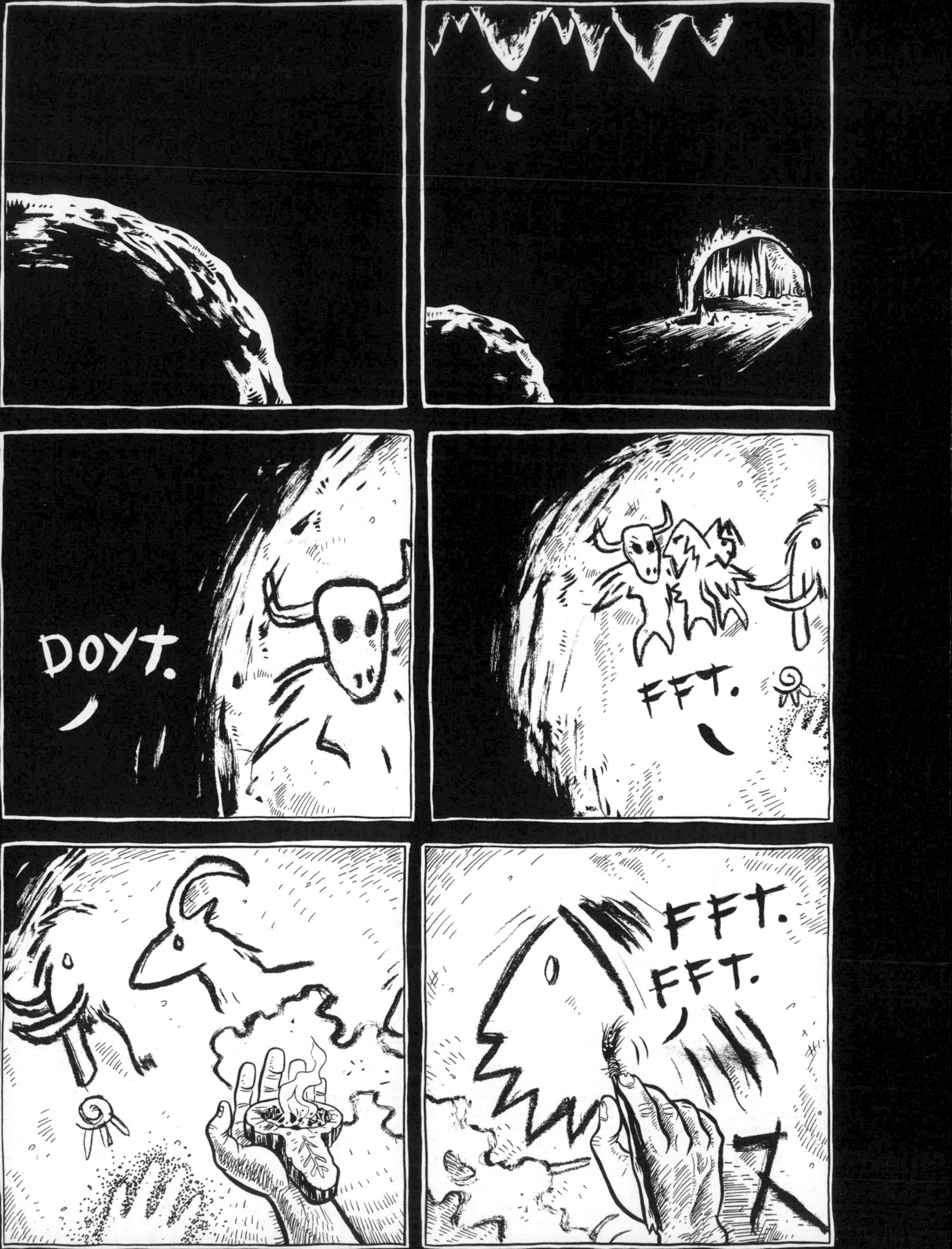
DOYT.
FFT.
FFT.
FFT.

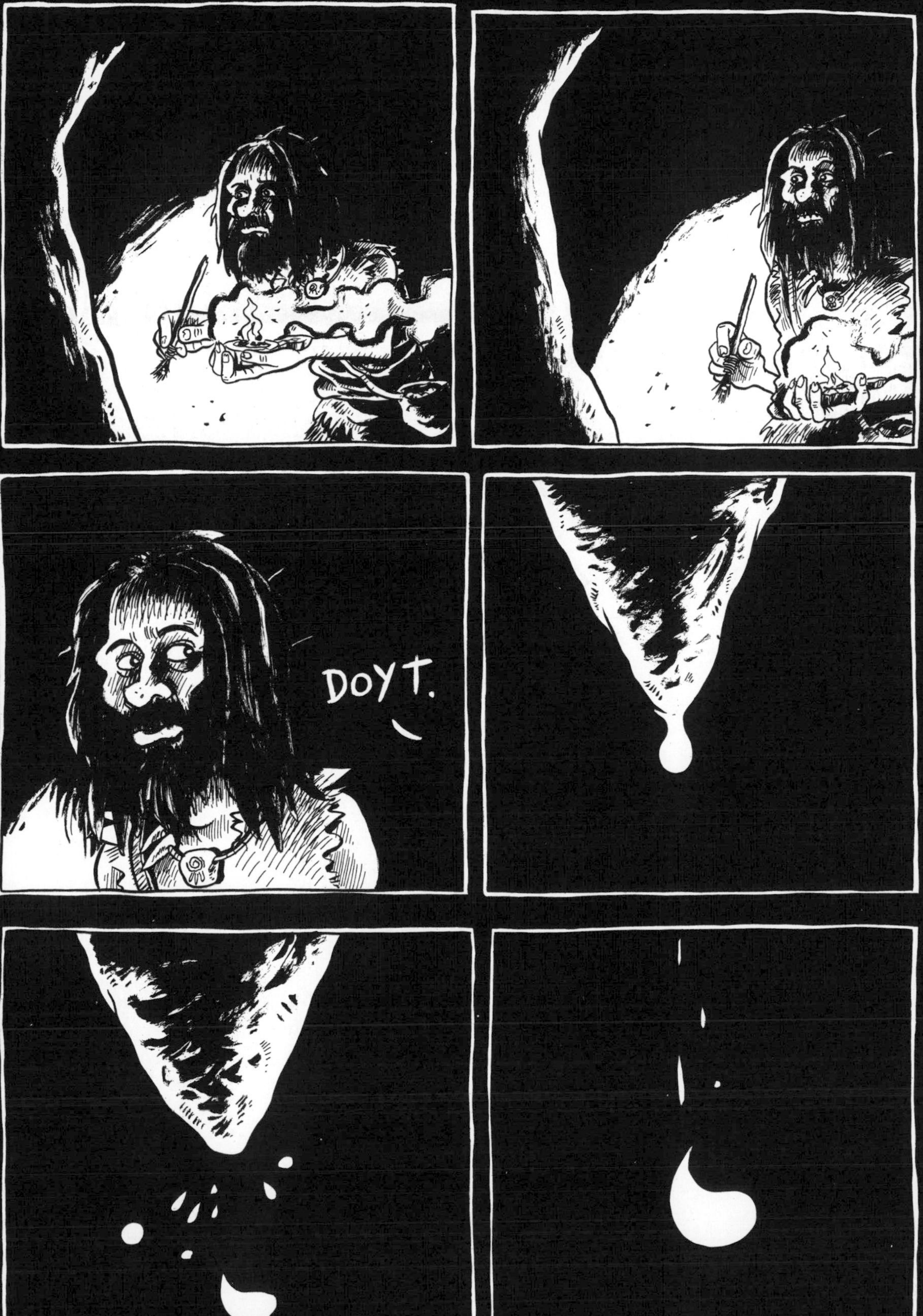
DOYT.

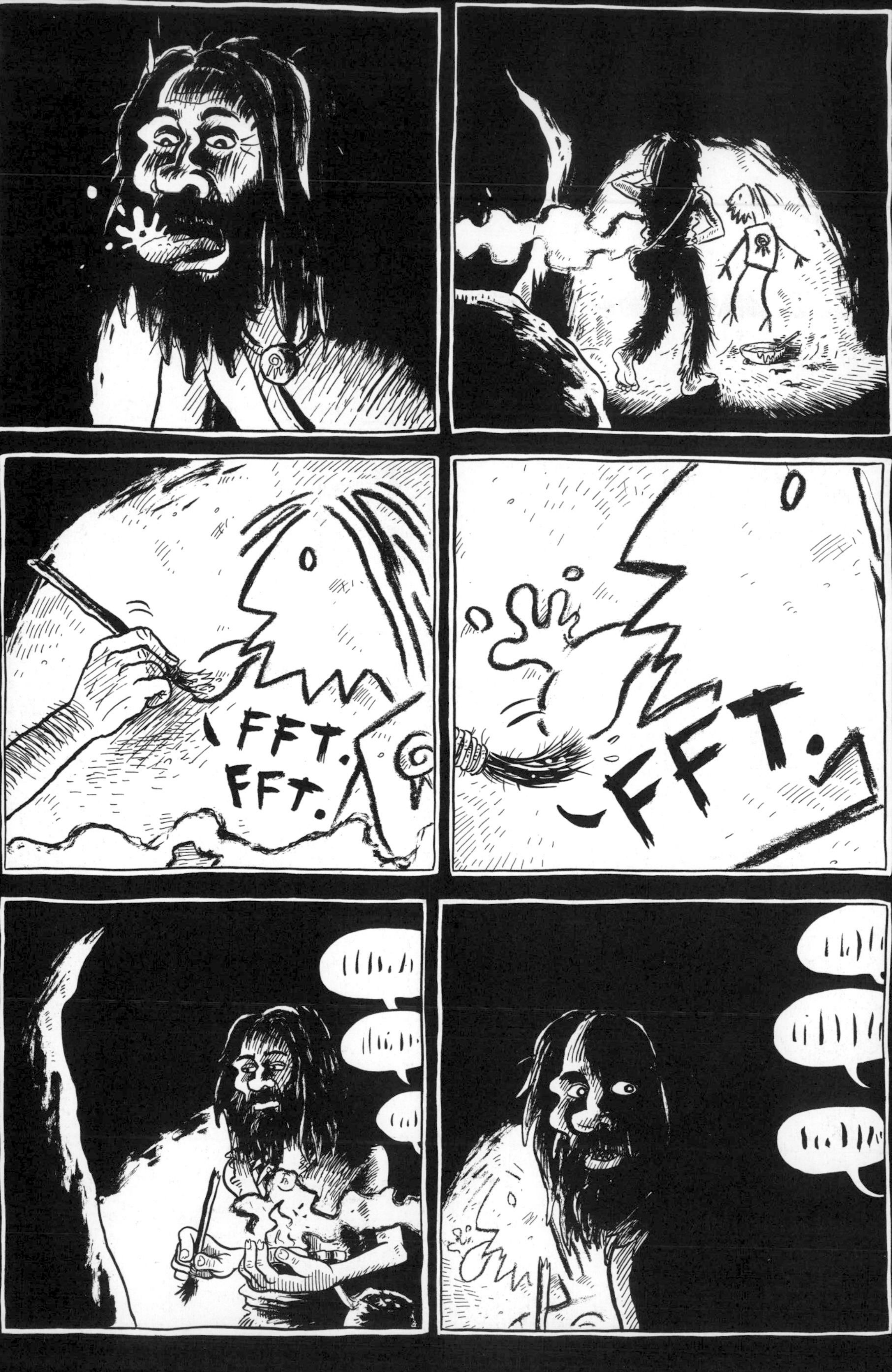
FFT.
FFT.
FFT.

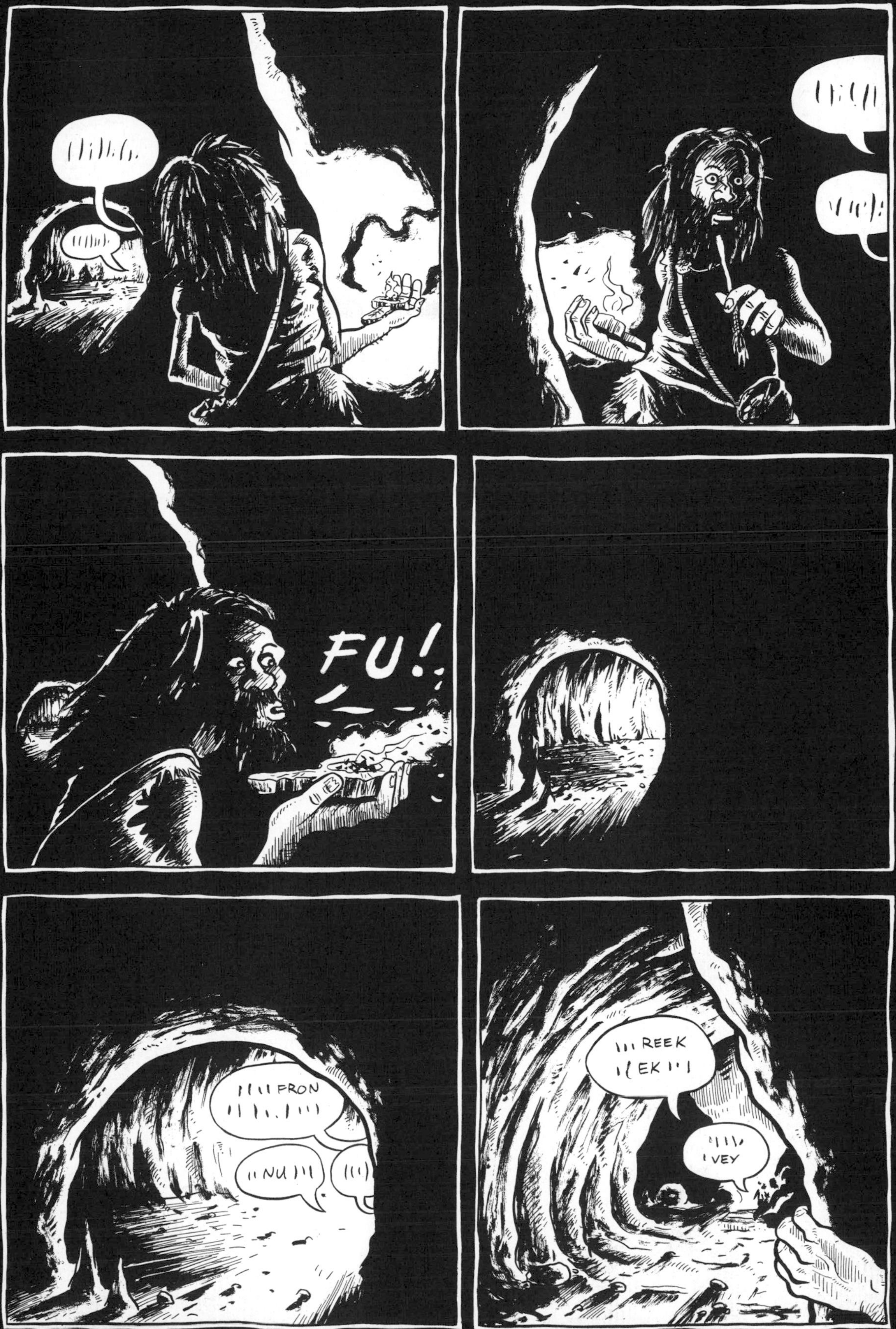
FU!
FRON
NU
REEK
EK
VEY

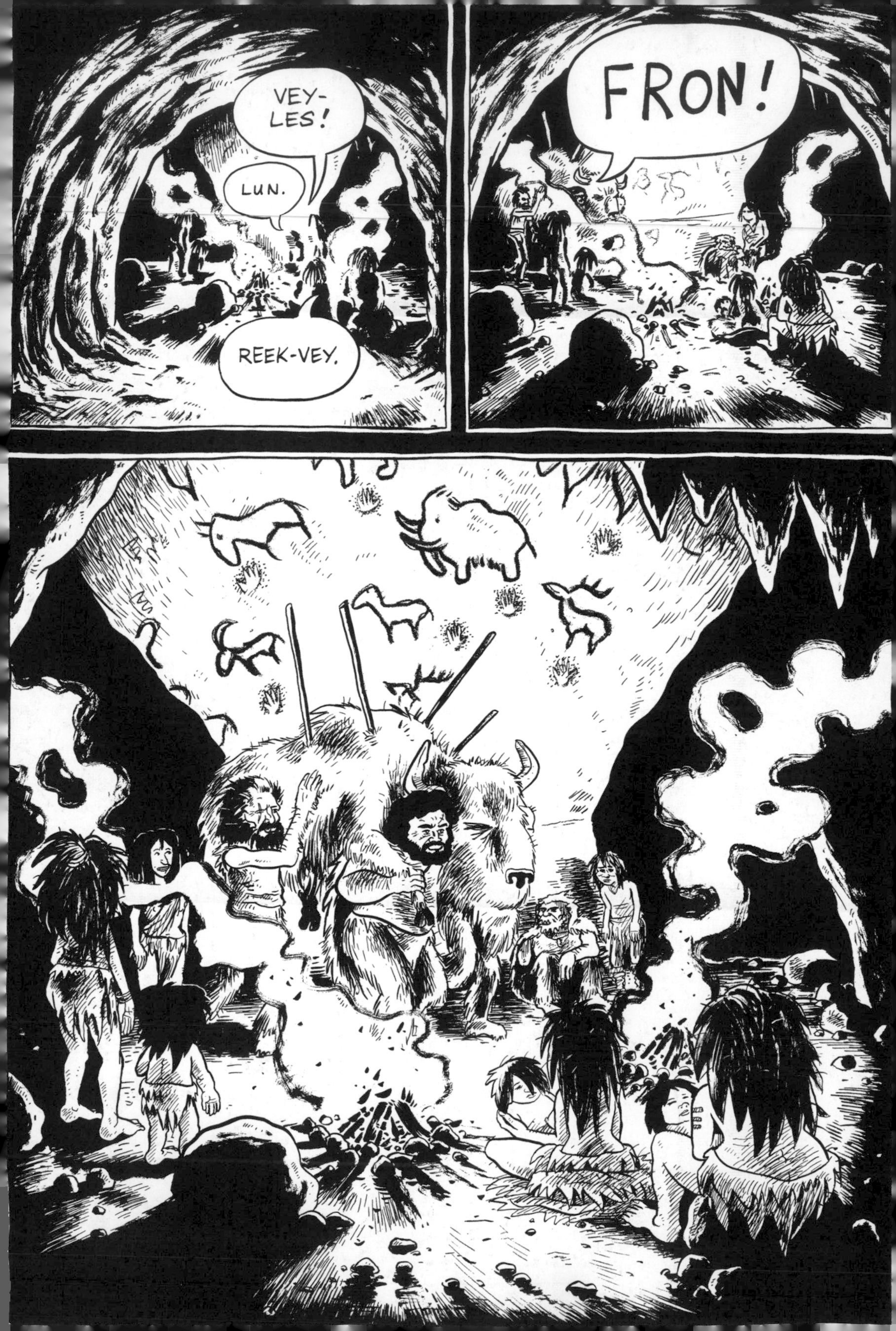
VEY-
LES!
LUN.
REEK-VEY.
FRON!

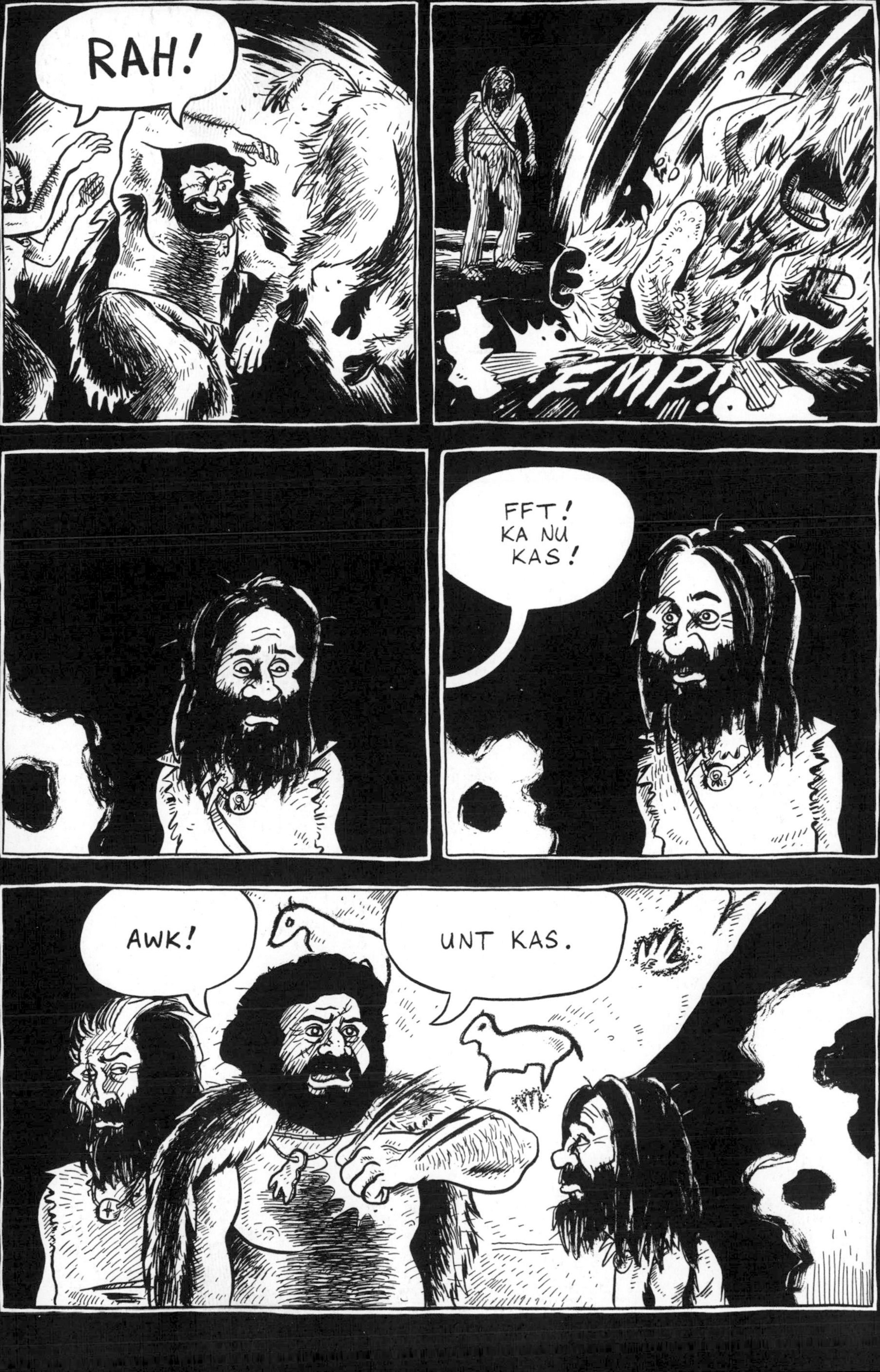
RAH!
FMP!
FFT! KA NU KAS!
AWK!
UNT KAS.

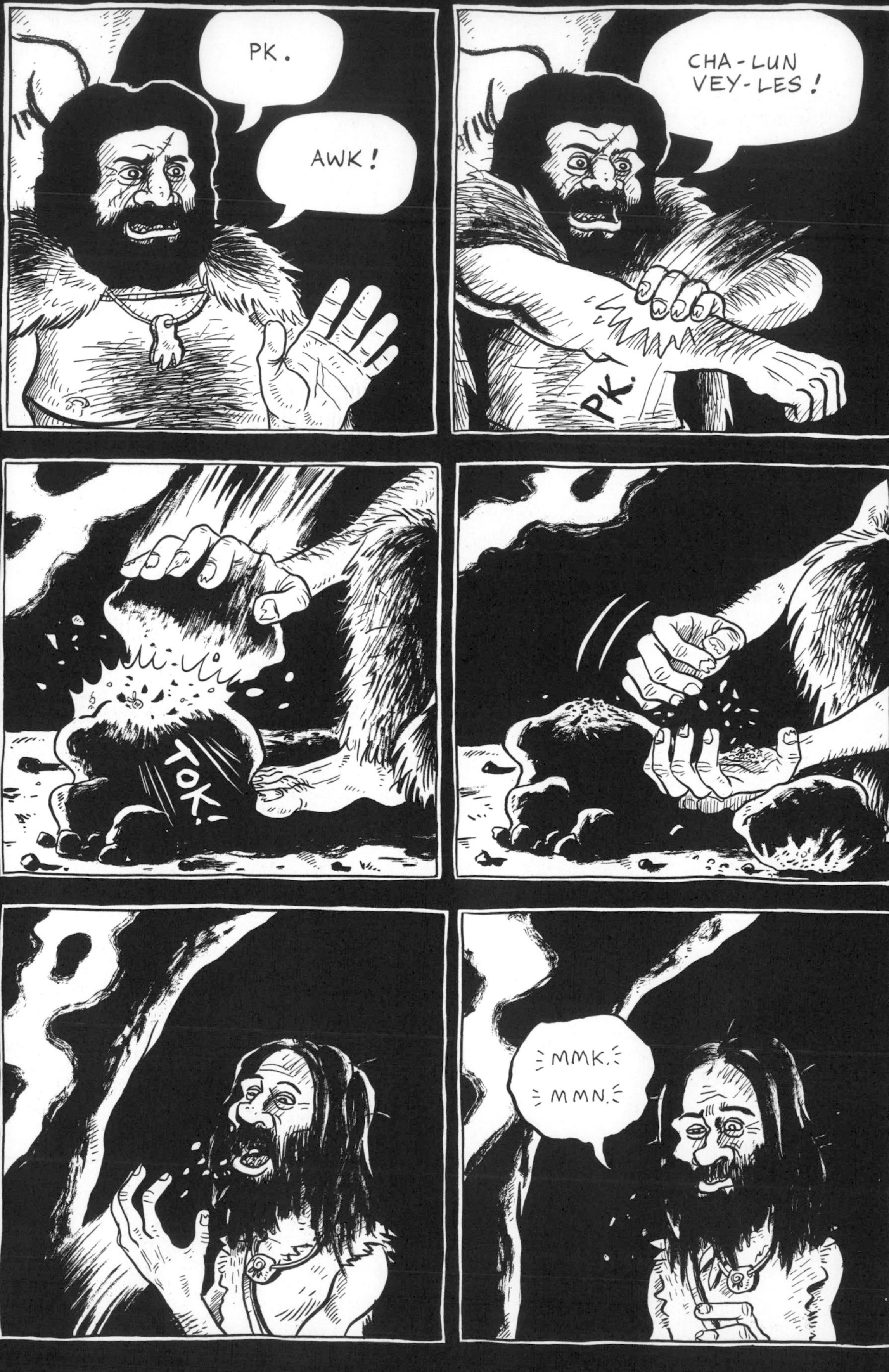
PK.
AWK!
CHA-LUN VEY-LES!
PK.
TOK!
MMK.
MMN.

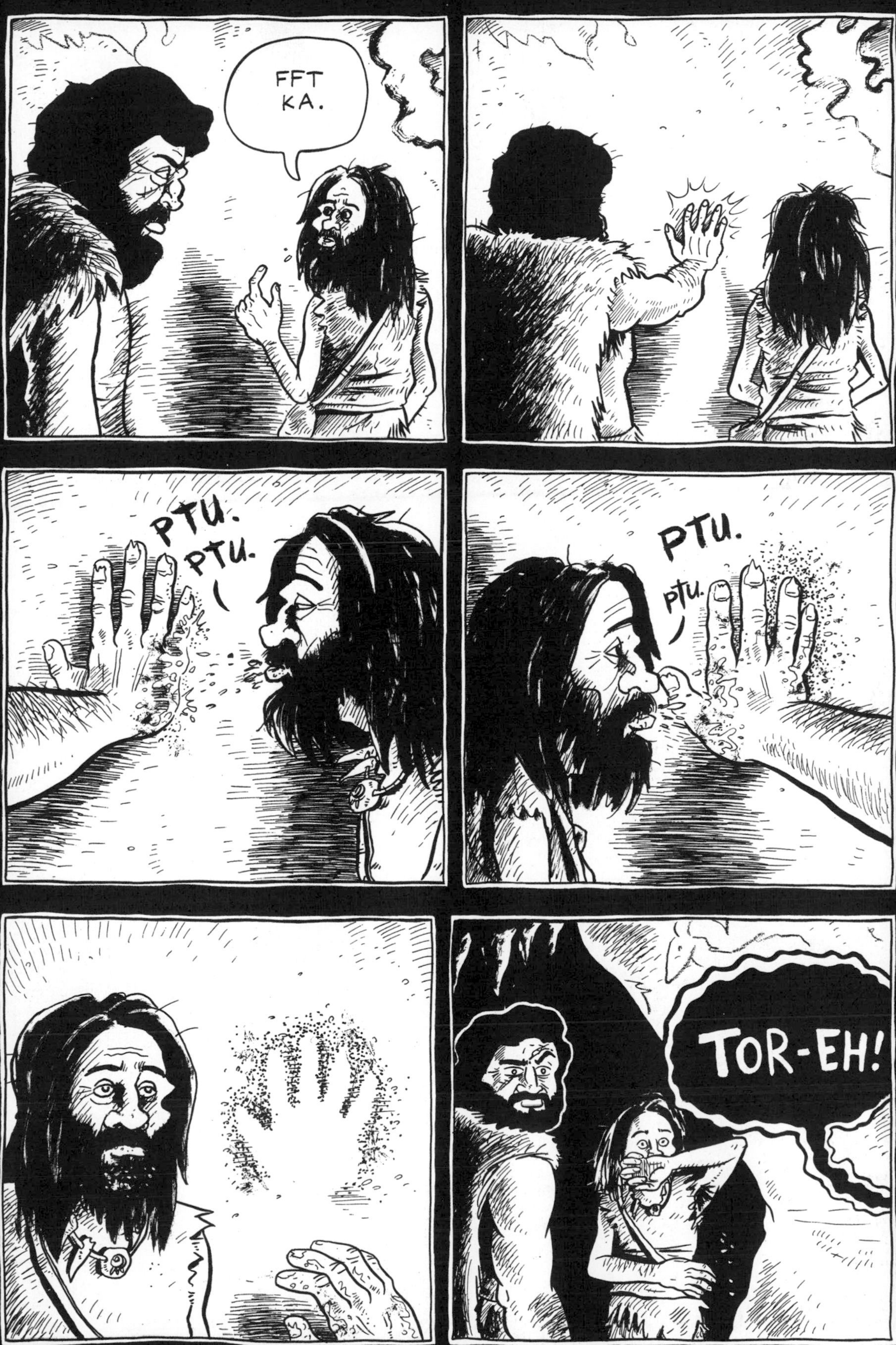
FFT KA.
PTU.
PTU.
PTU.
ptu.
TOR-EH!

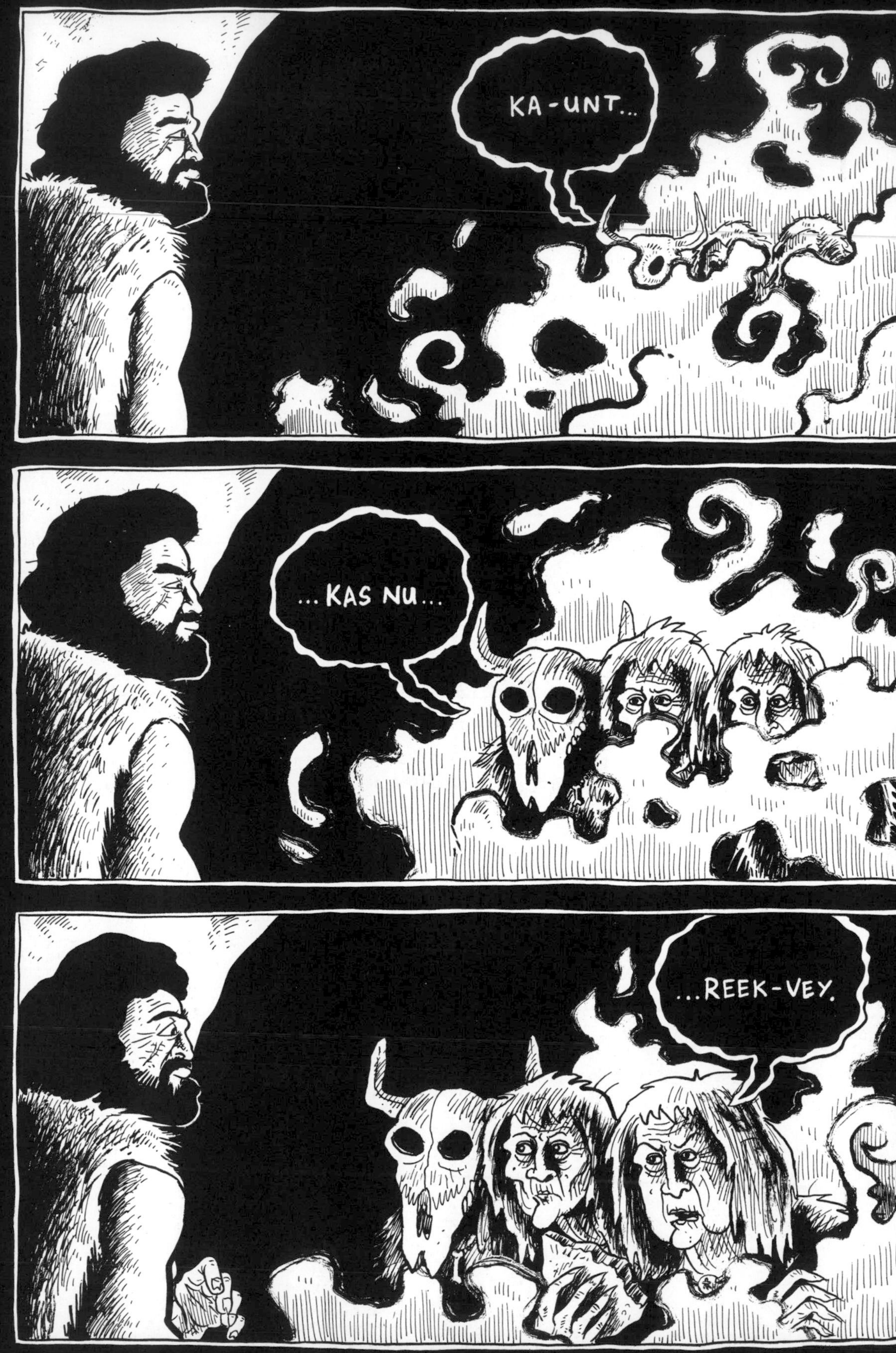
KA-UNT...
...KAS NU...
...REEK-VEY.

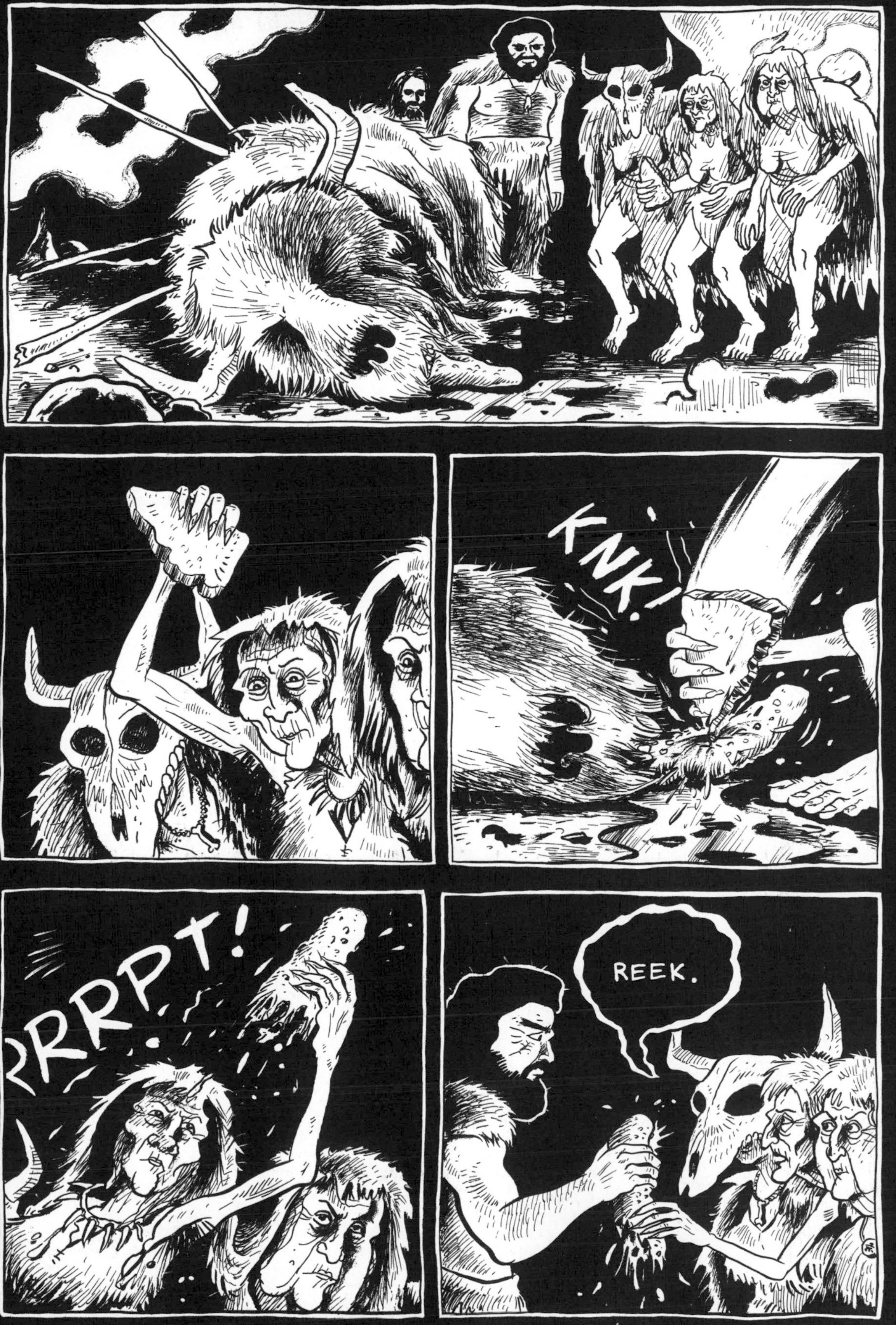
KNK!
RRRPT!
REEK.

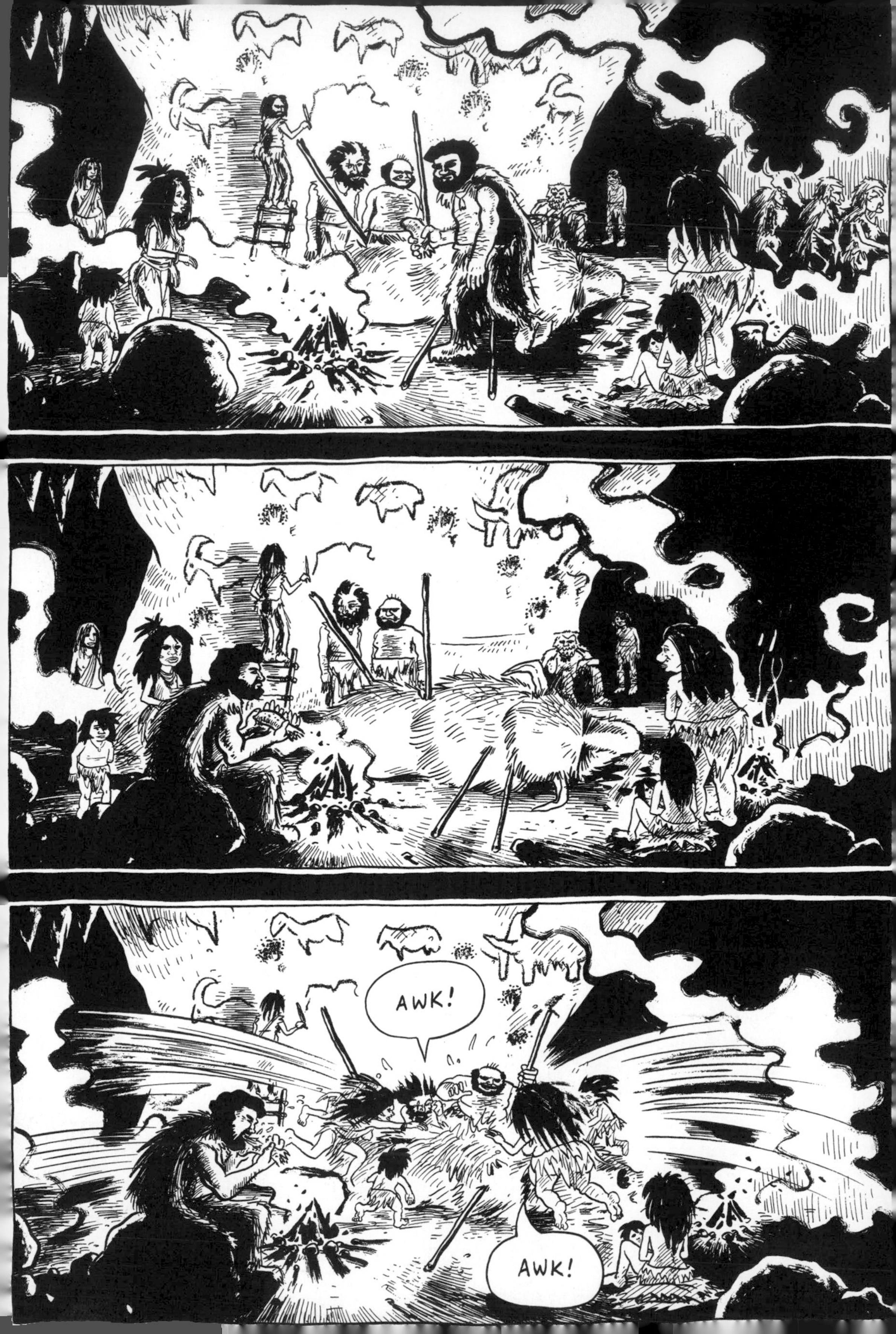
AWK!
AWK!

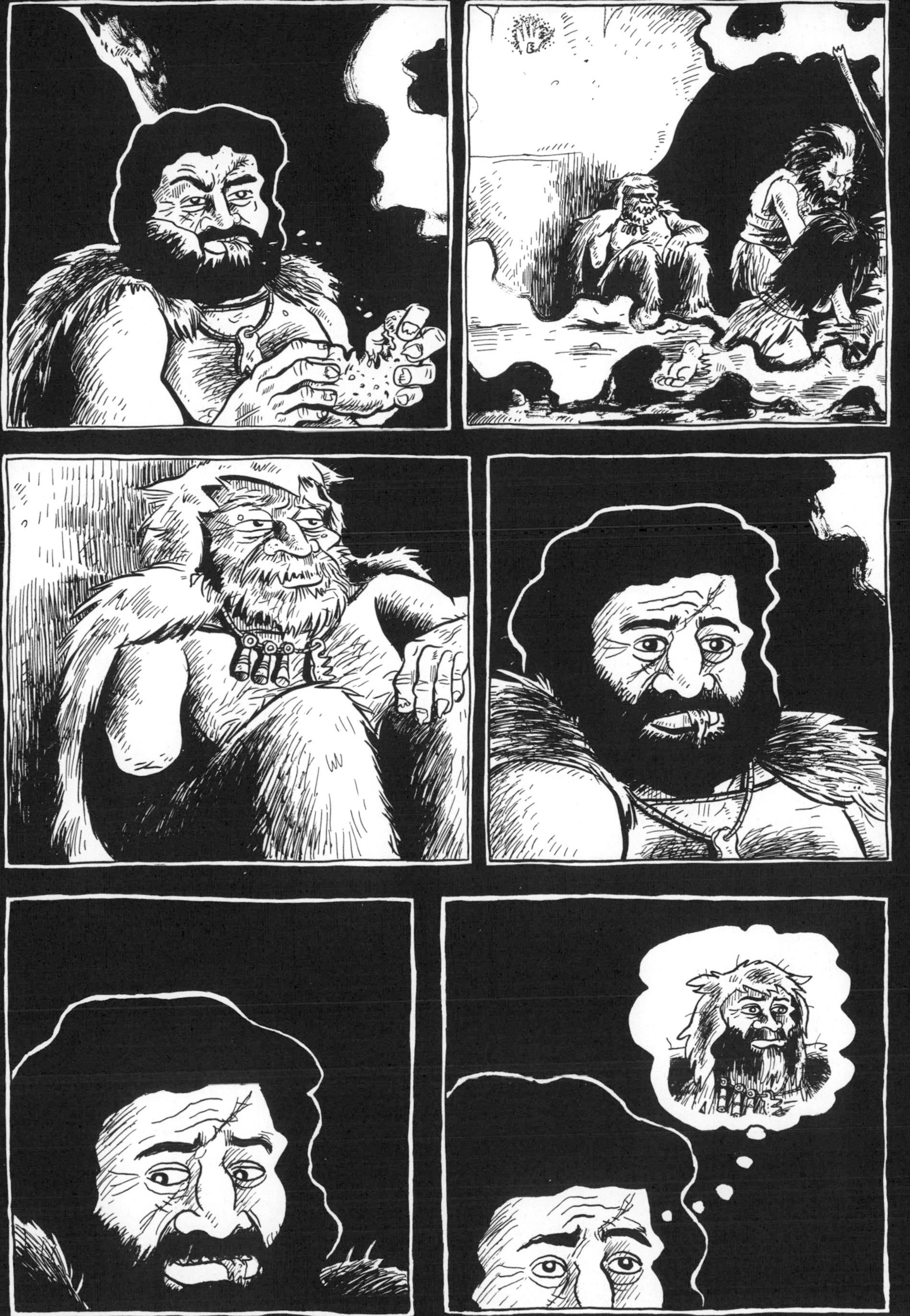

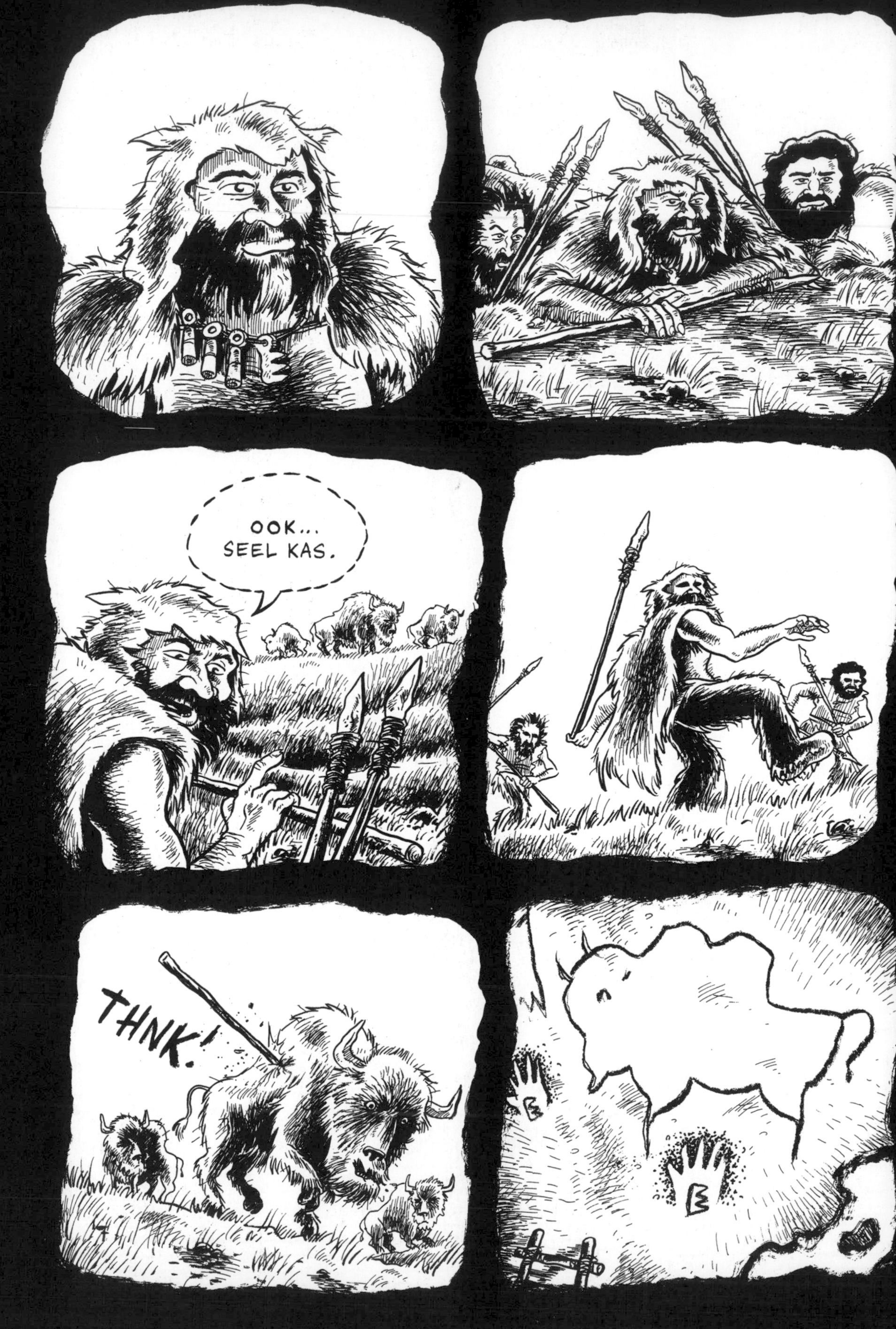
OOK...
SEEL KAS.
THNK!

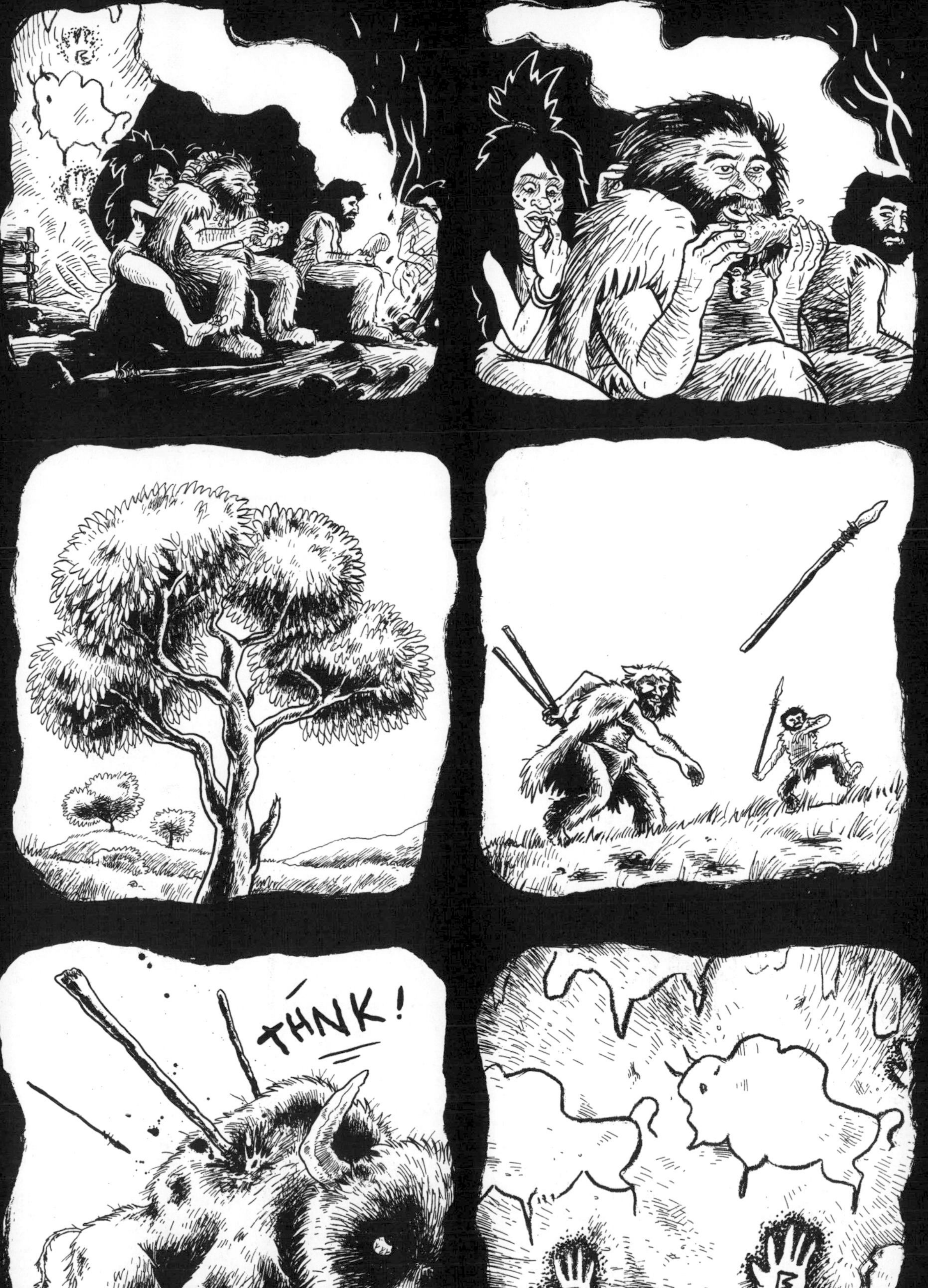
THNK!

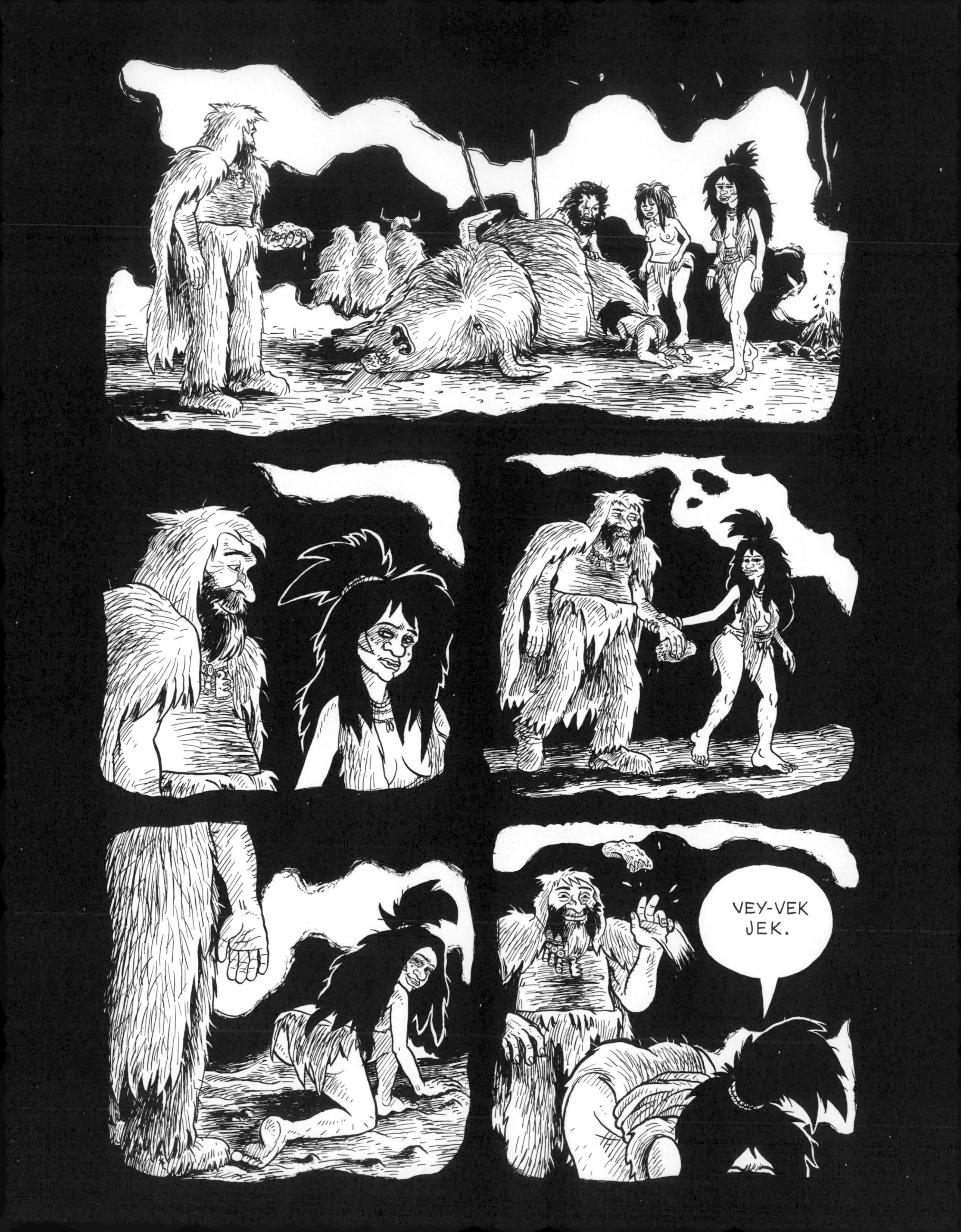
VEY-VEK
JEK.

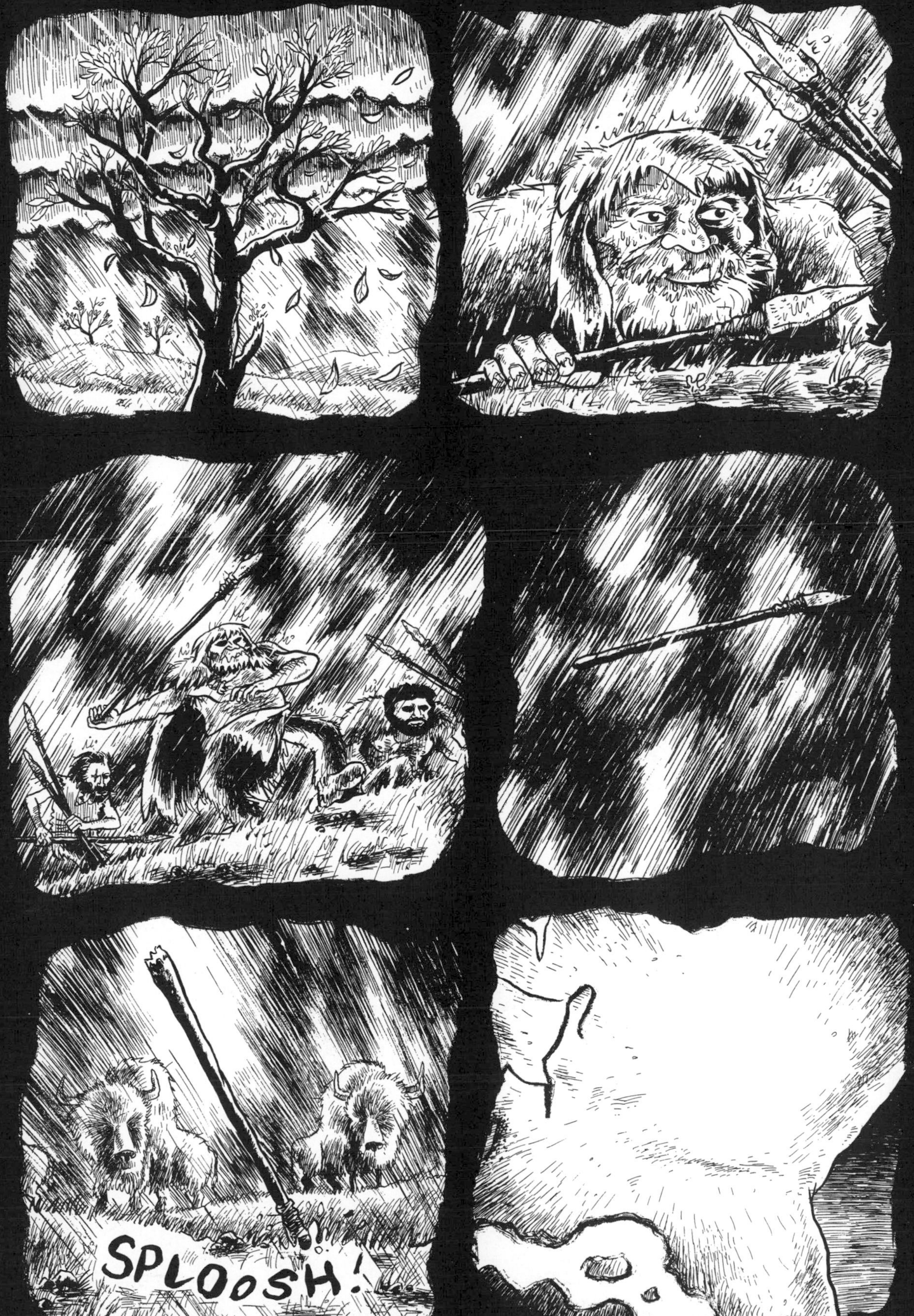
SPLOOSH!

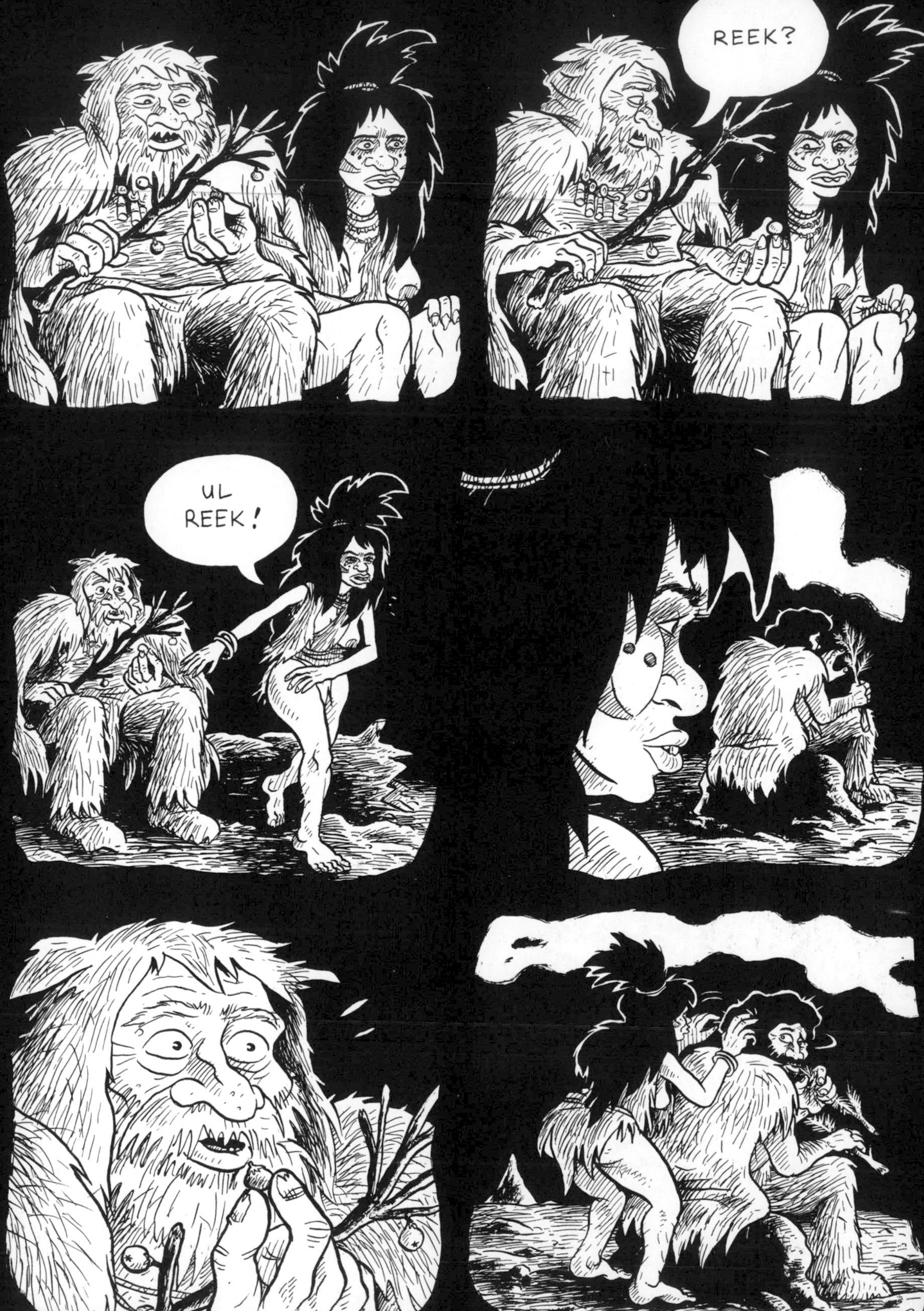
REEK?
UL REEK!

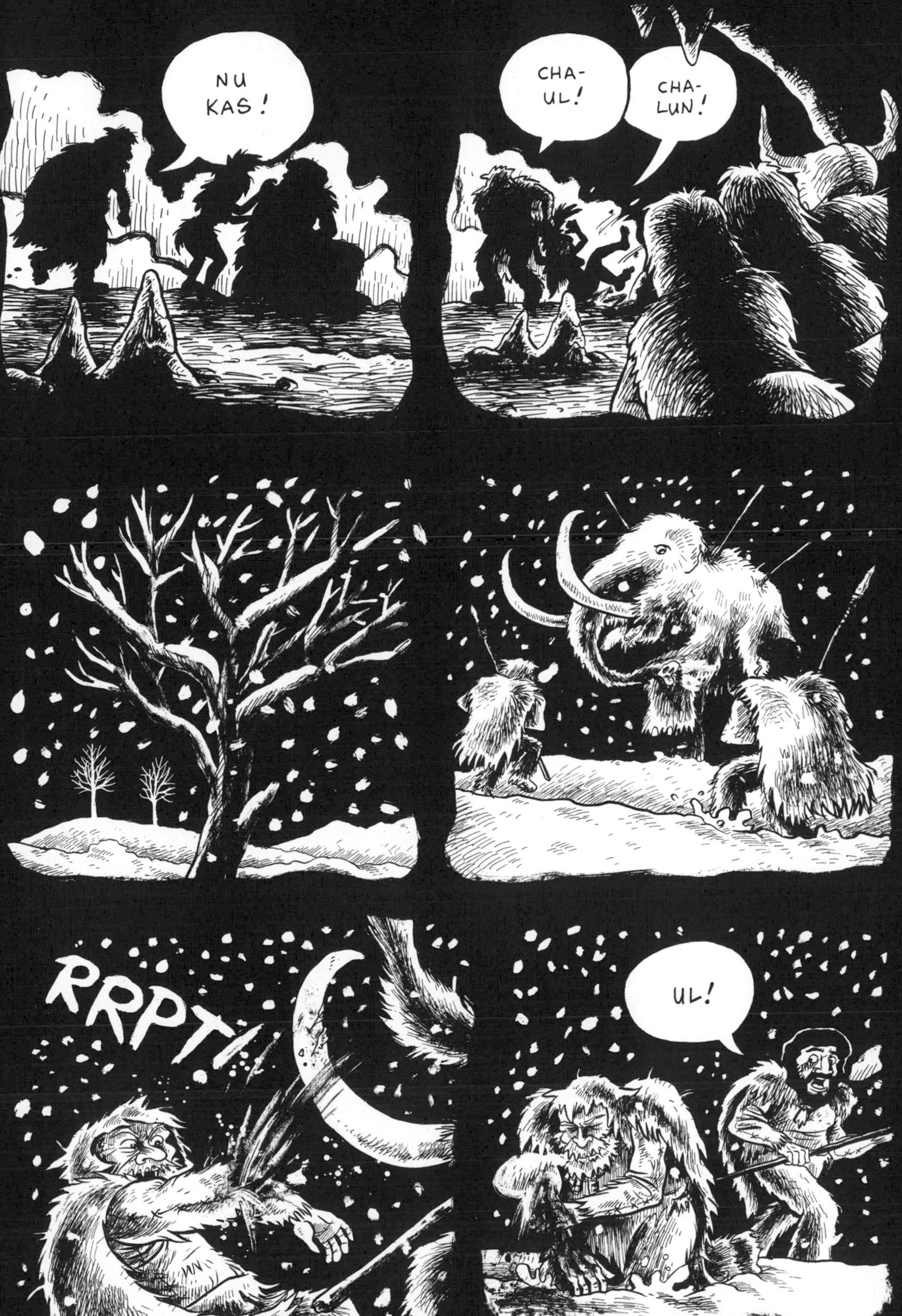

NU KAS!
CHA-UL!
CHA-LUN!
RRPT!
UL!

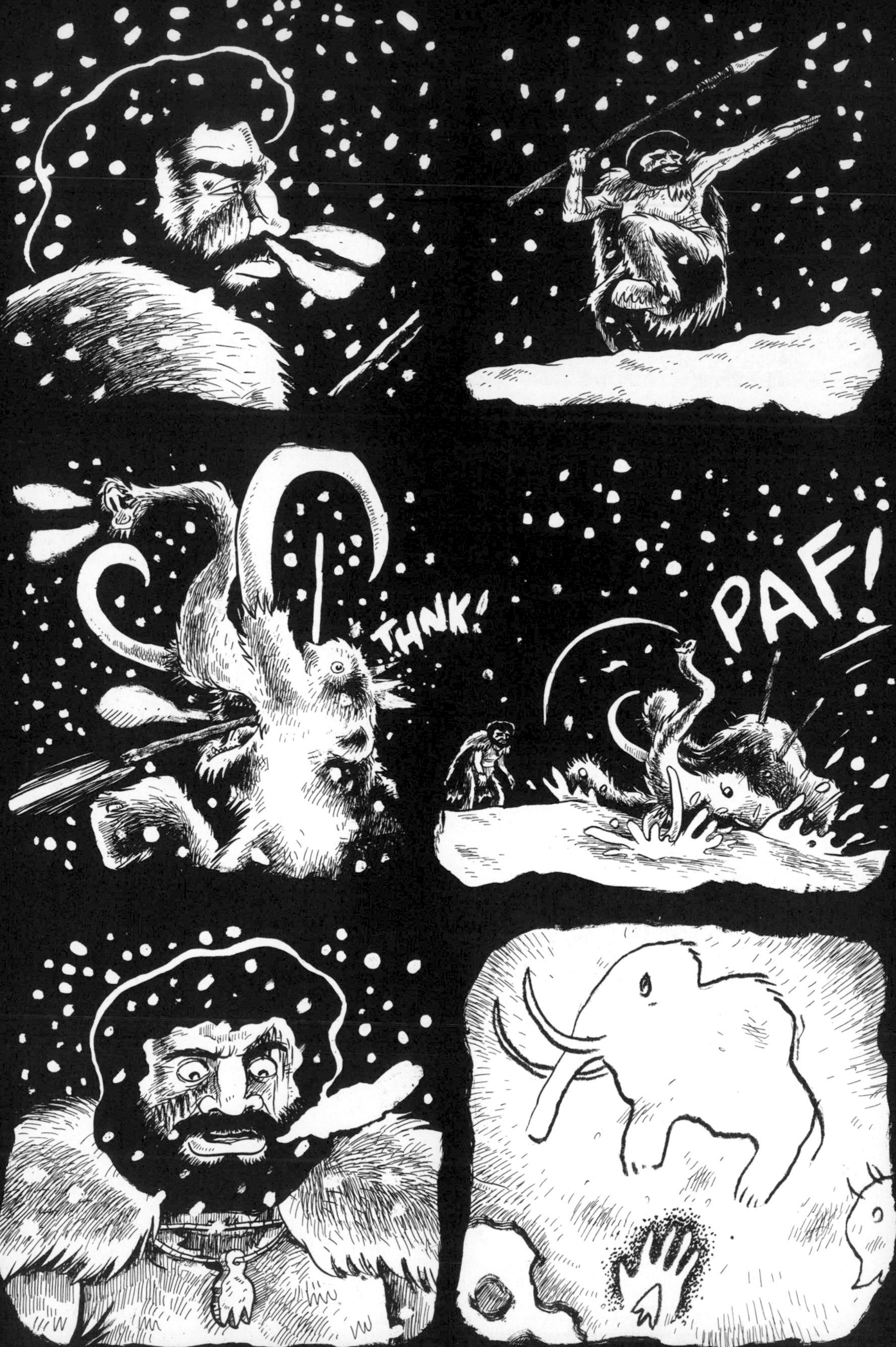
THNK!
PAF!

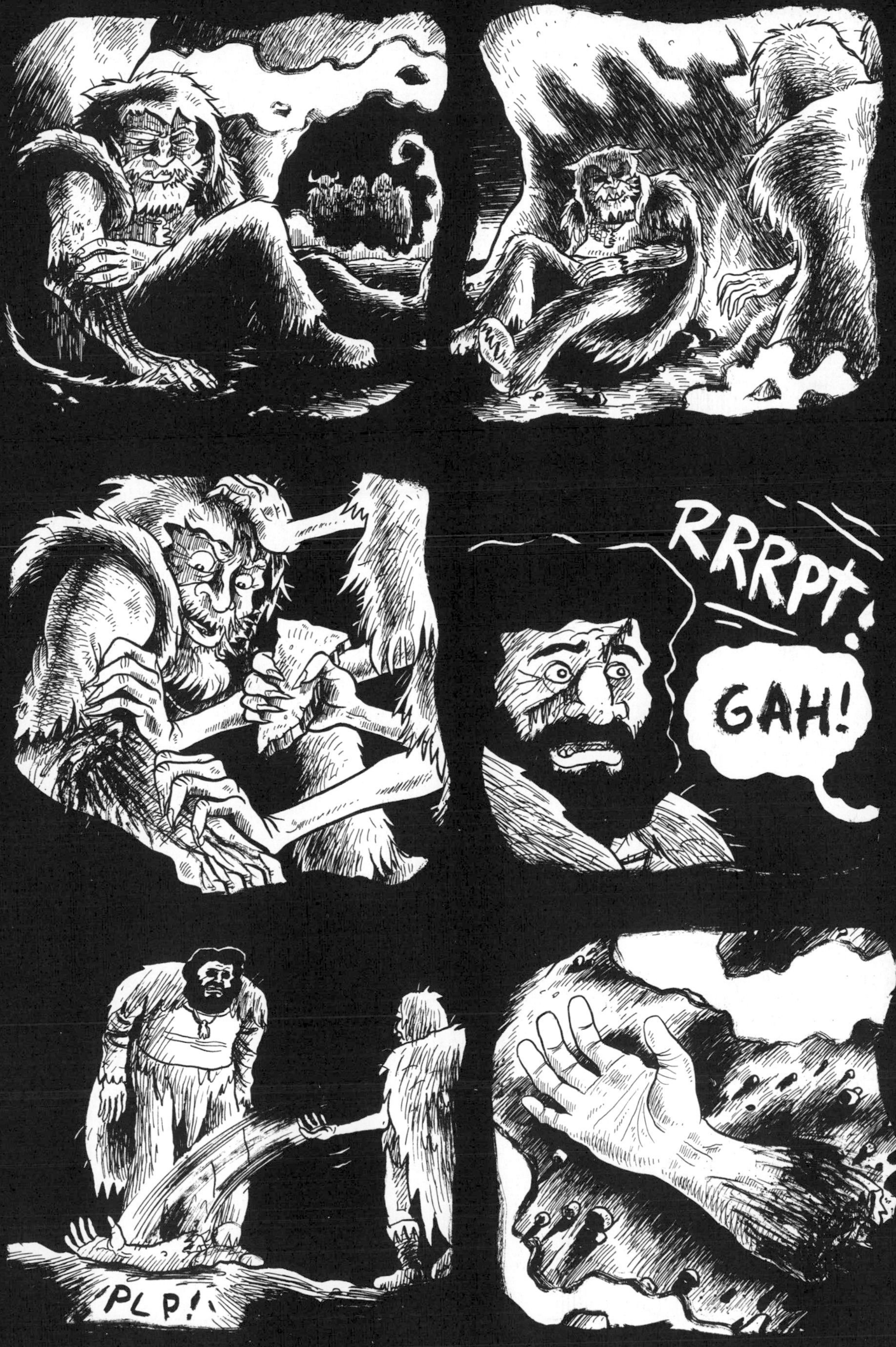
RRRPT!
GAH!
PLP!

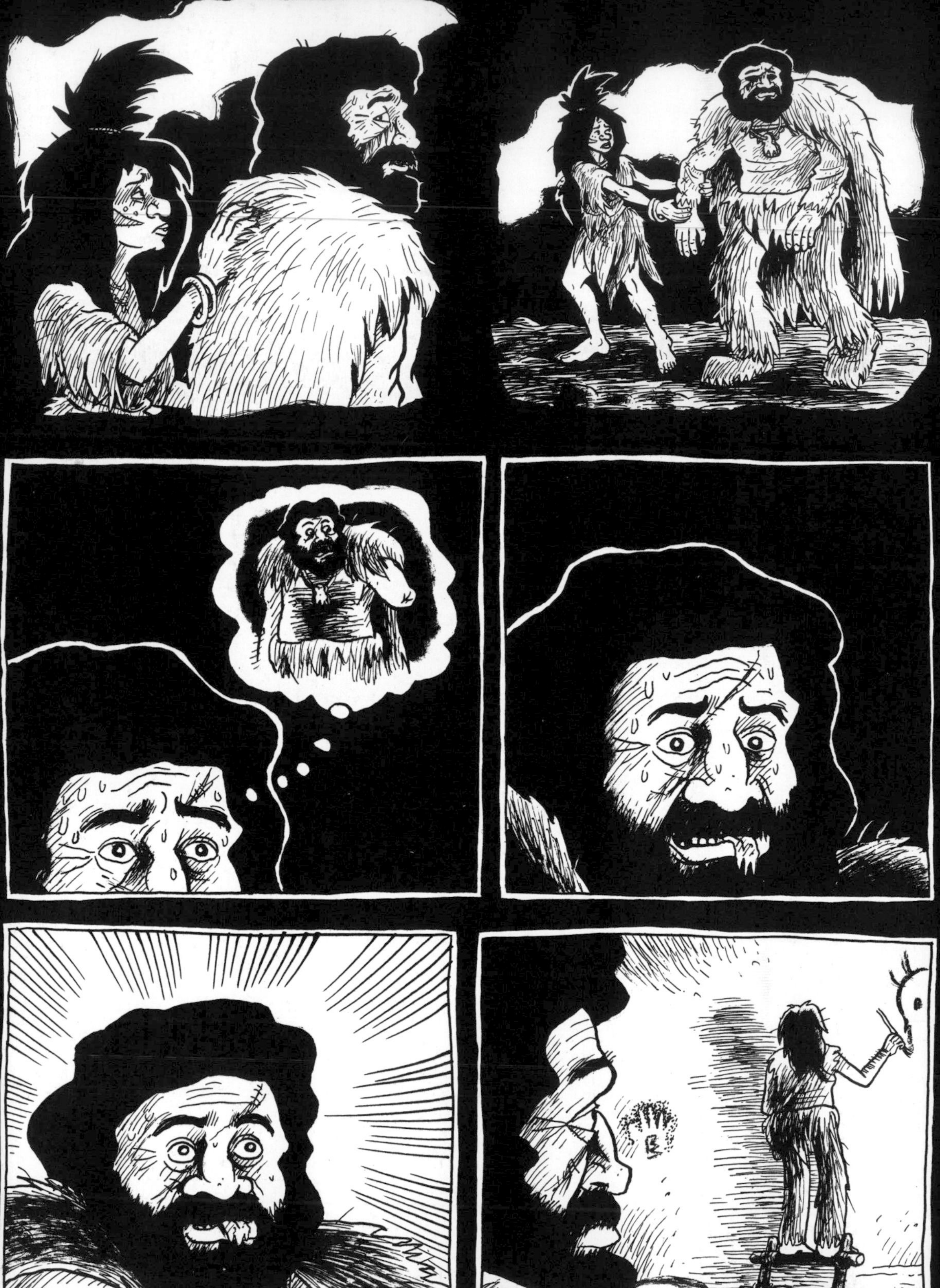

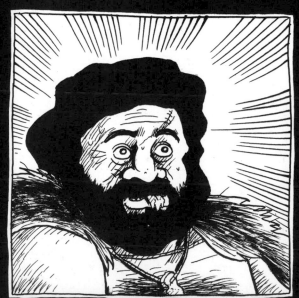

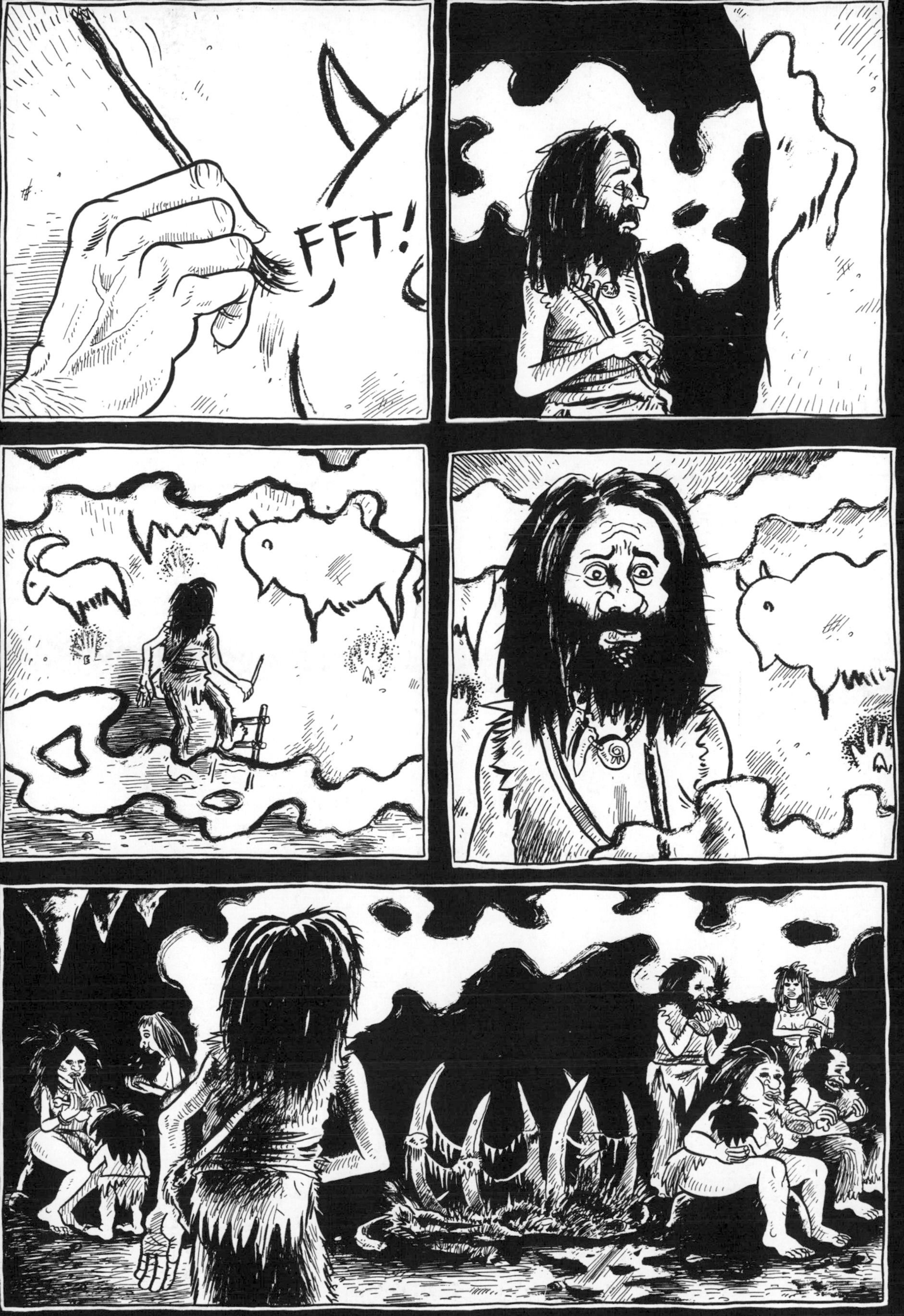
FFT!

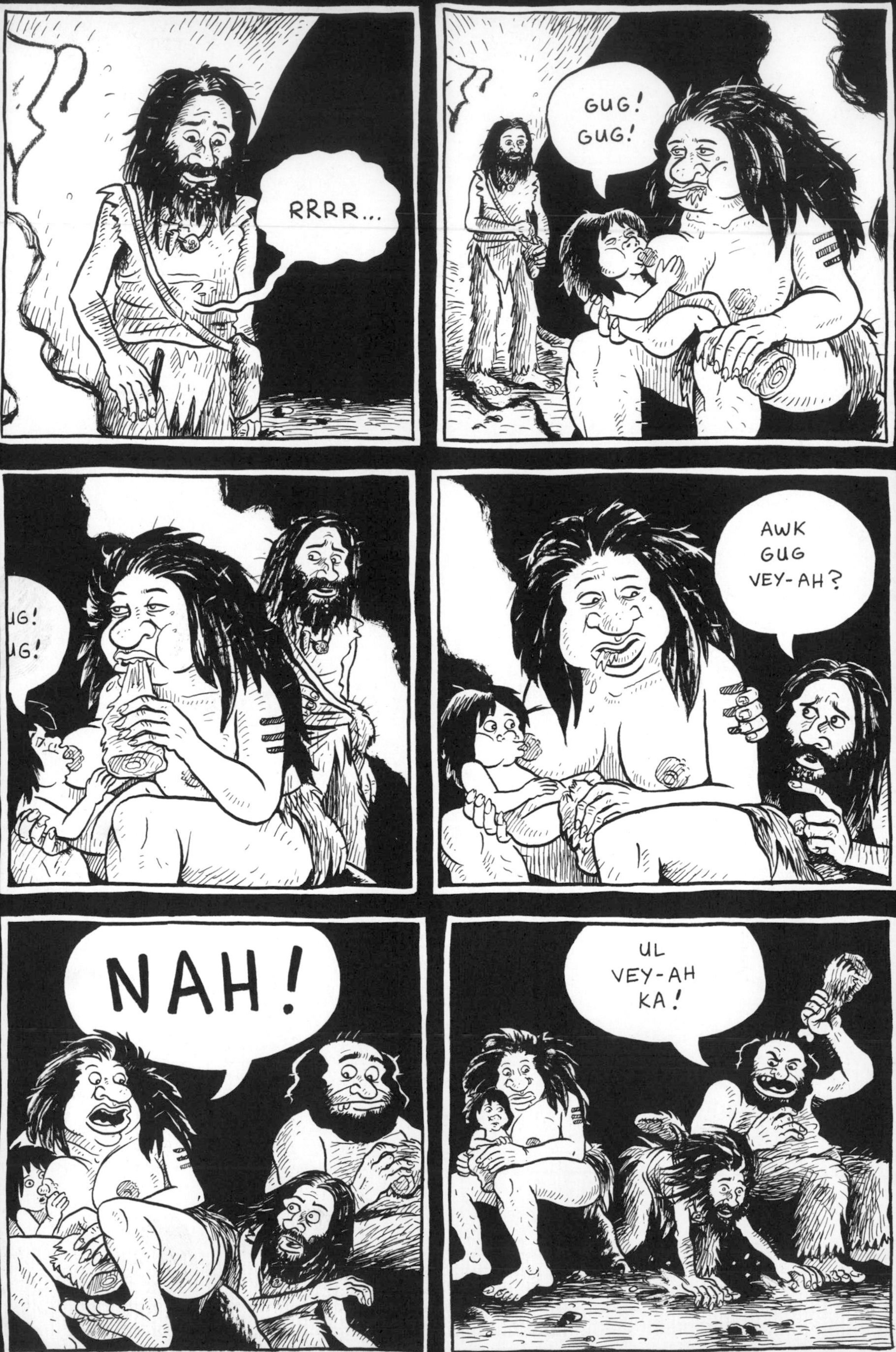
RRRR...
GUG! GUG!
UG! UG!
AWK GUG VEY-AH?
NAH!
UL VEY-AH KA!

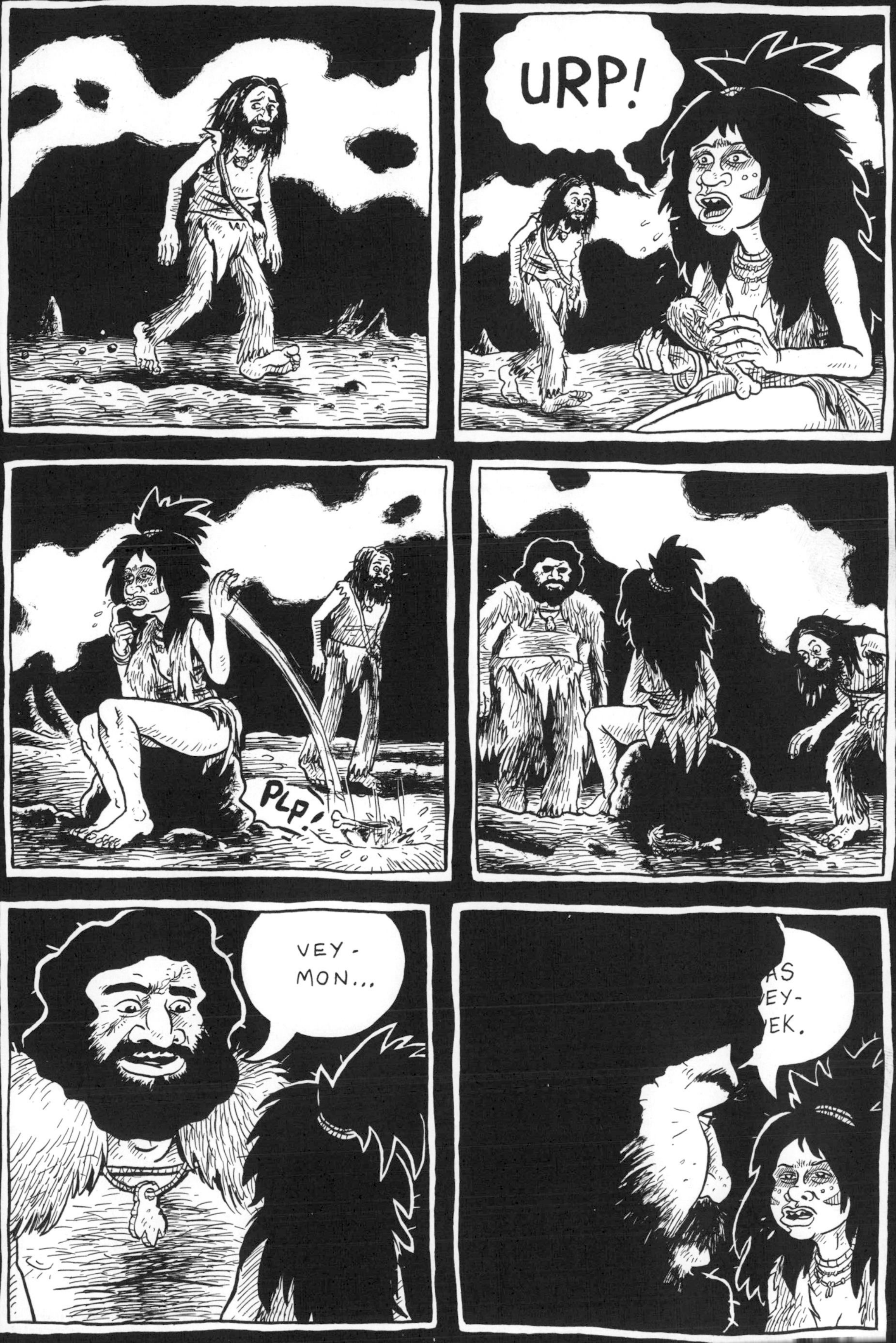
URP!
PLP!
VEY-
MON...
AS
EY-
EK.

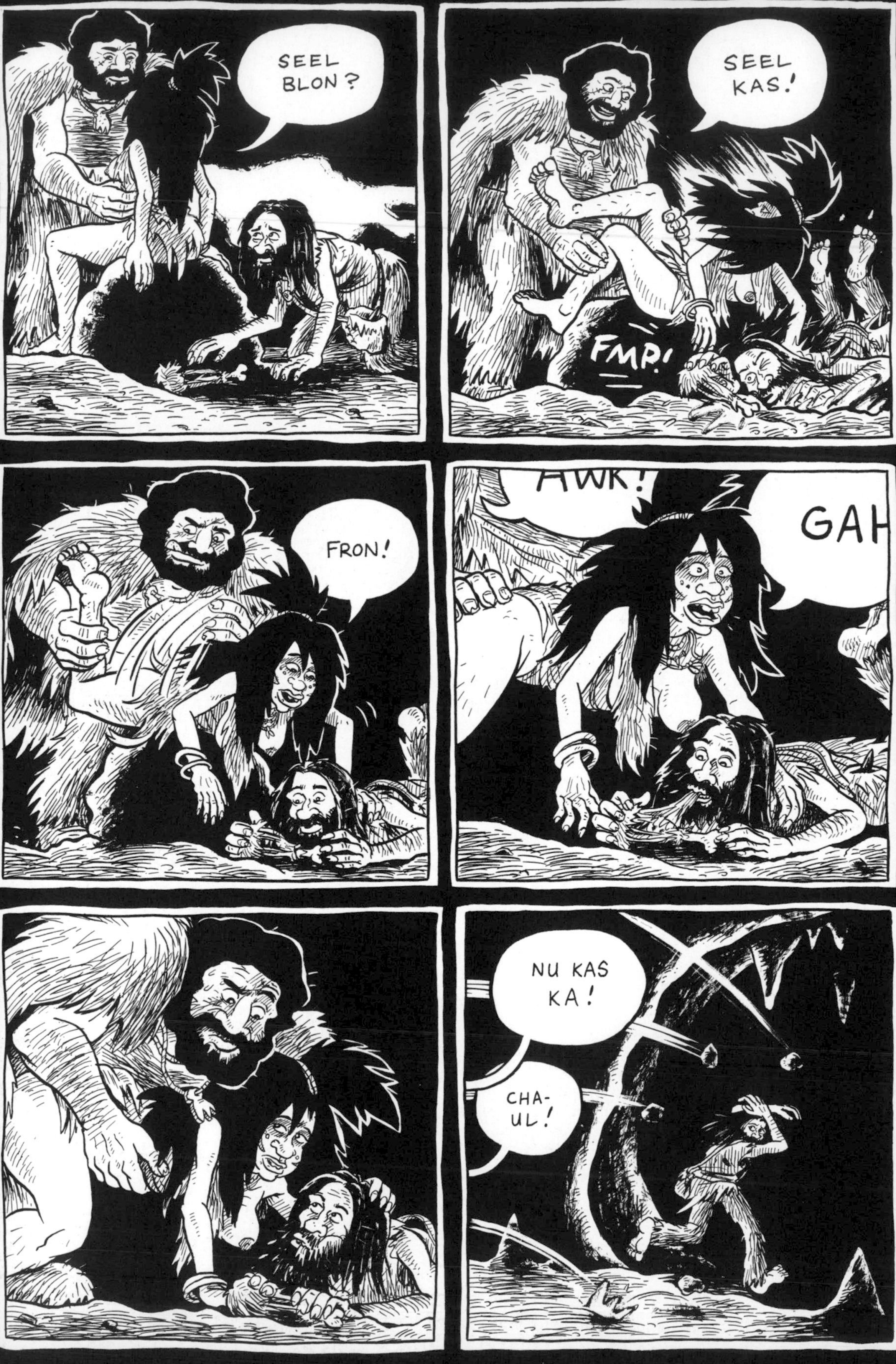
SEEL BLON?
SEEL KAS!
FMP!
FRON!
AWK!
GAH
NU KAS KA!
CHA-UL!

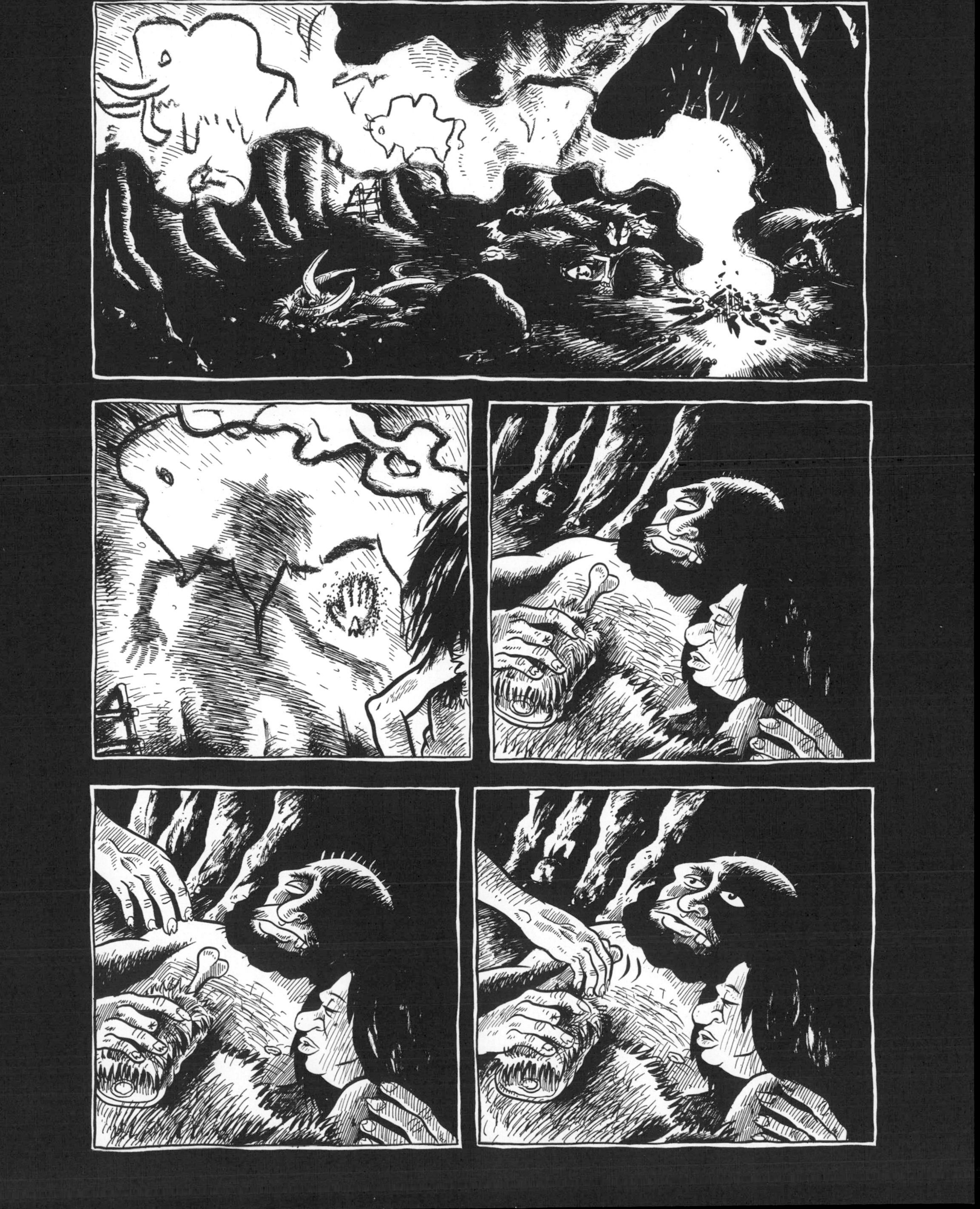

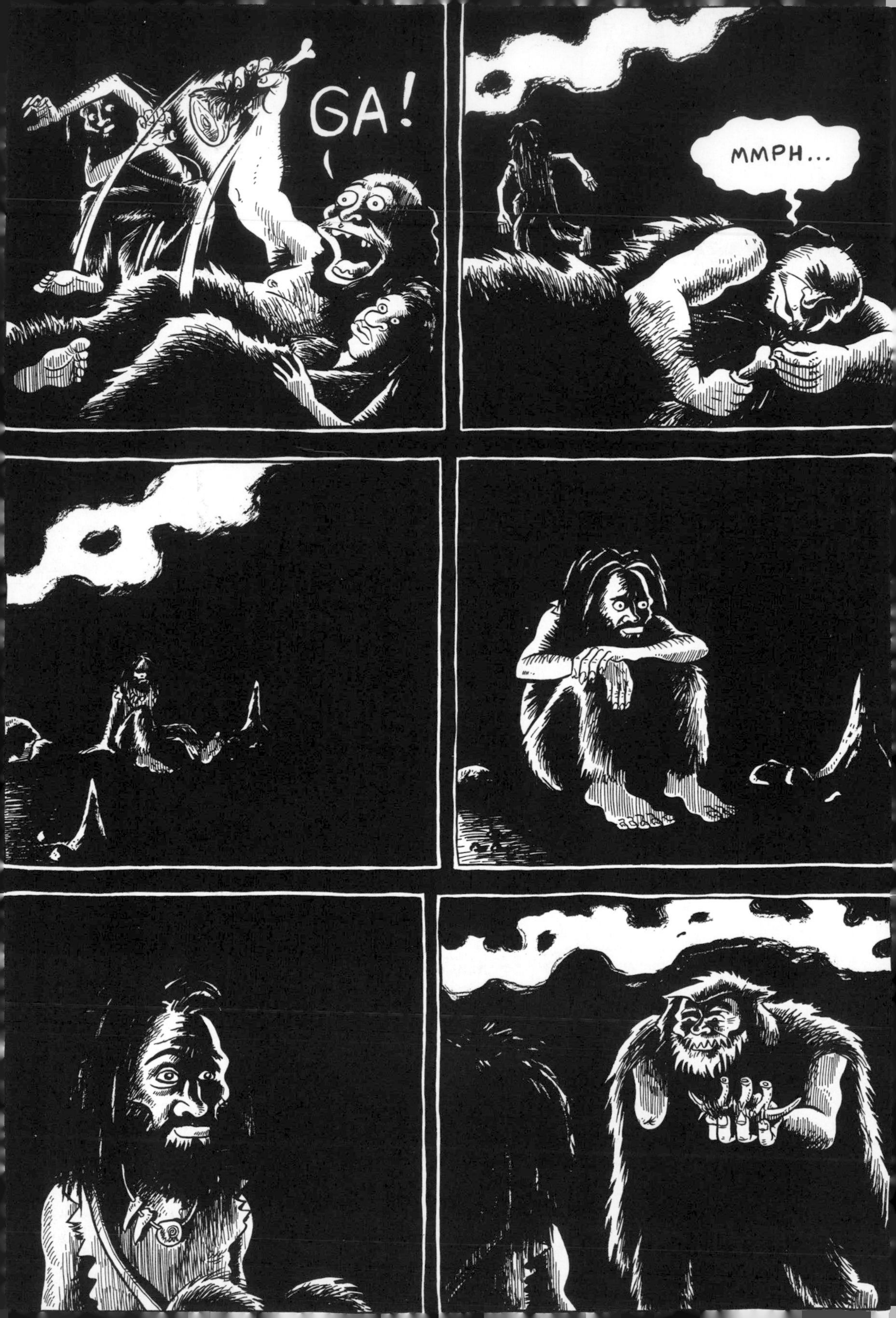
GA!
MMPH...

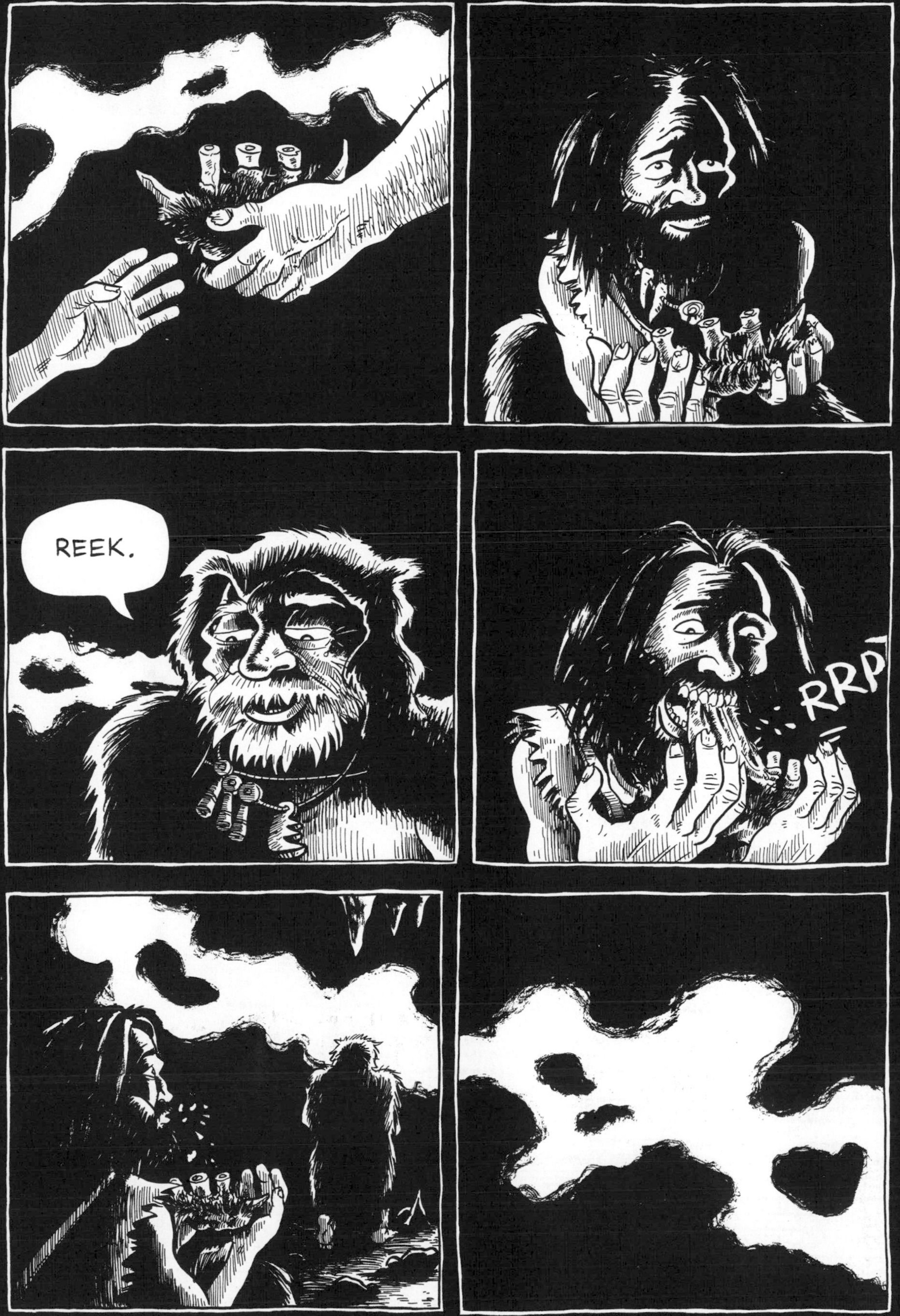
REEK.
RRP

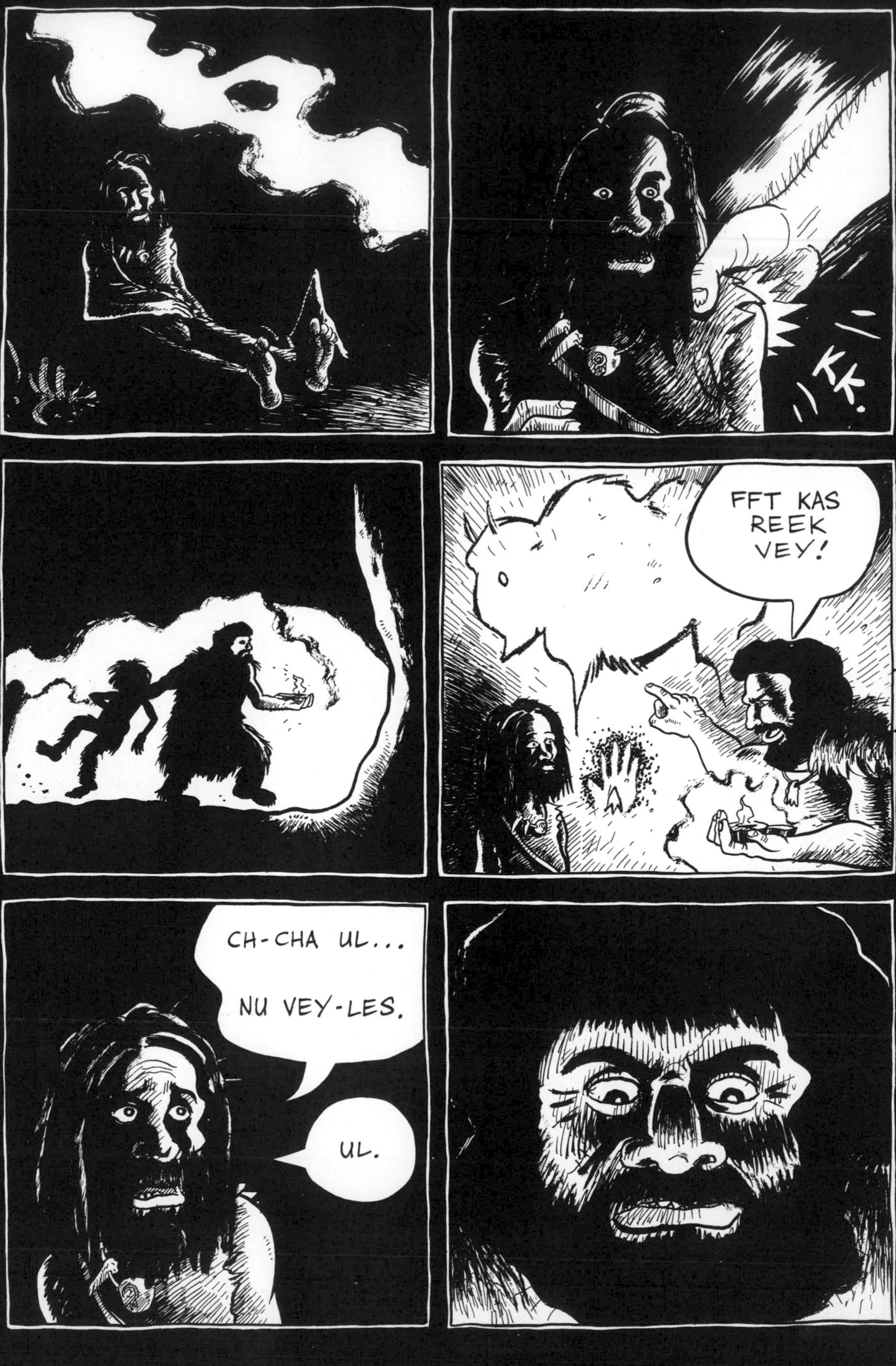
KK.
FFT KAS REEK VEY!
CH-CHA UL...
NU VEY-LES.
UL.

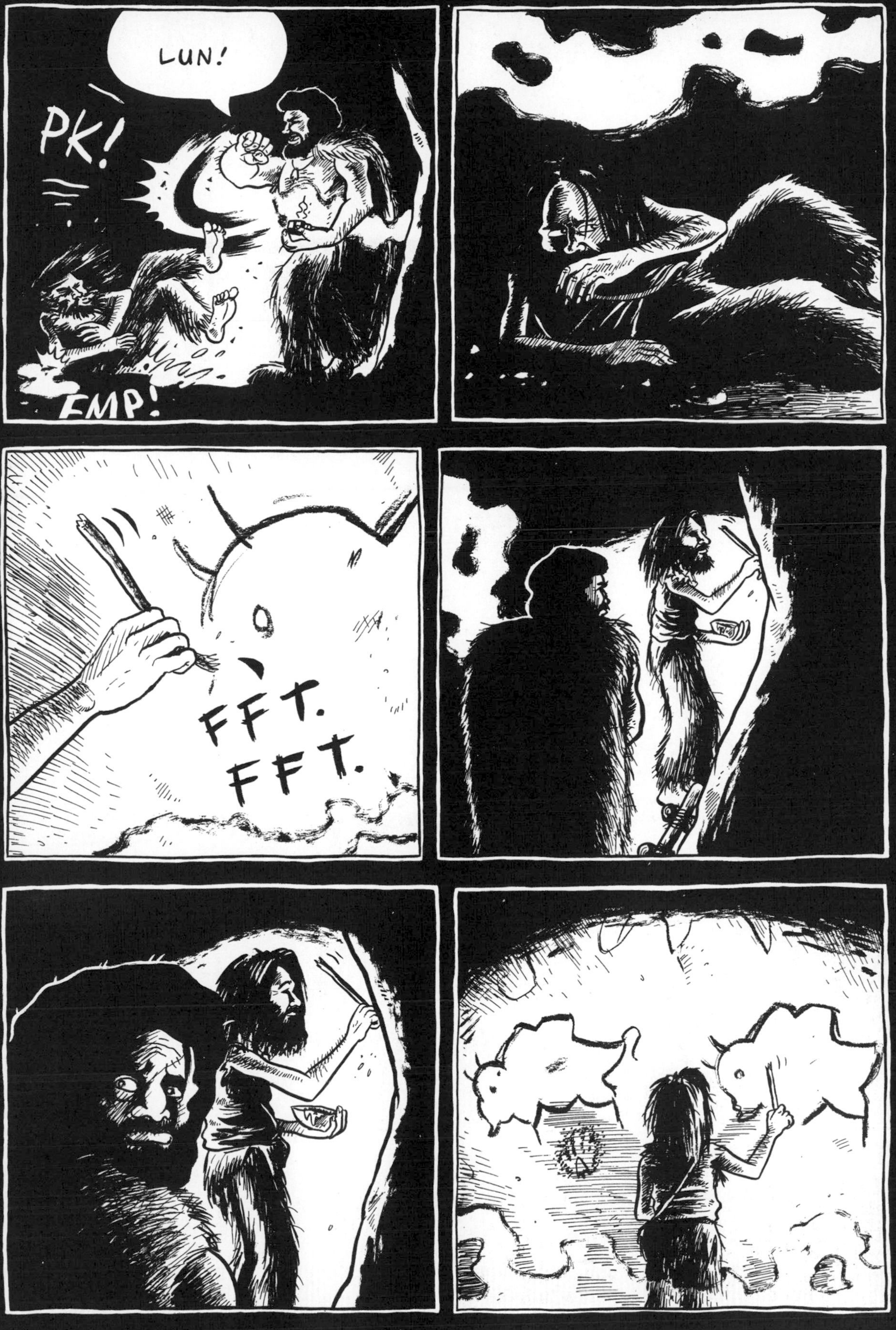
LUN!
PK!
EMP!
FFT.
FFT.

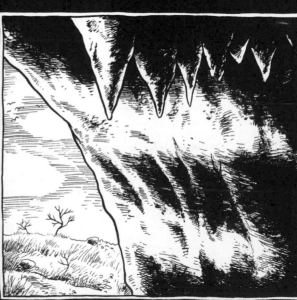

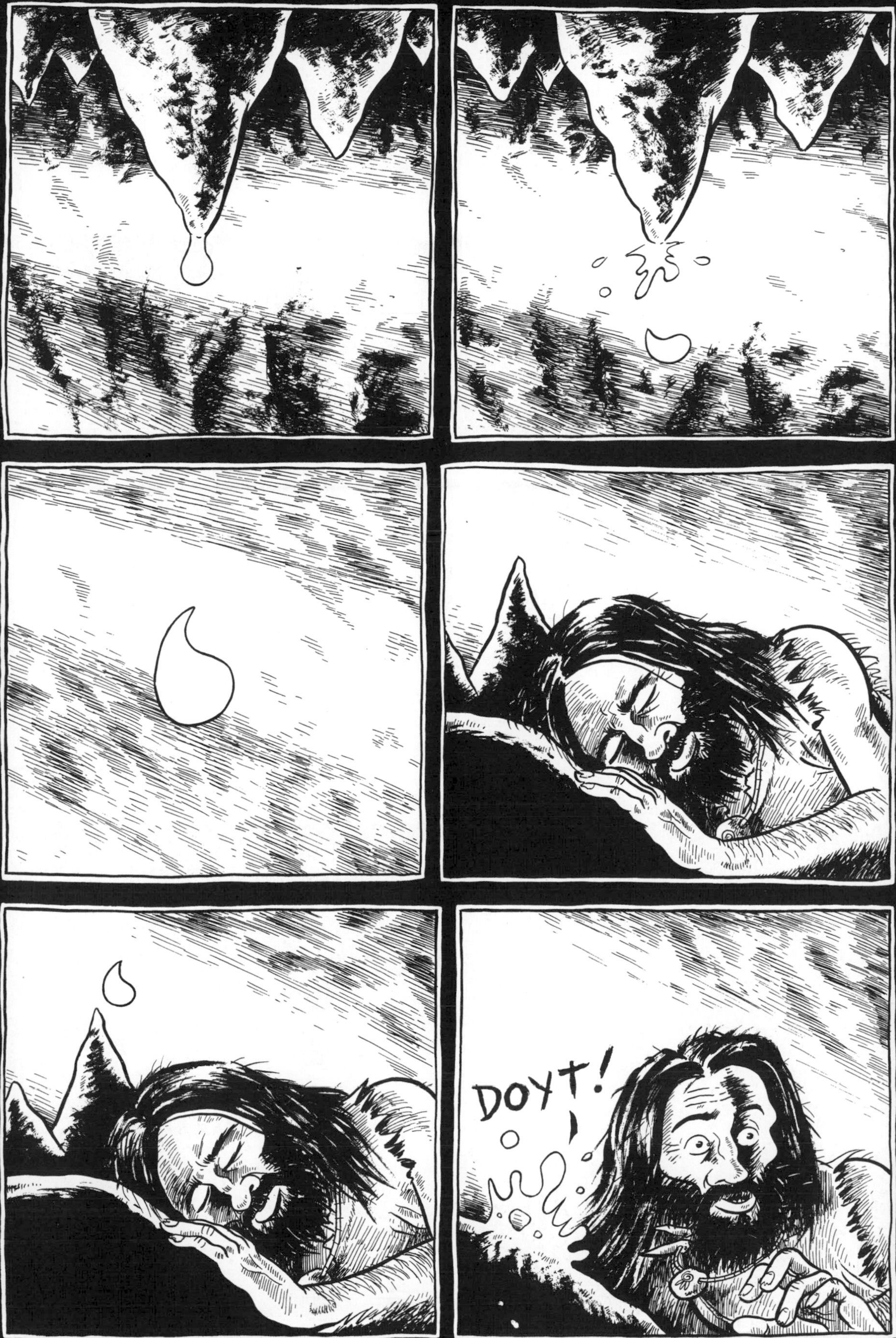
DOYT!

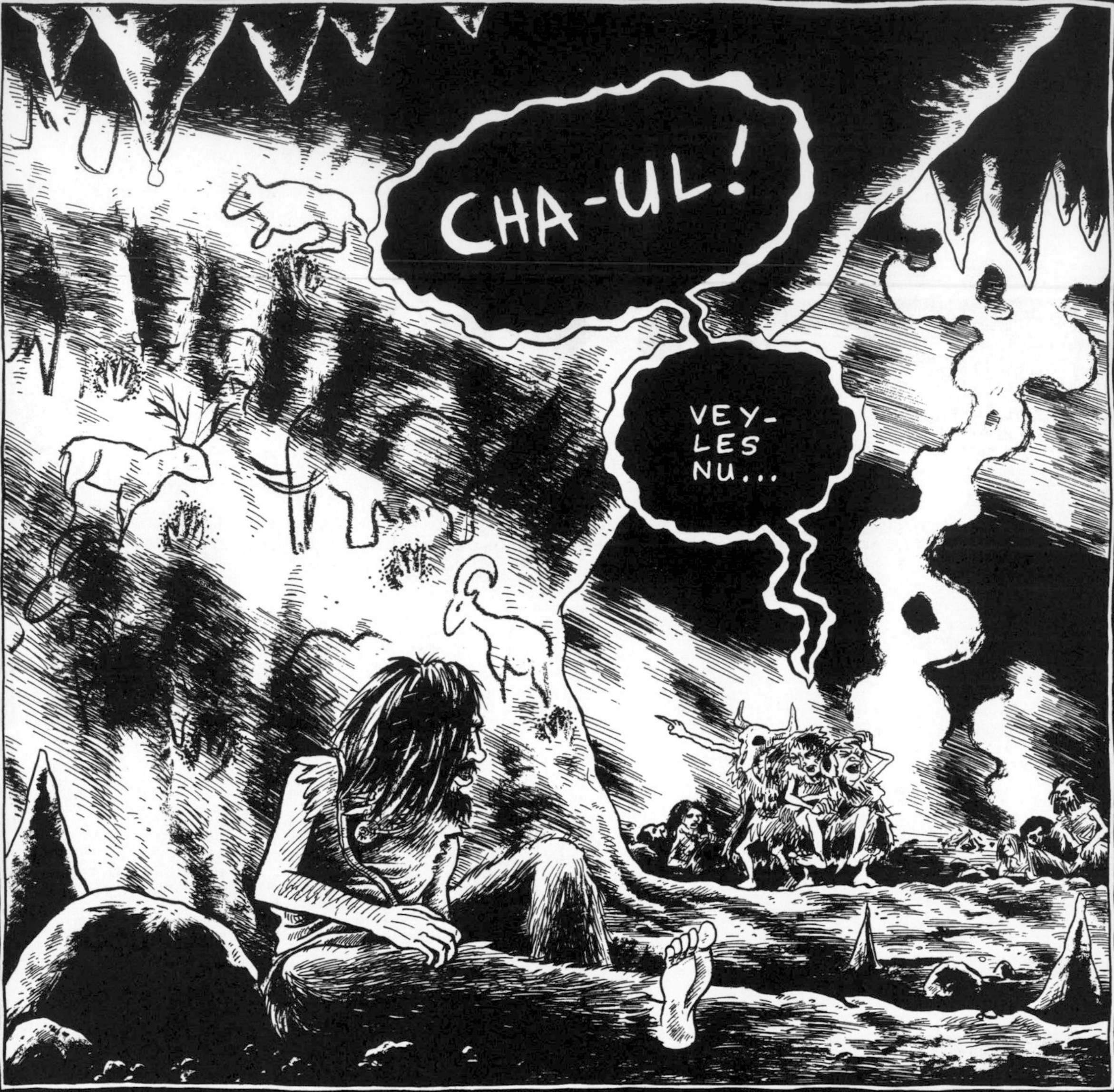
CHA-UL!
VEY-LES NU...

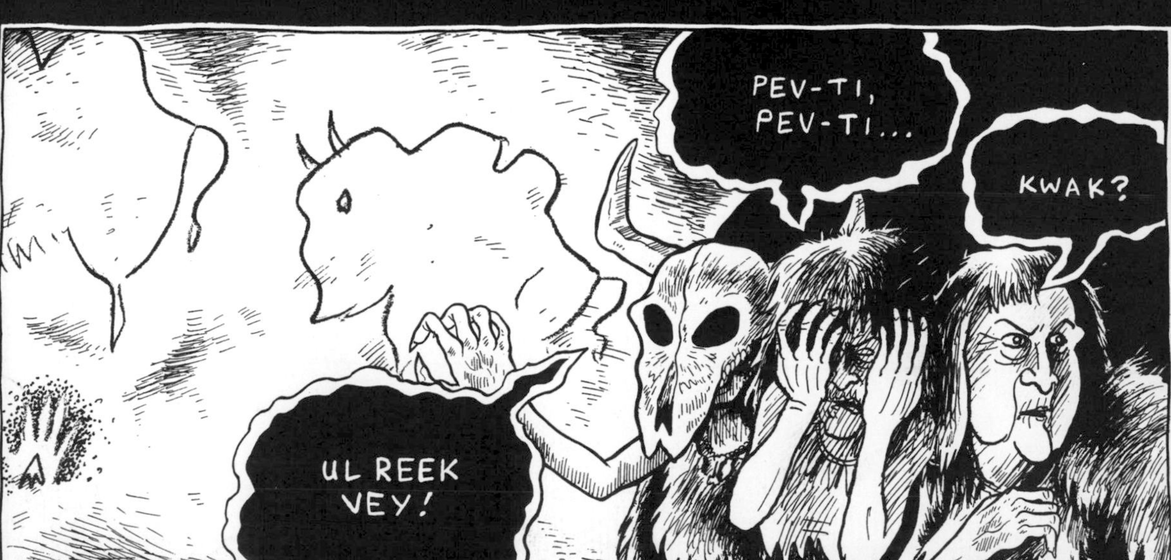
PEV-TI, PEV-TI...
KWAK?
UL REEK VEY!

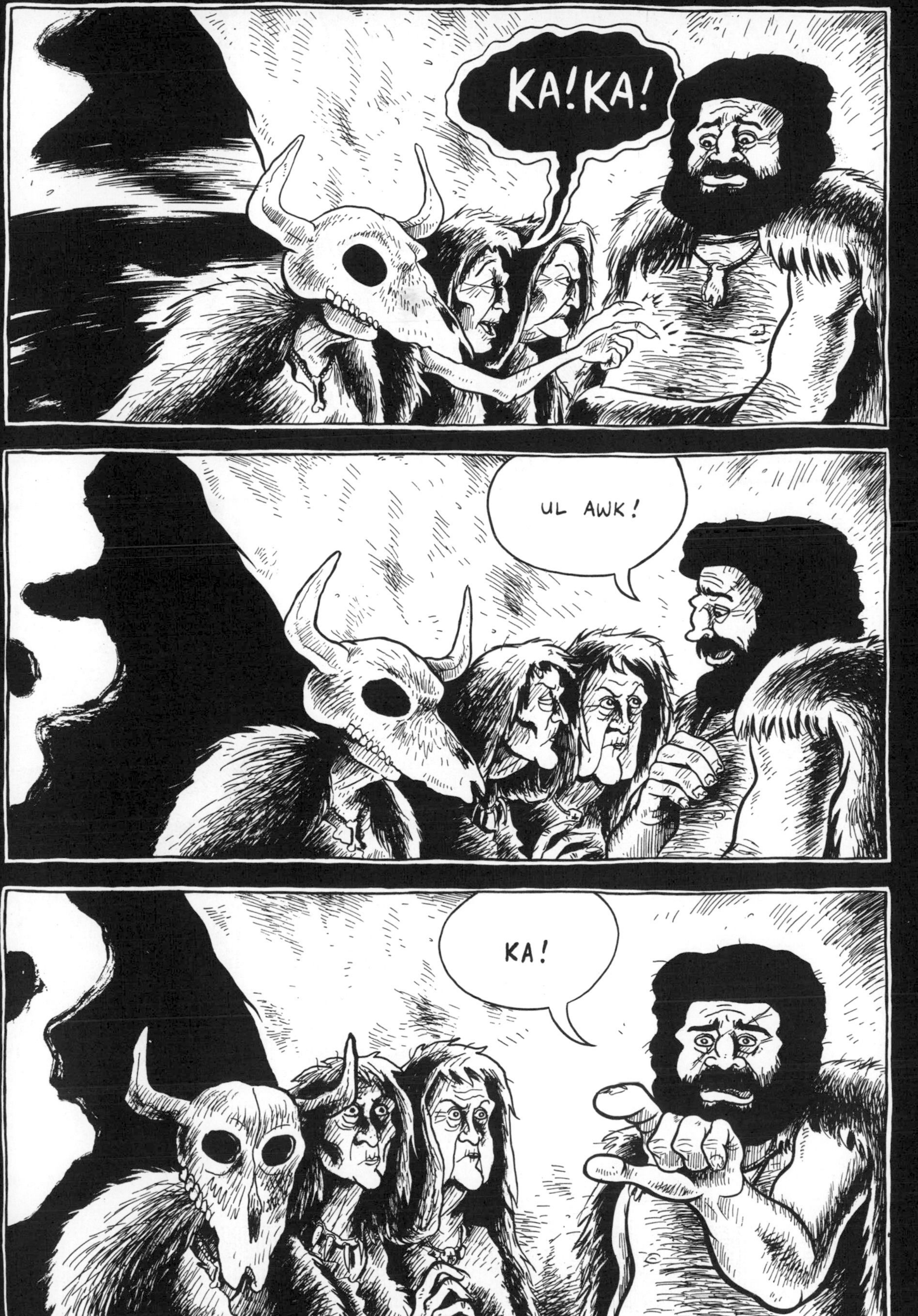
KA!KA!
UL AWK!
KA!

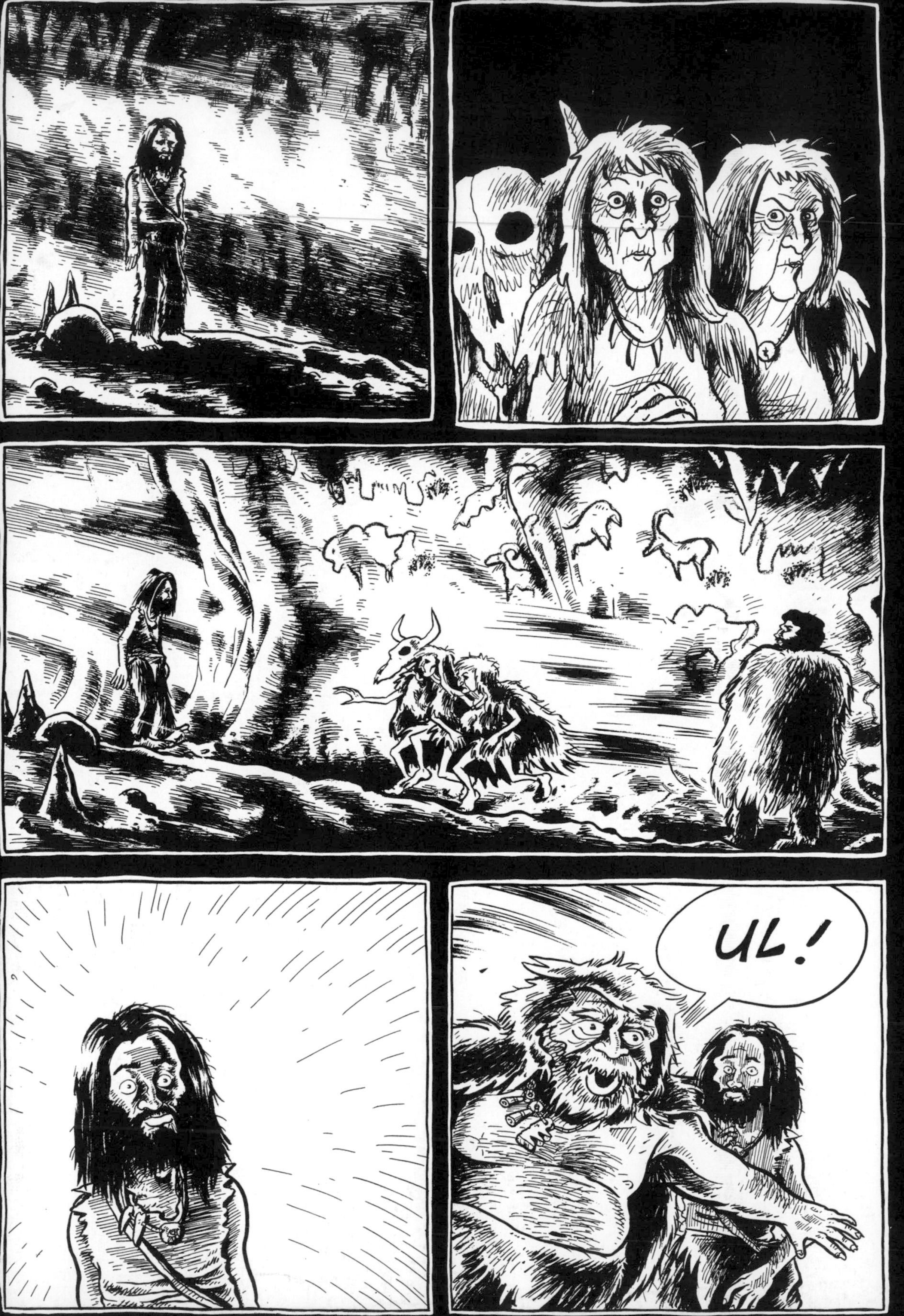
UL!

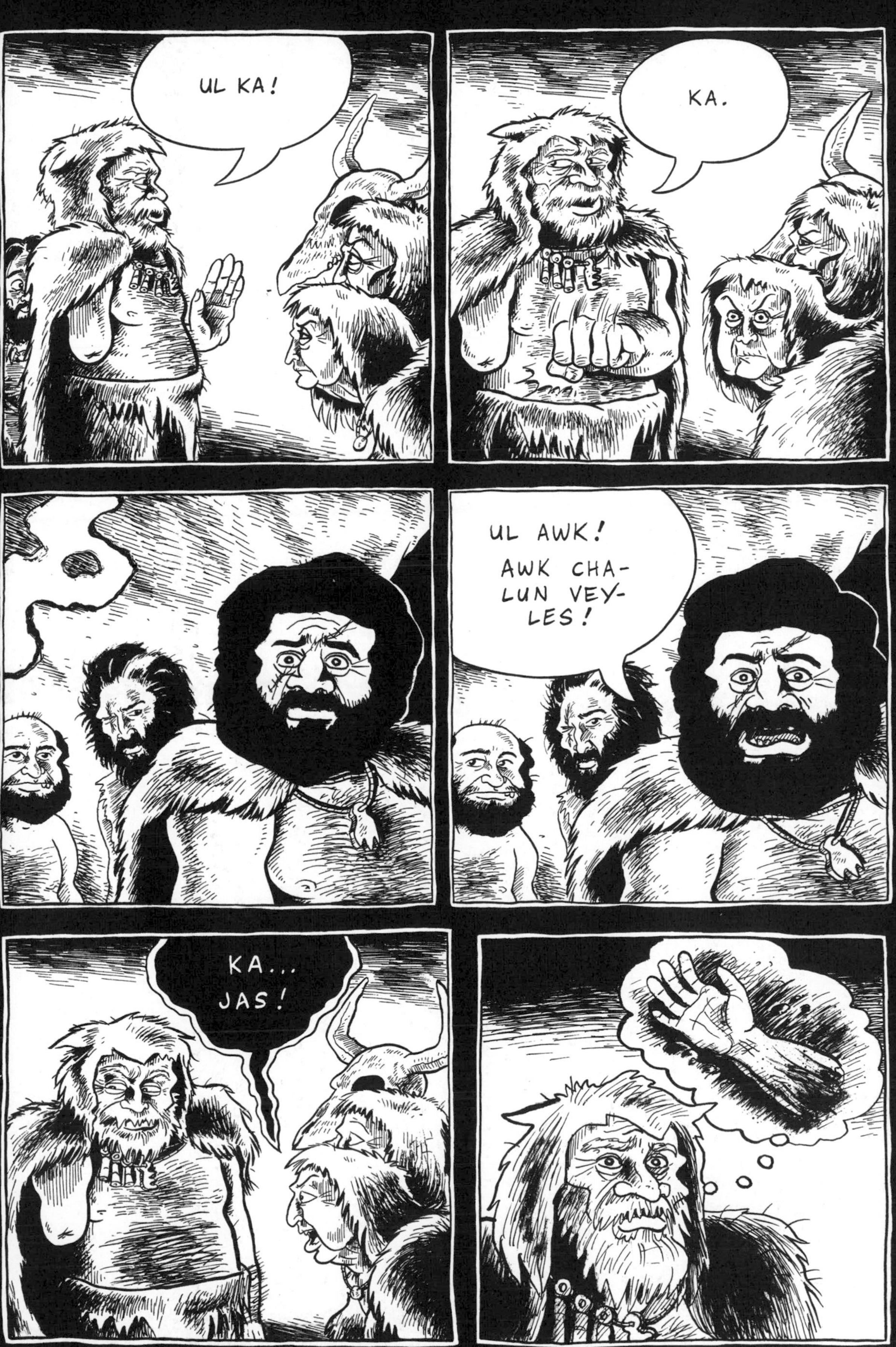
UL KA!
KA.
UL AWK! AWK CHA-LUN VEY-LES!
KA... JAS!

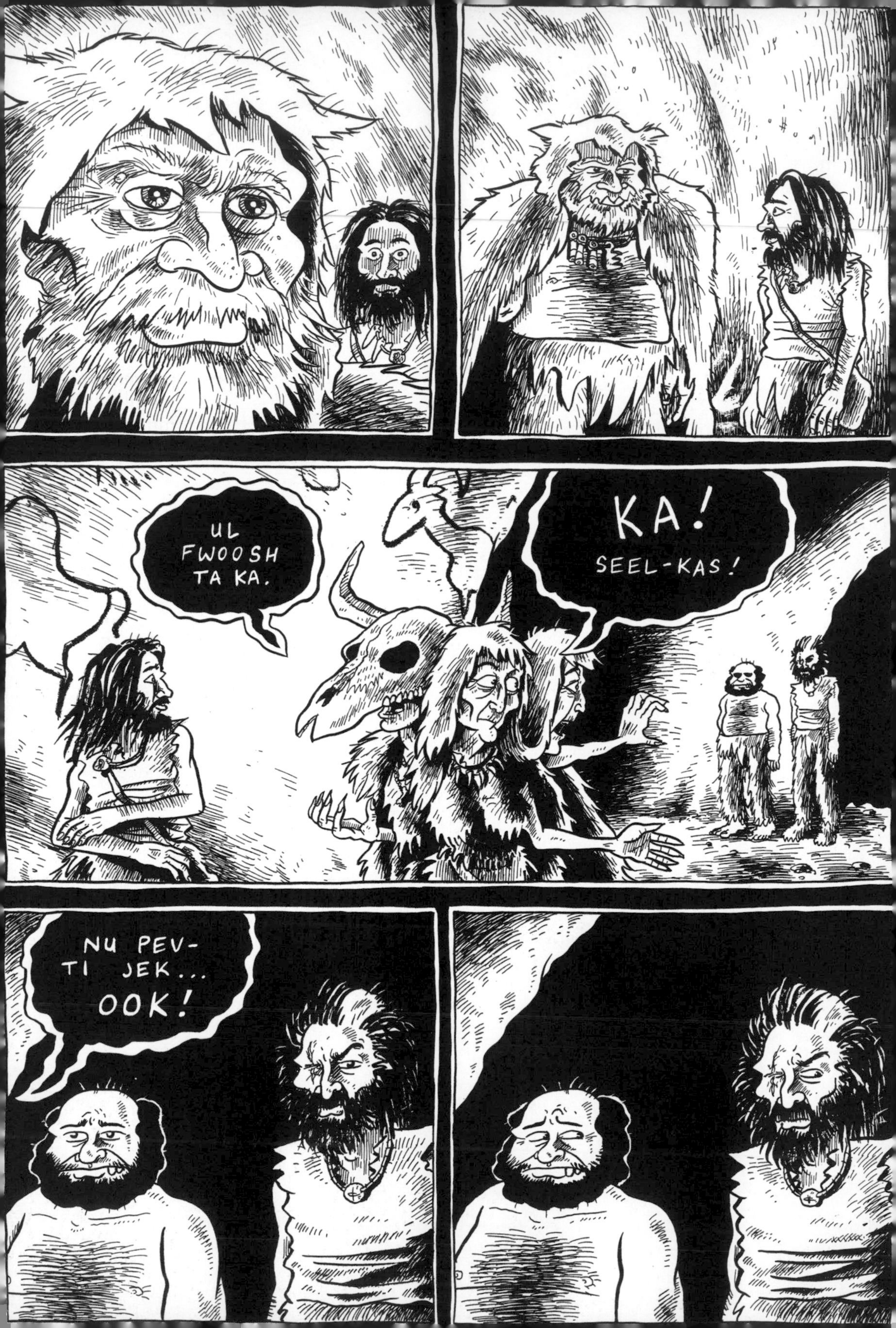
UL FWOOSH TA KA.
KA! SEEL-KAS!
NU PEV-TI JEK... OOK!

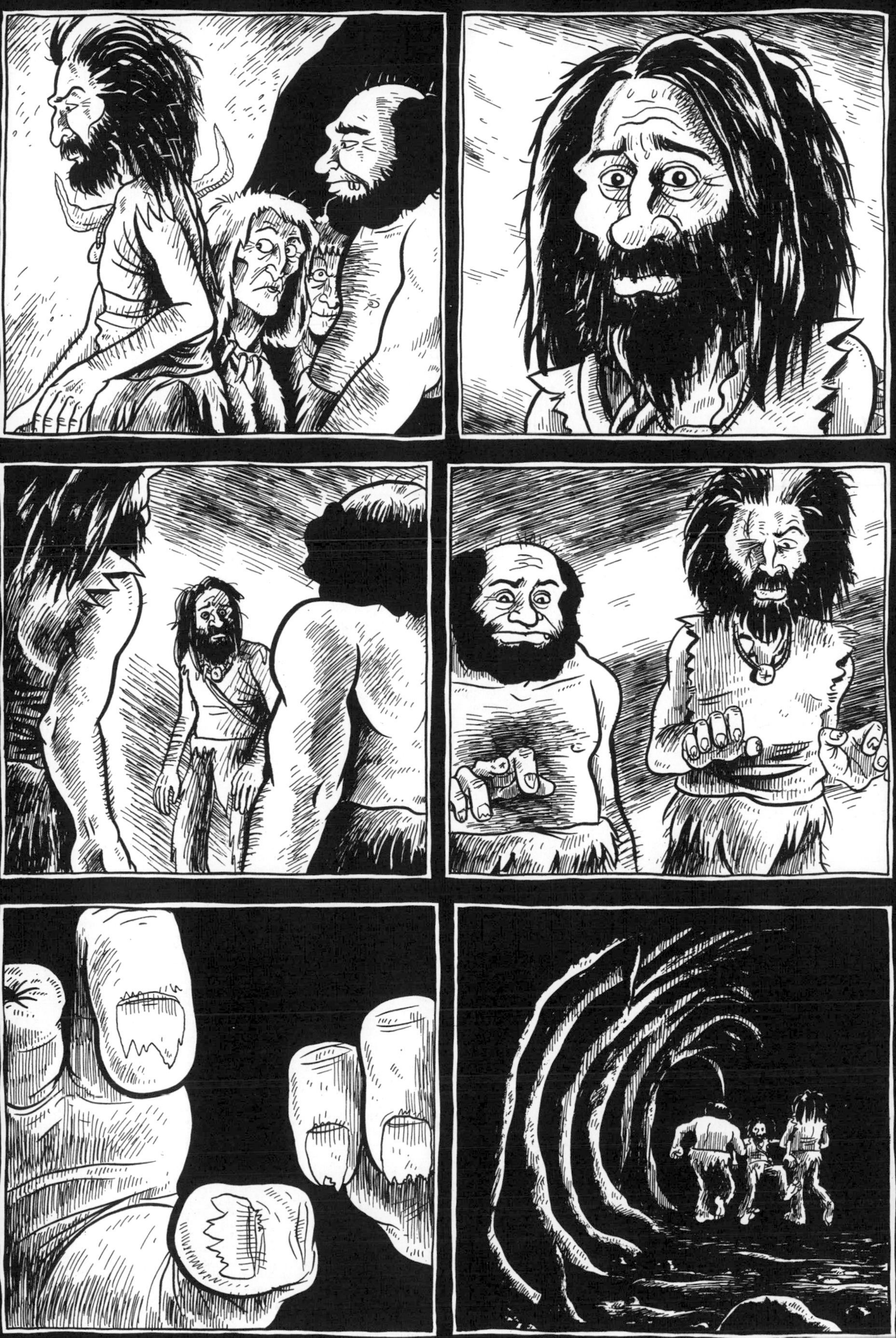

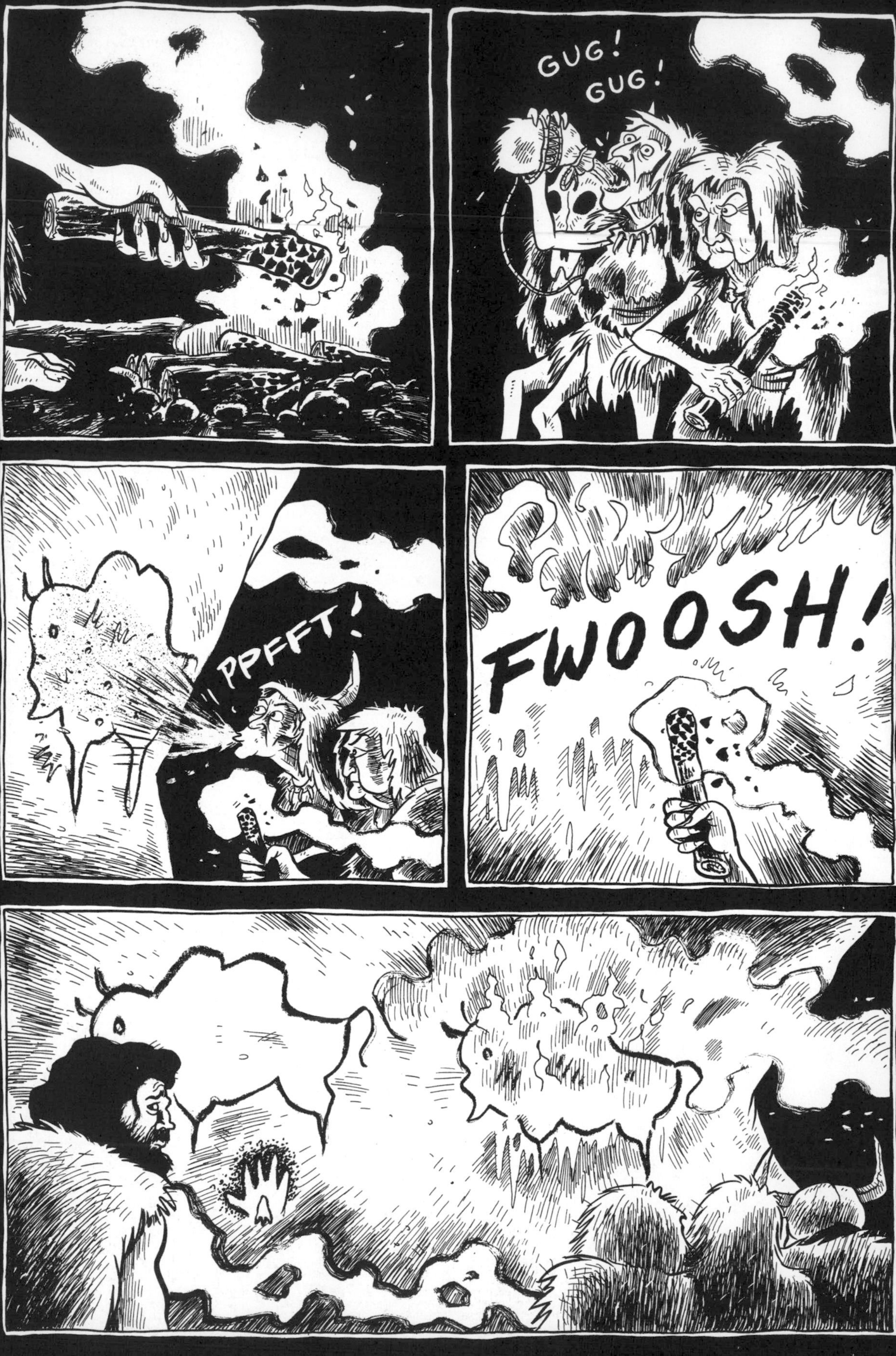
GUG!
GUG!
PPFFT!
FWOOSH!

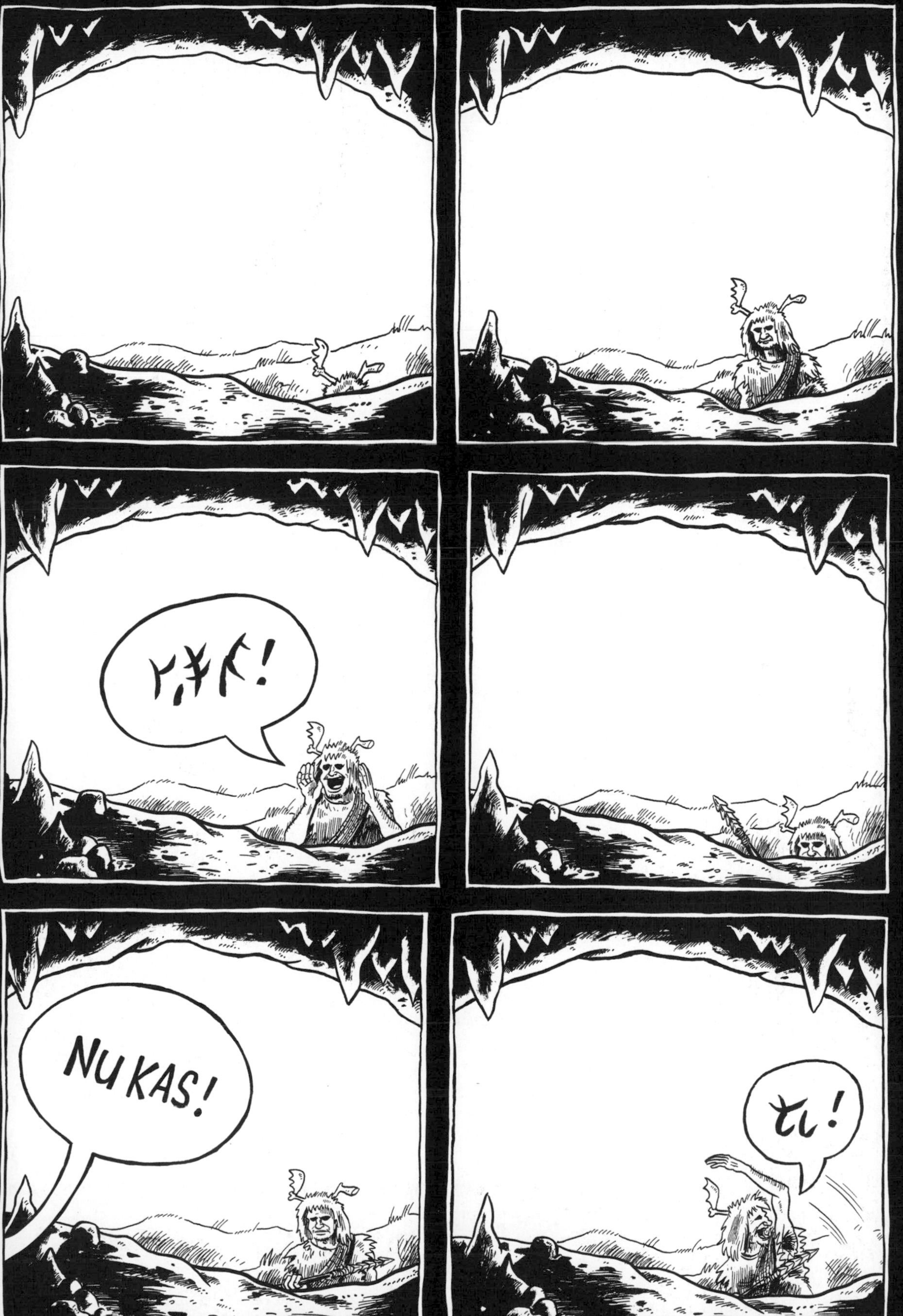
NU KAS!

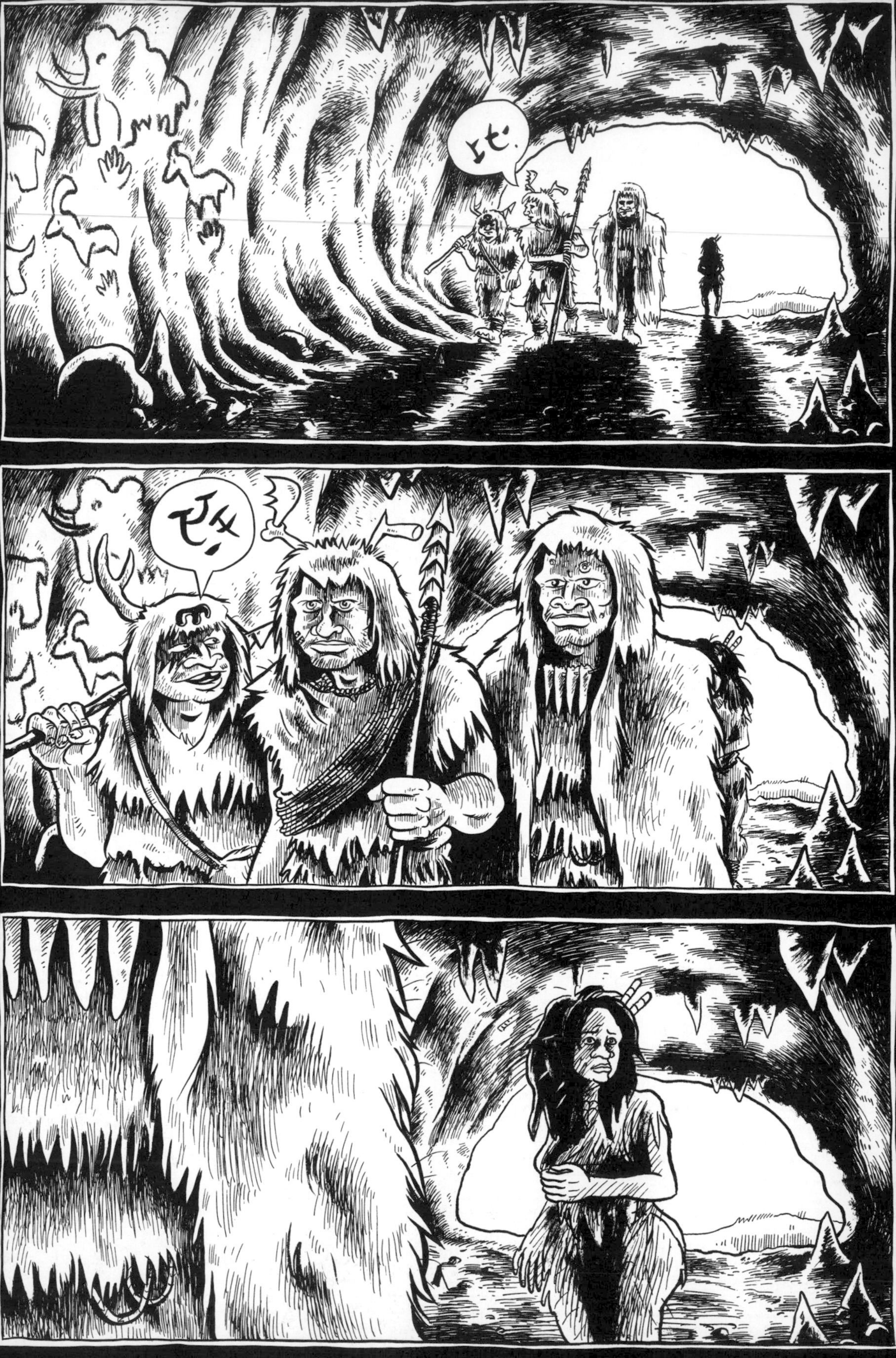

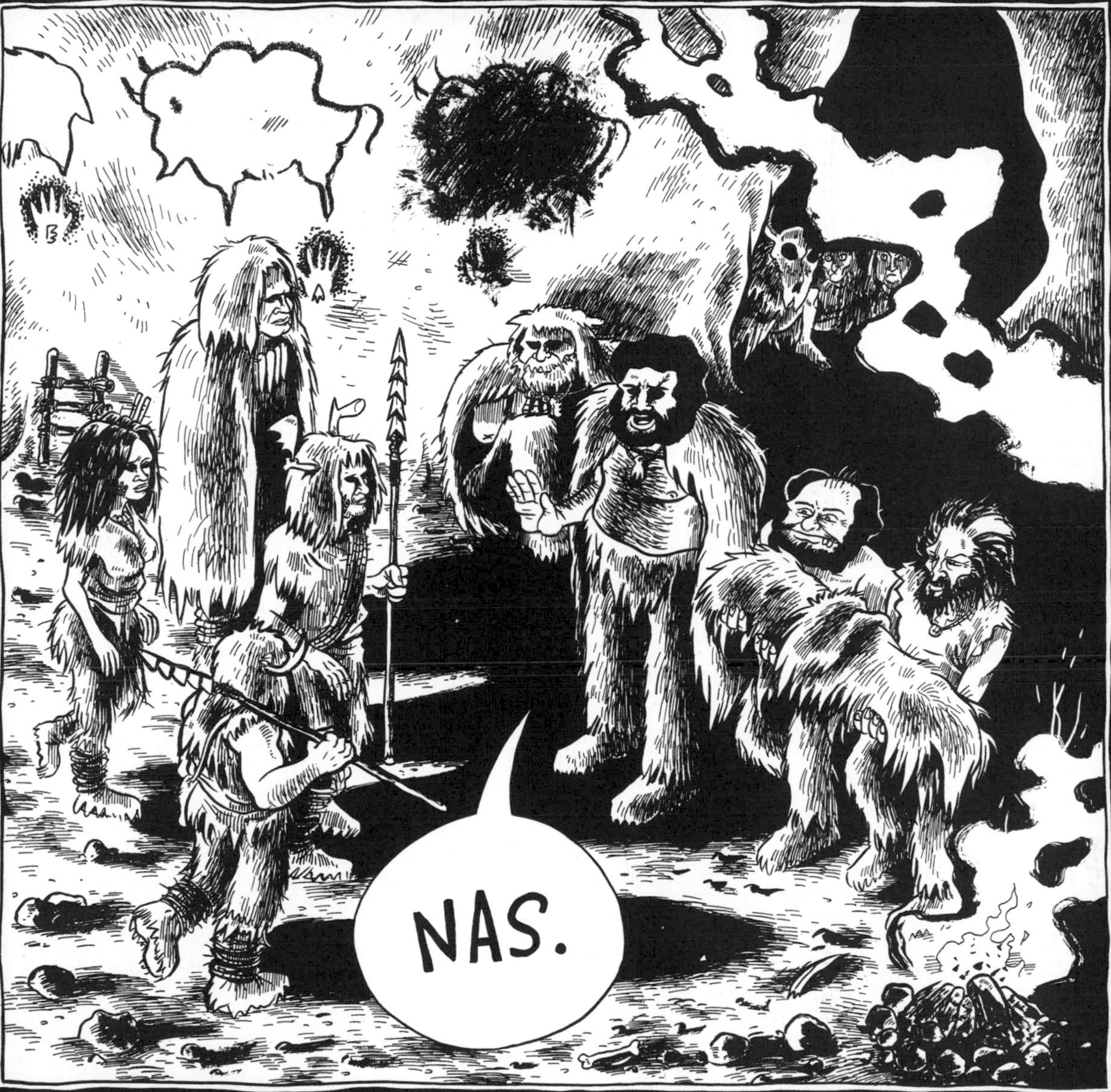
NAS.

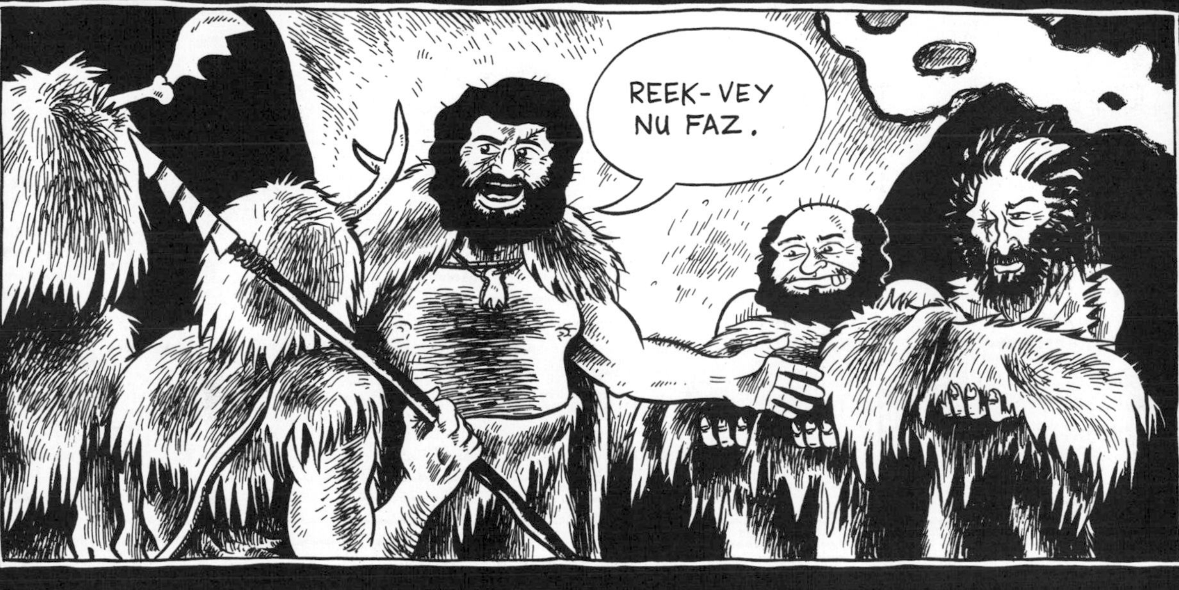
REEK-VEY
NU FAZ.

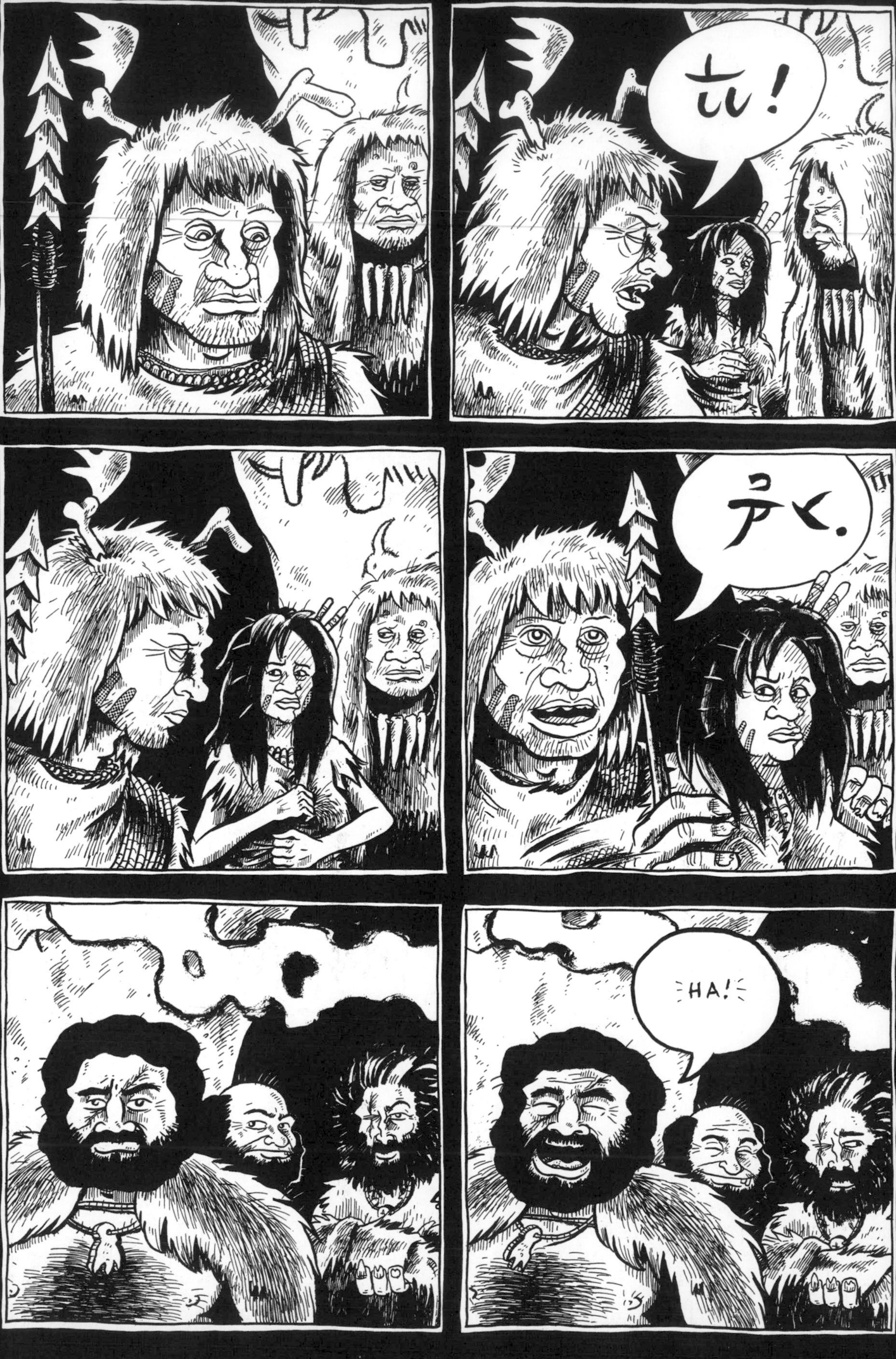
HA!

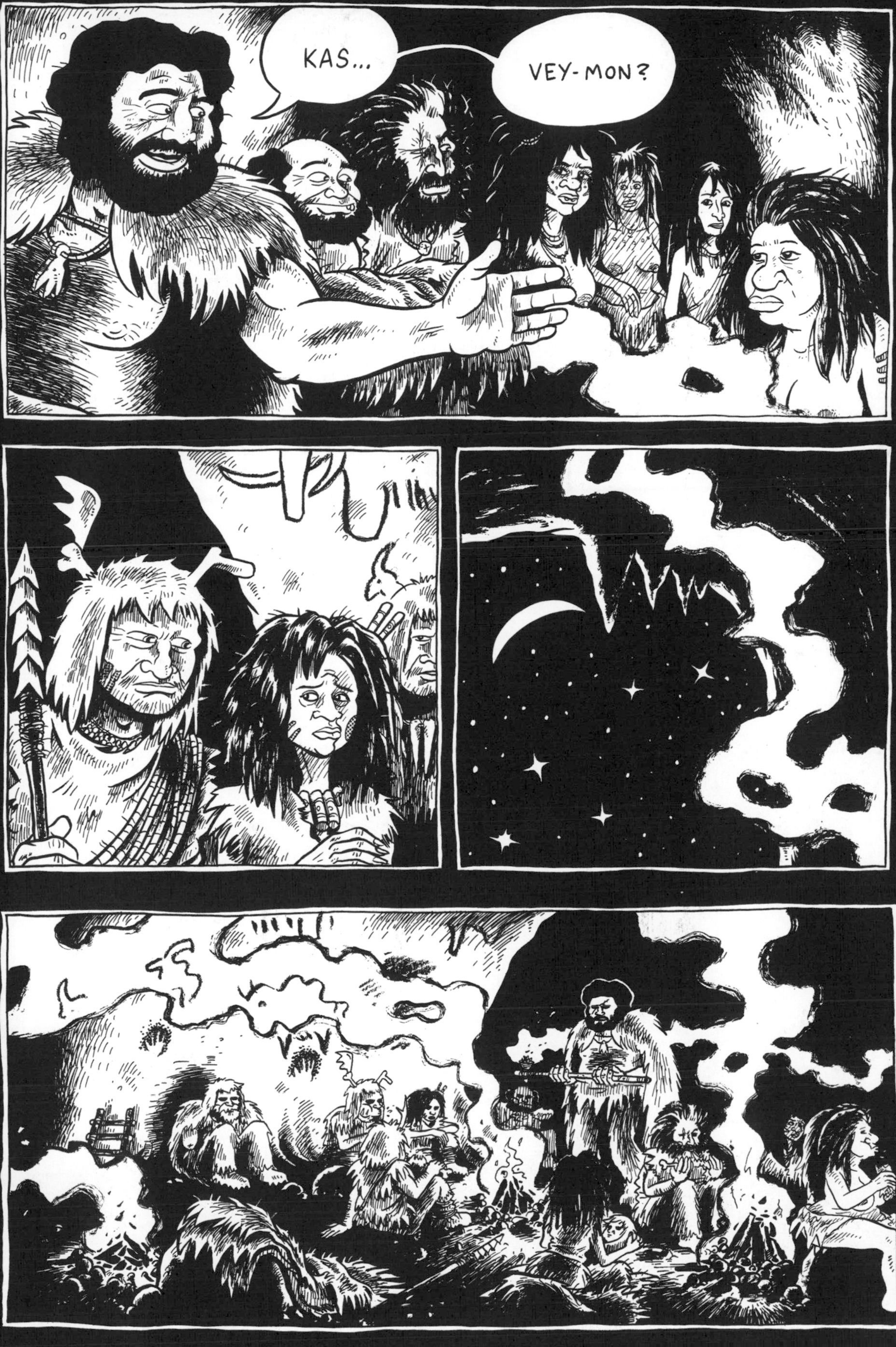
KAS...
VEY-MON?

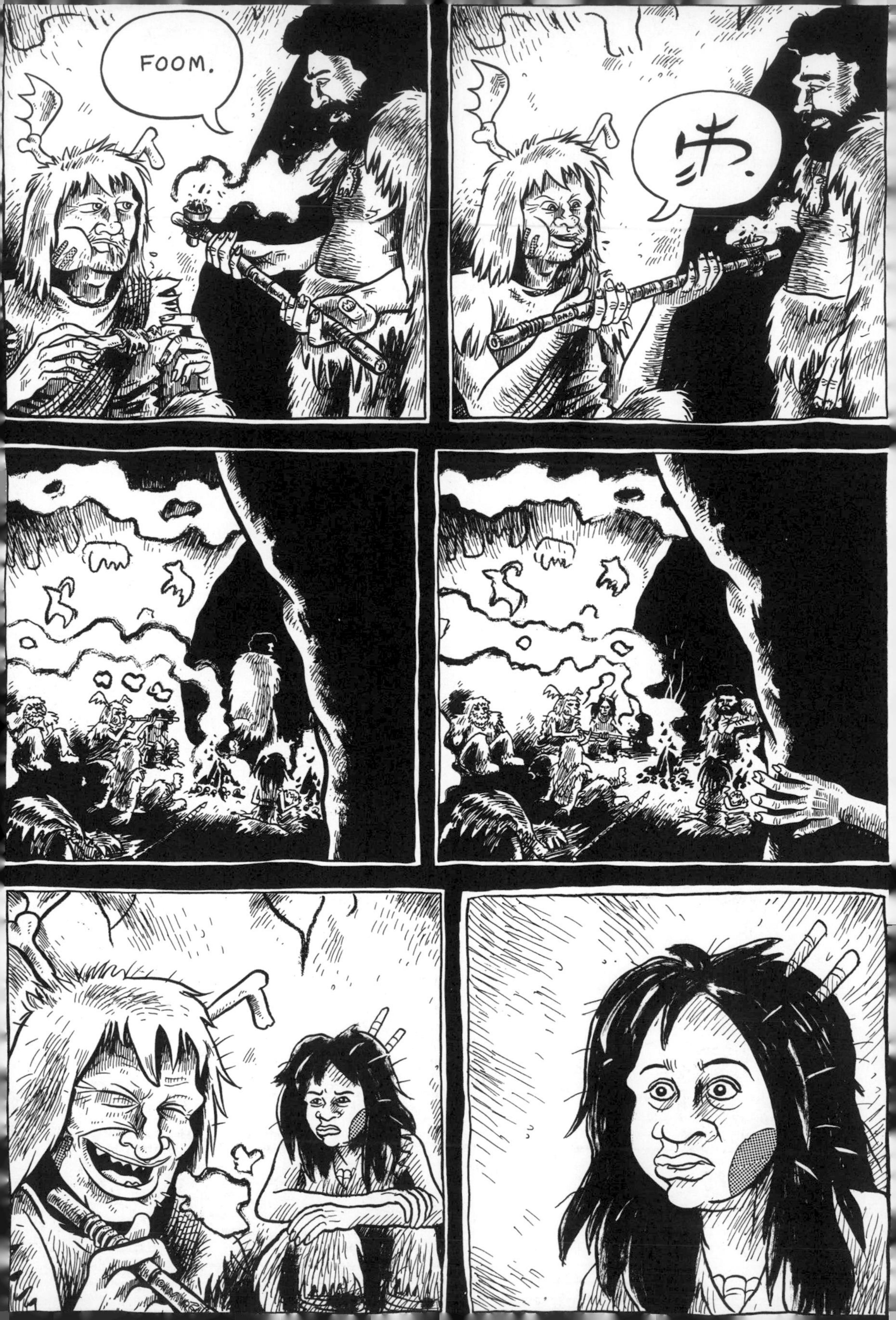
FOOM.

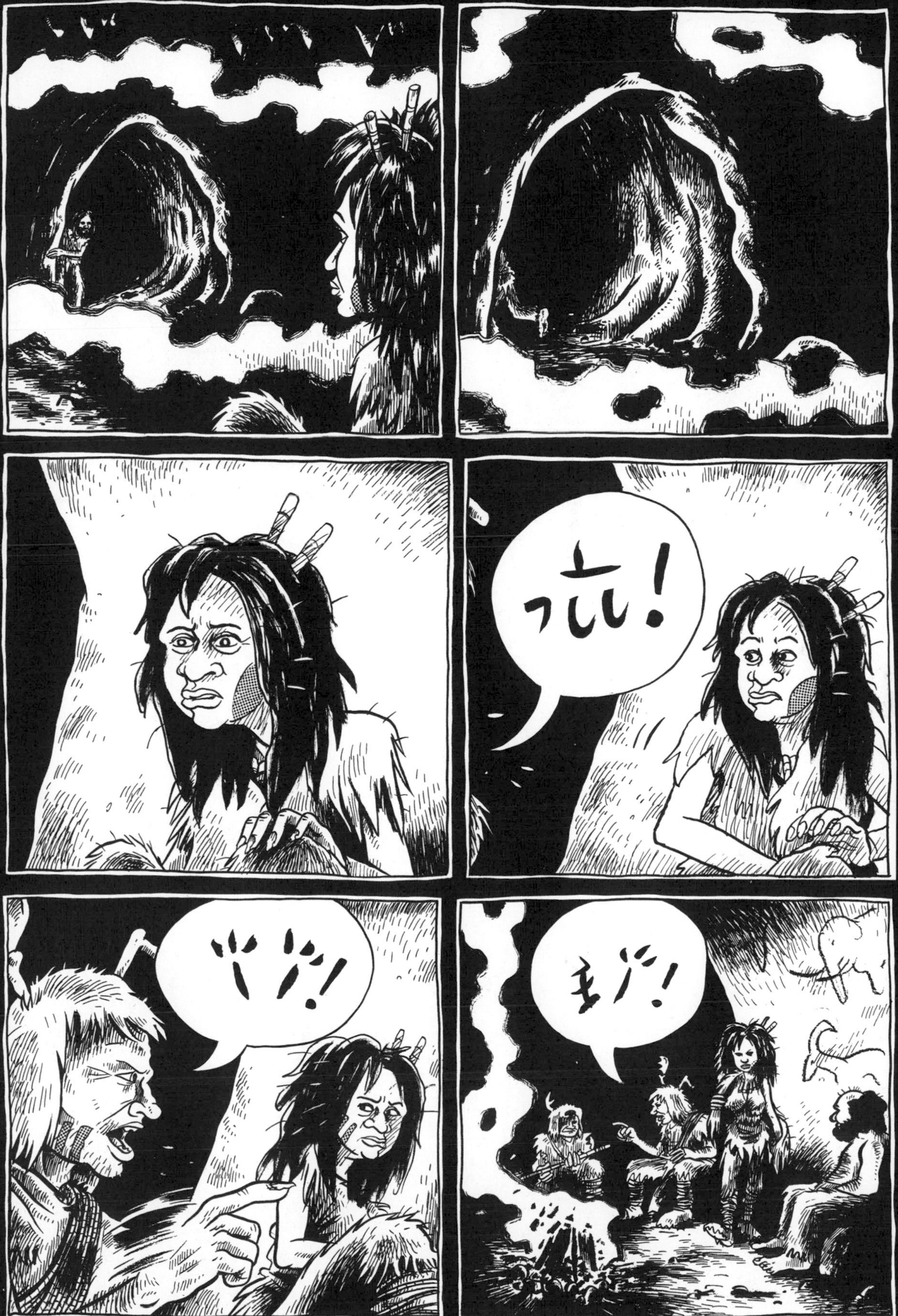

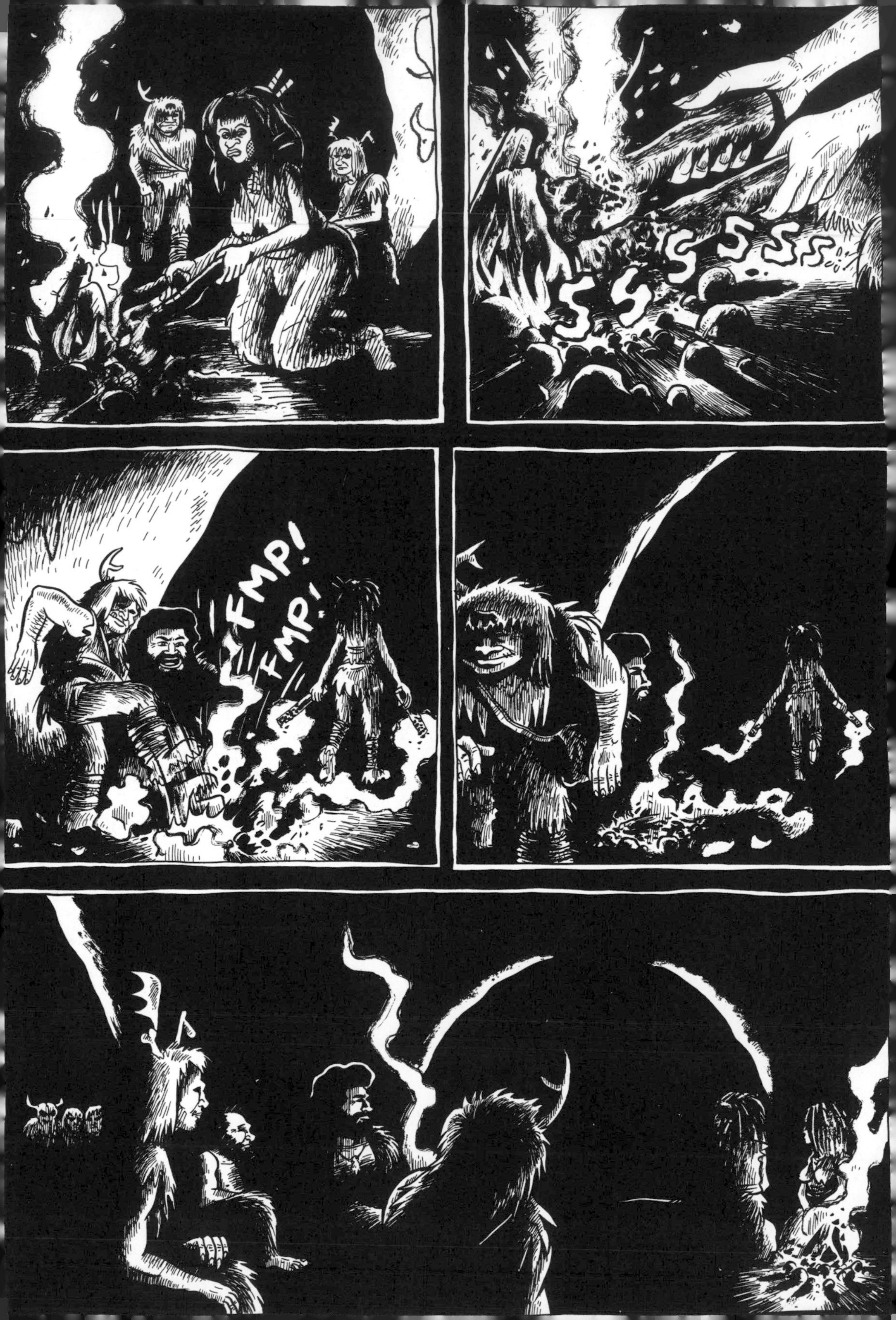
SSSSSSss...
FMP!
FMP!

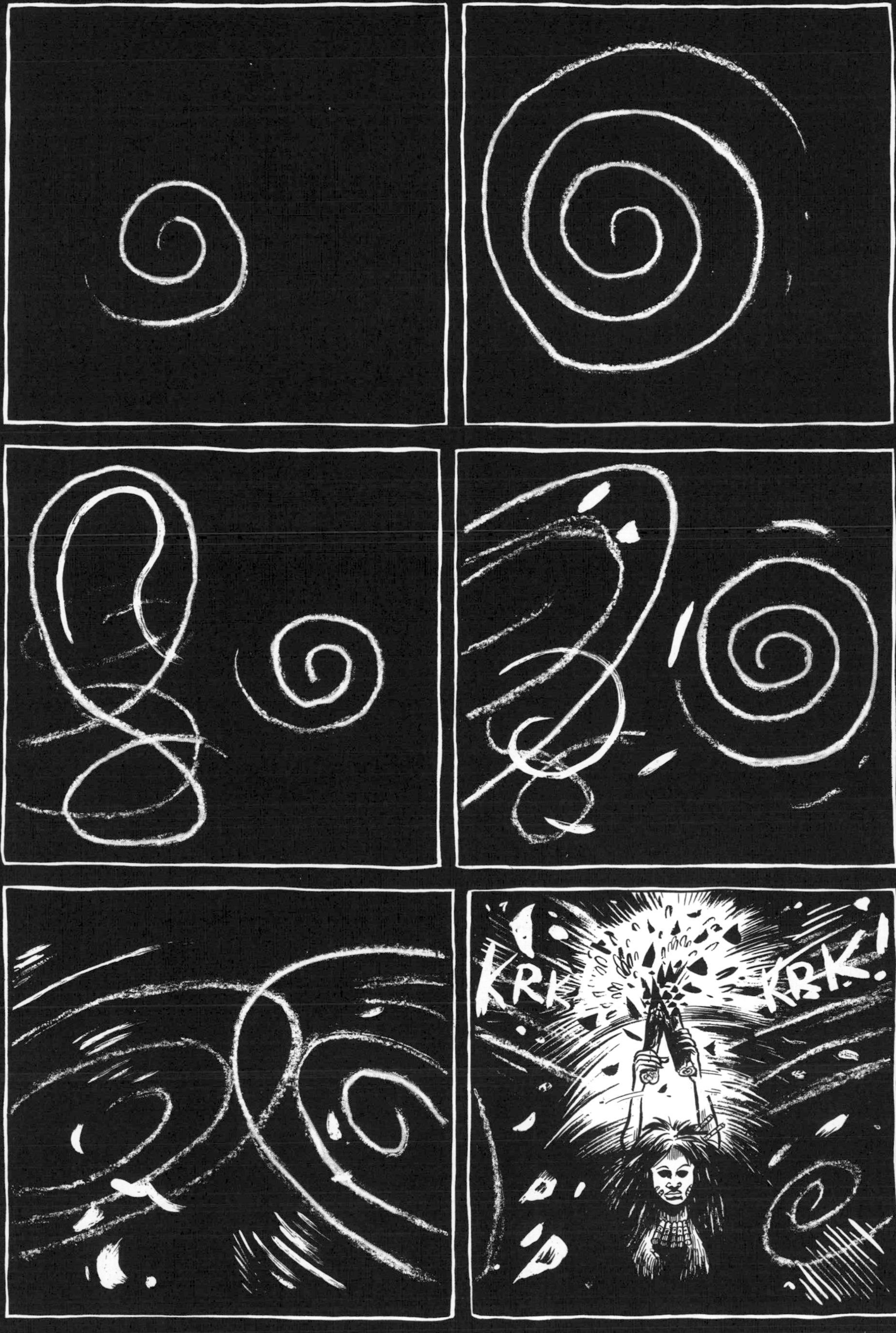
KRK
KRK!

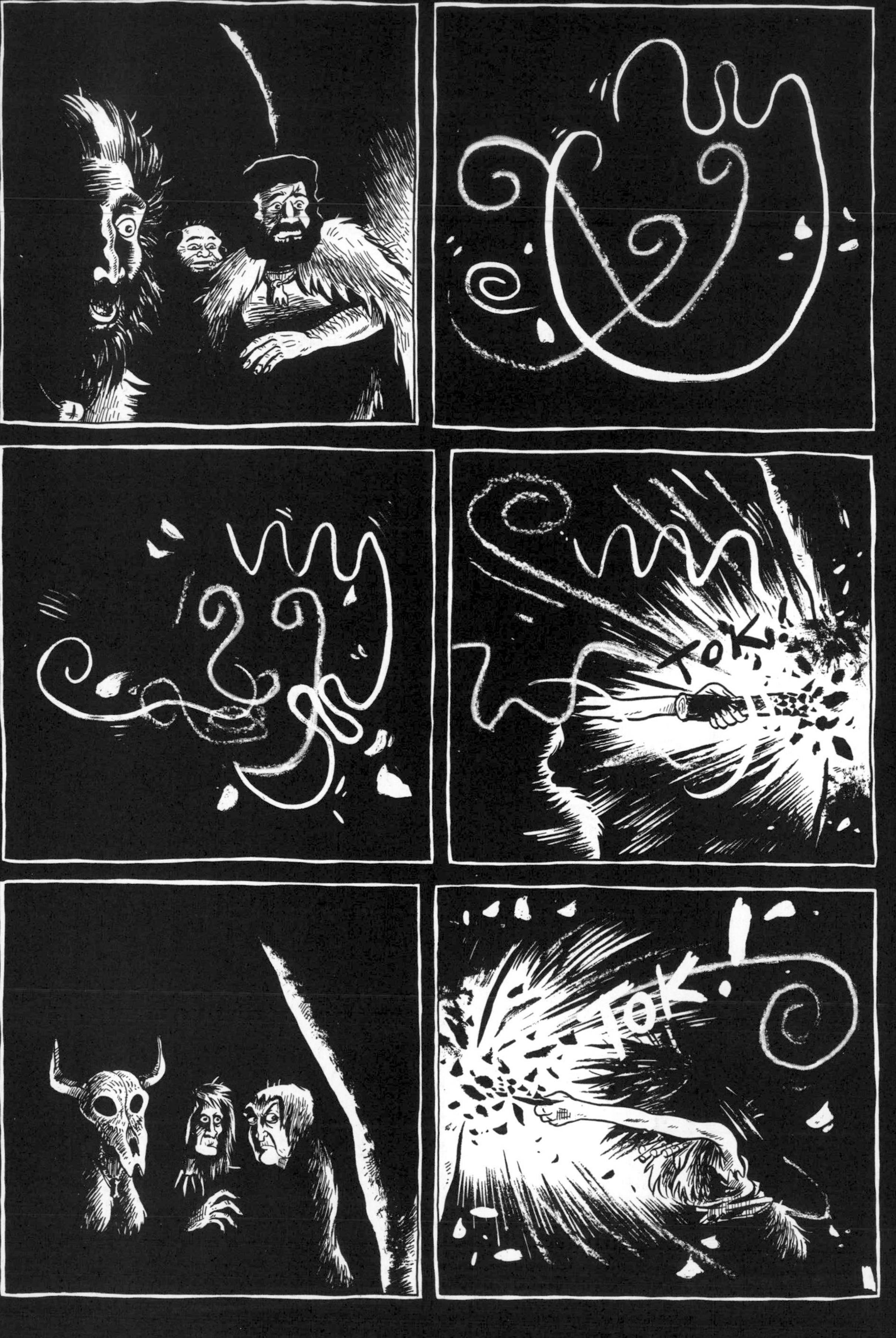
TOK!
TOK!

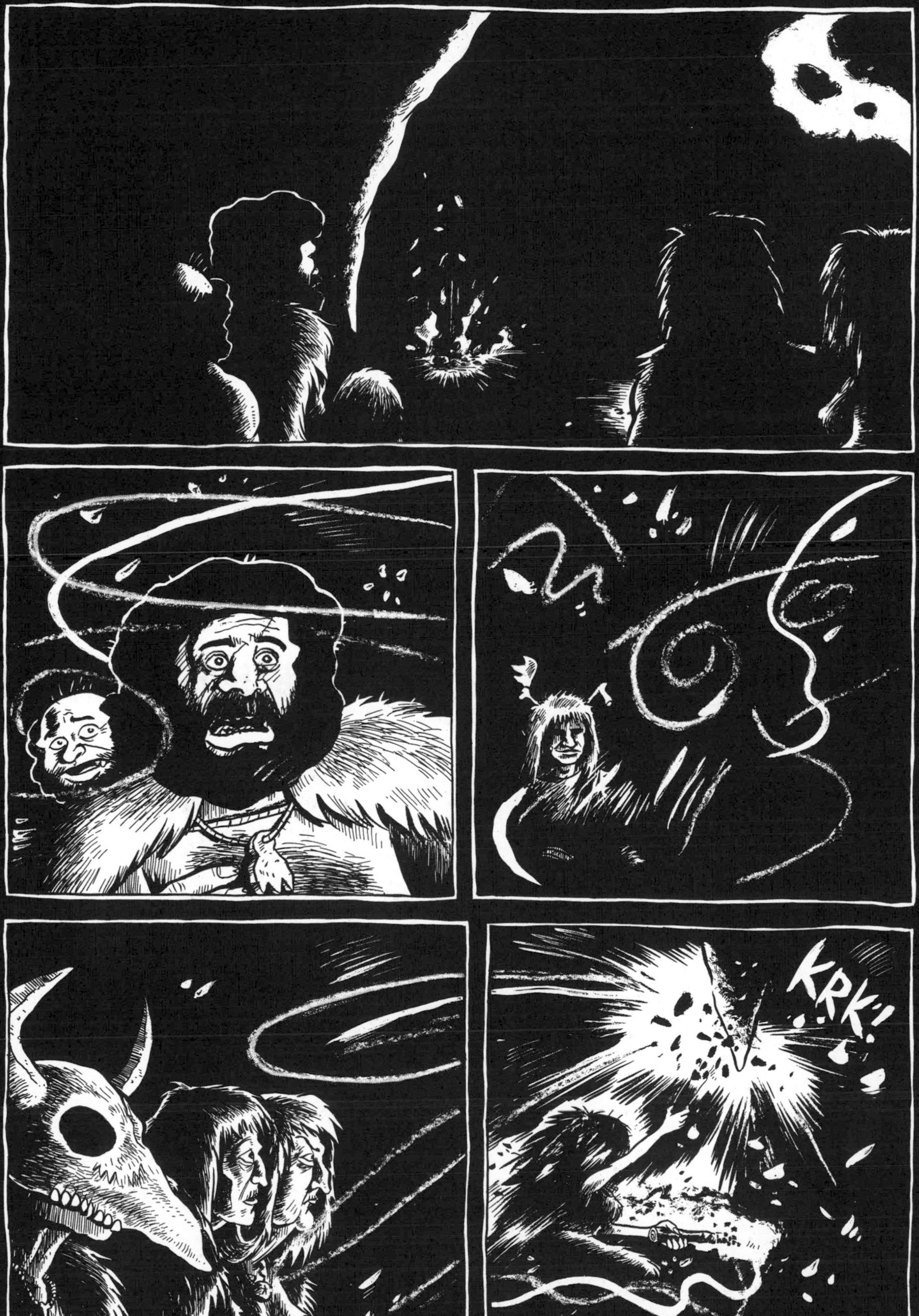
KRK!!

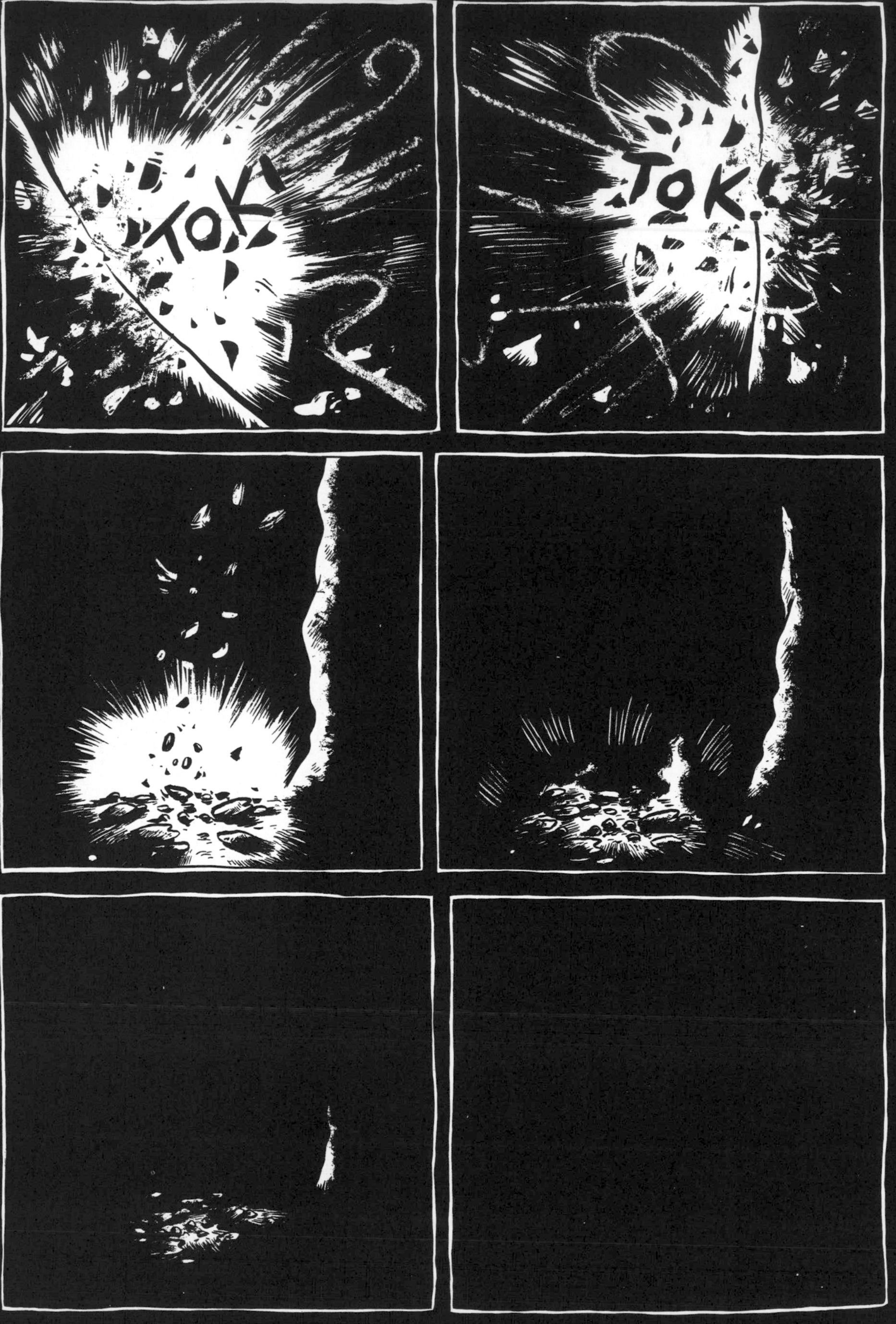
TOK
TOK

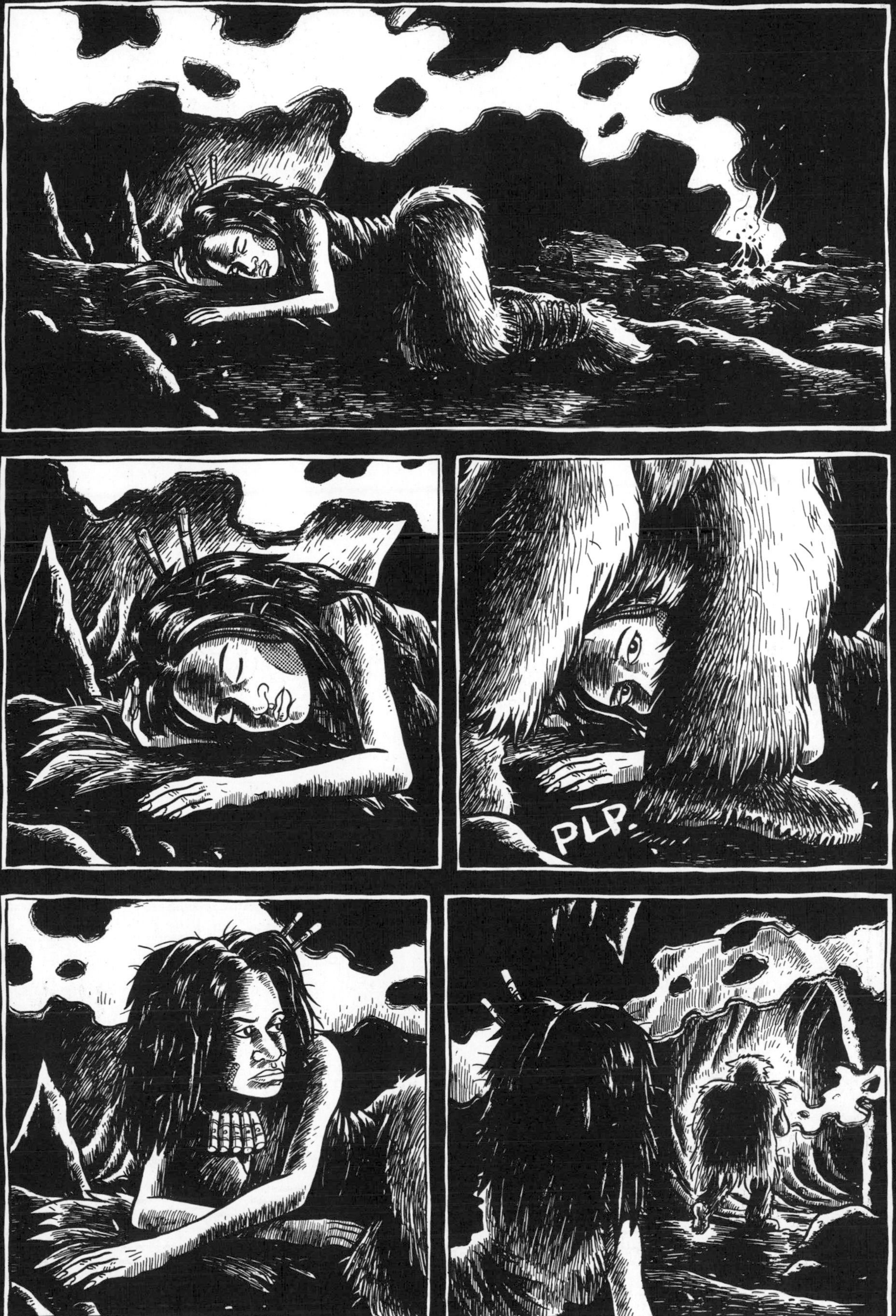
PLP.

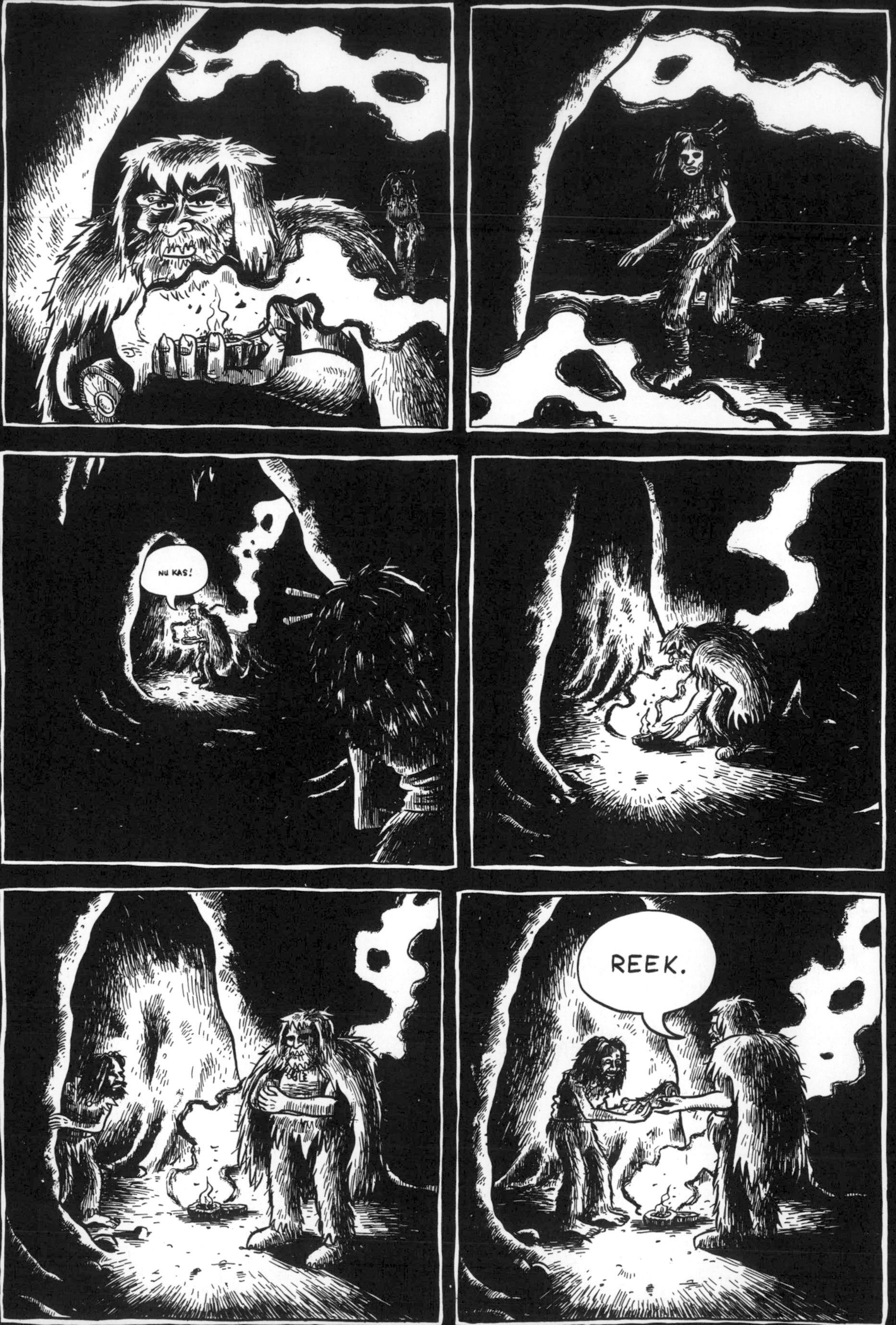
NU KAS!
REEK.

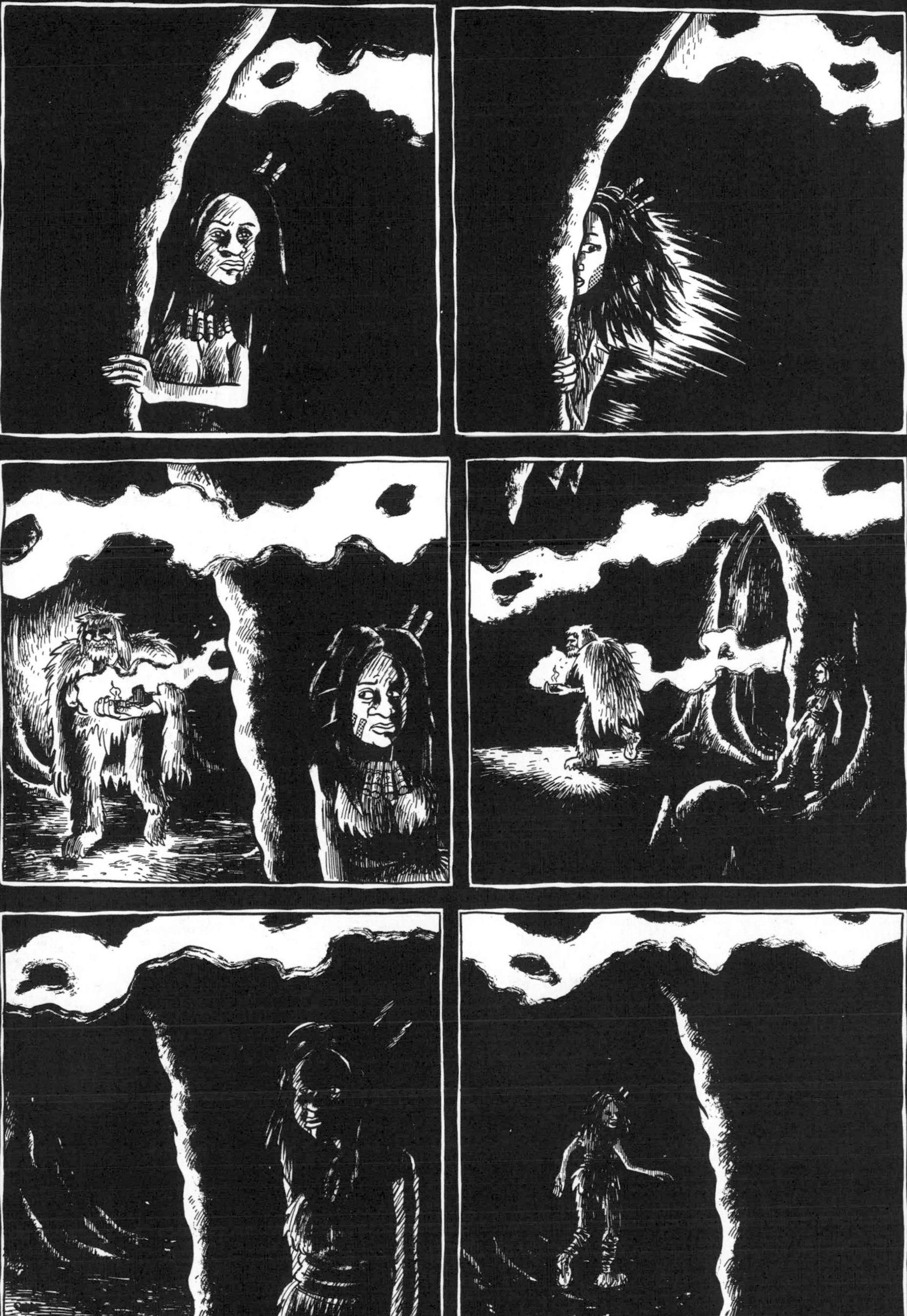

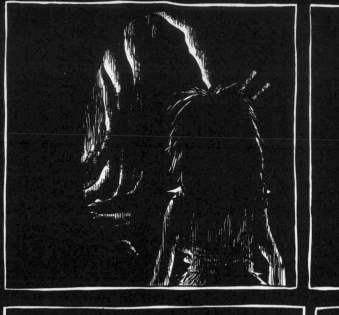
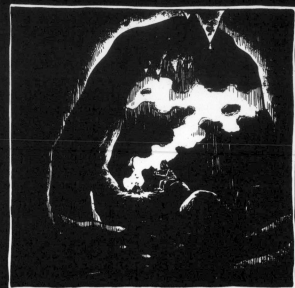

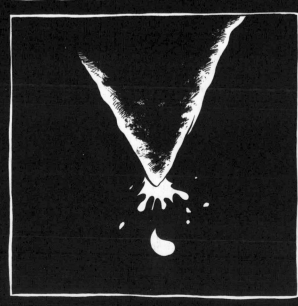

DOYT.

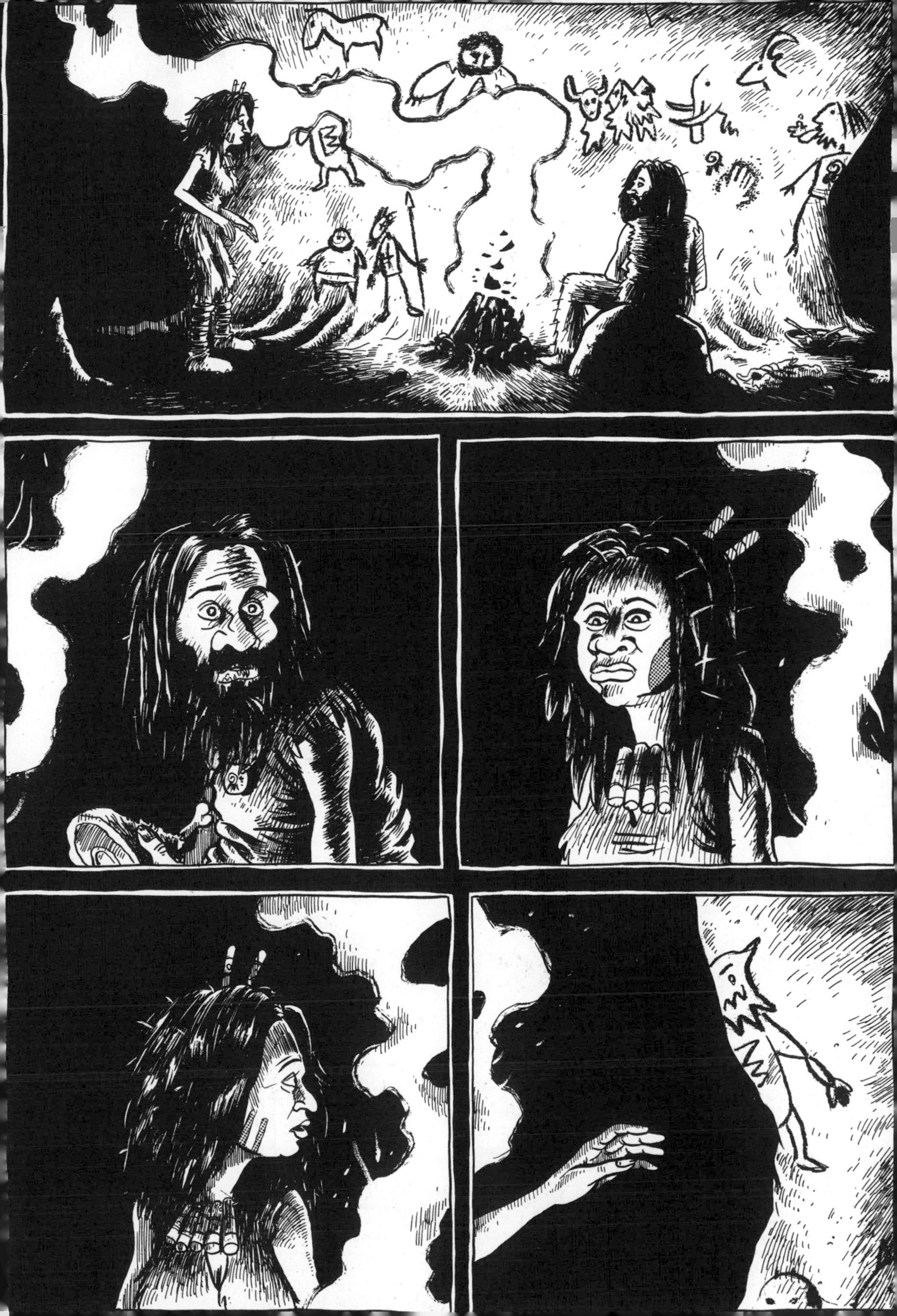

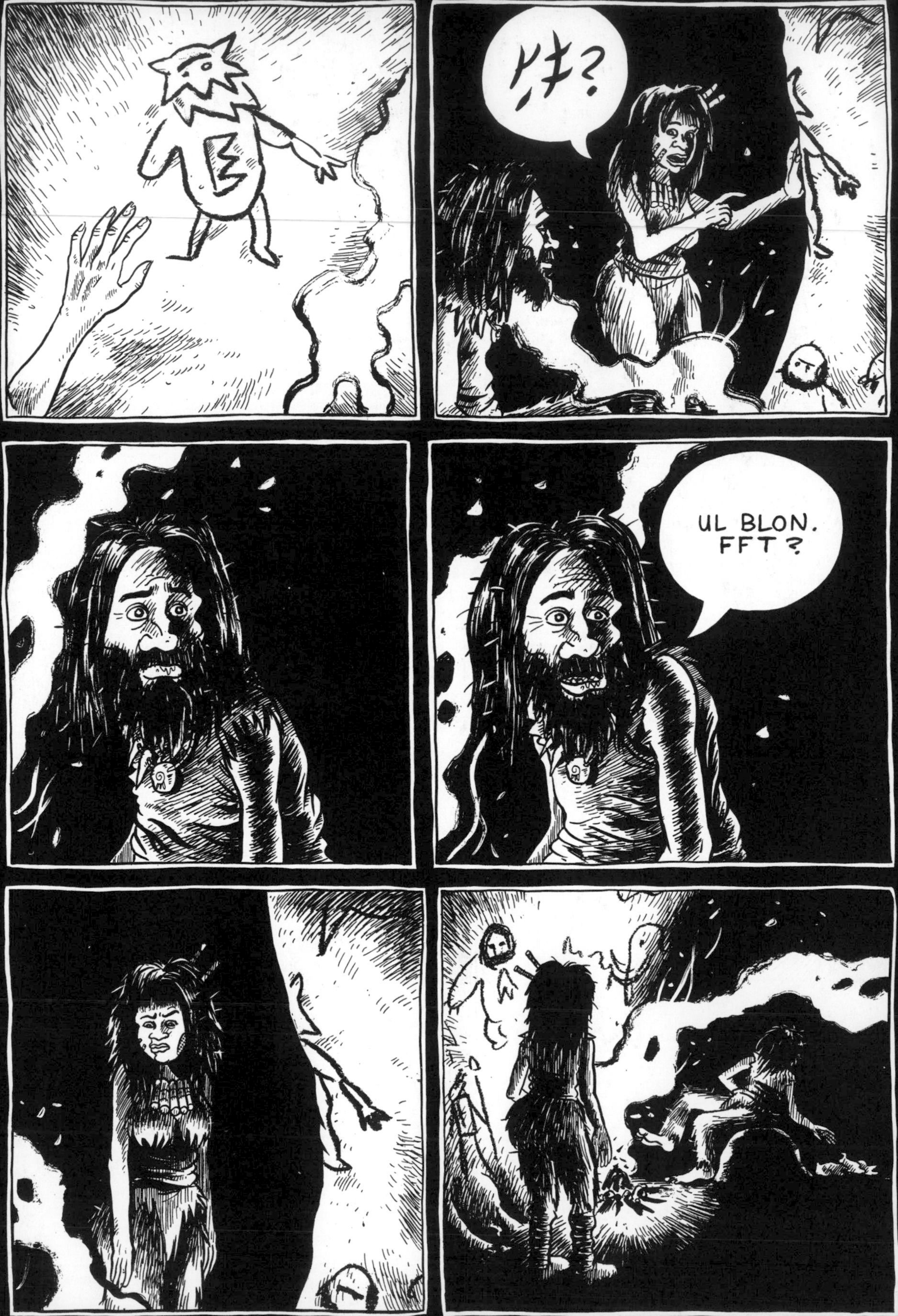
UL BLON.
FFT?

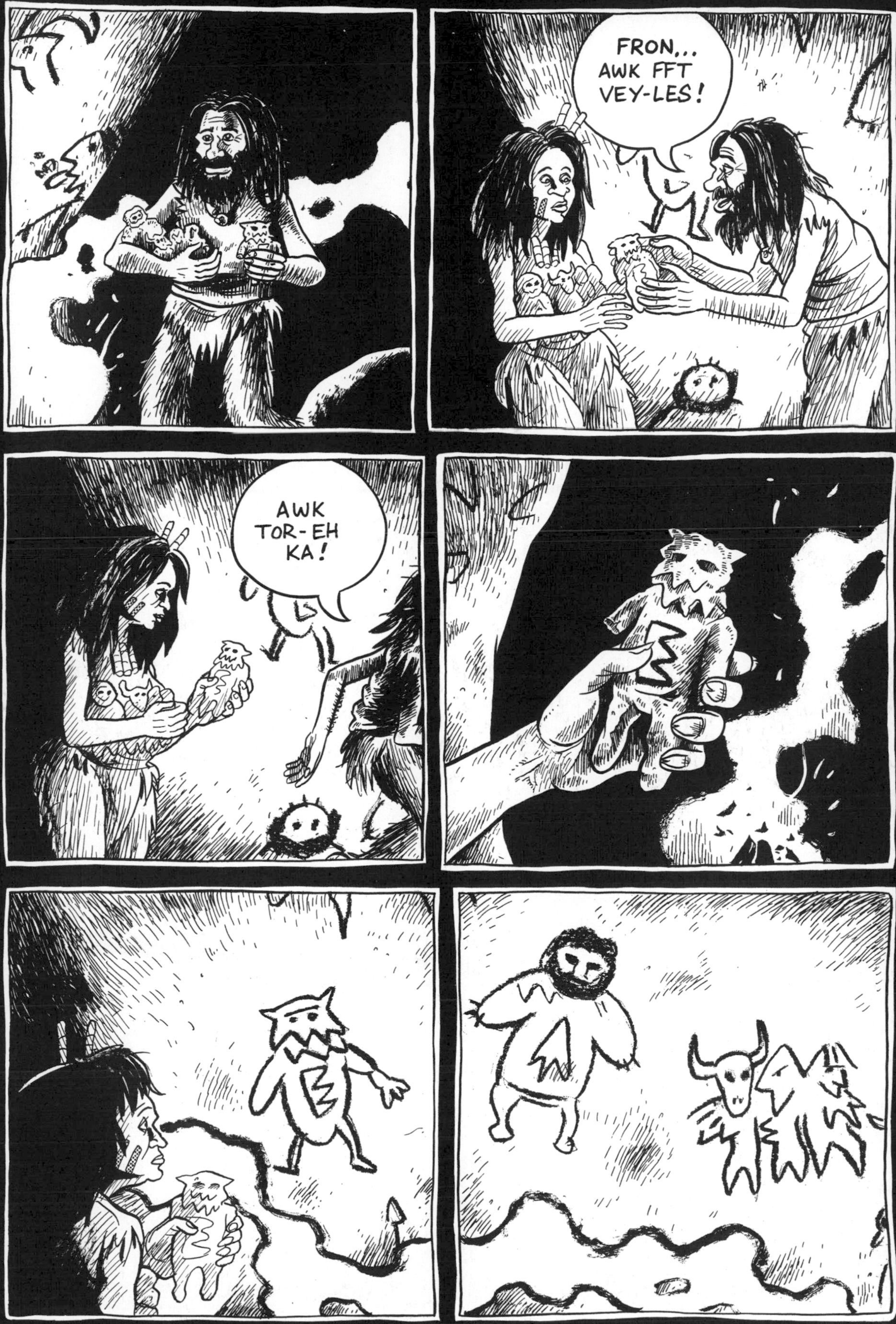
FRON... AWK FFT VEY-LES!
AWK TOR-EH KA!

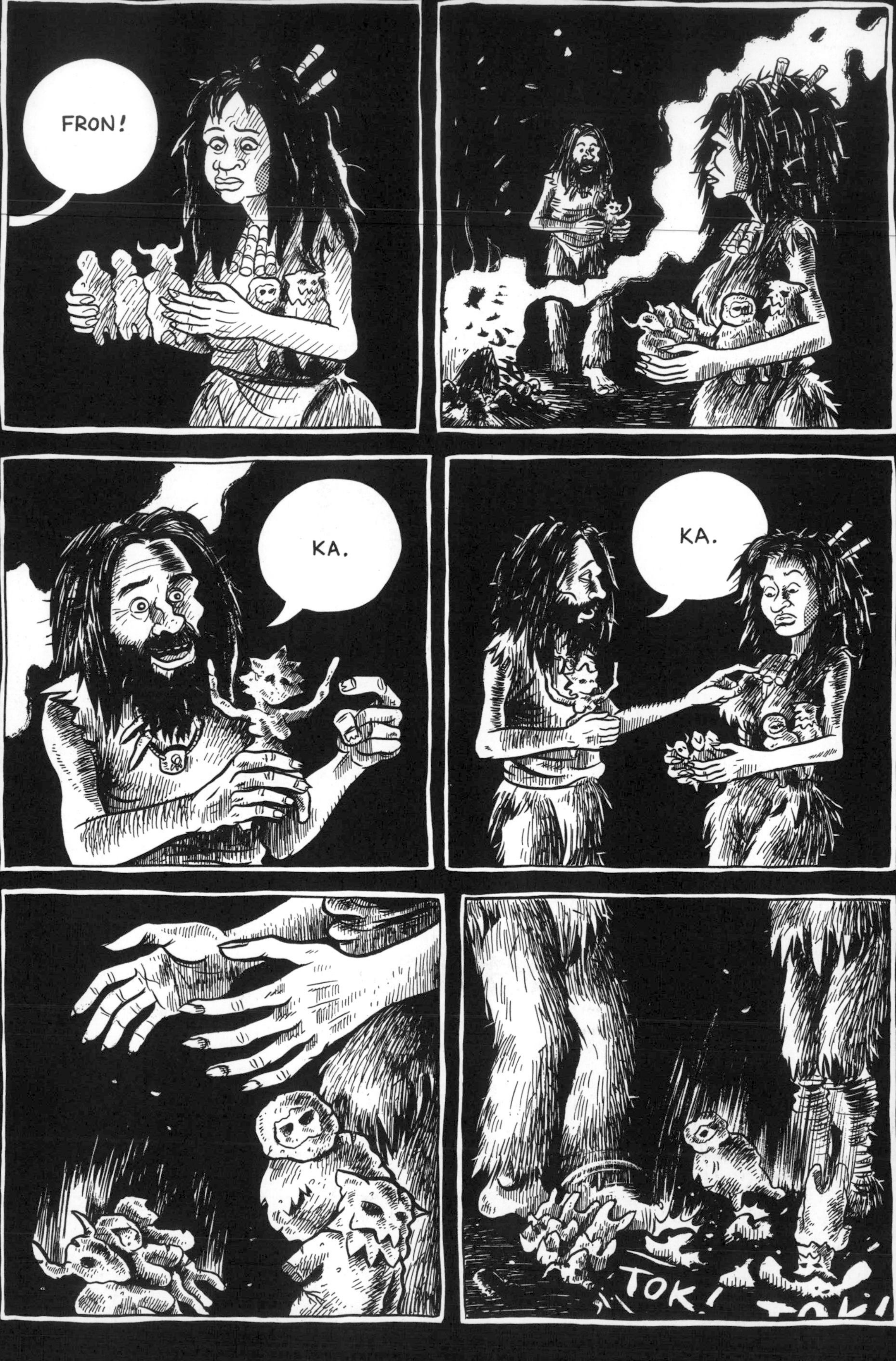
FRON!
KA.
KA.
TOK!

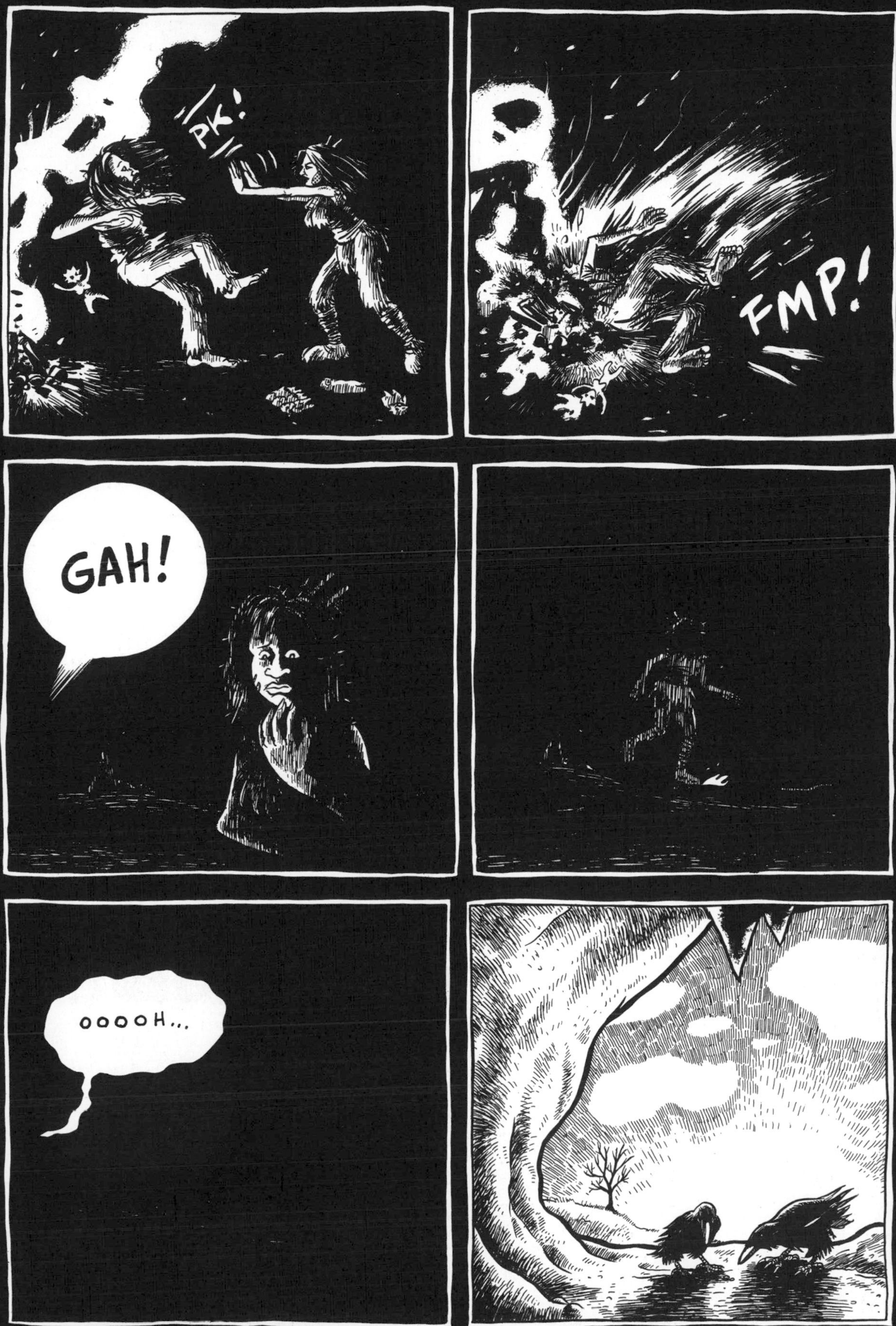
PK!
FMP!
GAH!
OOOOH...

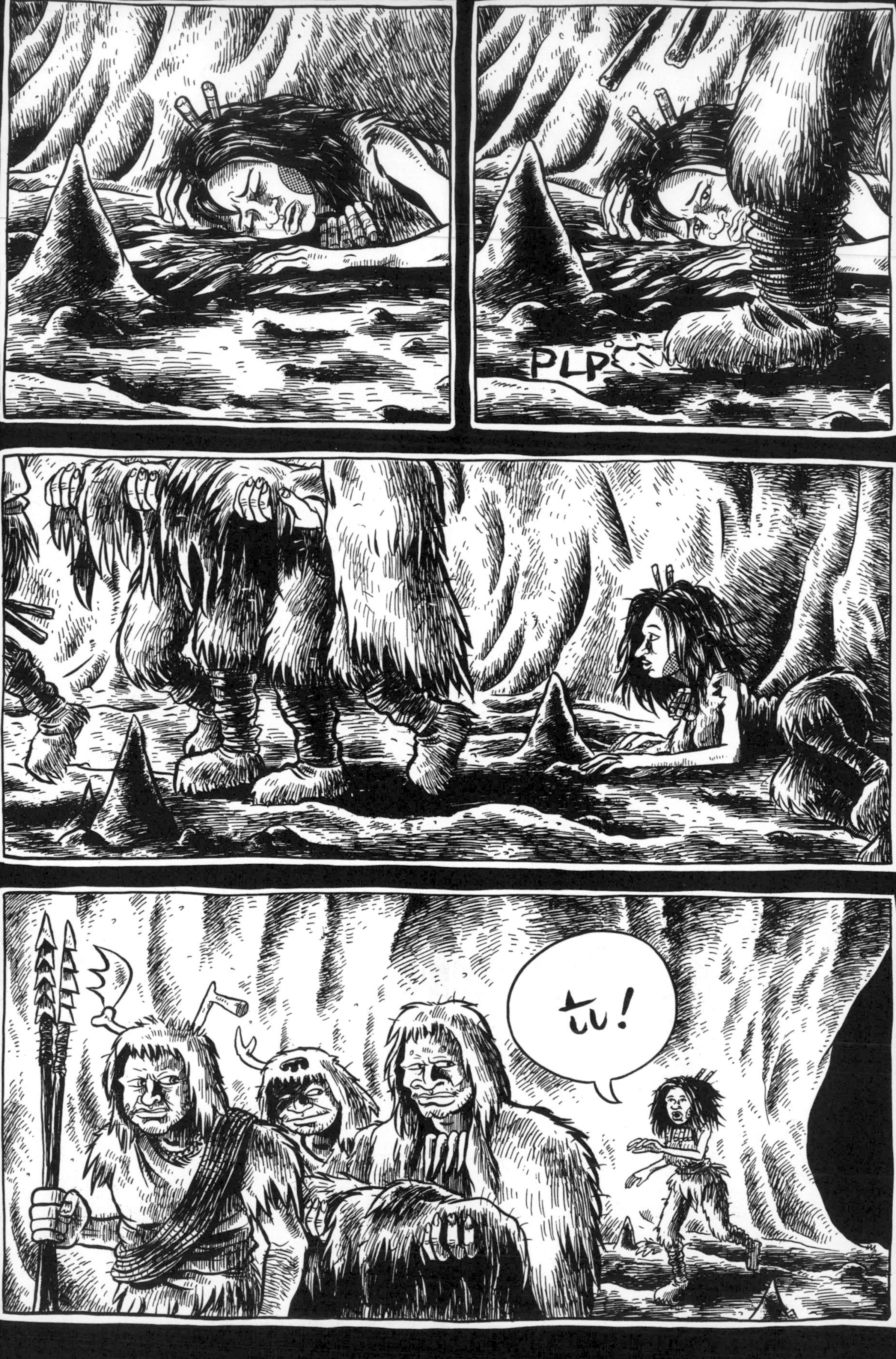
PLP
tu!

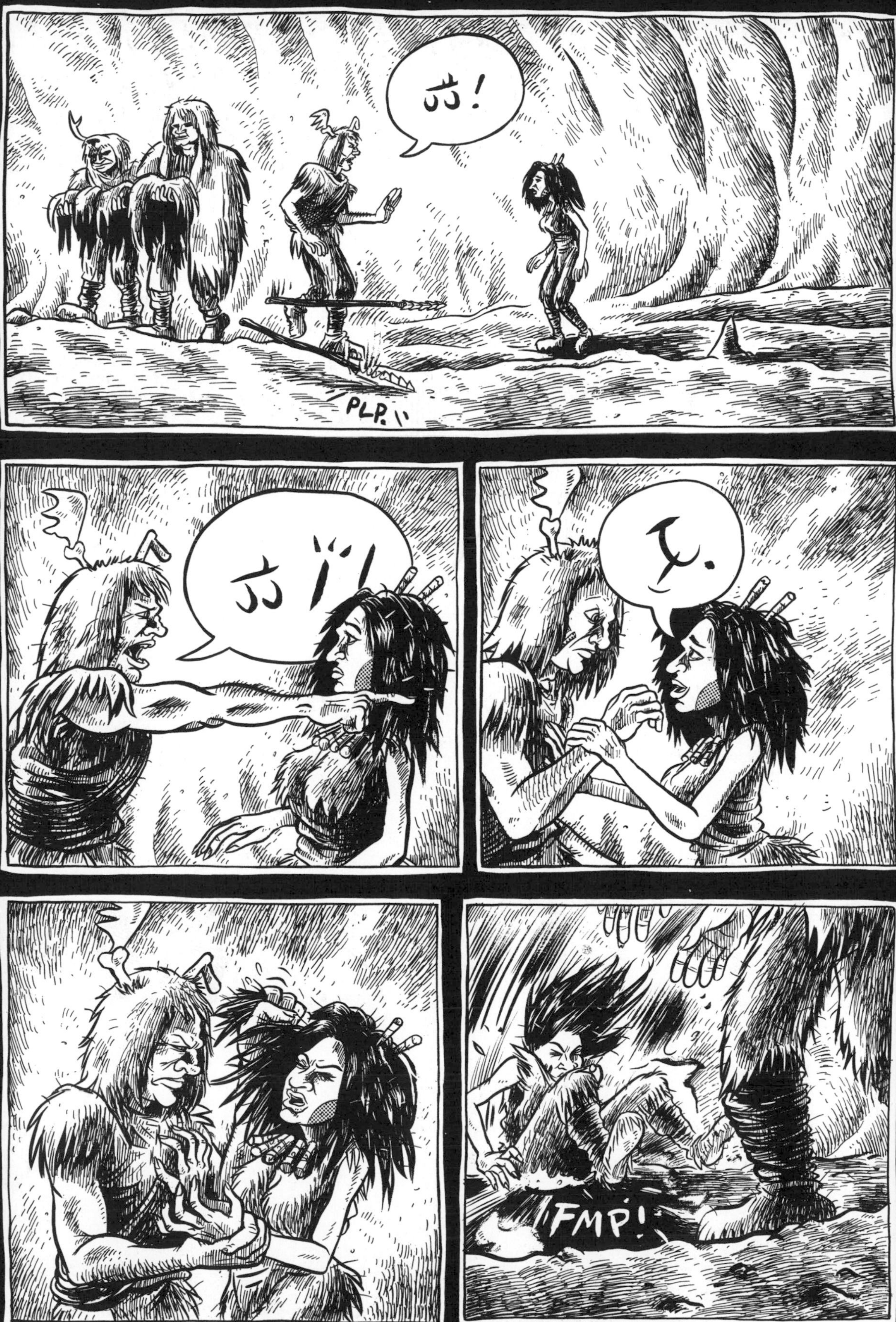
PLP.
FMP!

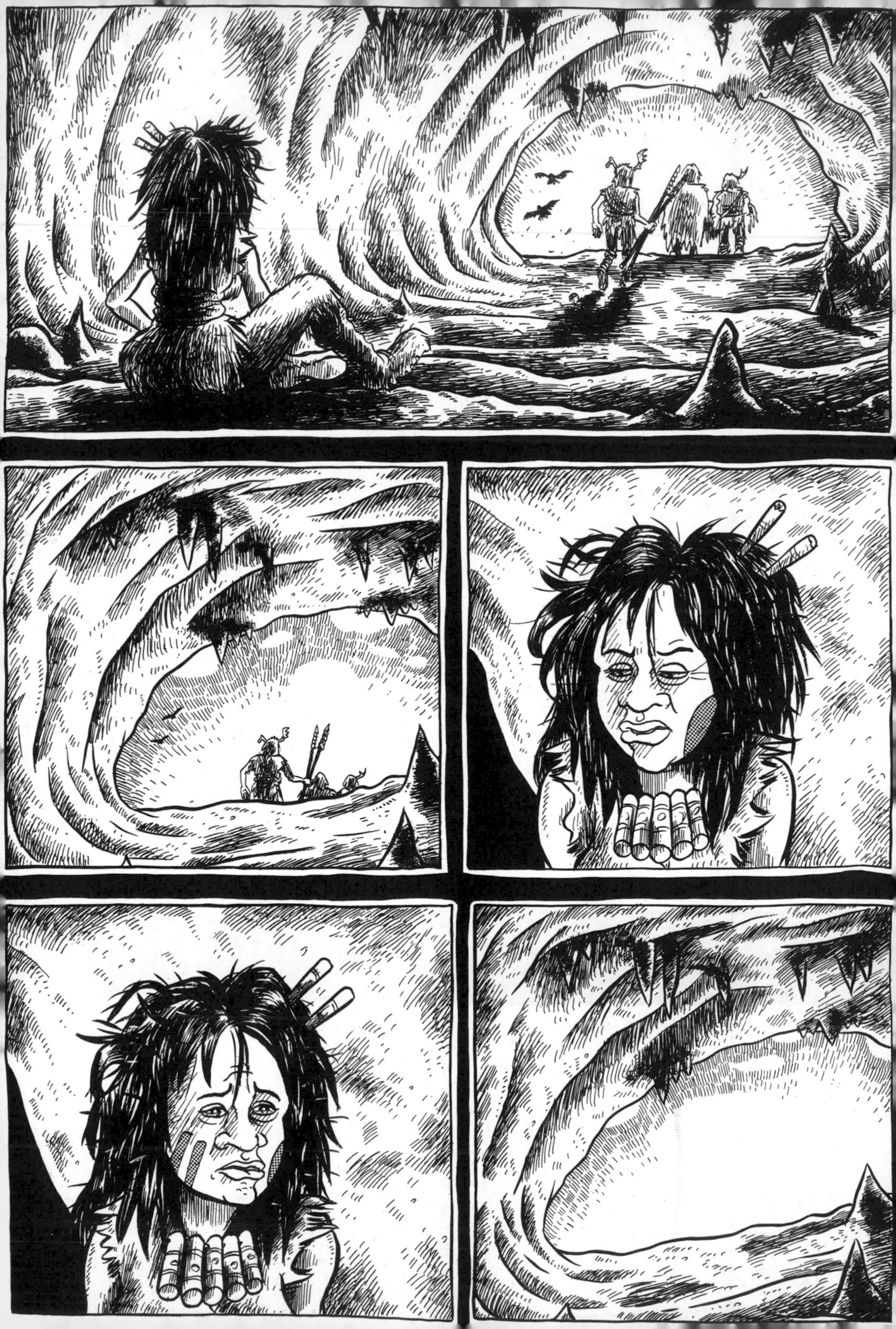

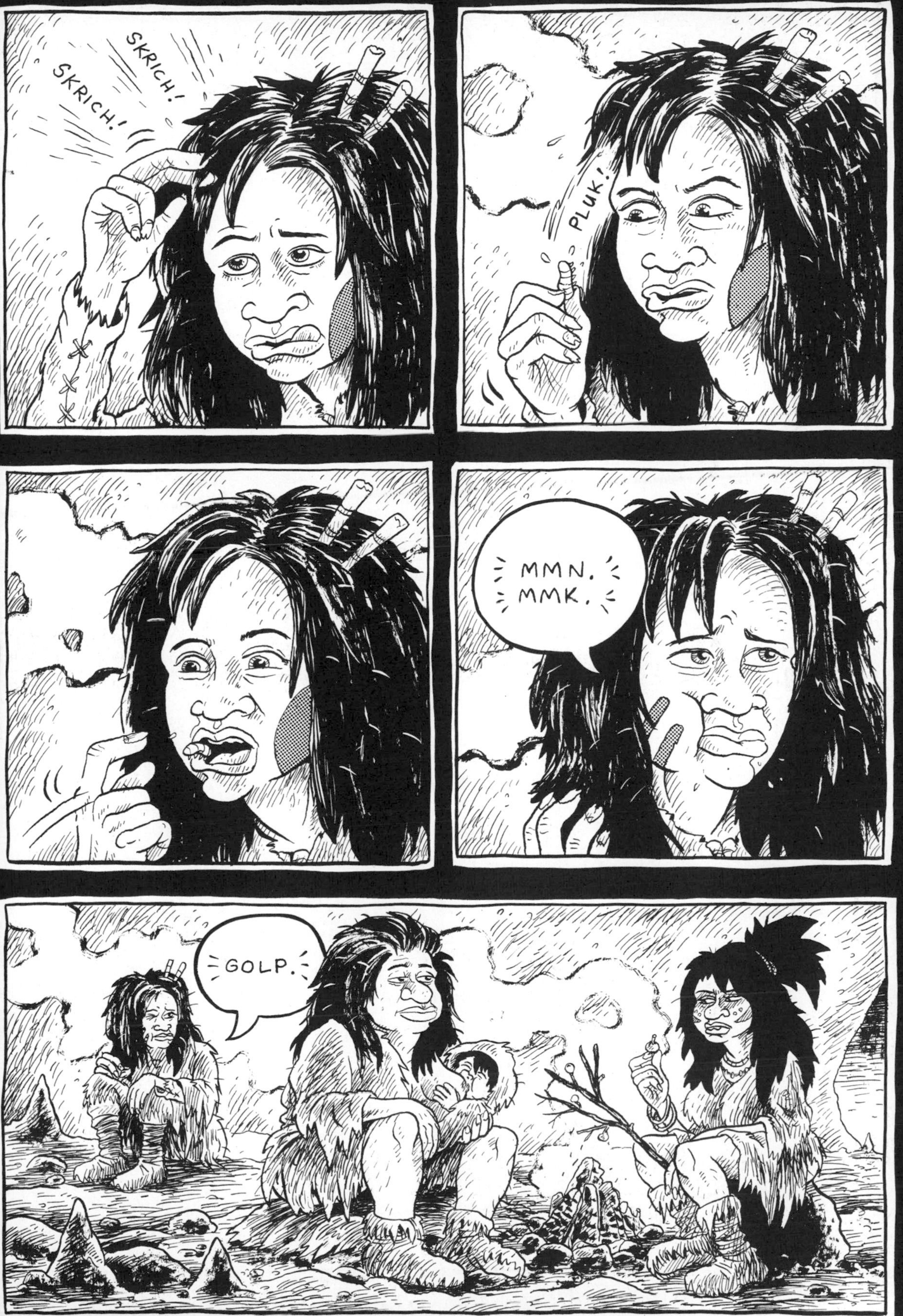

SKRICH!
SKRICH!
PLUK!
MMN. MMK.
GOLP.

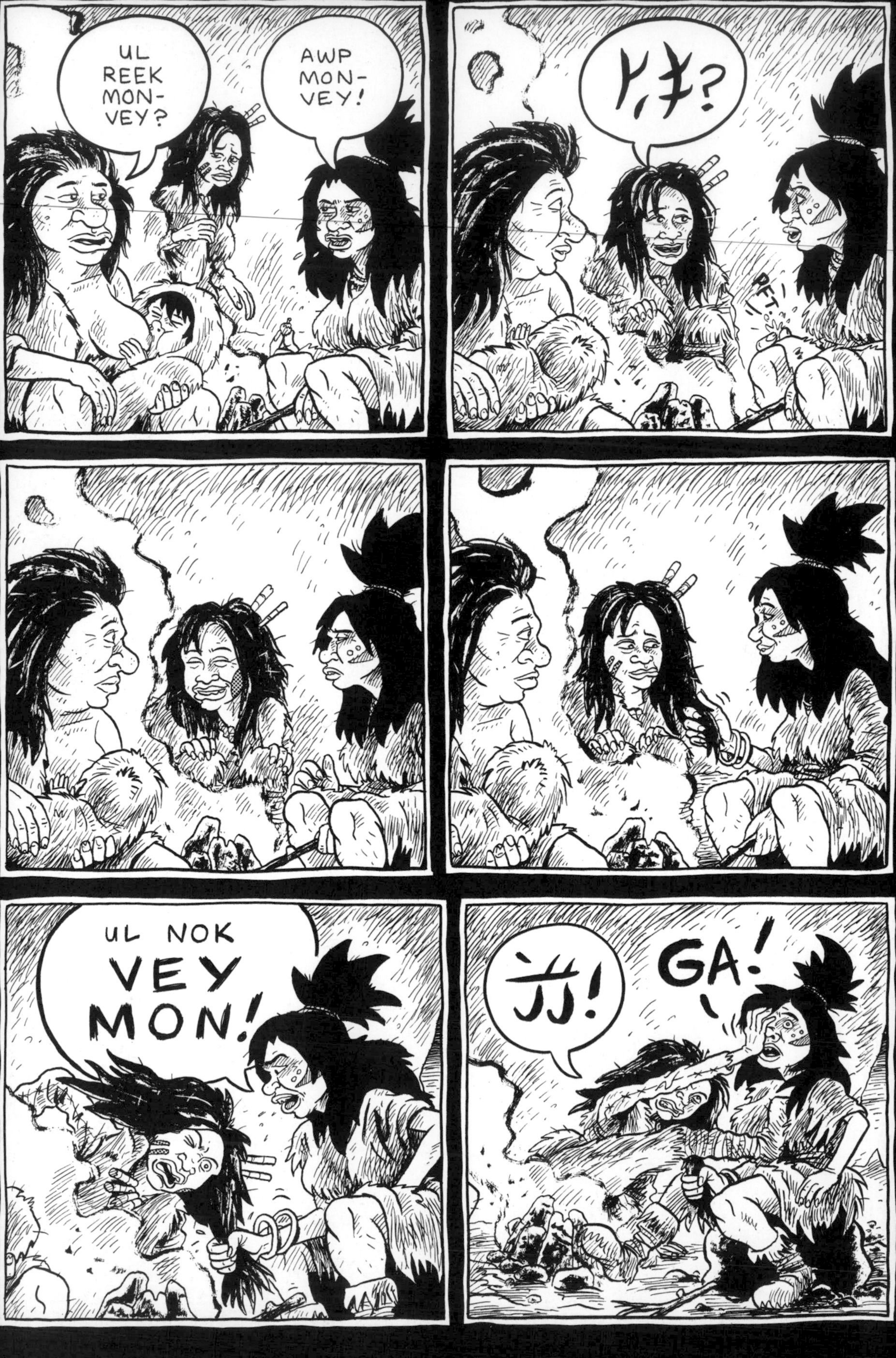
UL REEK MON-VEY?
AWP MON-VEY!
PFT
UL NOK VEY MON!
GA!

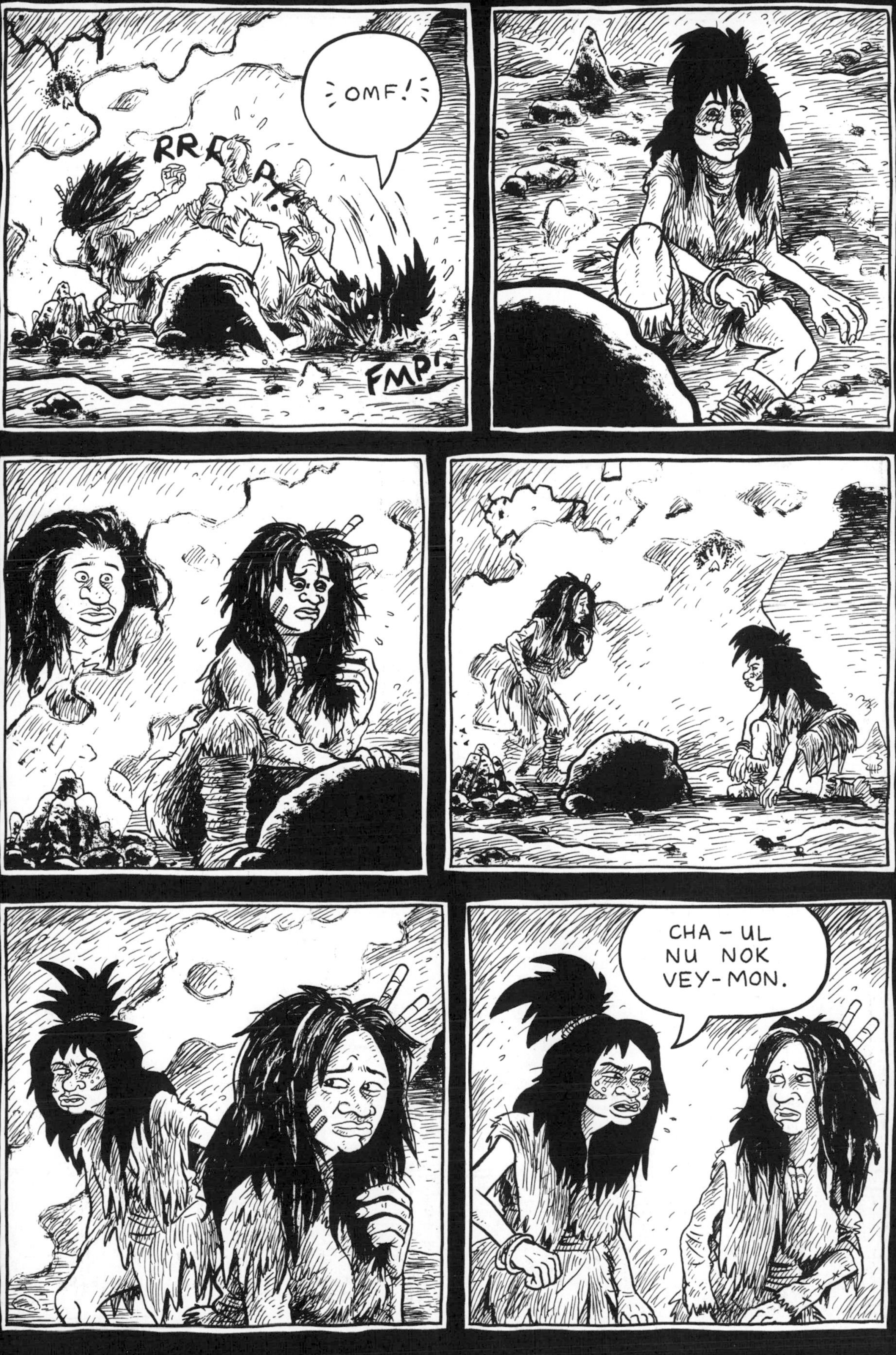
RRRIP!
OMF!
FMP!
CHA-UL
NU NOK
VEY-MON.

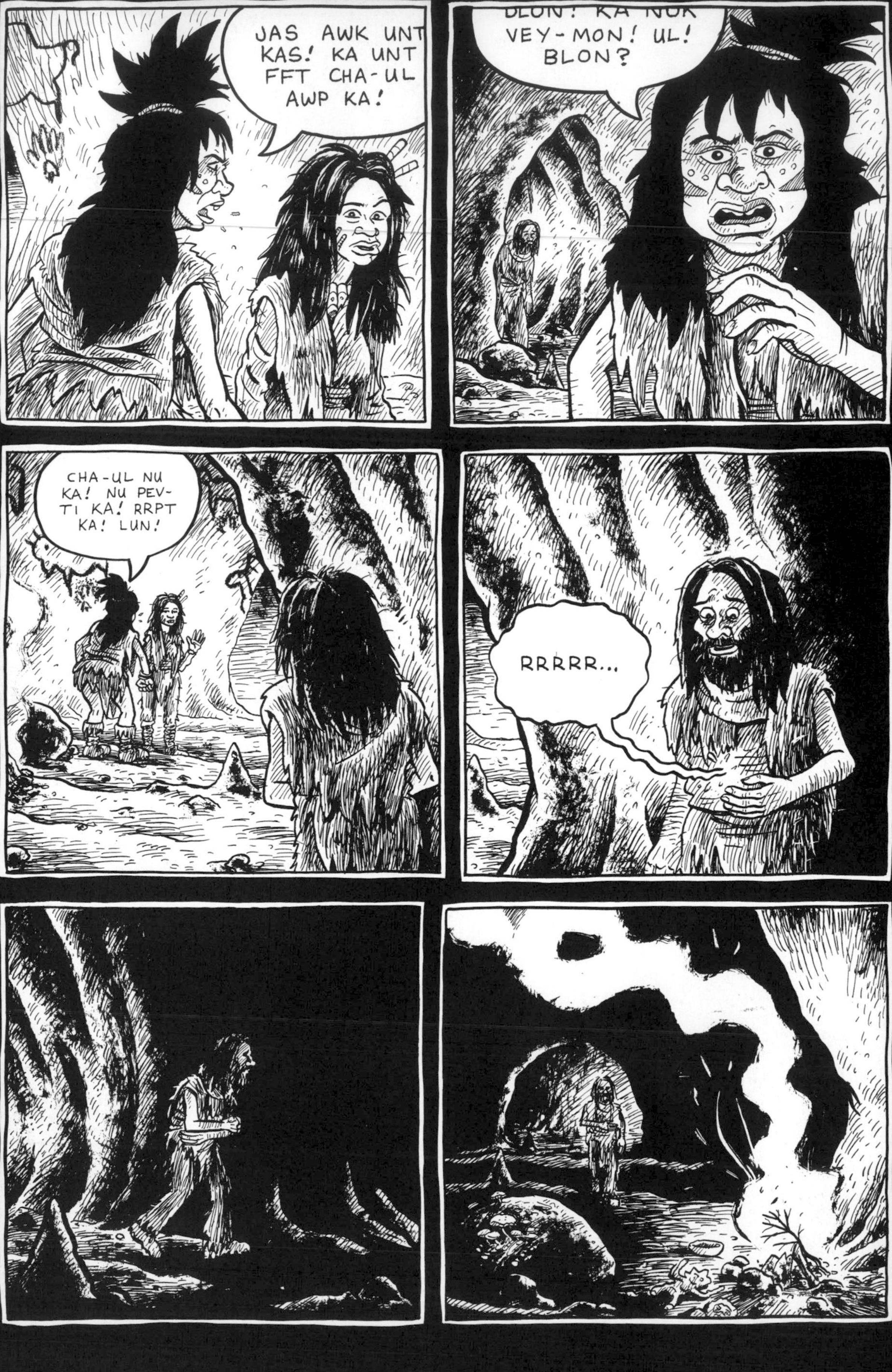

JAS AWK UNT KAS! KA UNT FFT CHA-UL AWP KA!
BLON! KA NUK VEY-MON! UL! BLON?
CHA-UL NU KA! NU PEV-TI KA! RRPT KA! LUN!
RRRRR...

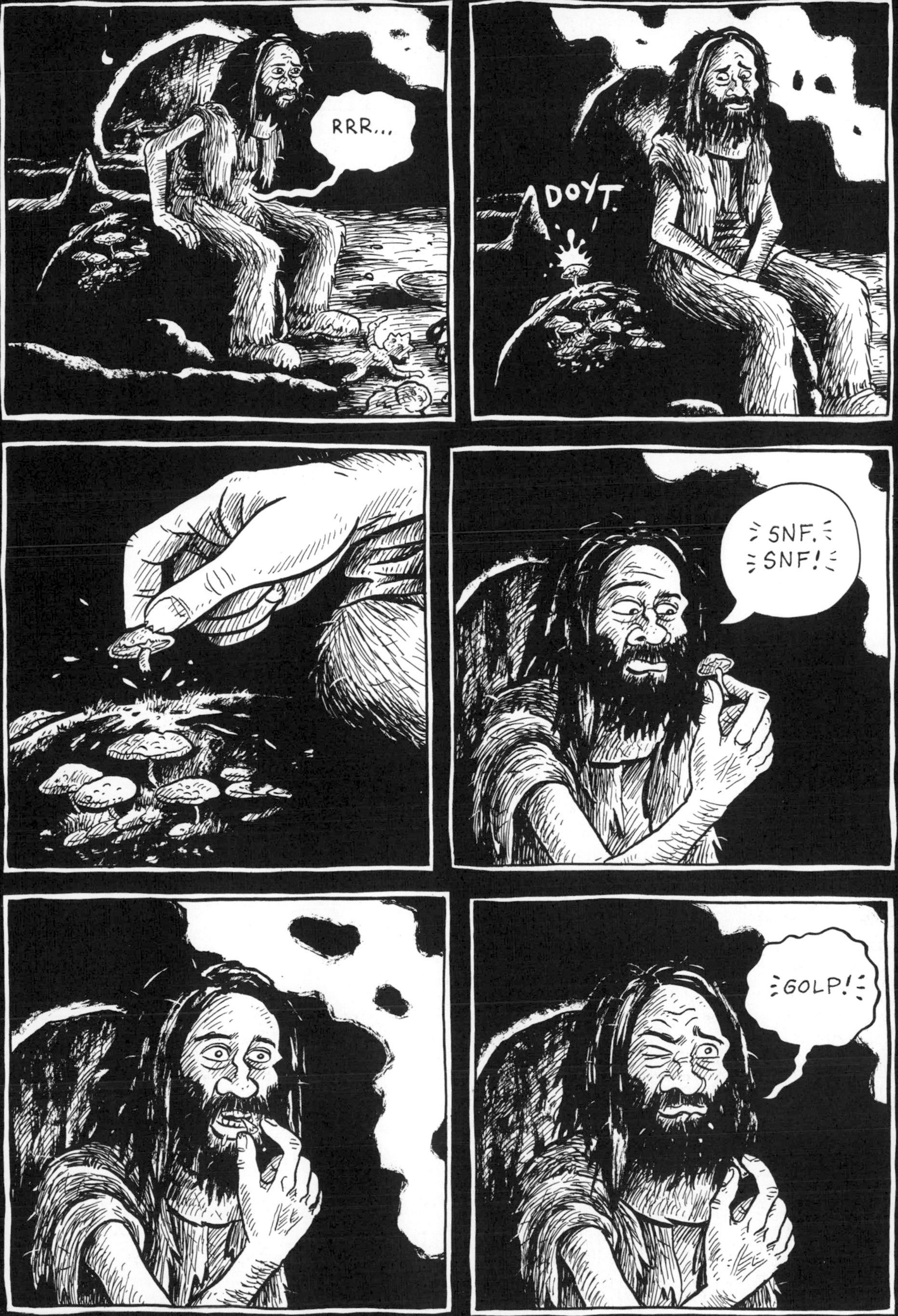
RRR...
DOYT.
SNF. SNF!
GOLP!

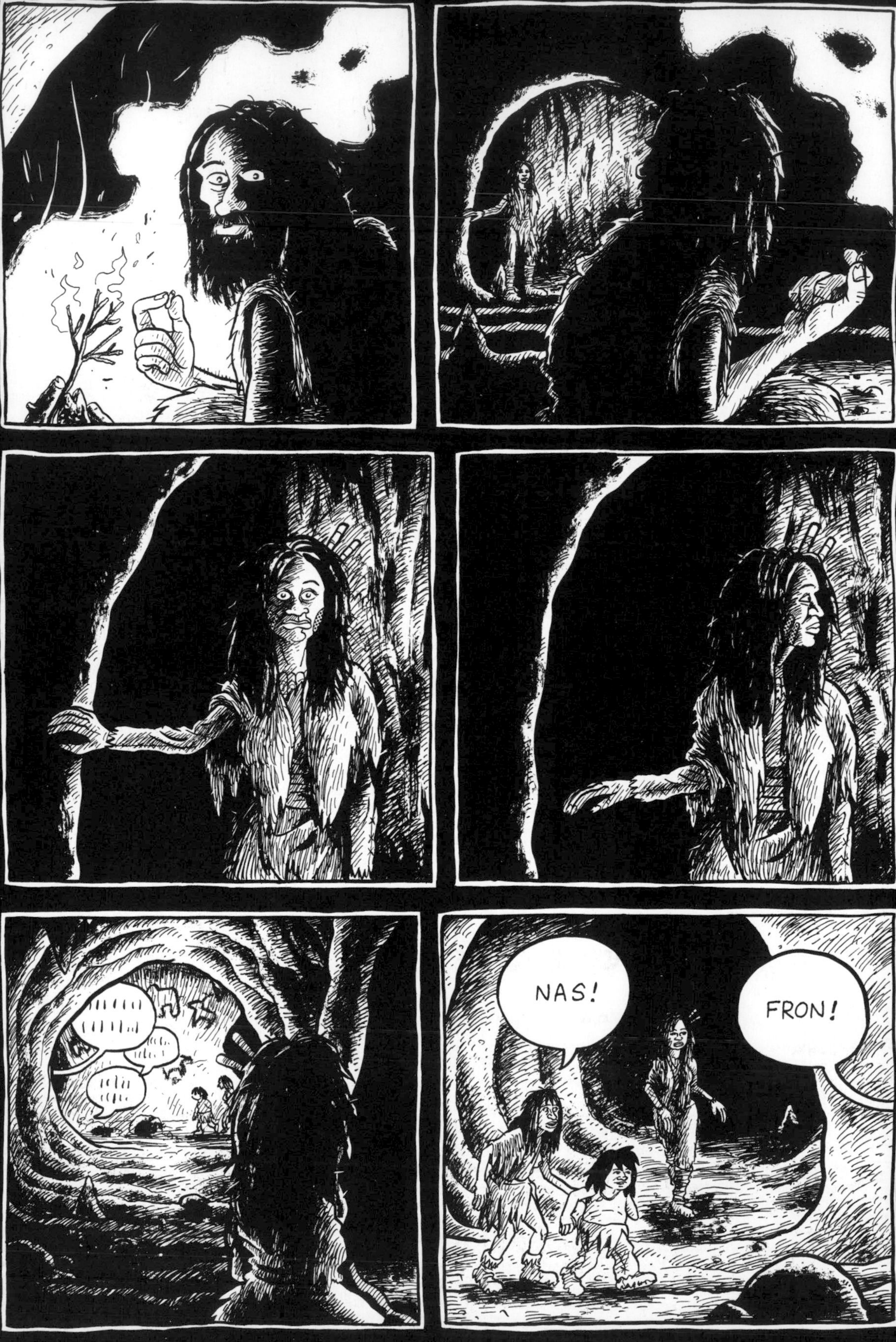
NAS!
FRON!

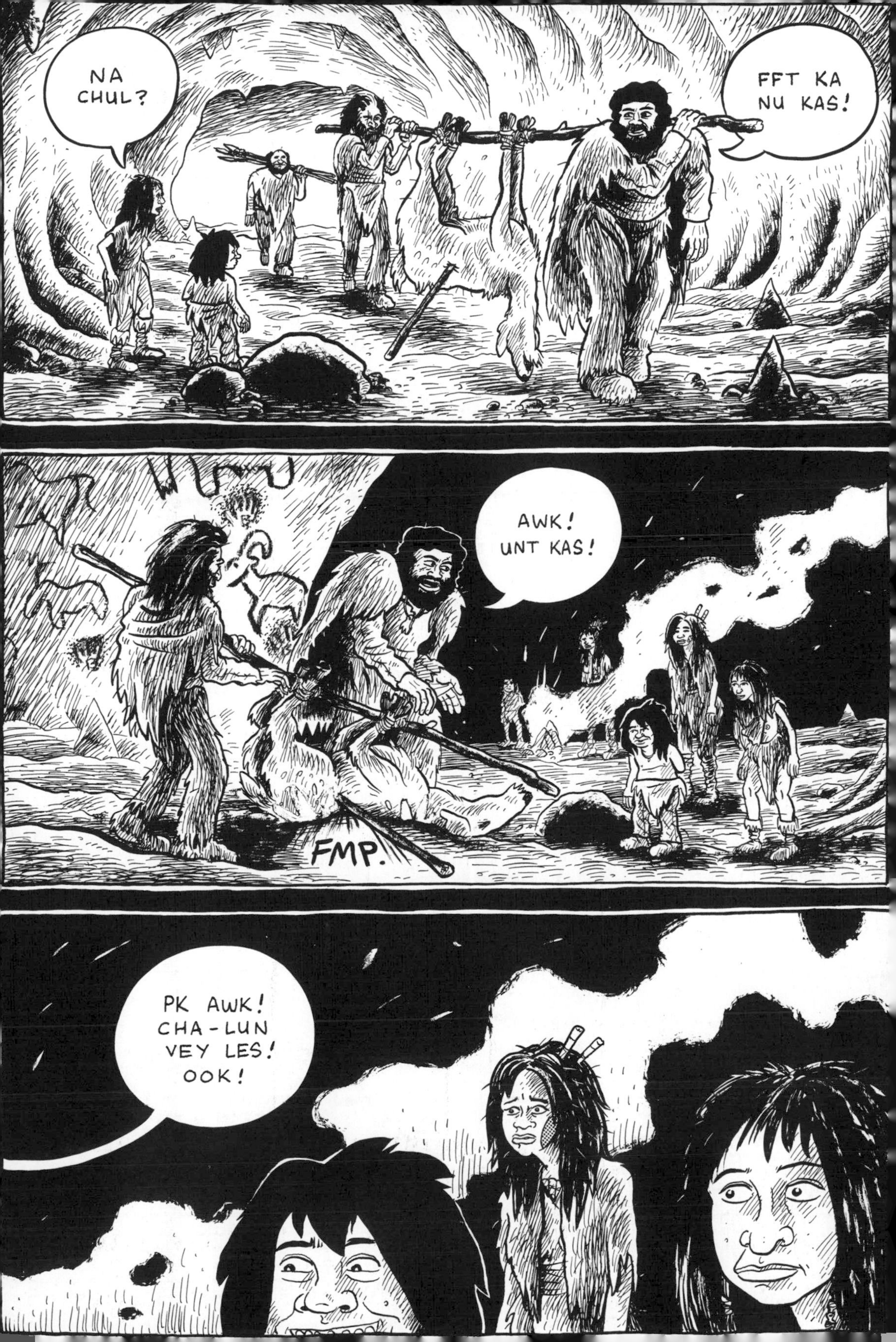
NA CHUL?
FFT KA NU KAS!
AWK! UNT KAS!
FMP.
PK AWK! CHA-LUN VEY LES! OOK!

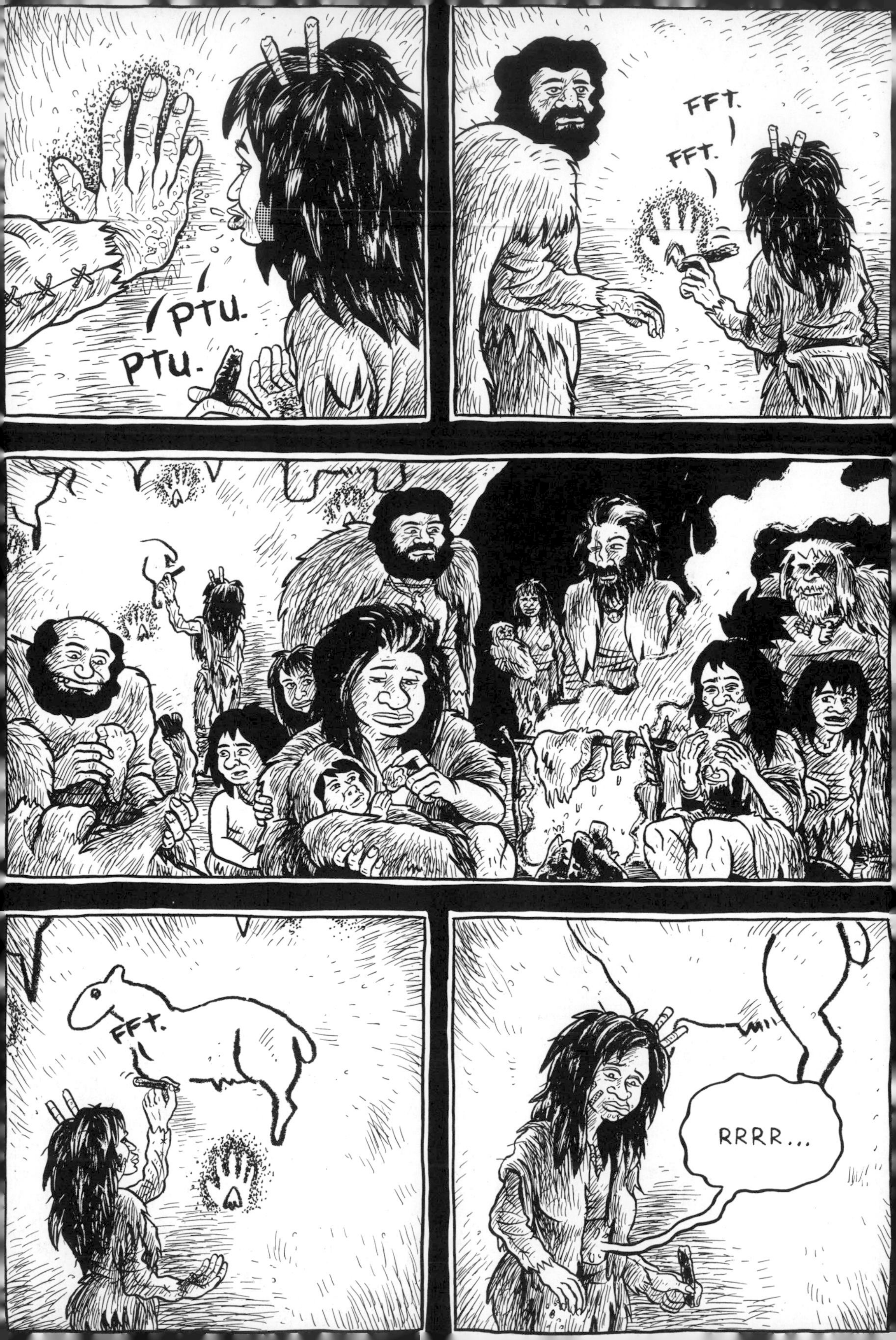
PTU.
PTU.
FFT.
FFT.
FFT.
RRRR...

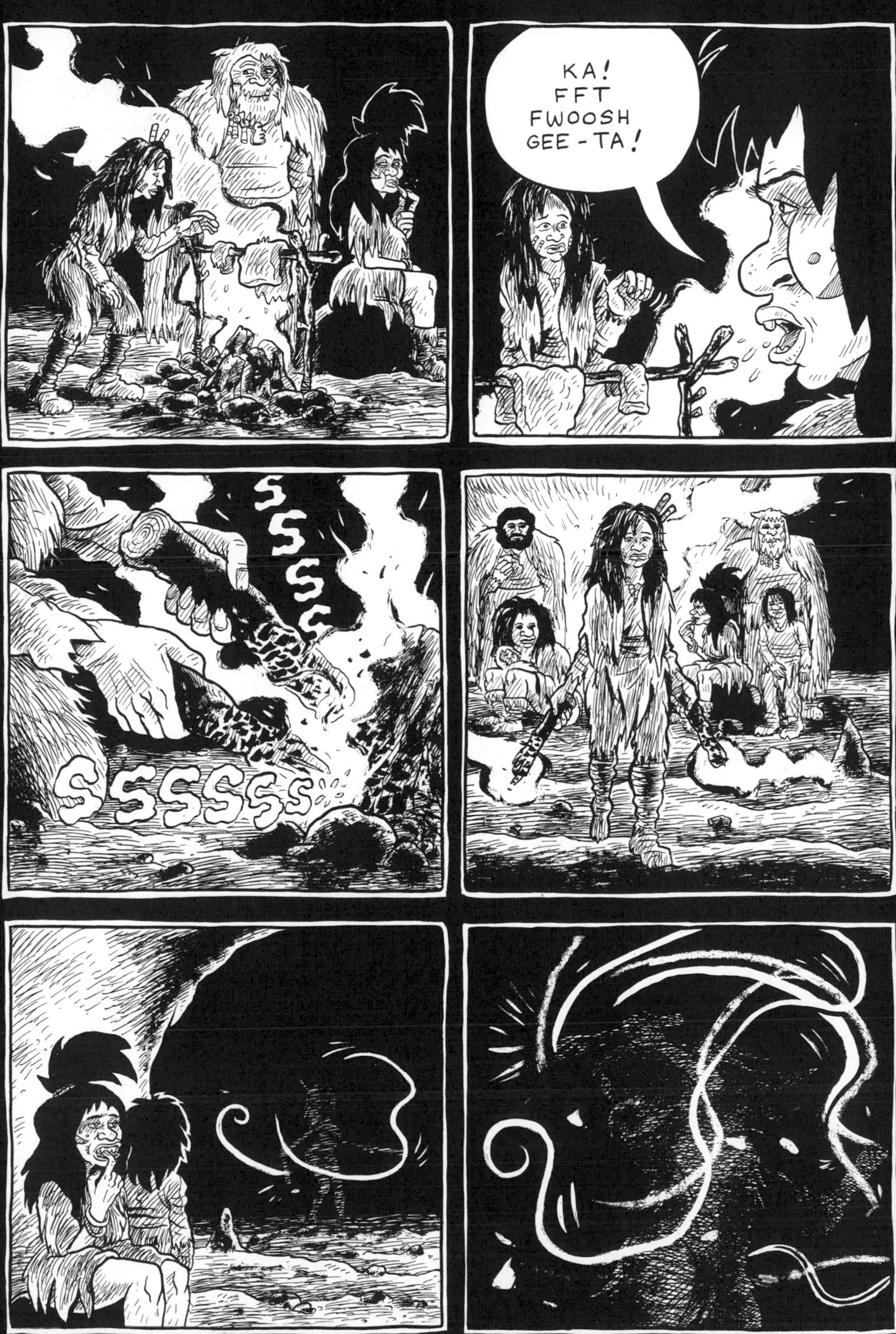
KA!
FFT
FWOOSH
GEE-TA!
SSSS
SSSSSS

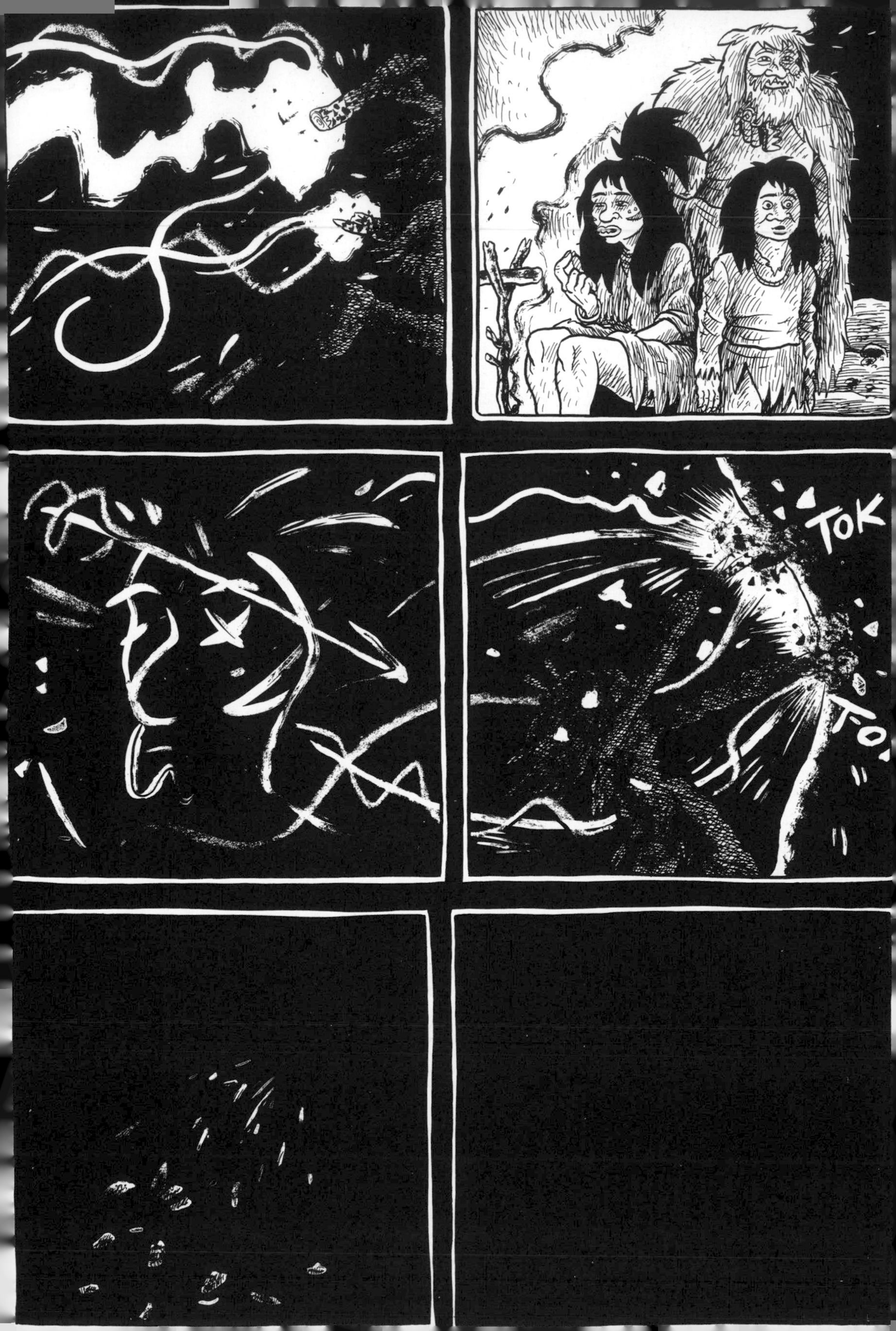
TOK
TOK

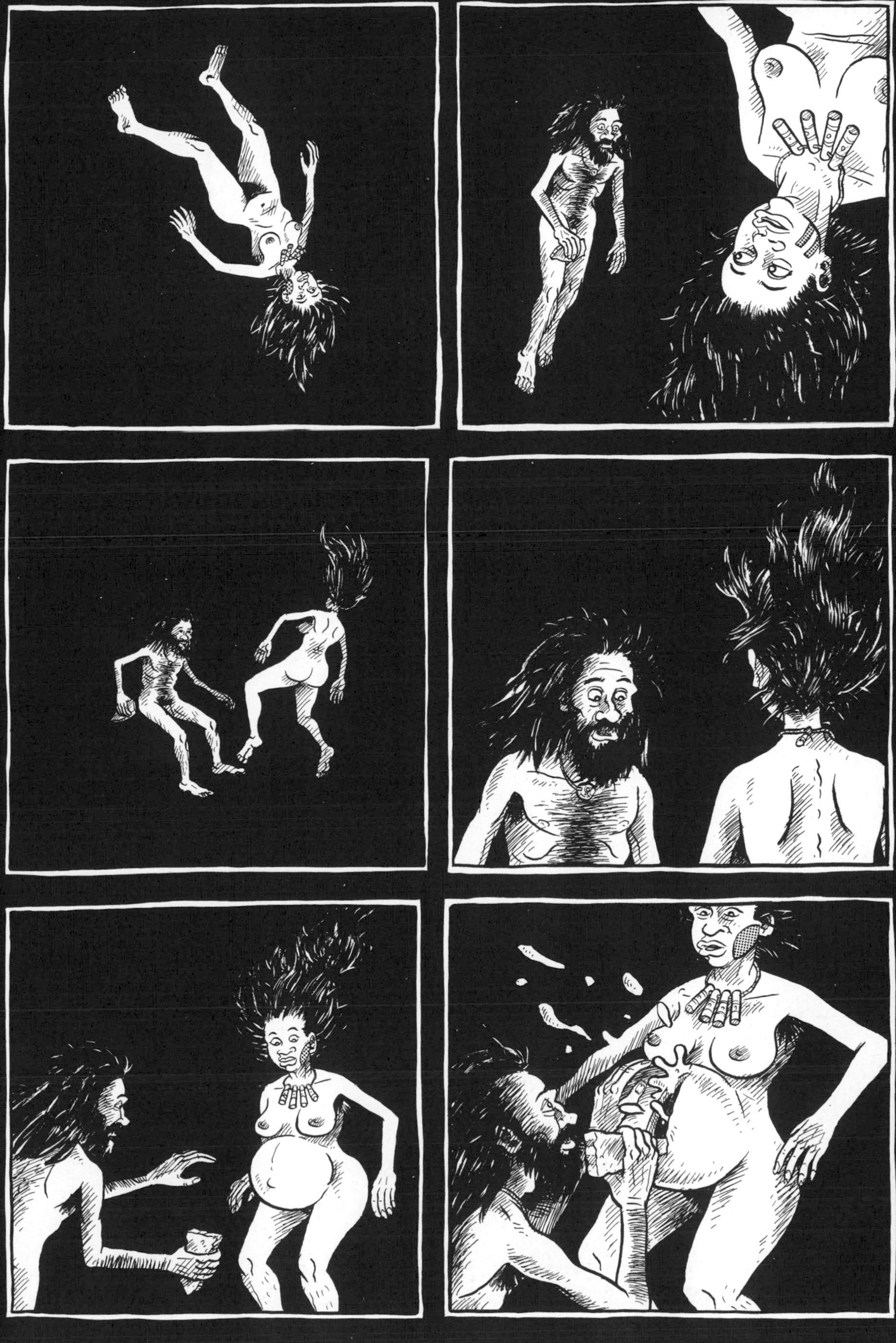

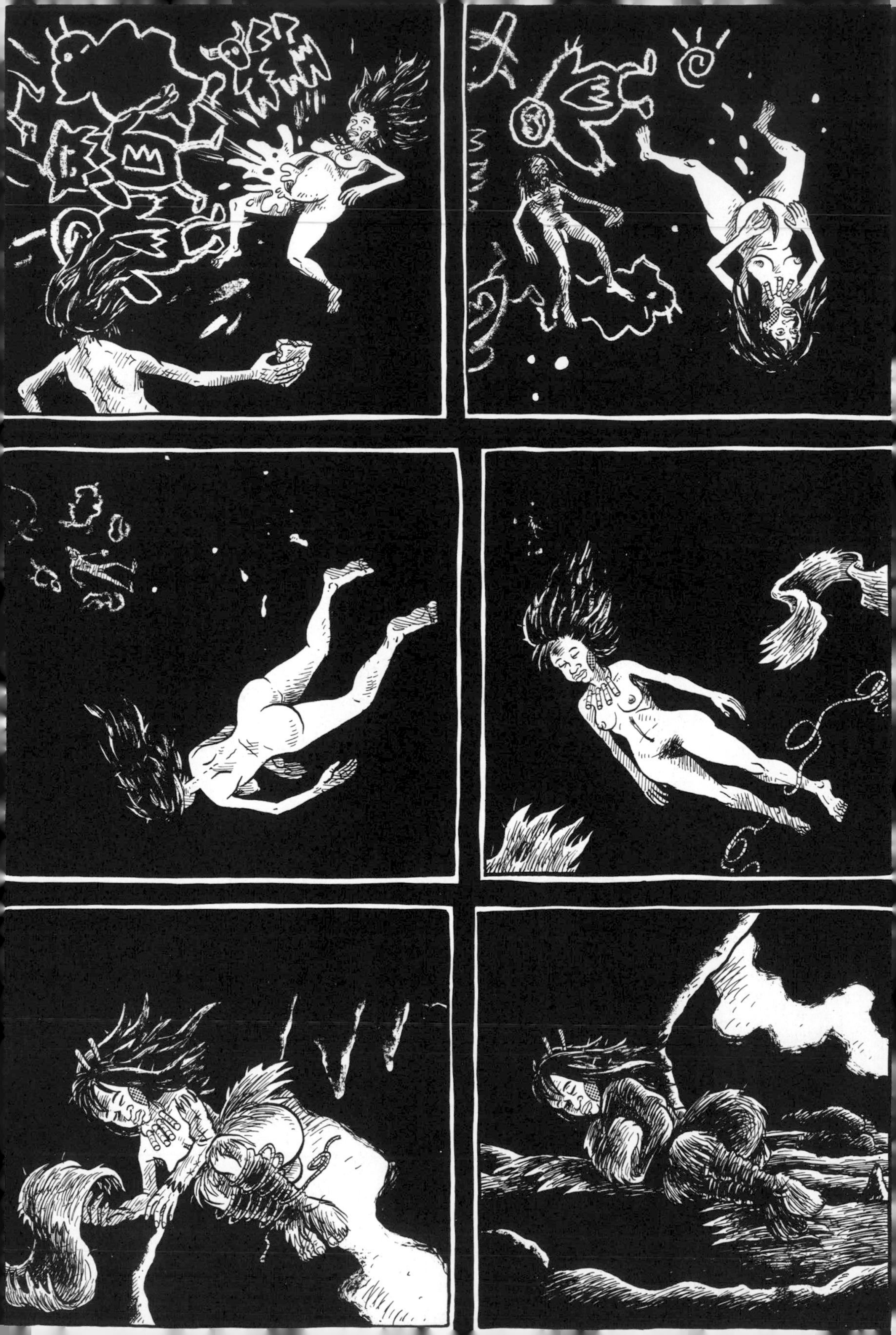

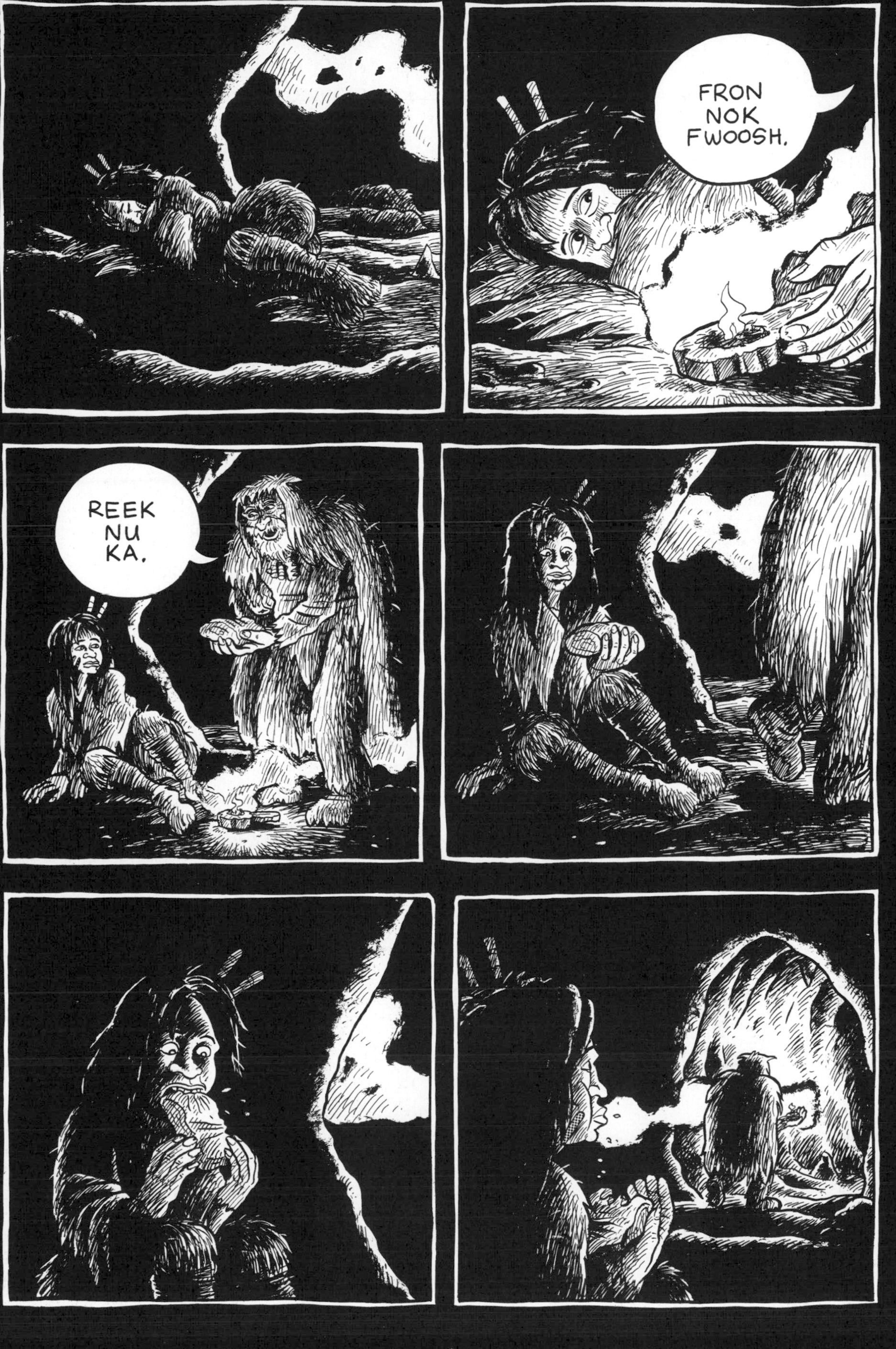
FRON NOK FWOOSH.
REEK NU KA.

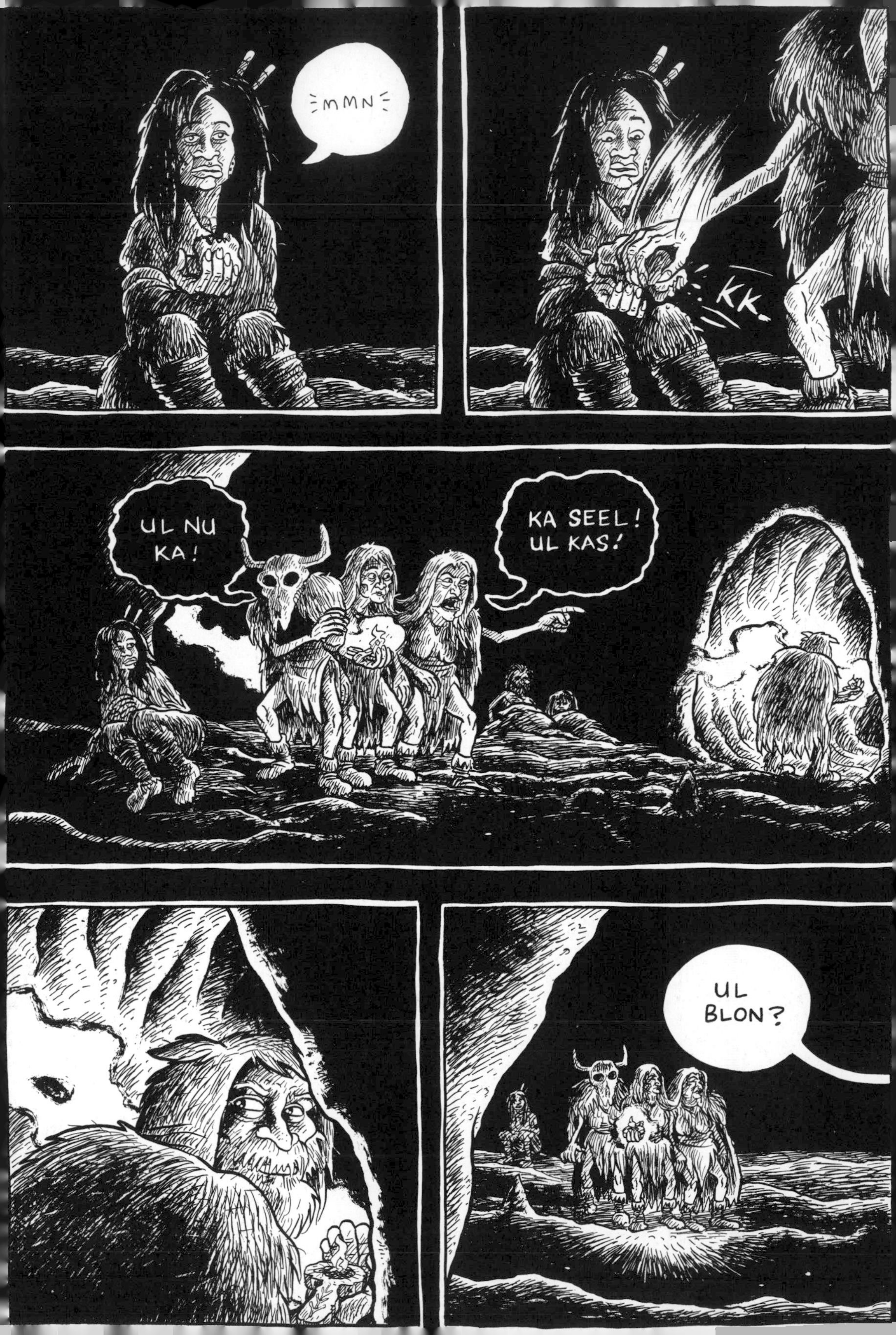
MMN
KK
UL NU KA!
KA SEEL! UL KAS!
UL BLON?

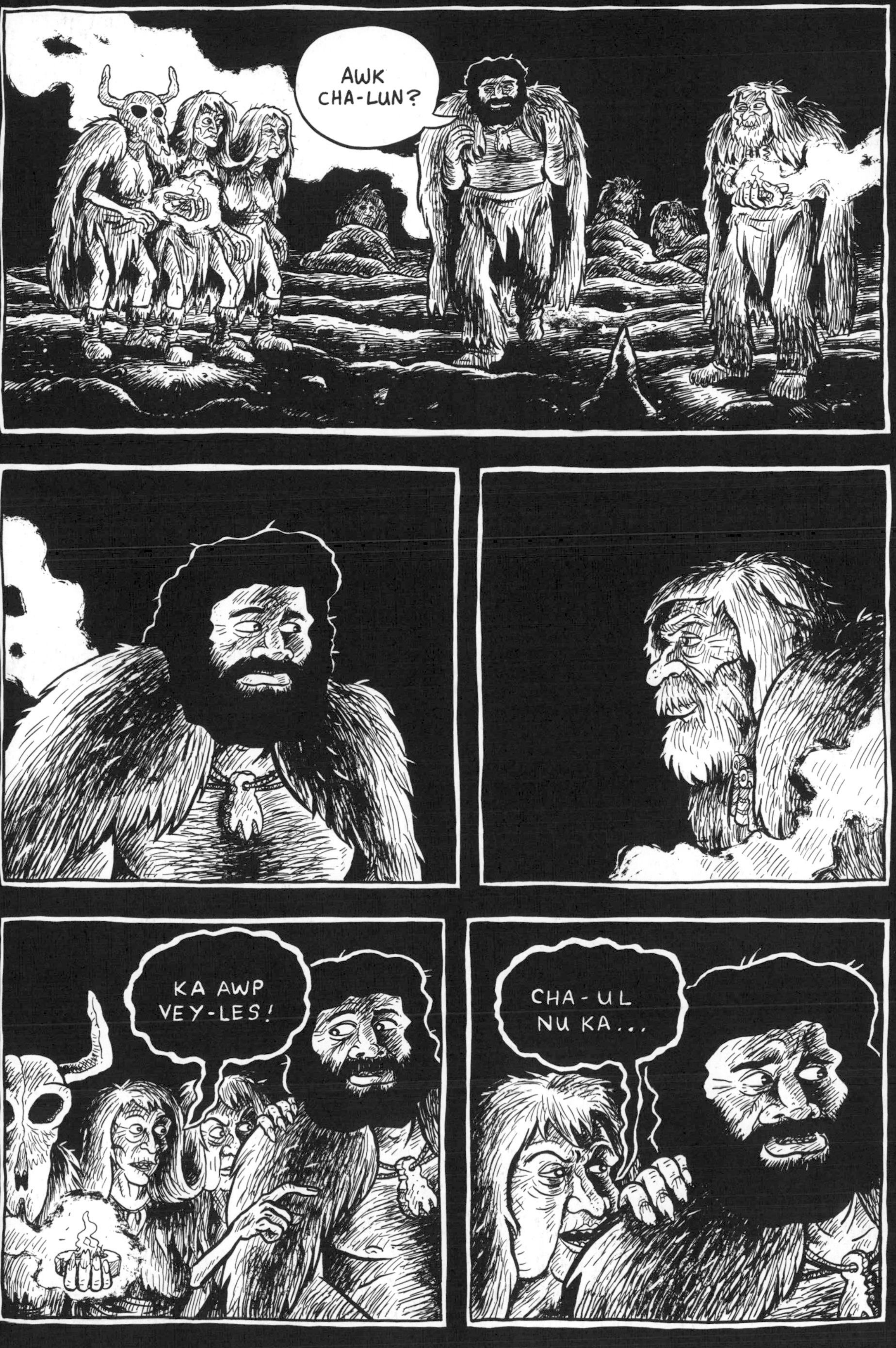
AWK CHA-LUN?
KA AWP VEY-LES!
CHA-UL NU KA...

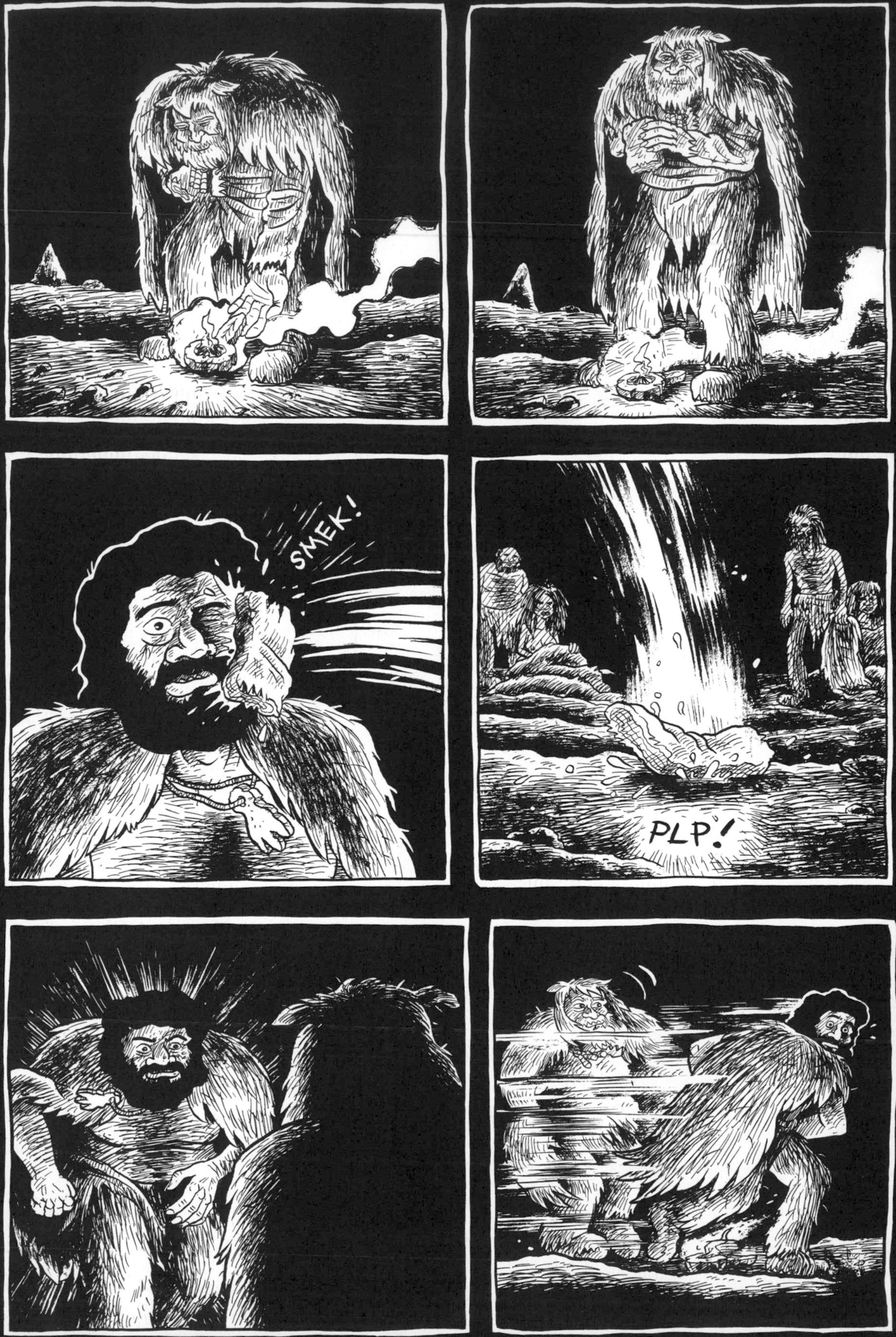
SMEK!
PLP!

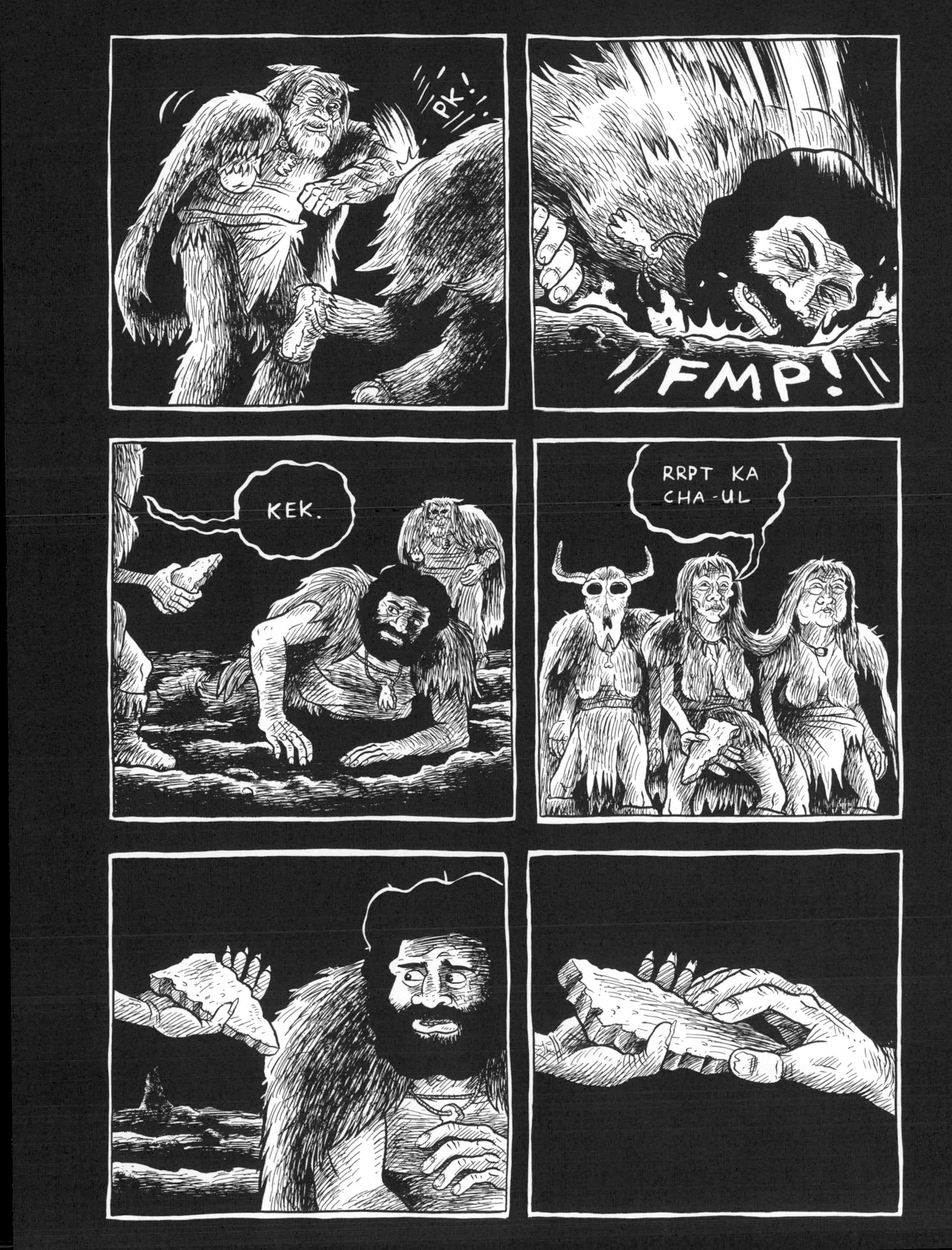
PK!
FMP!
KEK.
RRPT KA CHA-UL

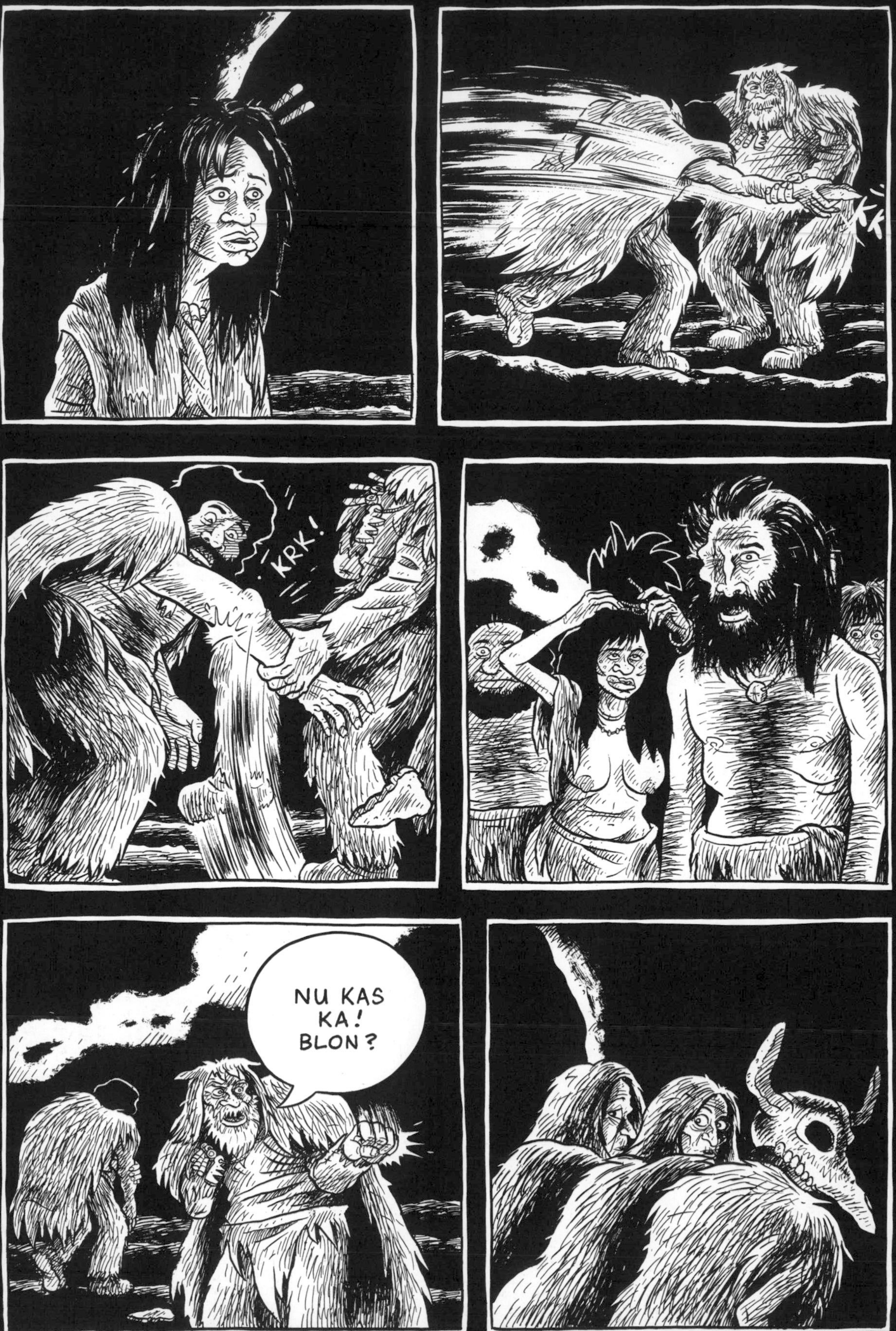
KK
KRK!
NU KAS KA! BLON?

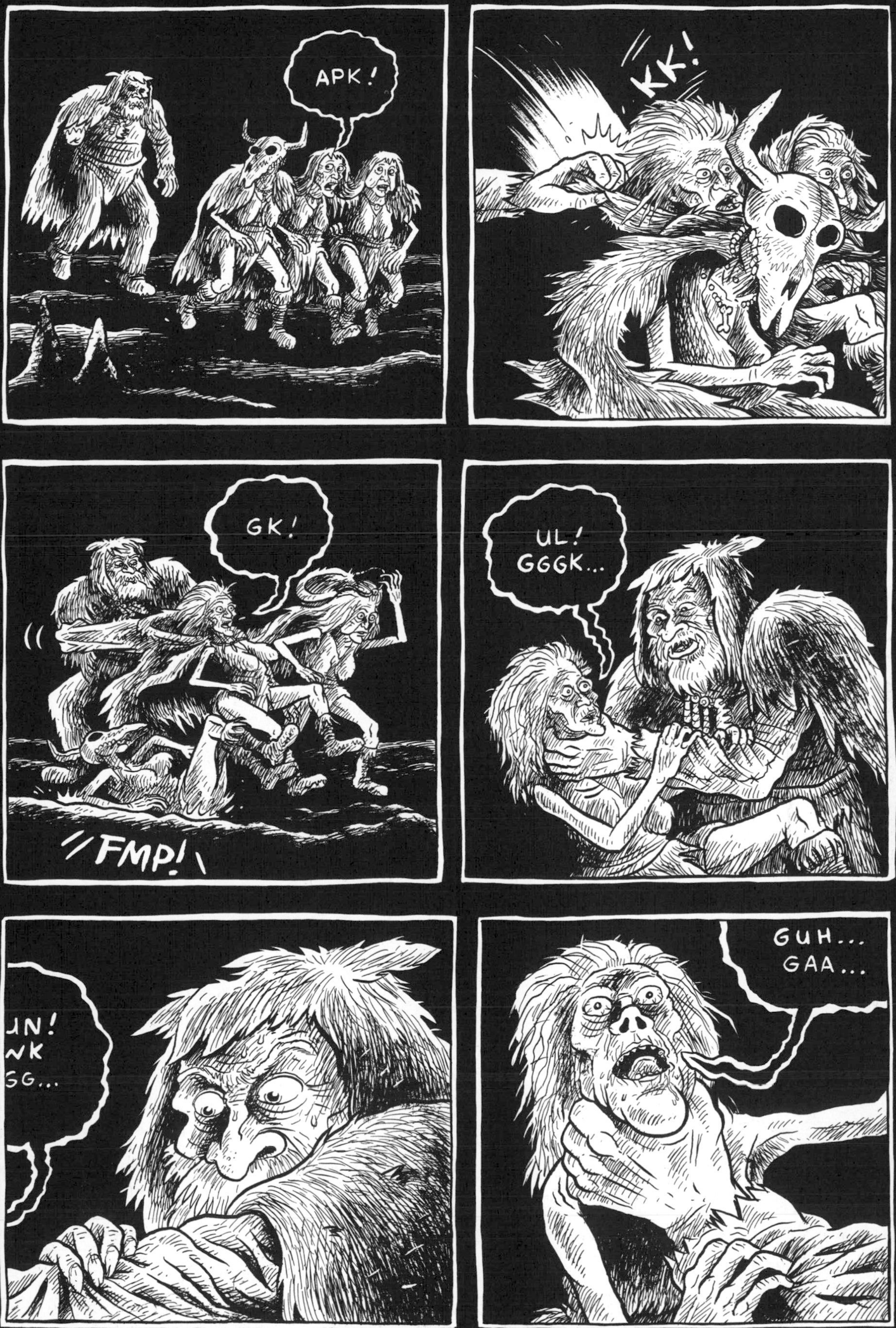
APK!
KK!
GK!
FMP!
UL! GGGK...
UN! NK GG...
GUH... GAA...

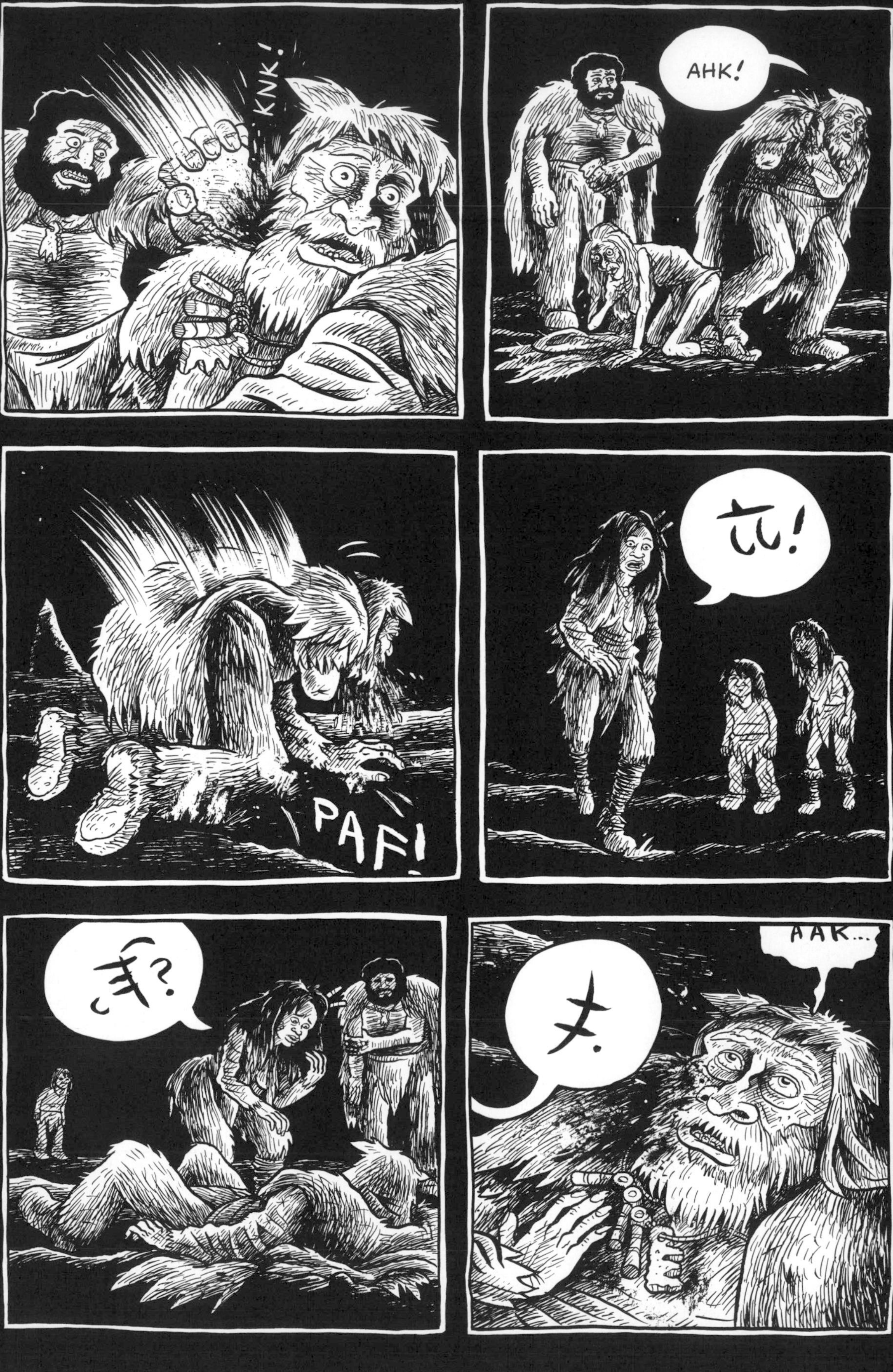
KNK!
AHK!
PAF!
AAK...

PK!

RRPT!

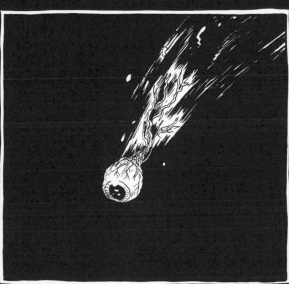

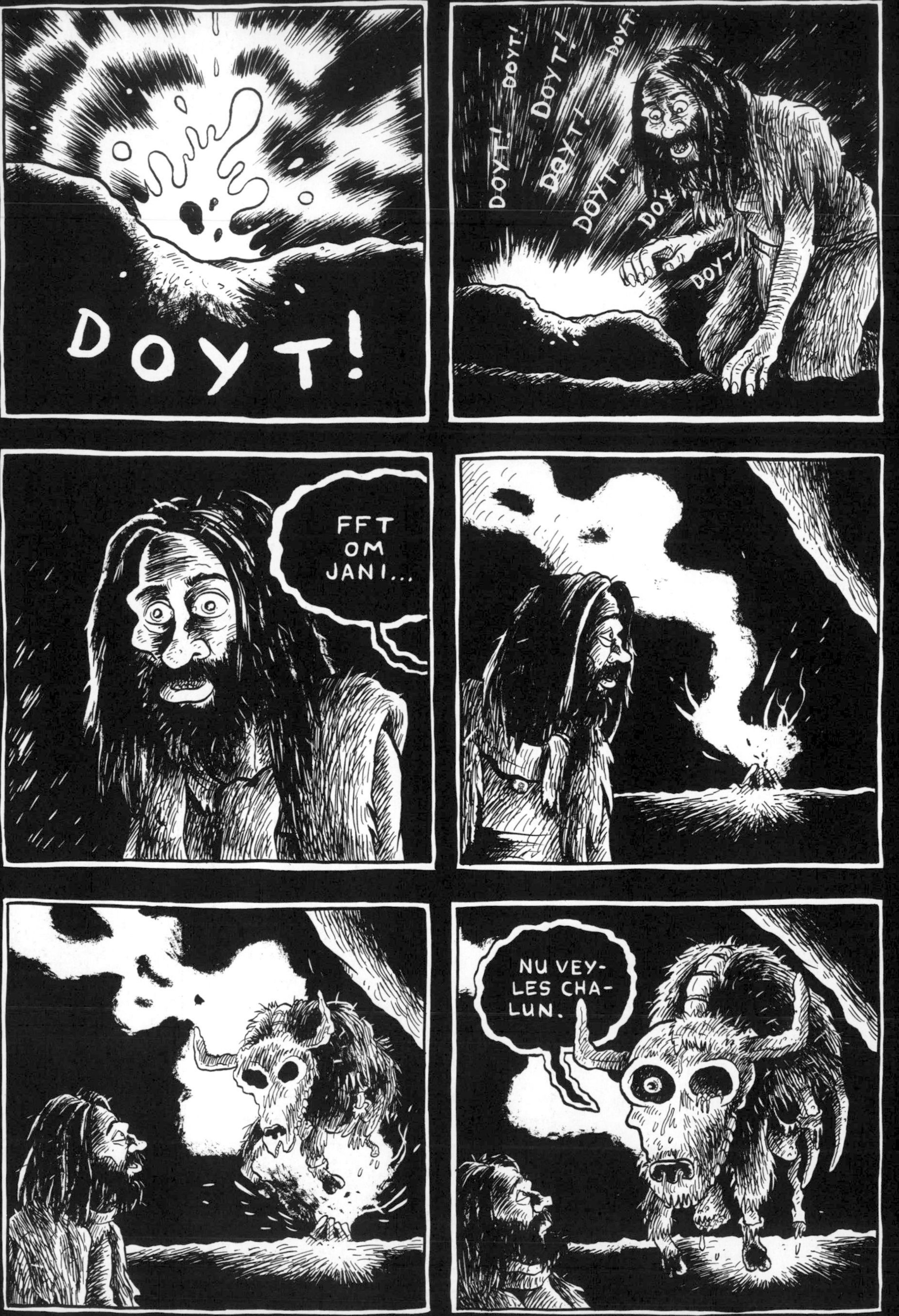
DOYT!
DOYT! DOYT! DOYT! DOYT.
DOYT! DOYT! DOYT! DOY
DOYT
FFT OM JANI...
NU VEY-LES CHA-LUN.

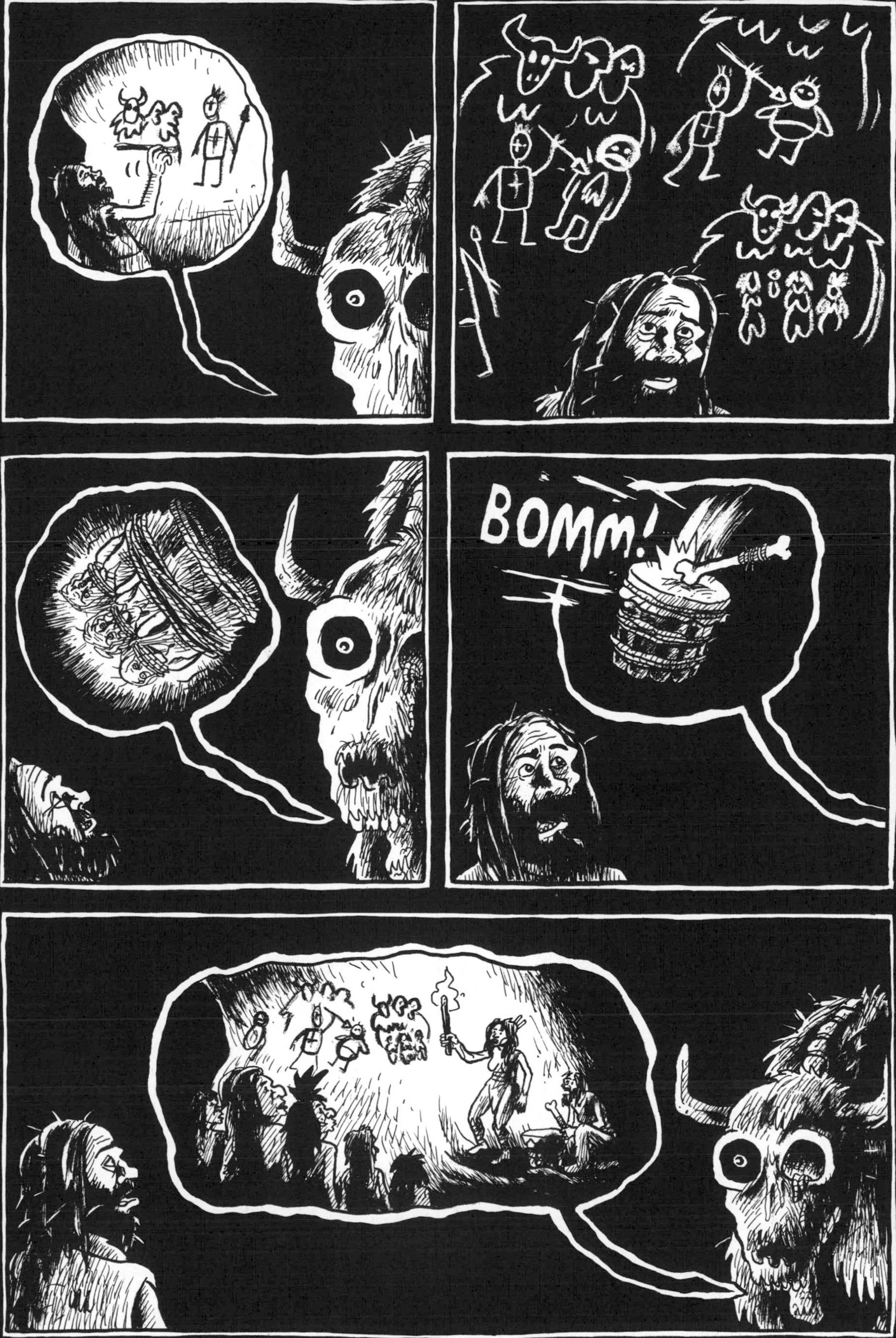
BOMM!

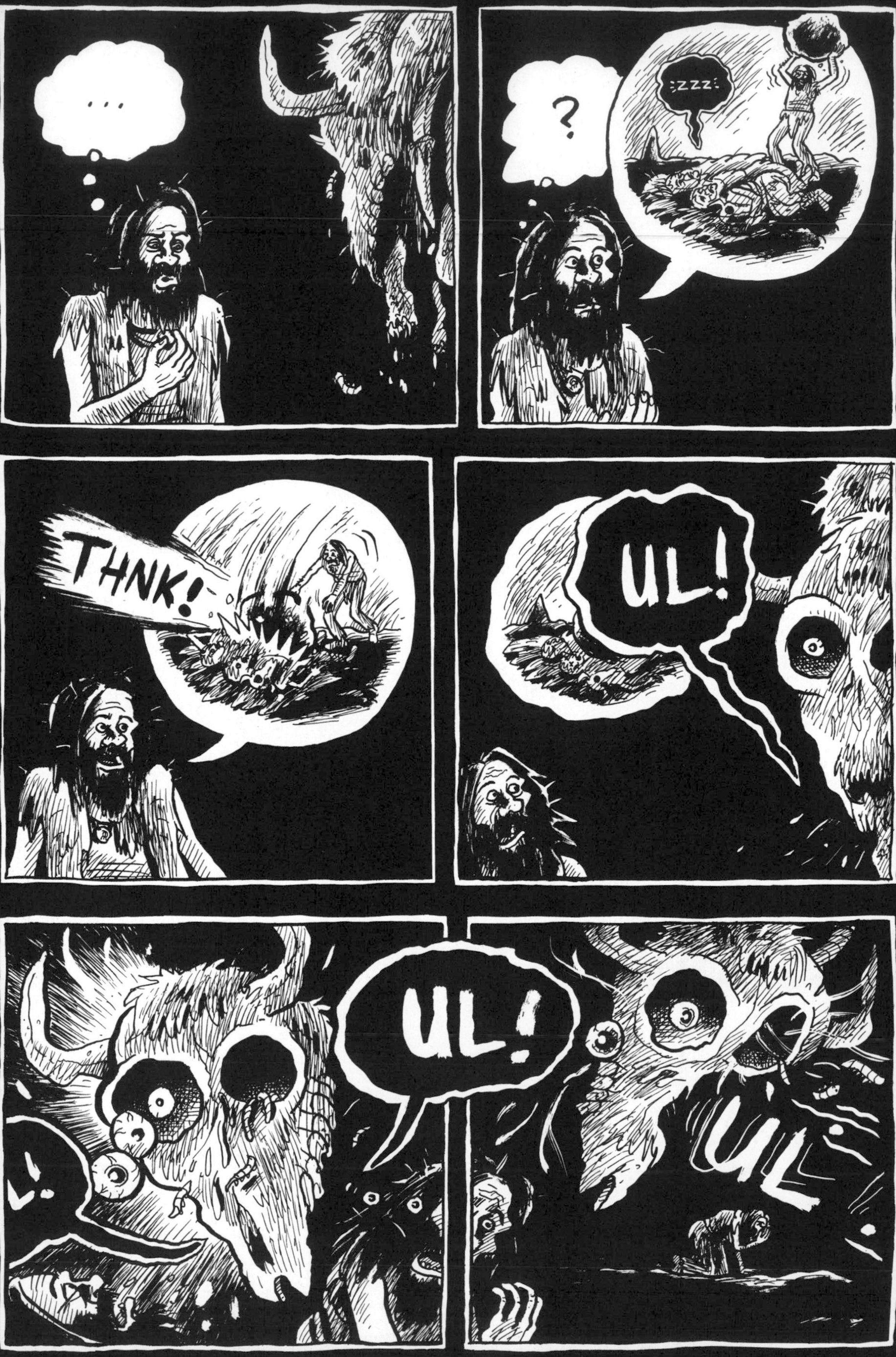
...
?
ZZZ
THNK!
UL!
UL!
UL

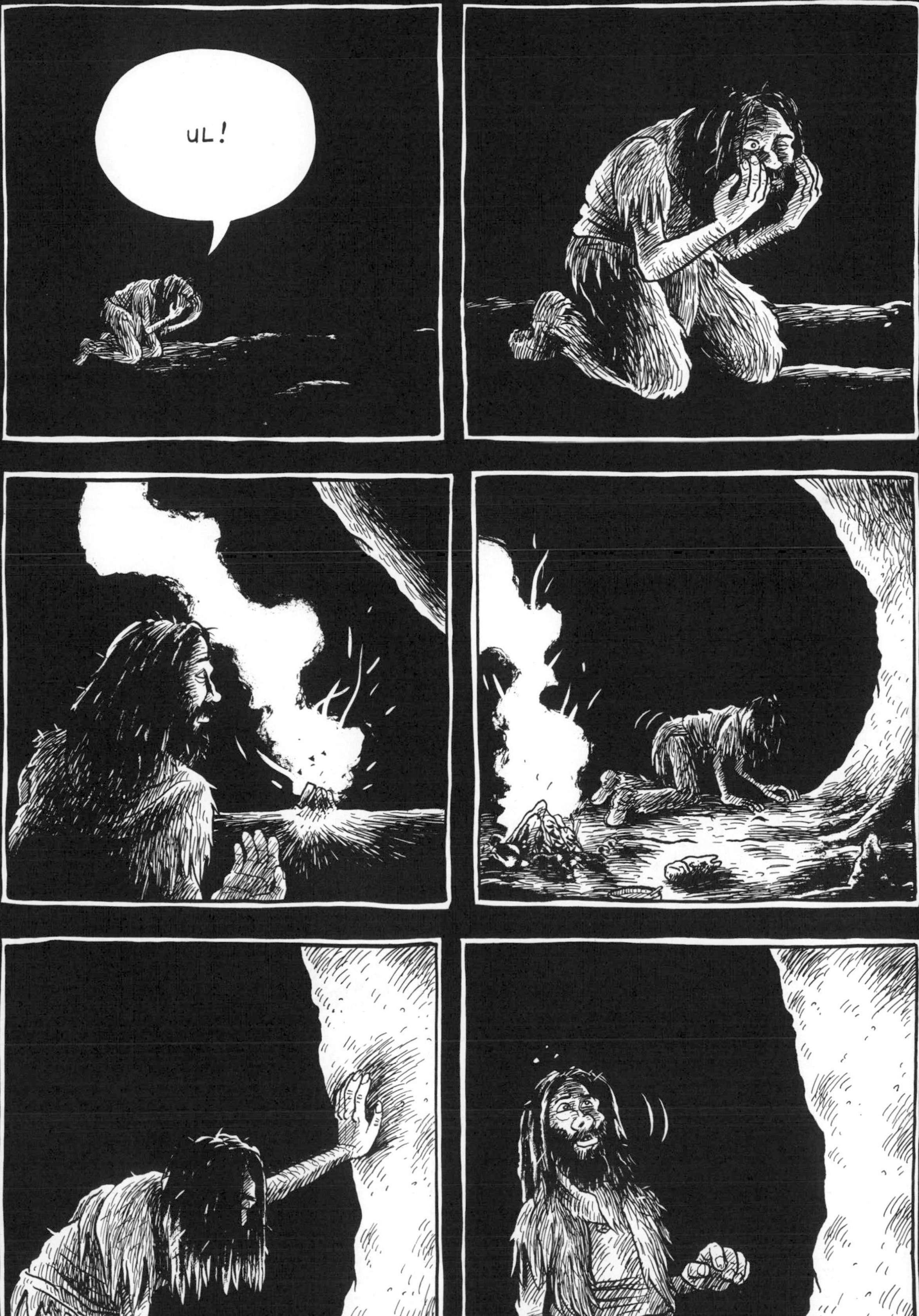
UL!

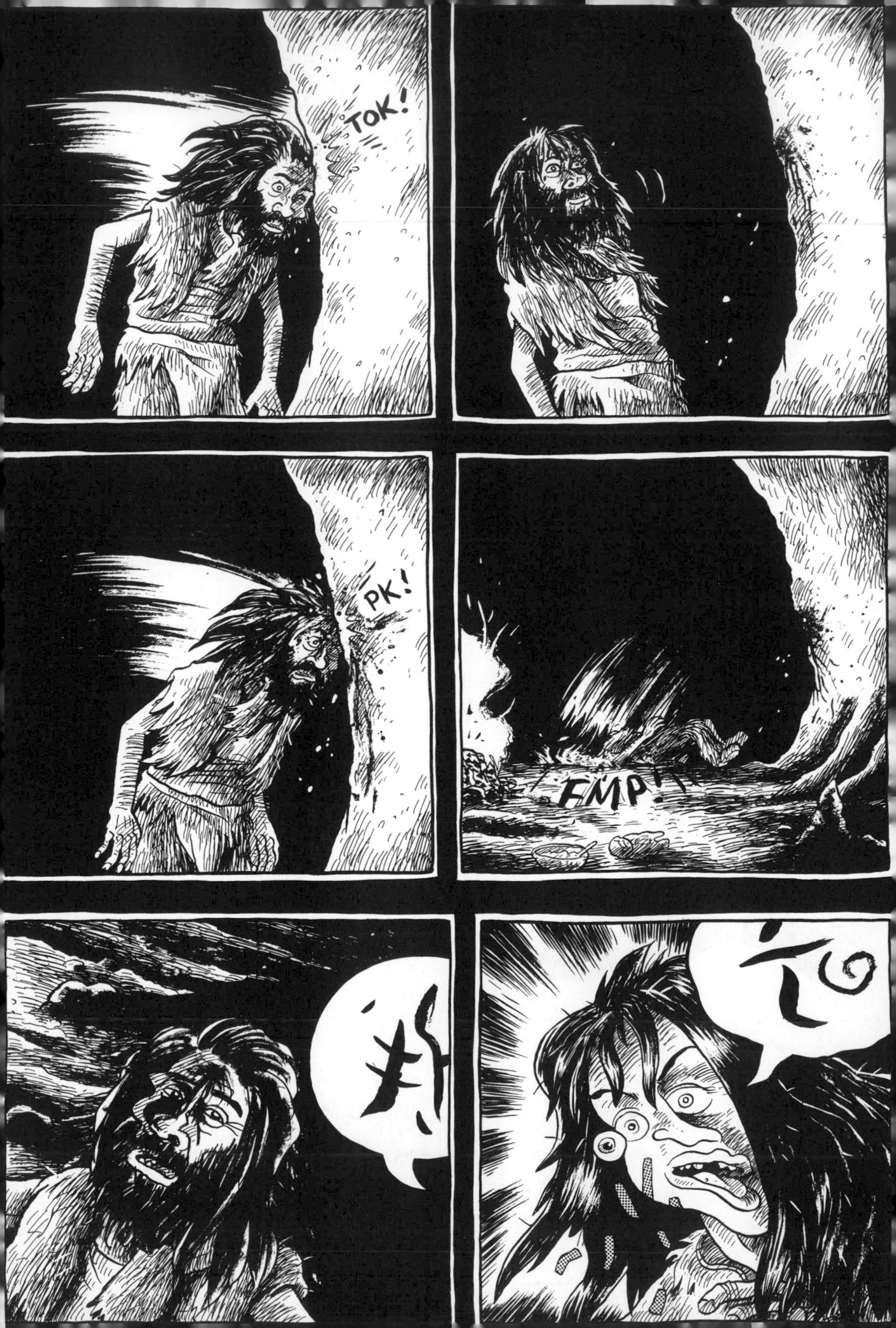
TOK!
PK!
FMP!

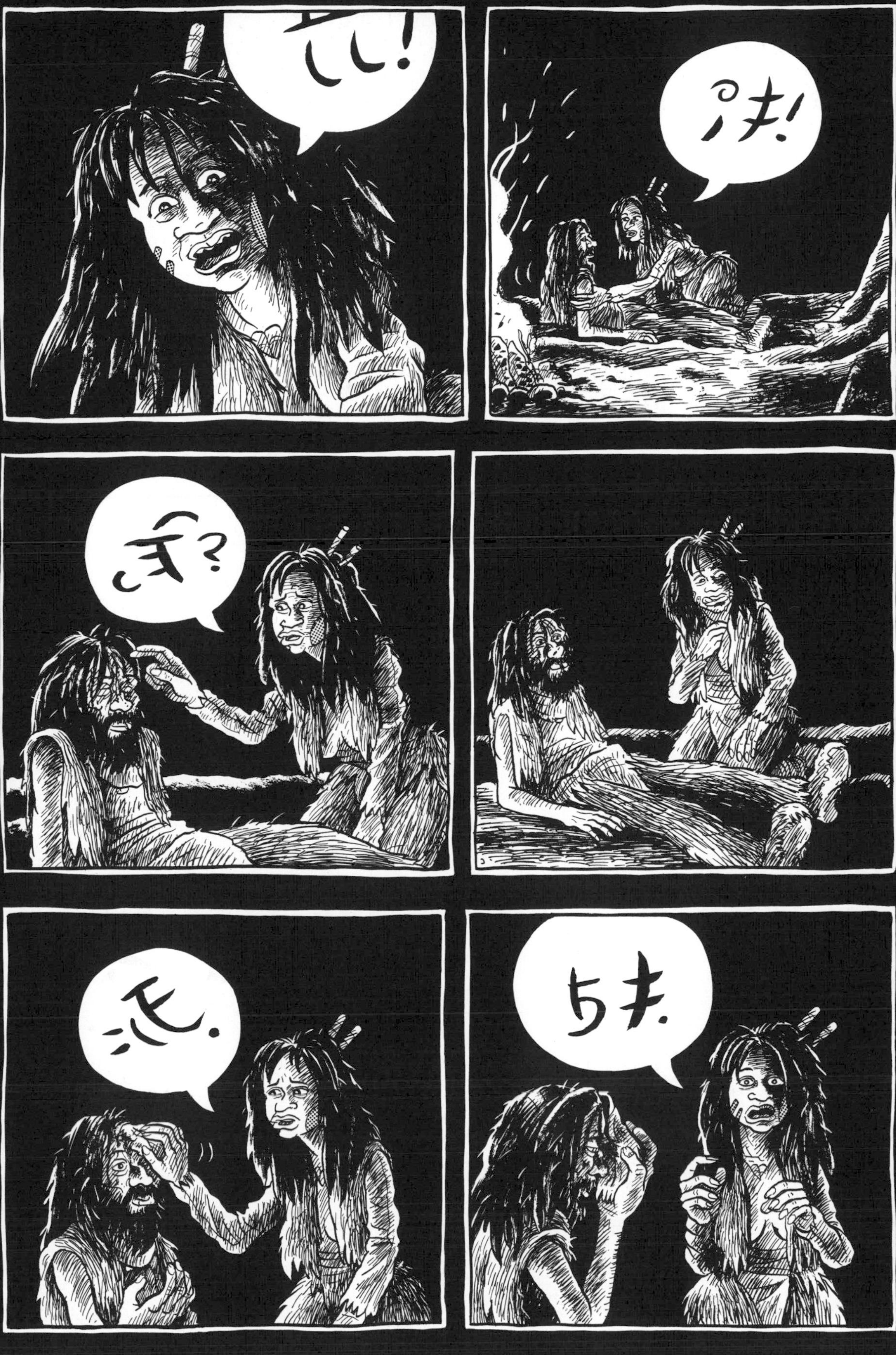

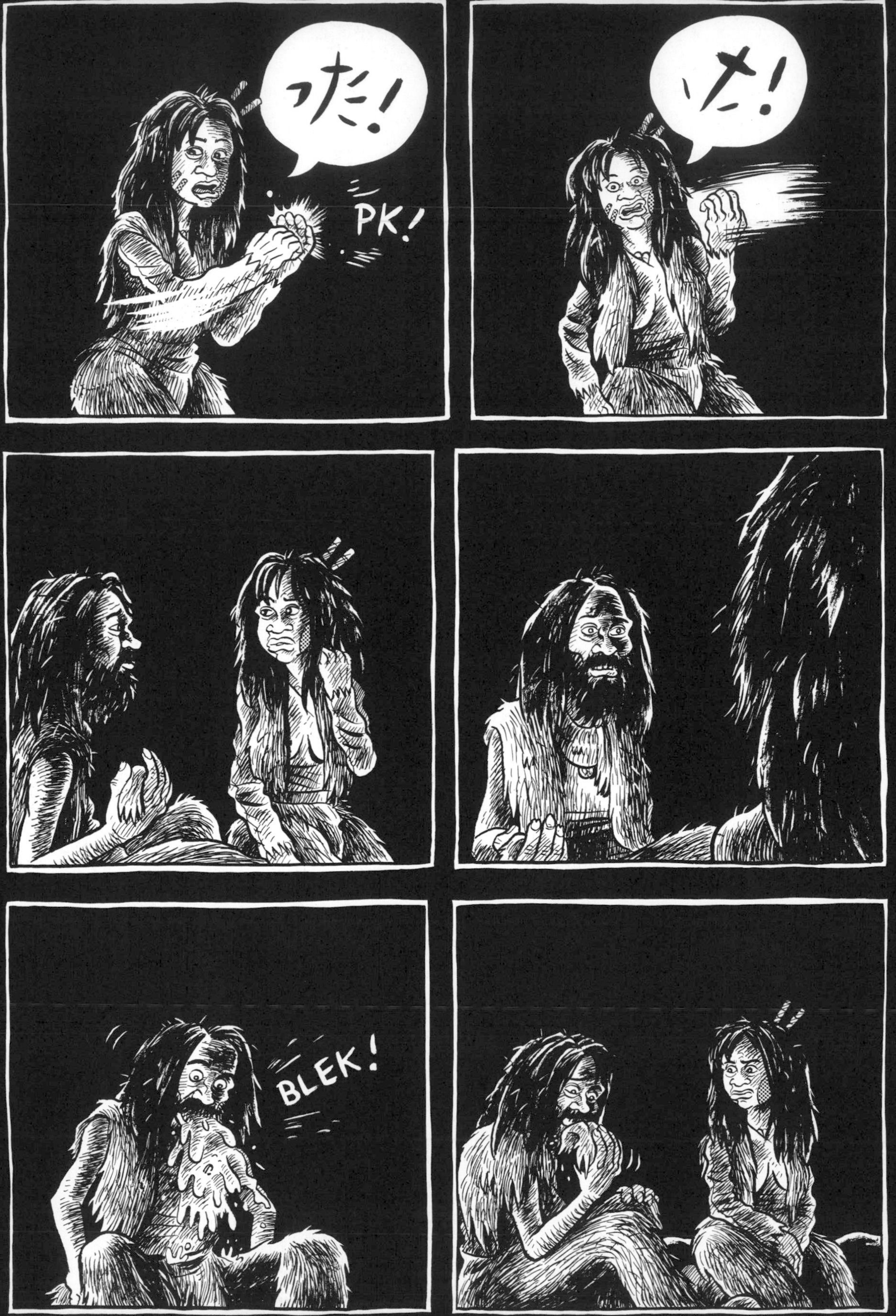
PK!
BLEK!

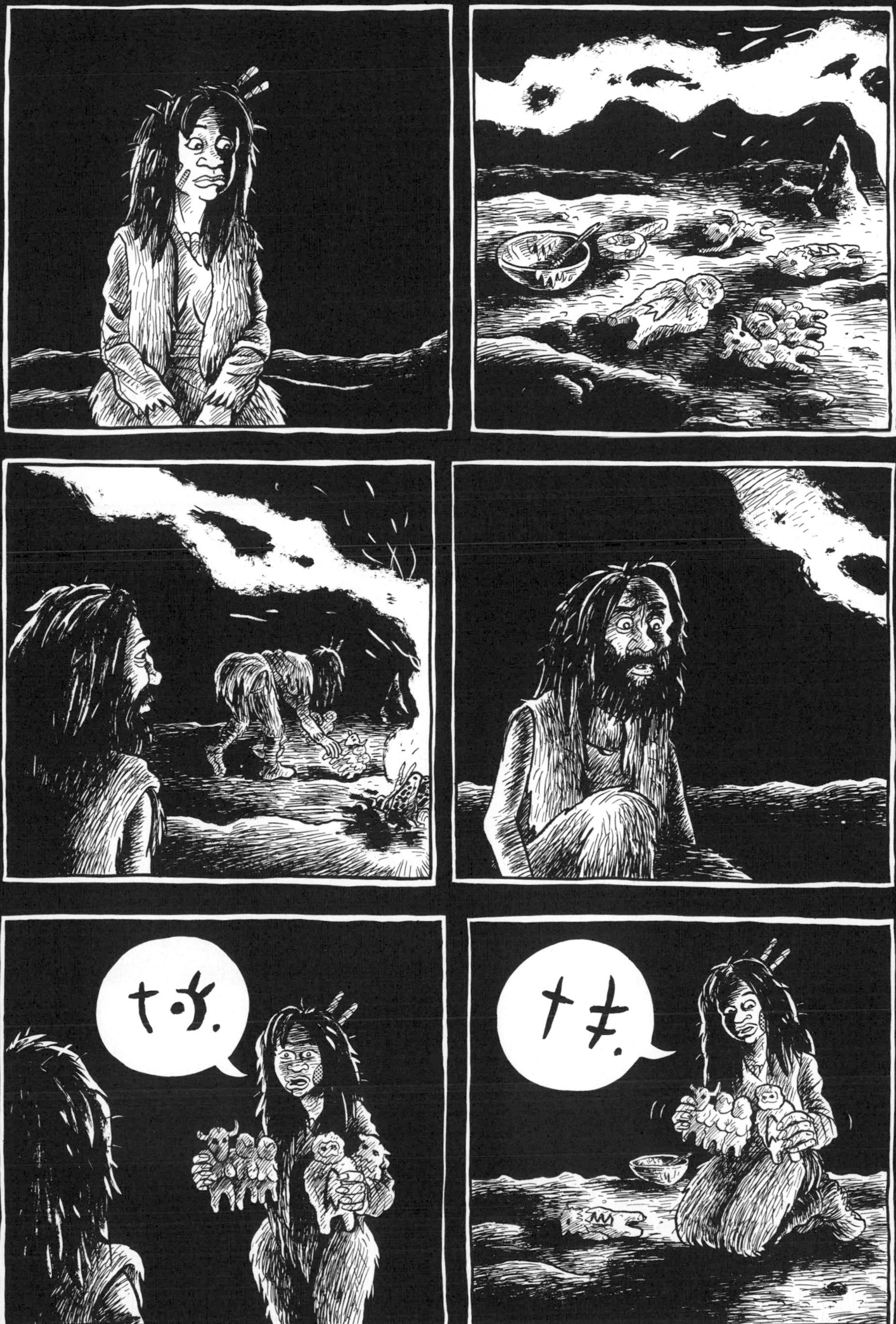

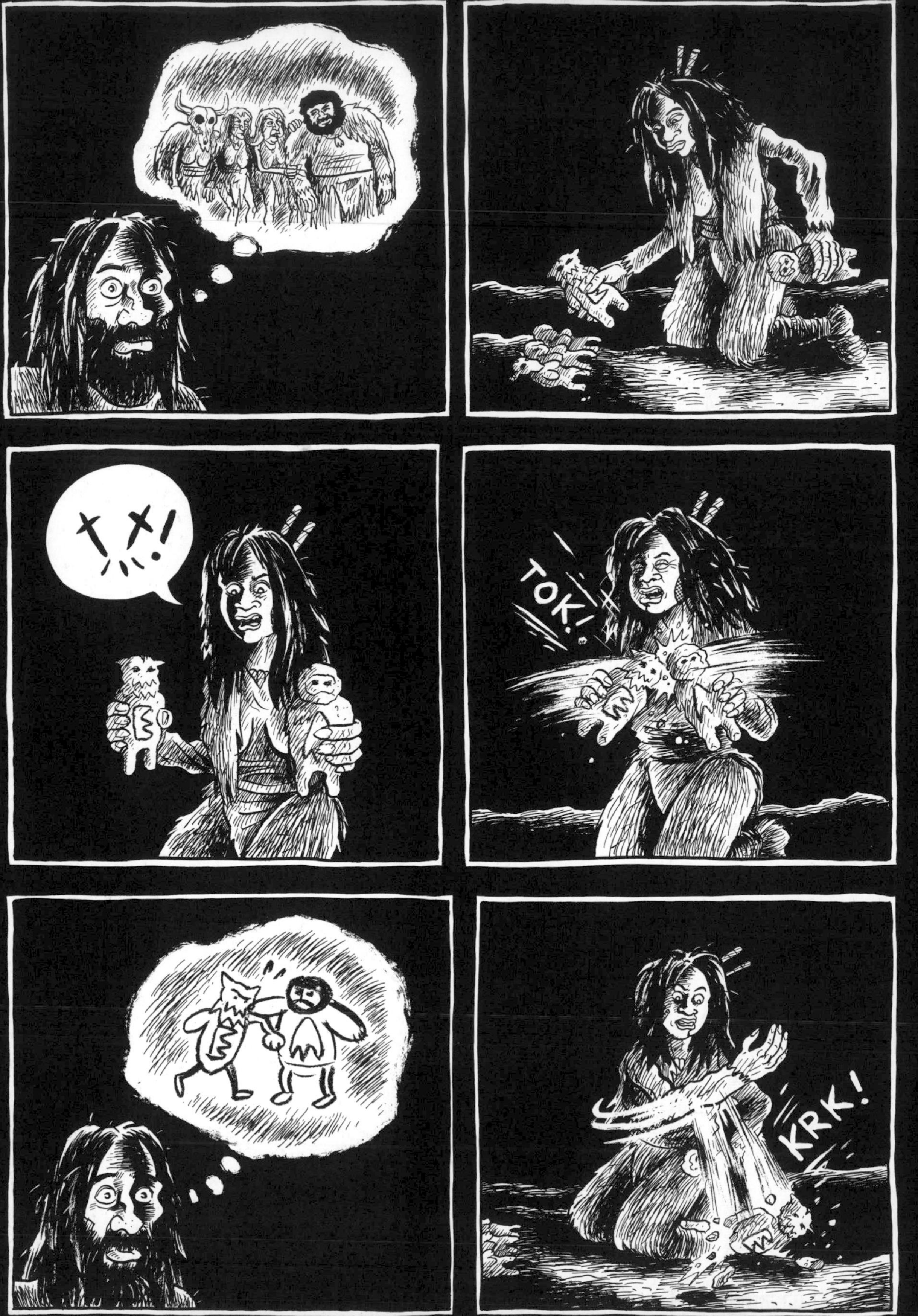
TOK!
KRK!

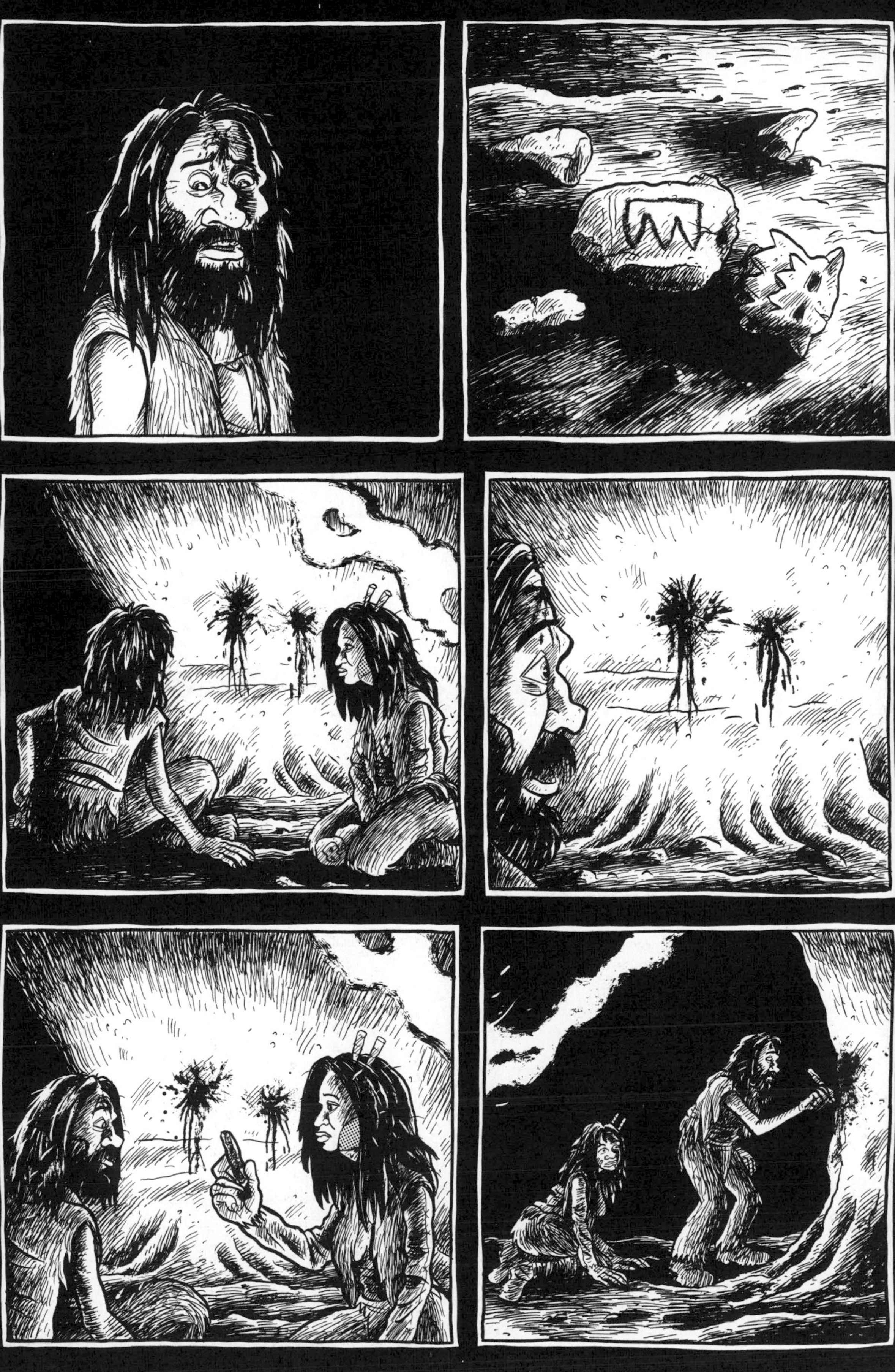

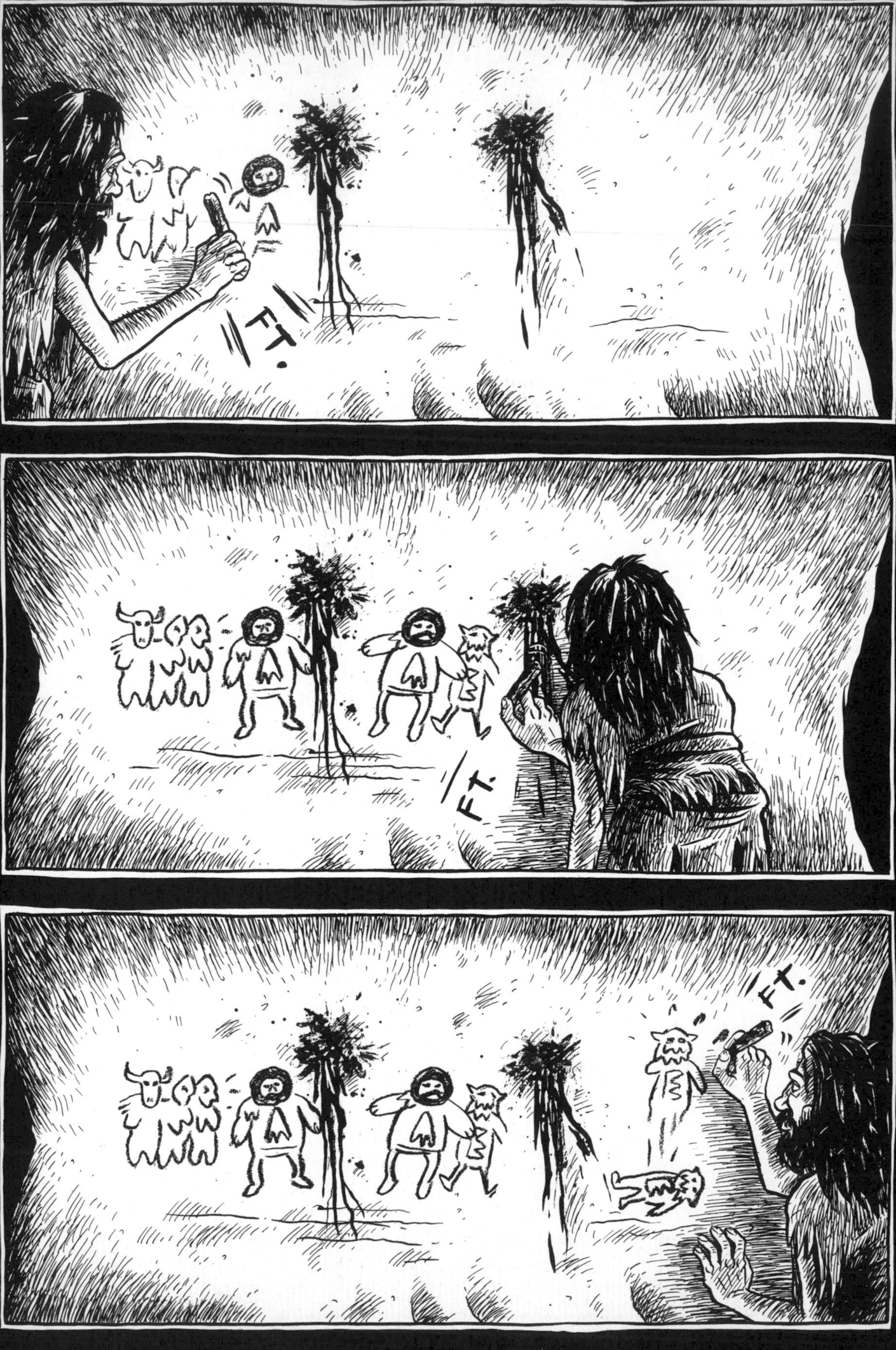
FT.
FT.
FT.

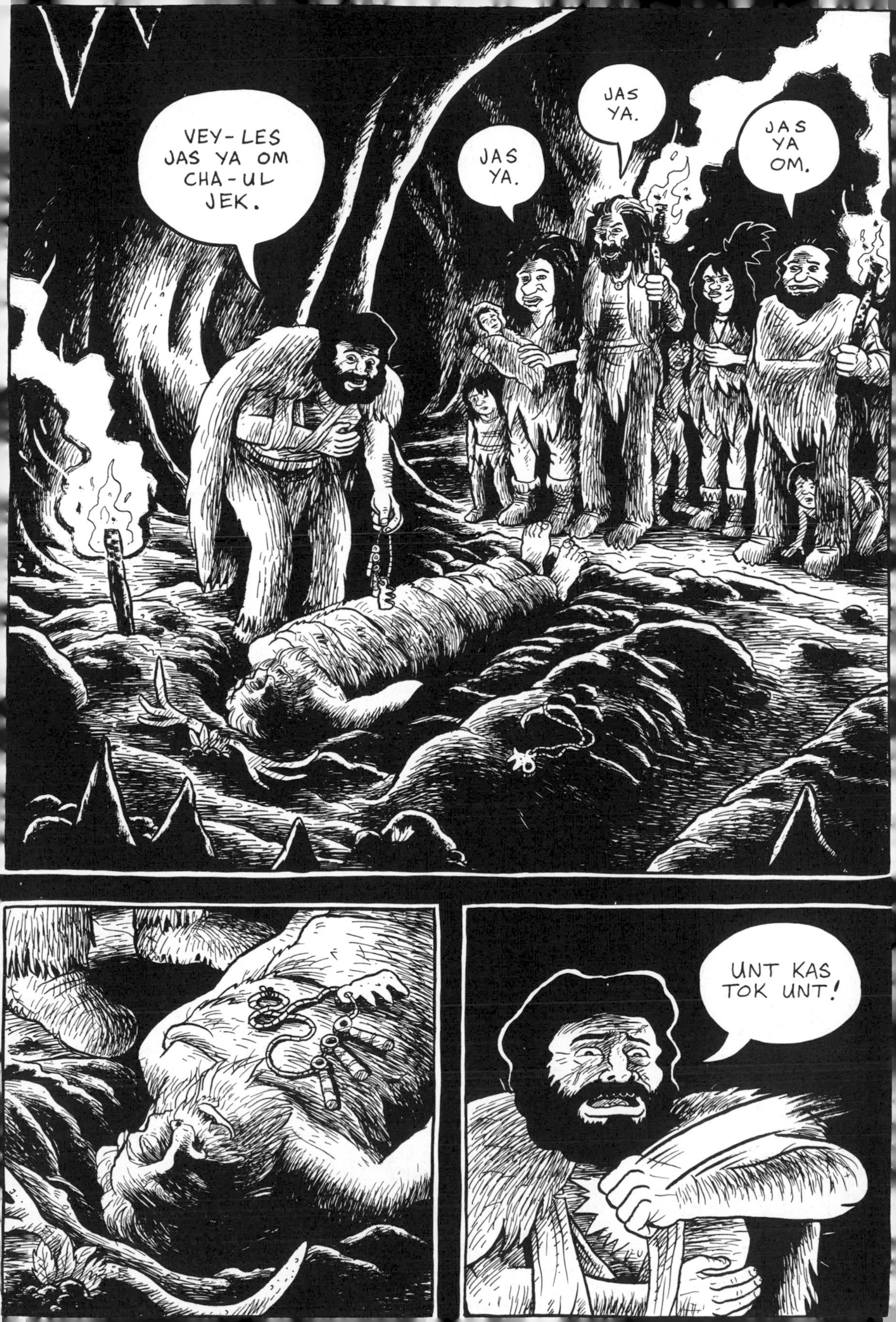
VEY-LES JAS YA OM CHA-UL JEK.
JAS YA.
JAS YA.
JAS YA OM.
UNT KAS TOK UNT!

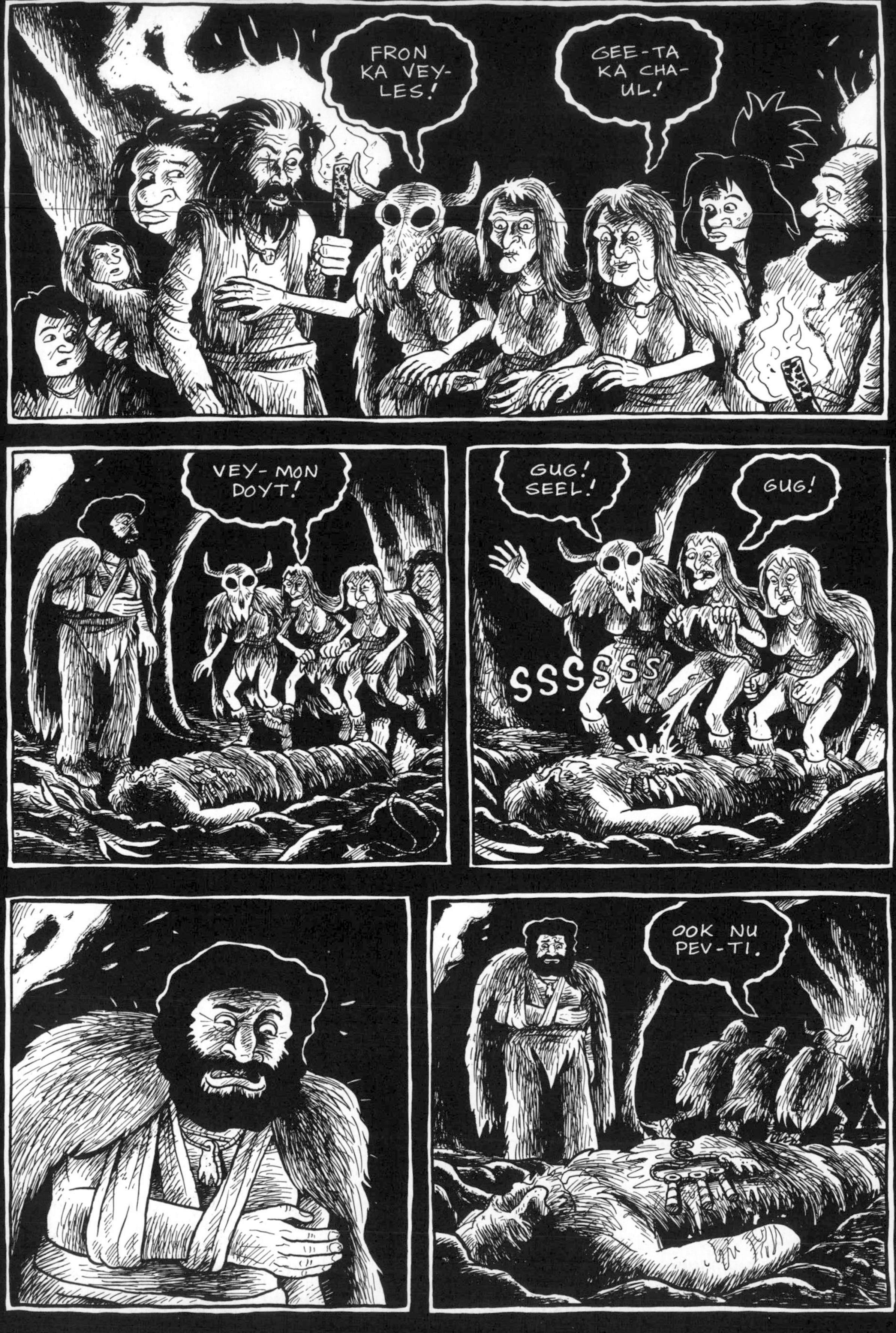
FRON KA VEY-LES!
GEE-TA KA CHA-UL!
VEY-MON DOYT!
GUG! SEEL!
GUG!
SSSSSS
OOK NU PEV-TI.

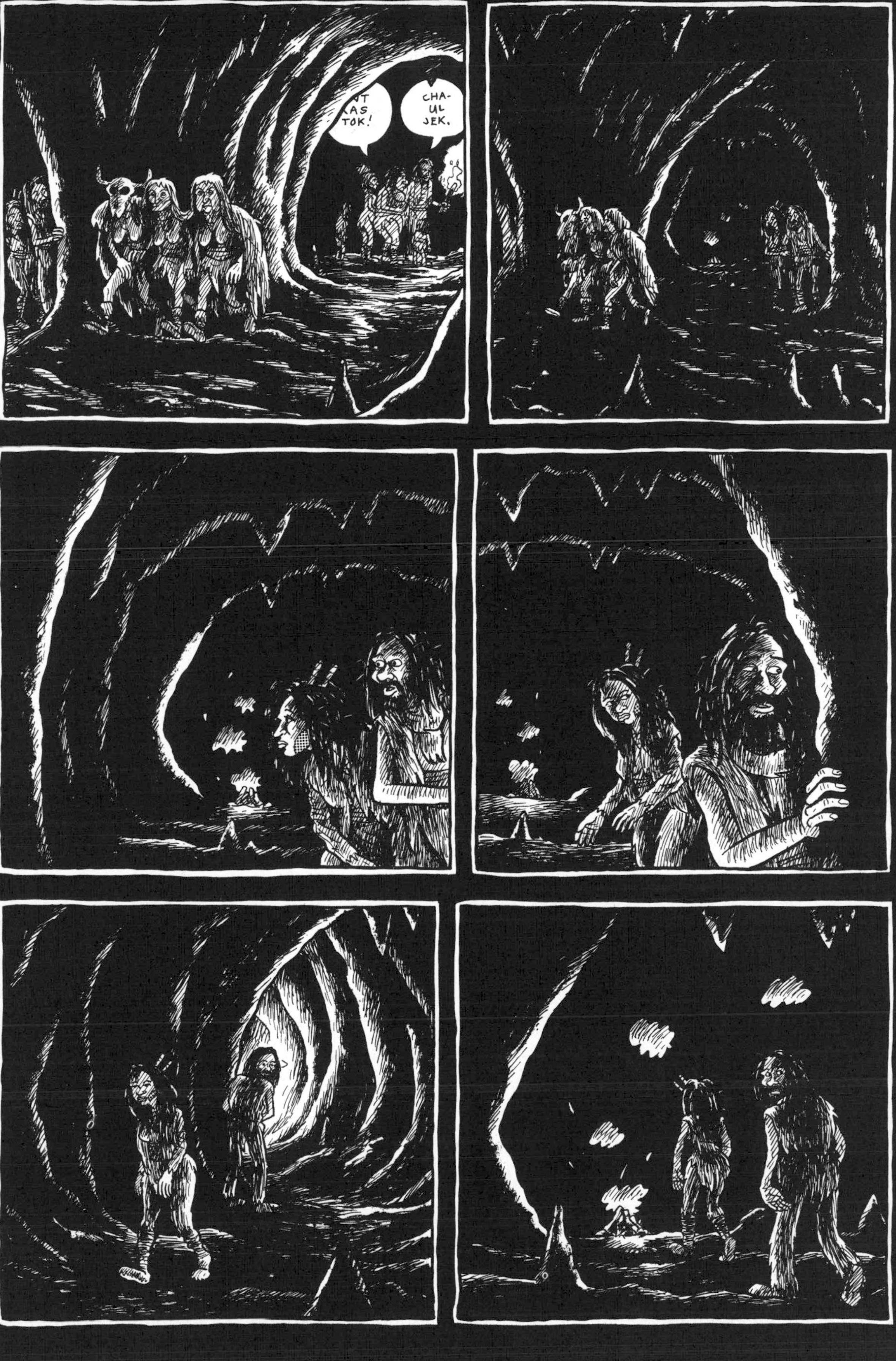
TOK!
CHA-UL JEK.

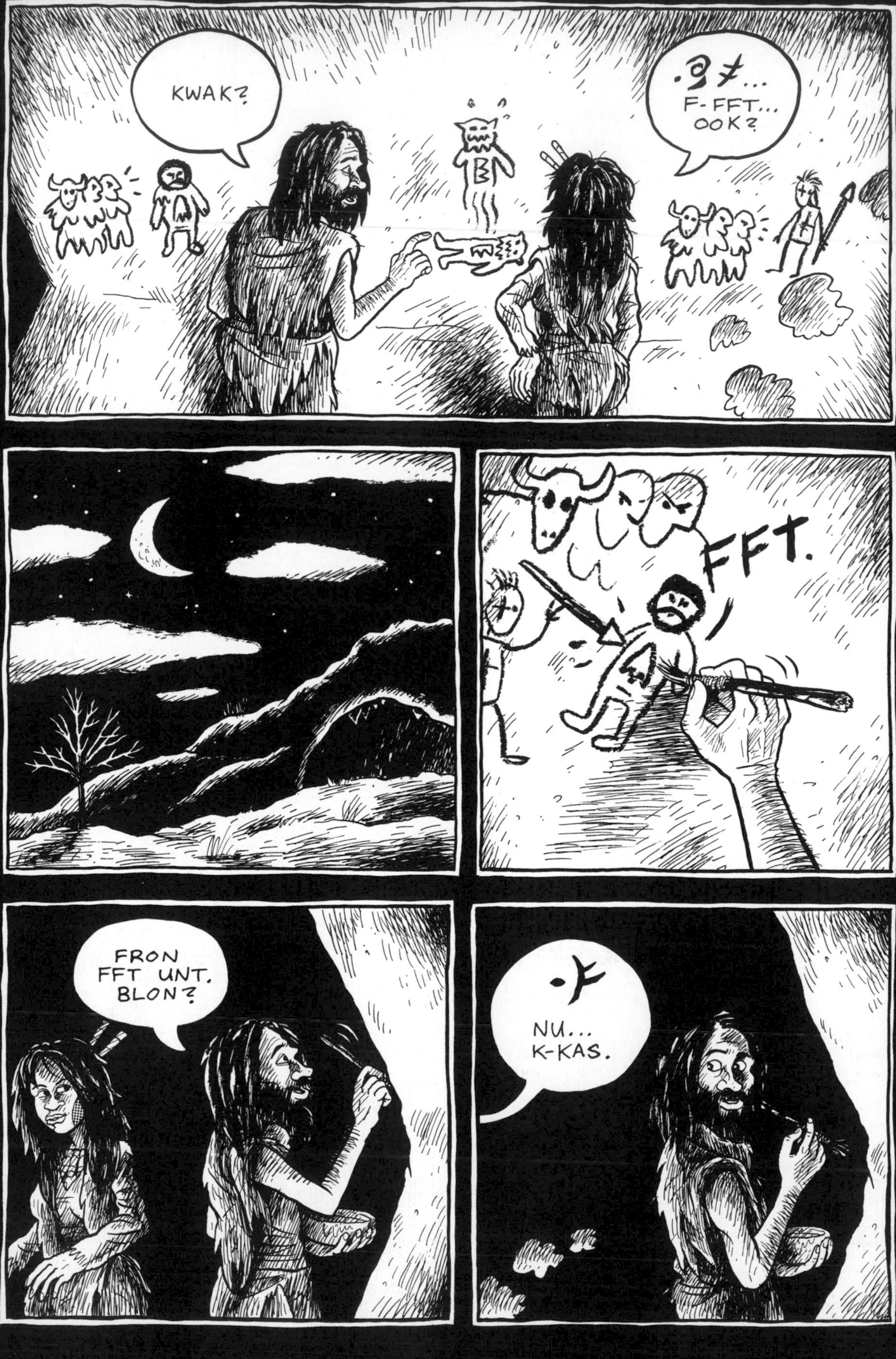
KWAK?
F-FFT... OOK?
FFT.
FRON FFT UNT. BLON?
NU... K-KAS.

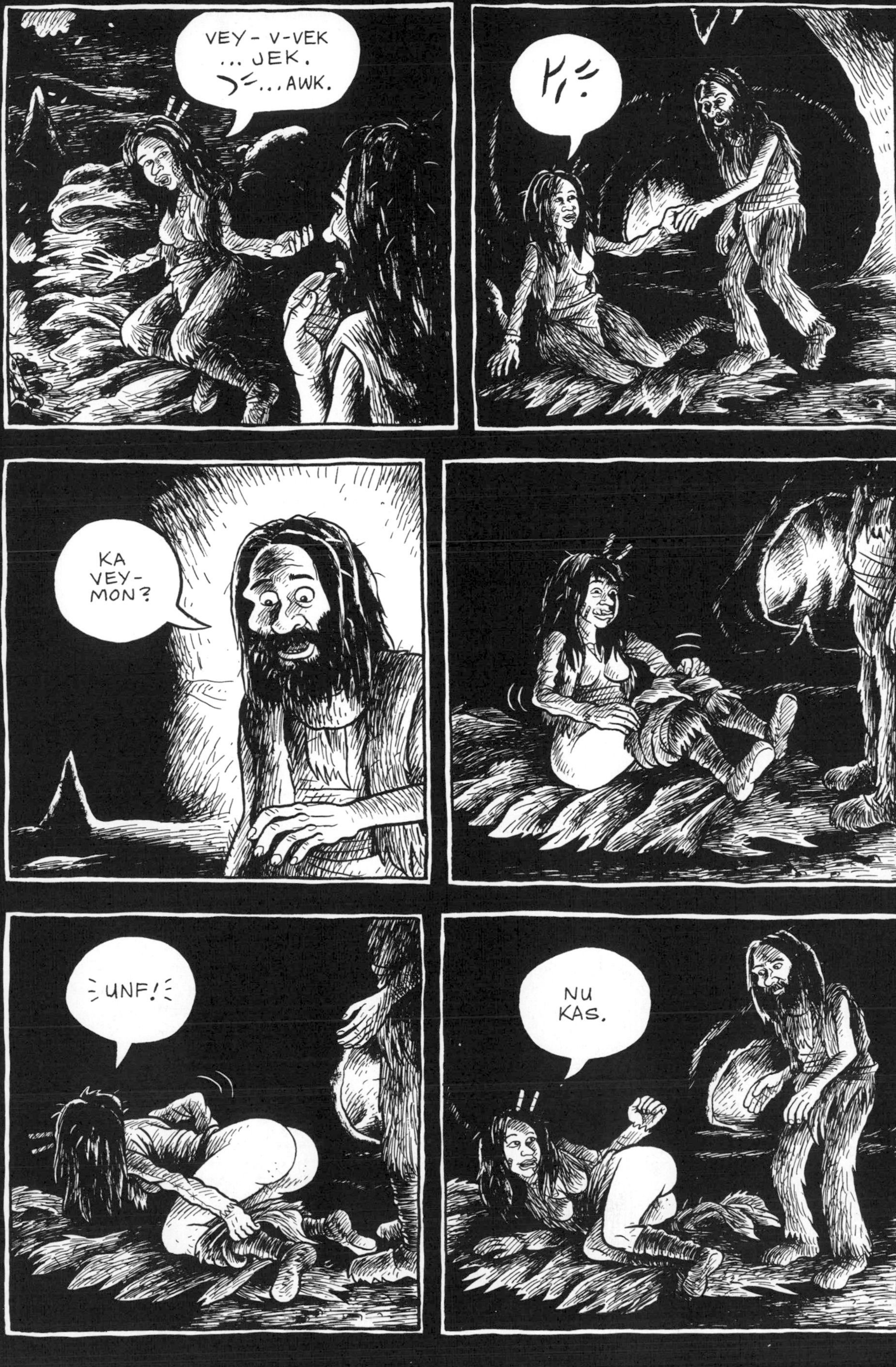
VEY - V-VEK
... JEK.
... AWK.
KA VEY-MON?
UNF!
NU KAS.

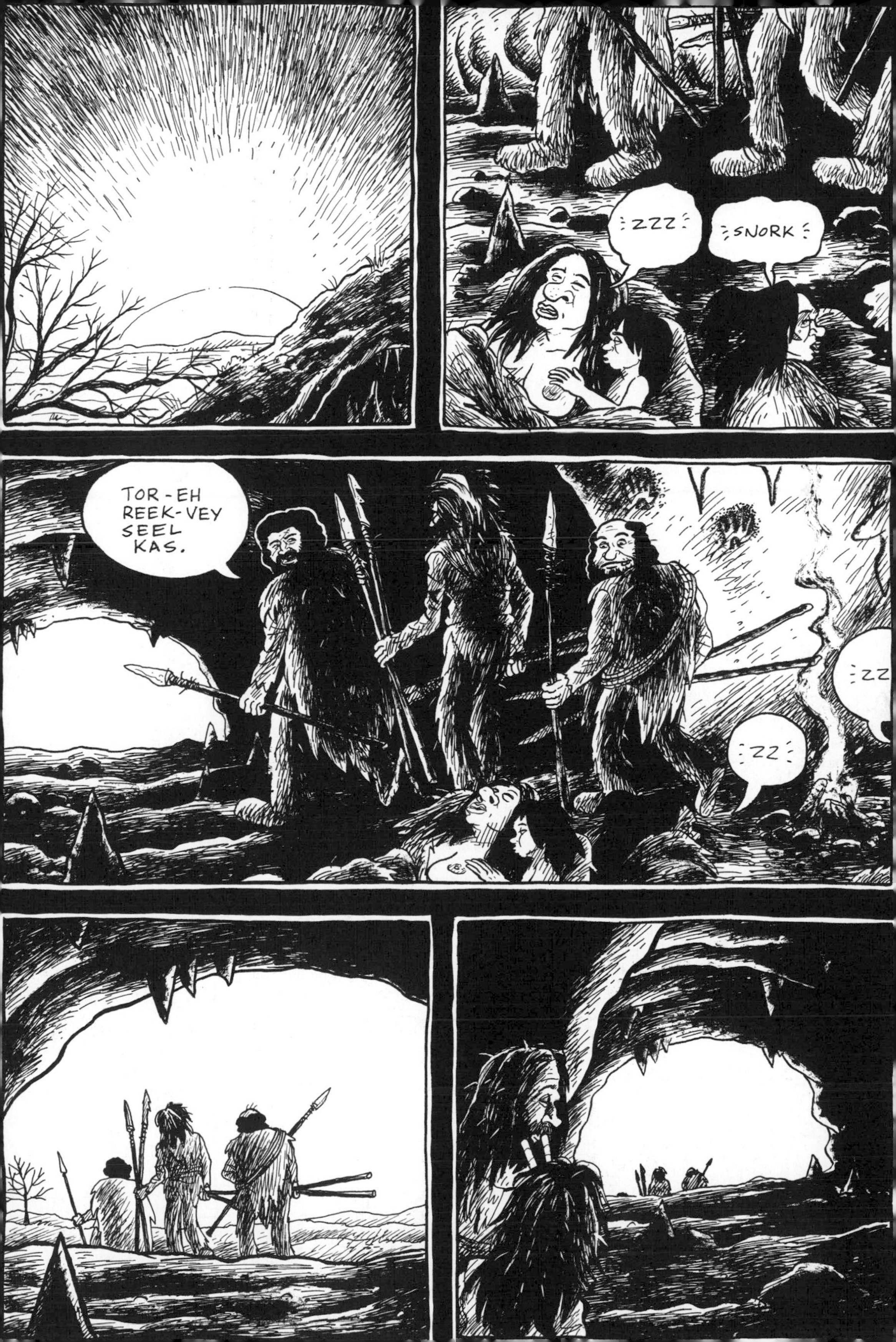
ZZZ
SNORK
TOR-EH REEK-VEY SEEL KAS.
ZZ
ZZ

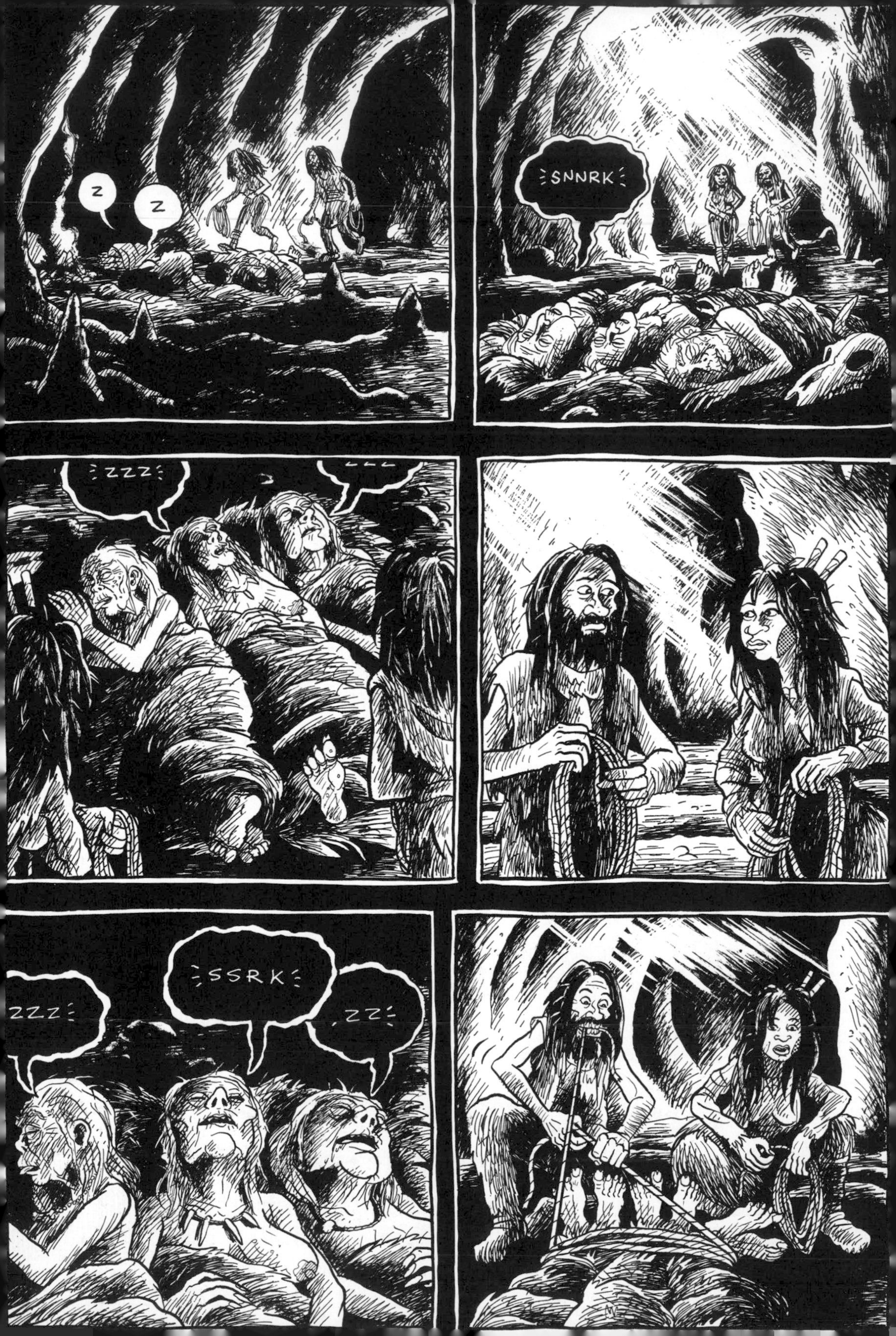
Z
Z
SNNRK
ZZZ
ZZZ
SSRK
ZZ

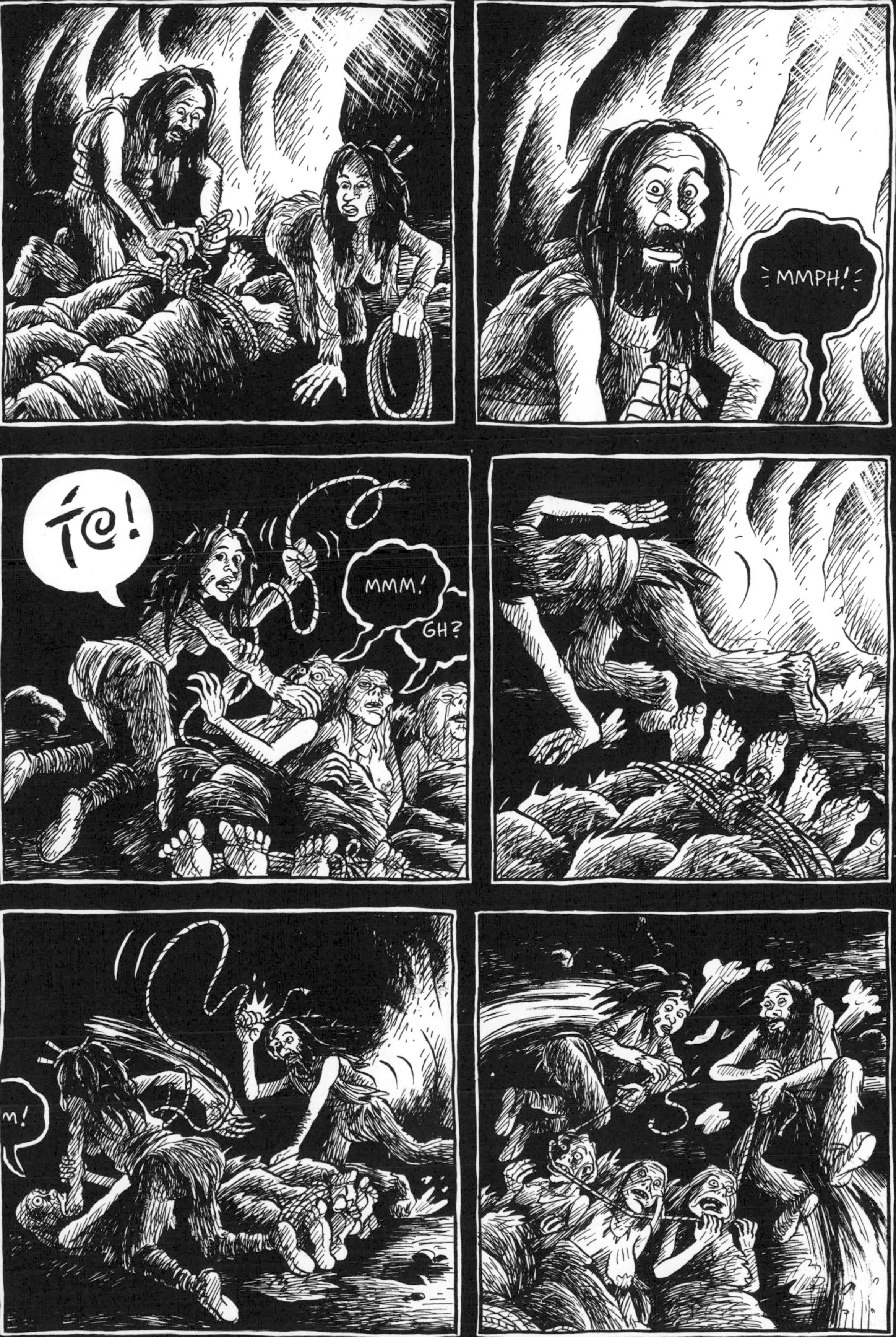
MMPH!
Ɨ@!
MMM!
GH?
M!

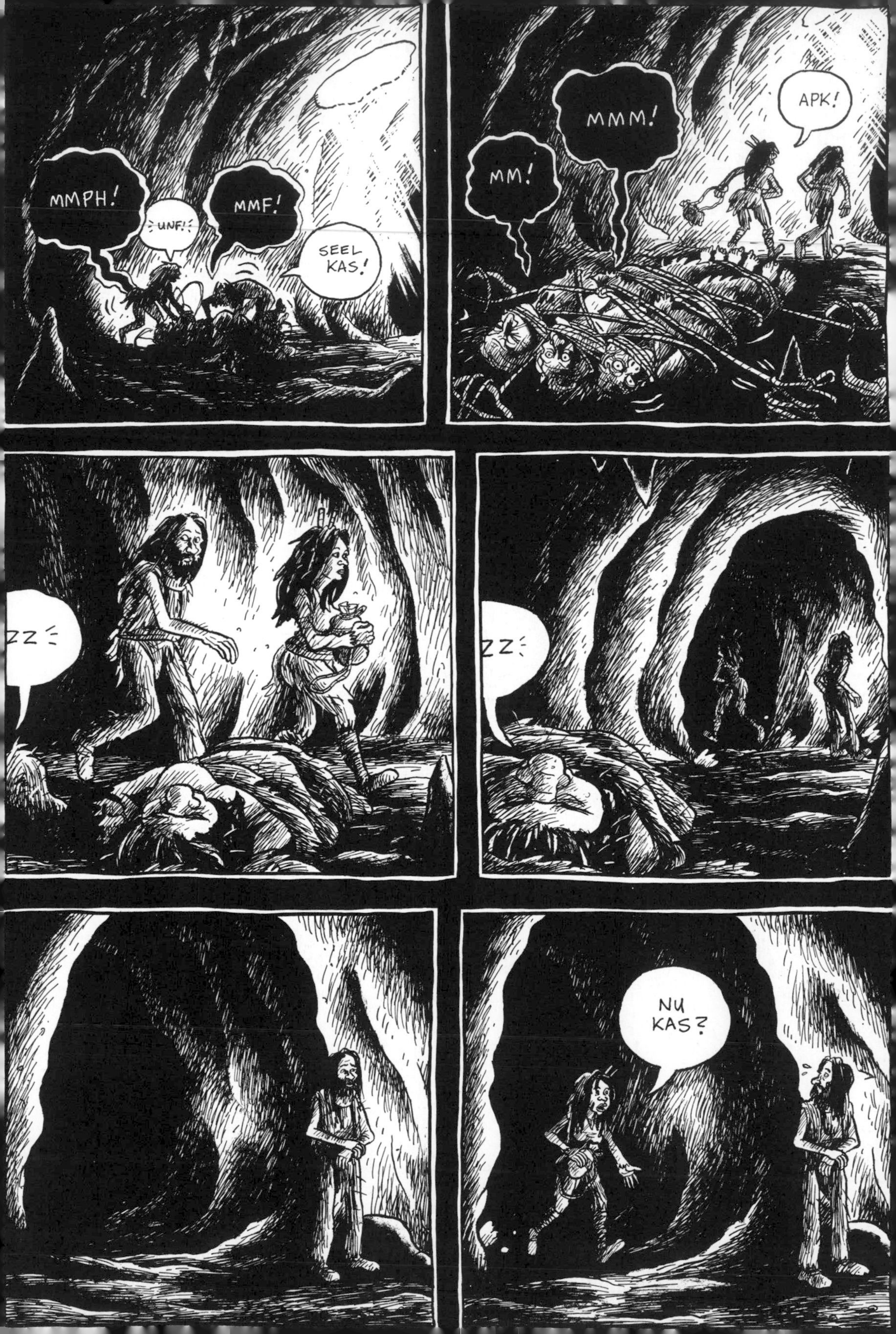
MMPH!
UNF!
MMF!
SEEL KAS!
MM!
MMM!
APK!
ZZ
ZZ
NU KAS?

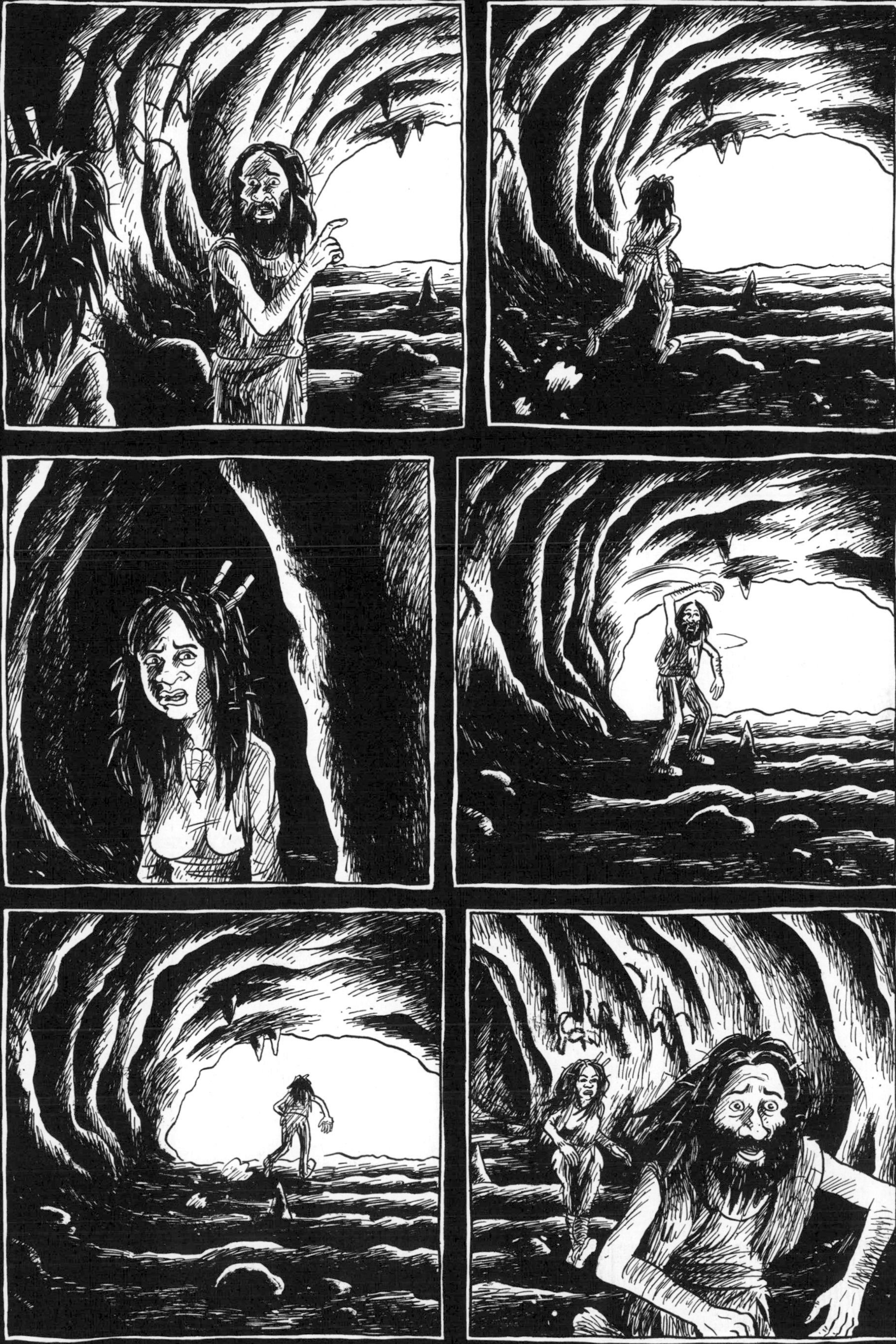

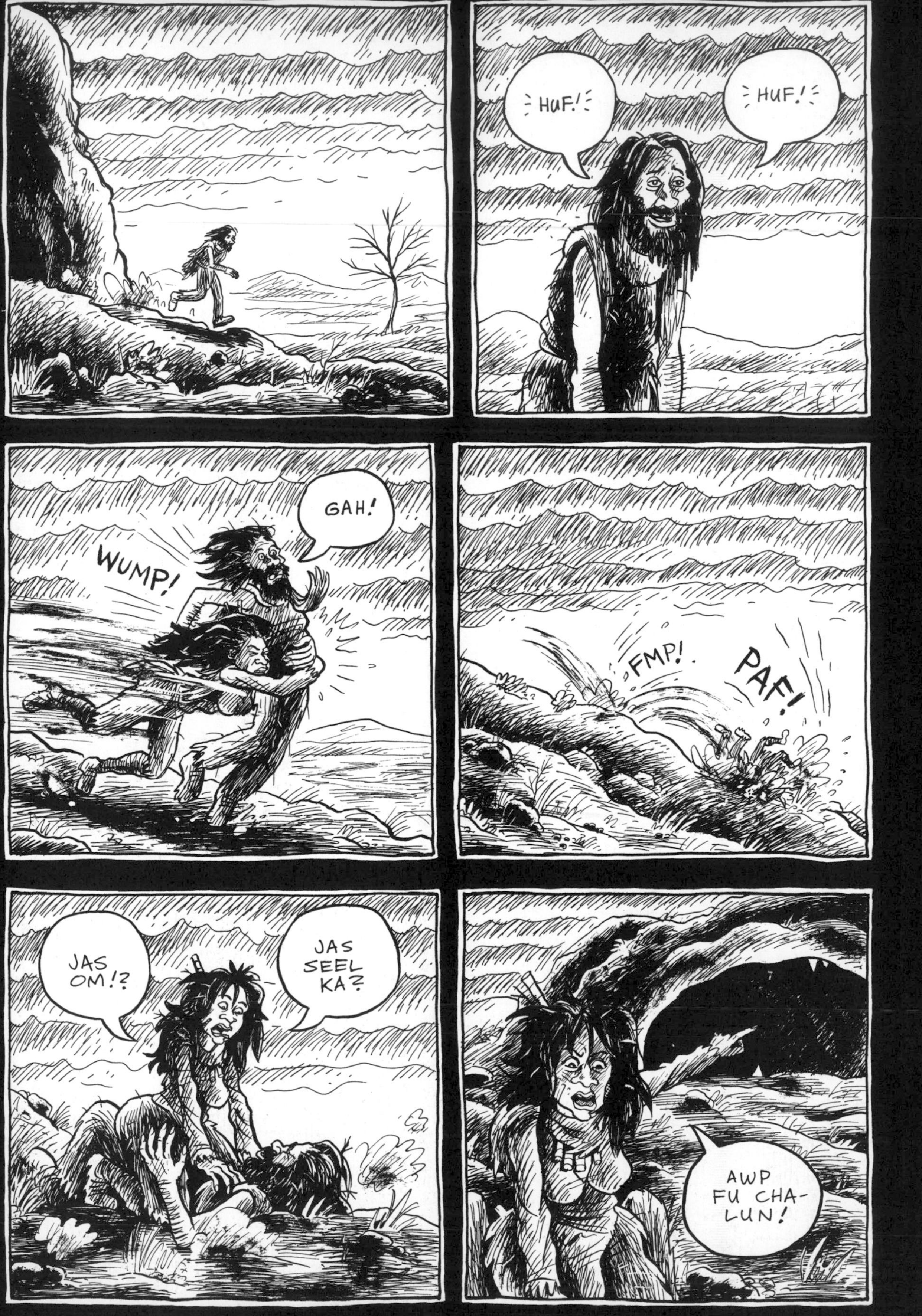
HUF!
HUF!
WUMP!
GAH!
FMP!
PAF!
JAS OM!?
JAS SEEL KA?
AWP FU CHA-LUN!

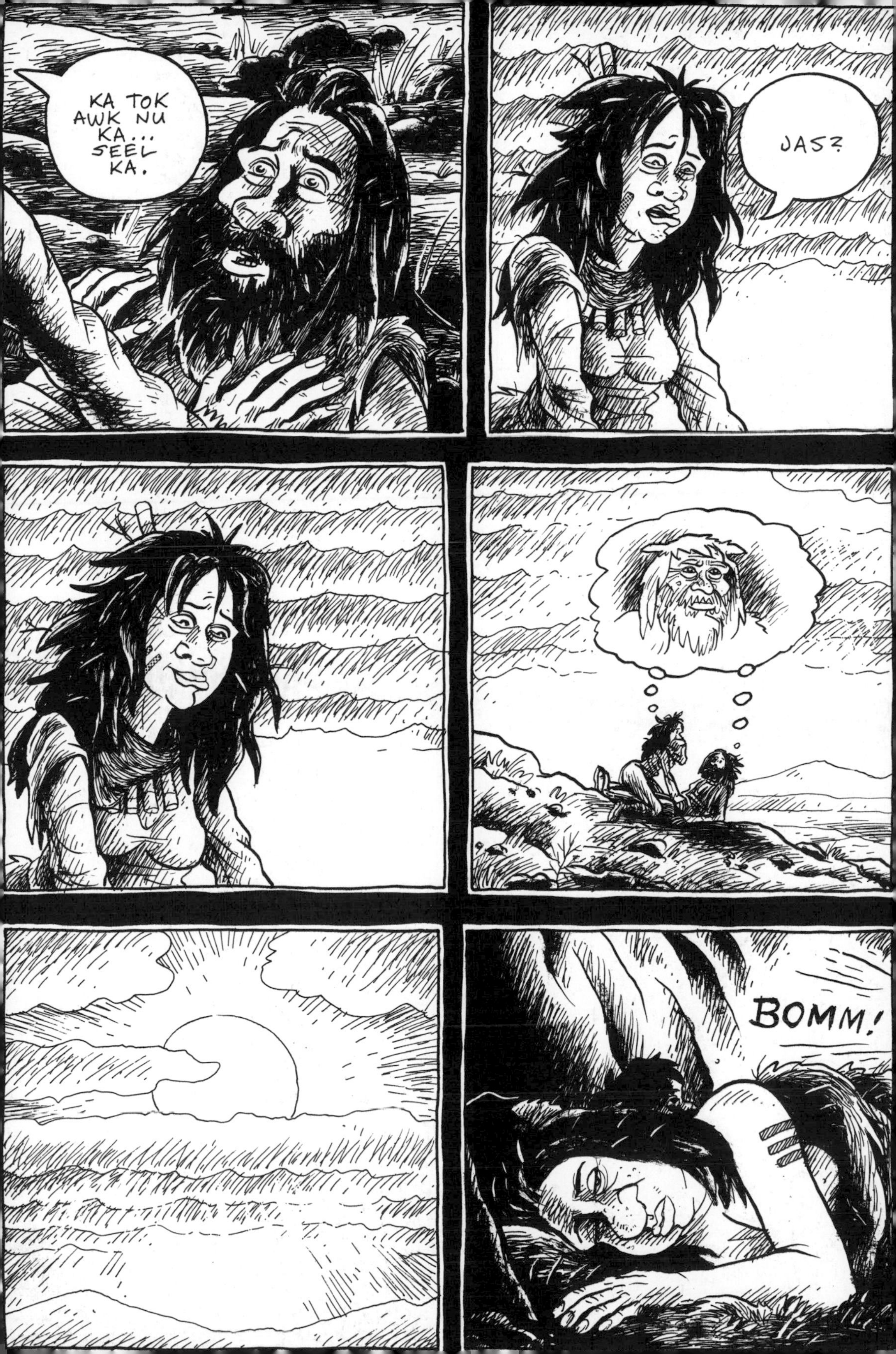
KA TOK AWK NU KA... SEEL KA.
JAS?
BOMM!

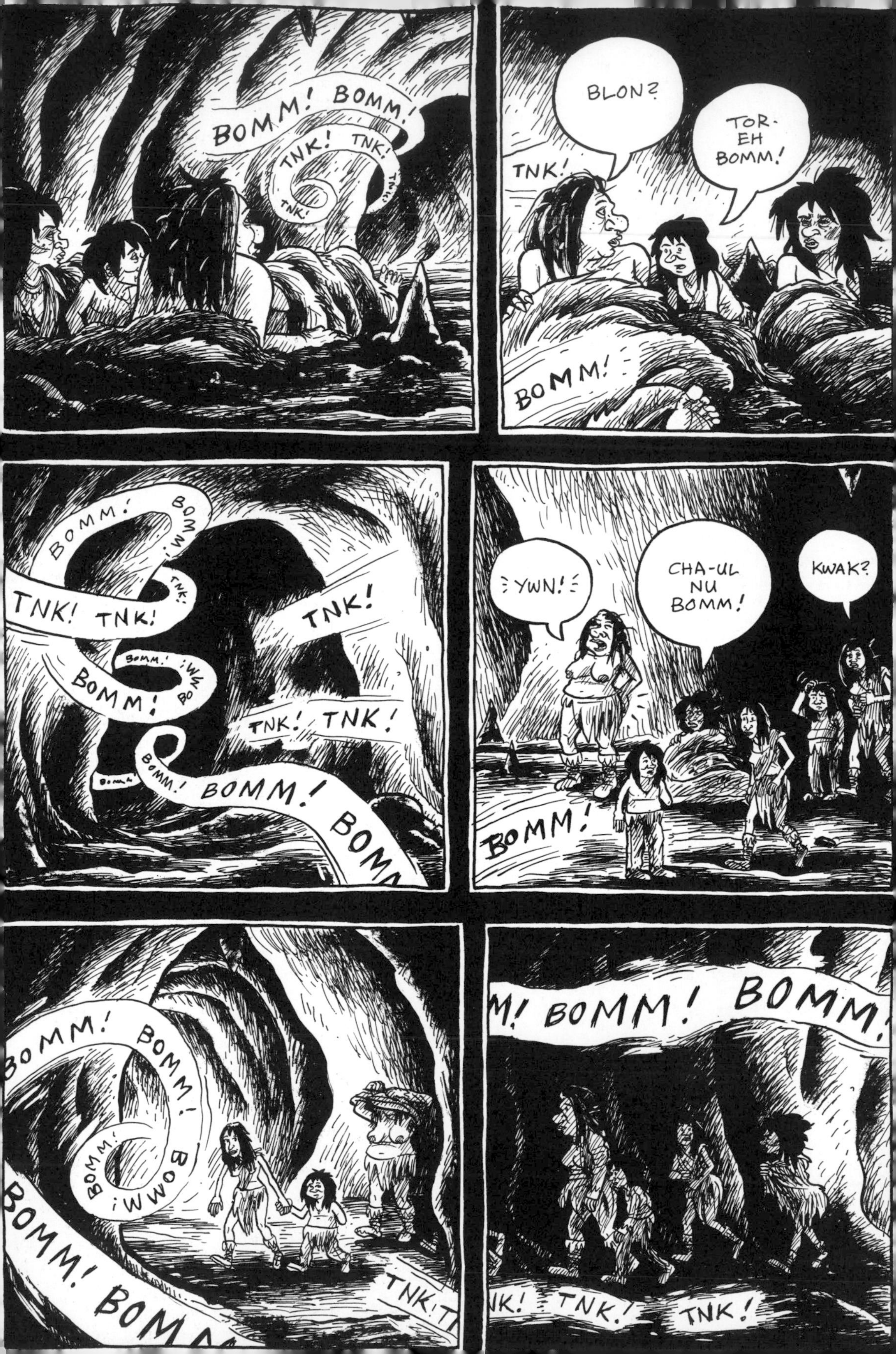
BOMM! BOMM!
TNK! TNK!
TNK!
TNK!
TNK!
BLON?
TOR-EH BOMM!
BOMM!
BOMM! BOMM!
TNK! TNK!
TNK!
BOMM!
TNK! TNK!
BOMM! BOMM
YWN!
CHA-UL NU BOMM!
KWAK?
BOMM!
BOMM! BOMM! BOMM!
BOMM! BOMM!
TNK!
M! BOMM! BOMM!
NK! TNK! TNK!

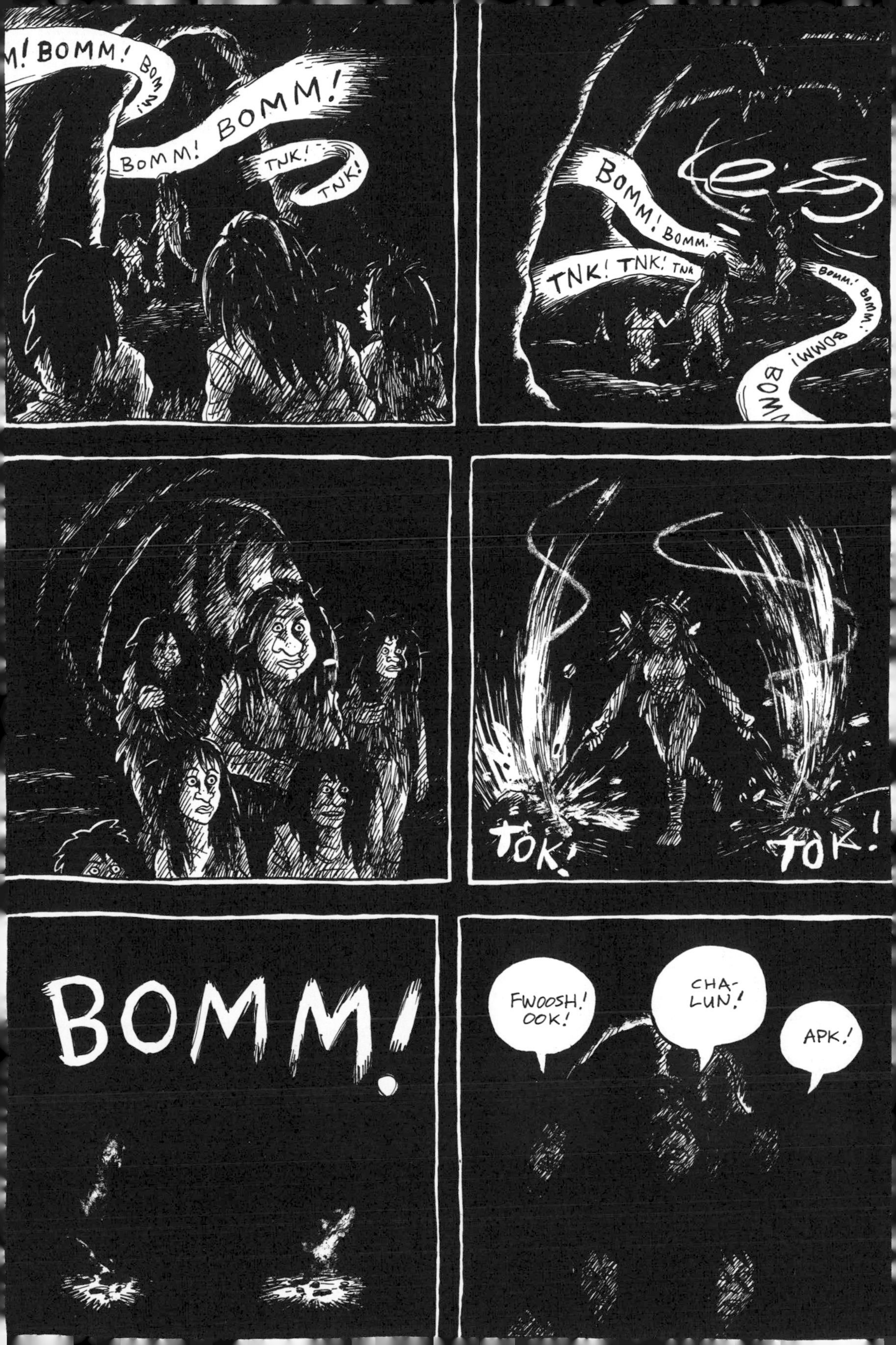
M! BOMM! BOMM!
BOMM! BOMM!
TNK! TNK!
BOMM! BOMM!
TNK! TNK! TNK
BOMM! BOMM! BOMM! BOMM
TOK!
TOK!
BOMM!
FWOOSH! OOK!
CHA-LUN!
APK!

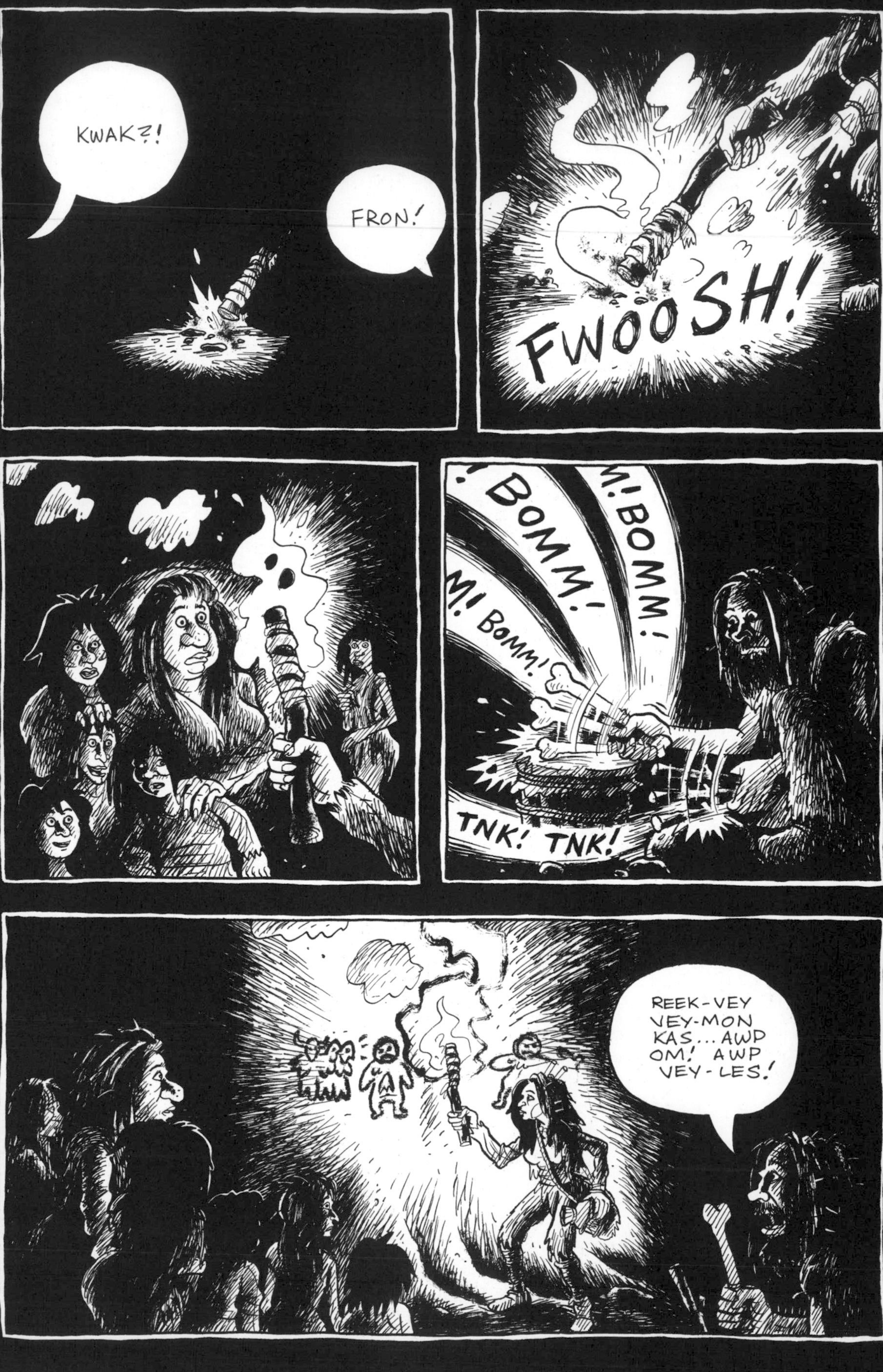
KWAK?!
FRON!
FWOOSH!
! BOMM!
M! BOMM!
M! BOMM!
TNK! TNK!
REEK-VEY VEY-MON KAS... AWP OM! AWP VEY-LES!

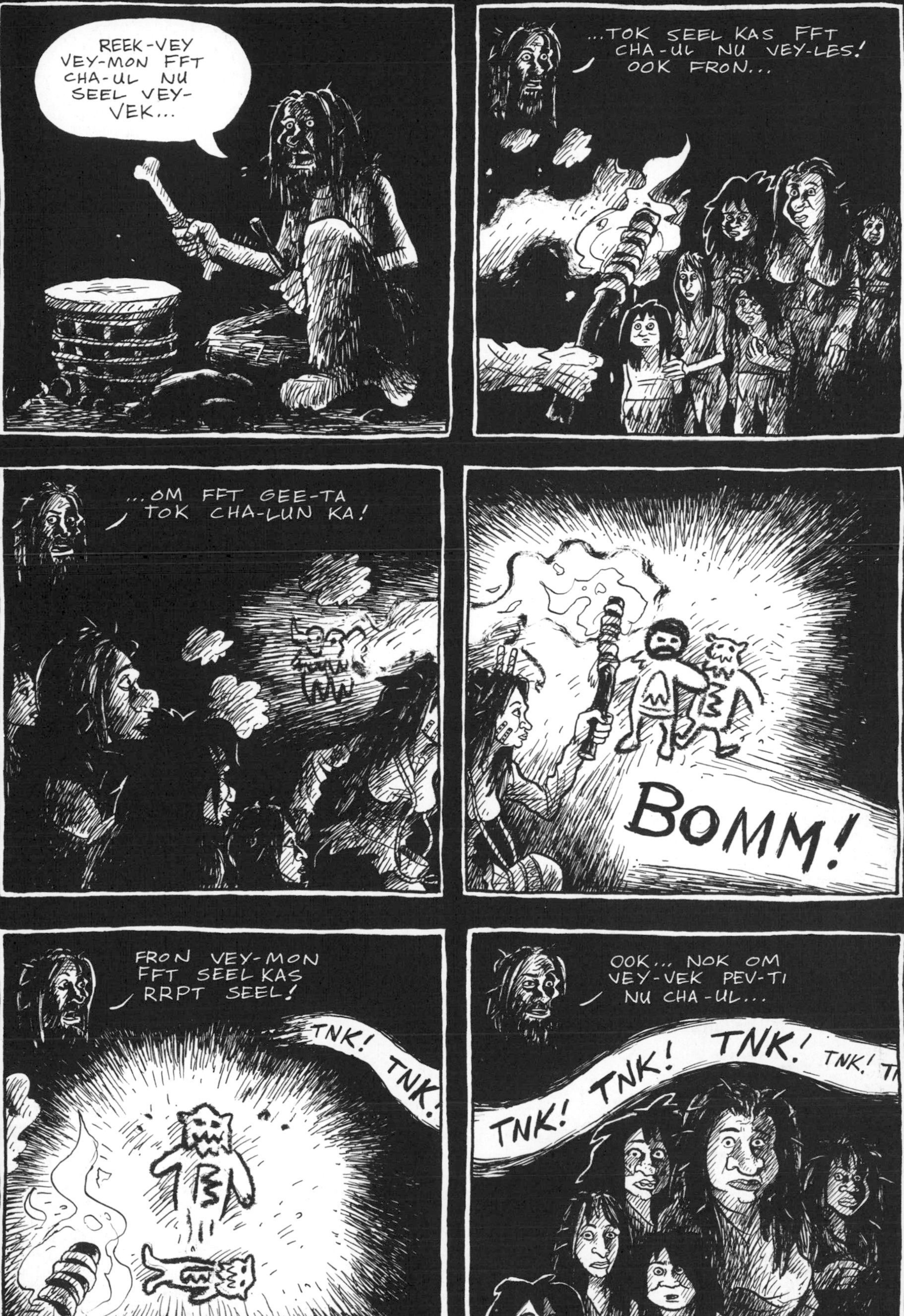
REEK-VEY VEY-MON FFT CHA-UL NU SEEL VEY-VEK...
...TOK SEEL KAS FFT CHA-UL NU VEY-LES! OOK FRON...
...OM FFT GEE-TA TOK CHA-LUN KA!
BOMM!
FRON VEY-MON FFT SEEL-KAS RRPT SEEL!
TNK! TNK! TNK!
OOK... NOK OM VEY-VEK PEV-TI NU CHA-UL...
TNK! TNK! TNK! TNK! TNK!

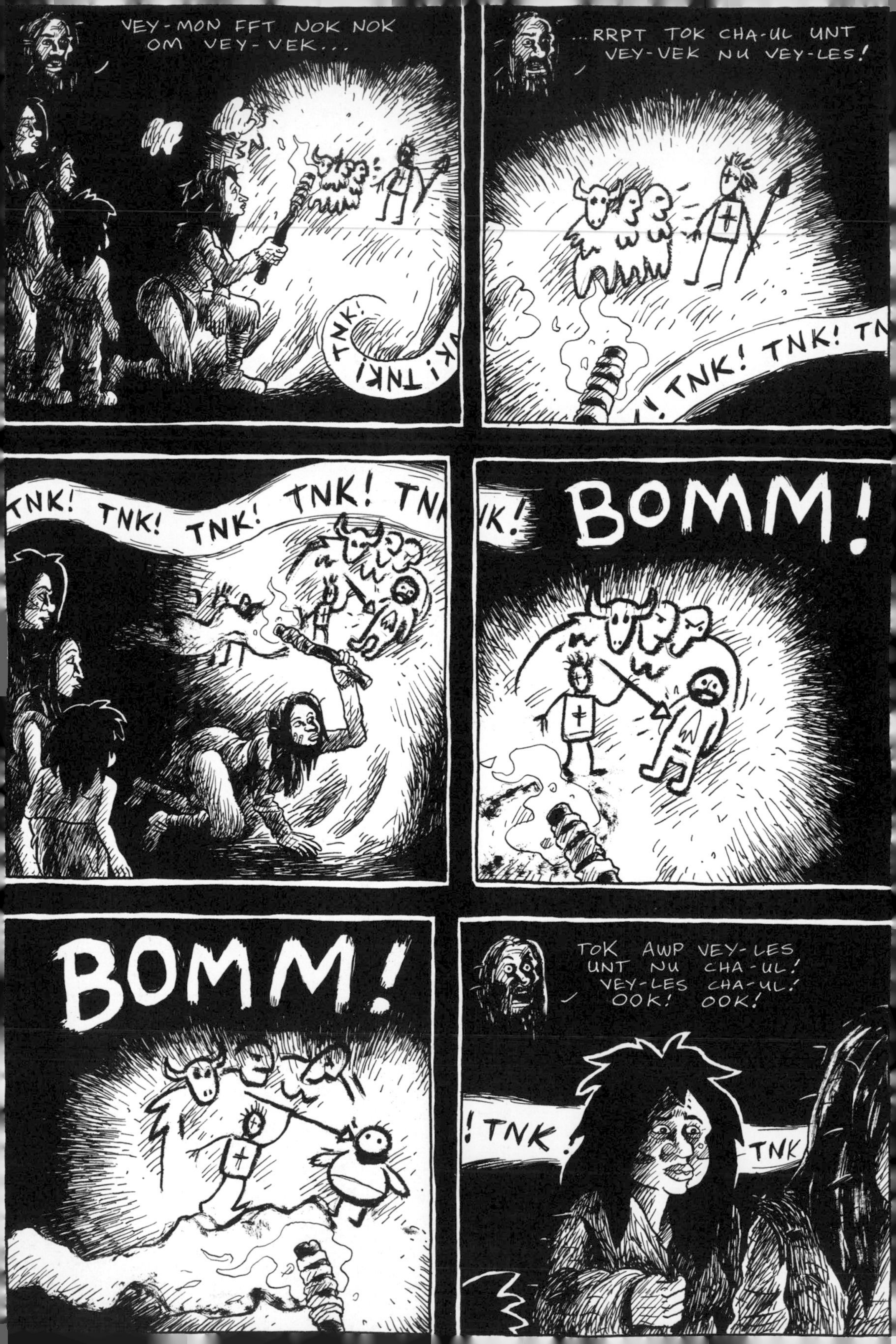
VEY-MON FFT NOK NOK OM VEY-VEK...
TNK! TNK! TNK!
...RRPT TOK CHA-UL UNT VEY-VEK NU VEY-LES!
TNK! TNK! TNK! TN
TNK! TNK! TNK! TNK! TN
K!
BOMM!
BOMM!
TOK AWP VEY-LES UNT NU CHA-UL! VEY-LES CHA-UL! OOK! OOK!
TNK
TNK

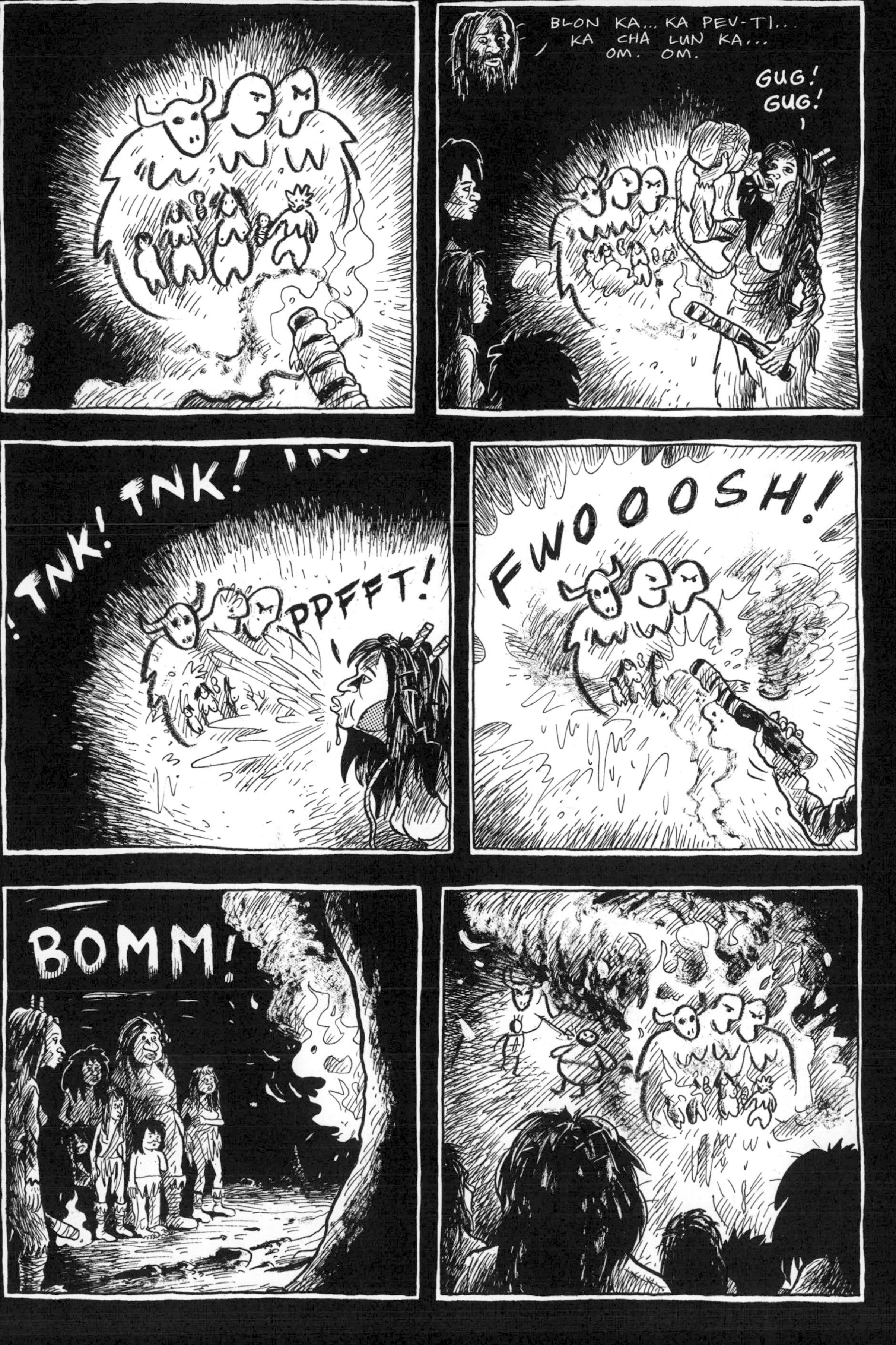
BLON KA... KA PEV-TI... KA CHA LUN KA... OM. OM.
GUG! GUG!
TNK! TNK! TNK!
PPFFT!
FWOOOSH!
BOMM!

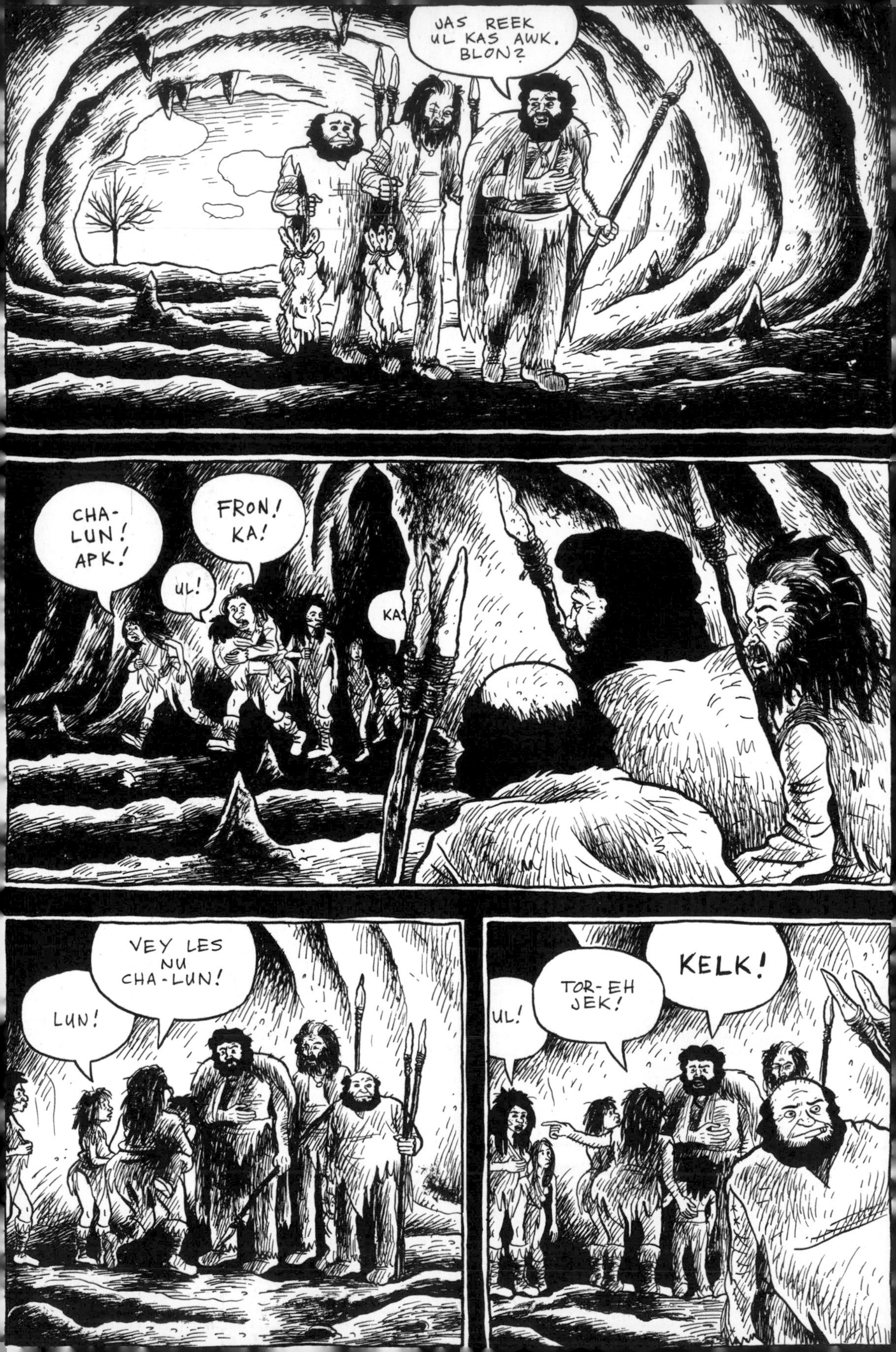
JAS REEK UL KAS AWK. BLON?
CHA-LUN! APK!
FRON! KA!
UL!
KA
LUN!
VEY LES NU CHA-LUN!
UL!
TOR-EH JEK!
KELK!

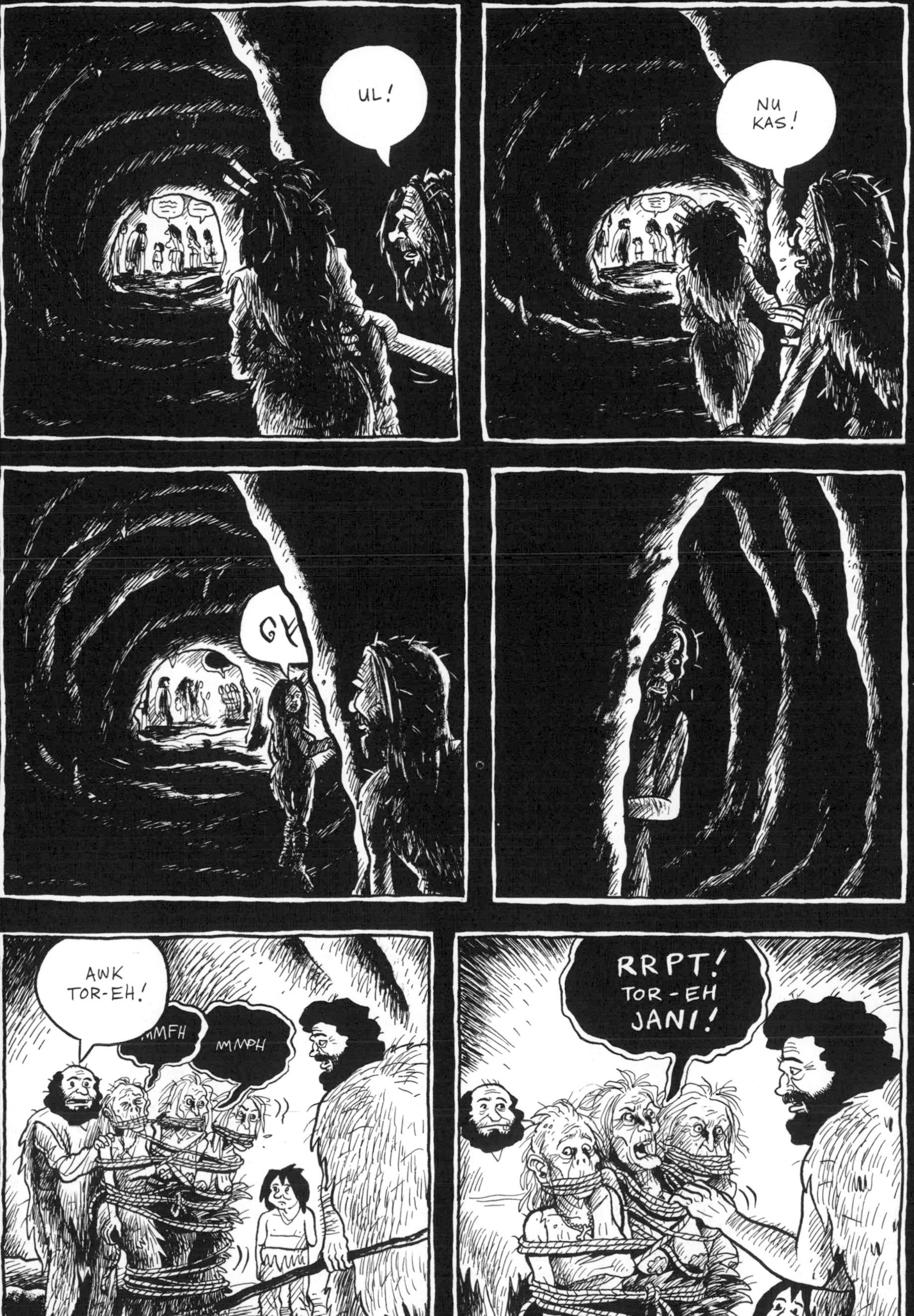
UL!
NU KAS!
GH
AWK TOR-EH!
MMFH
MMPH
RRPT! TOR-EH JANI!

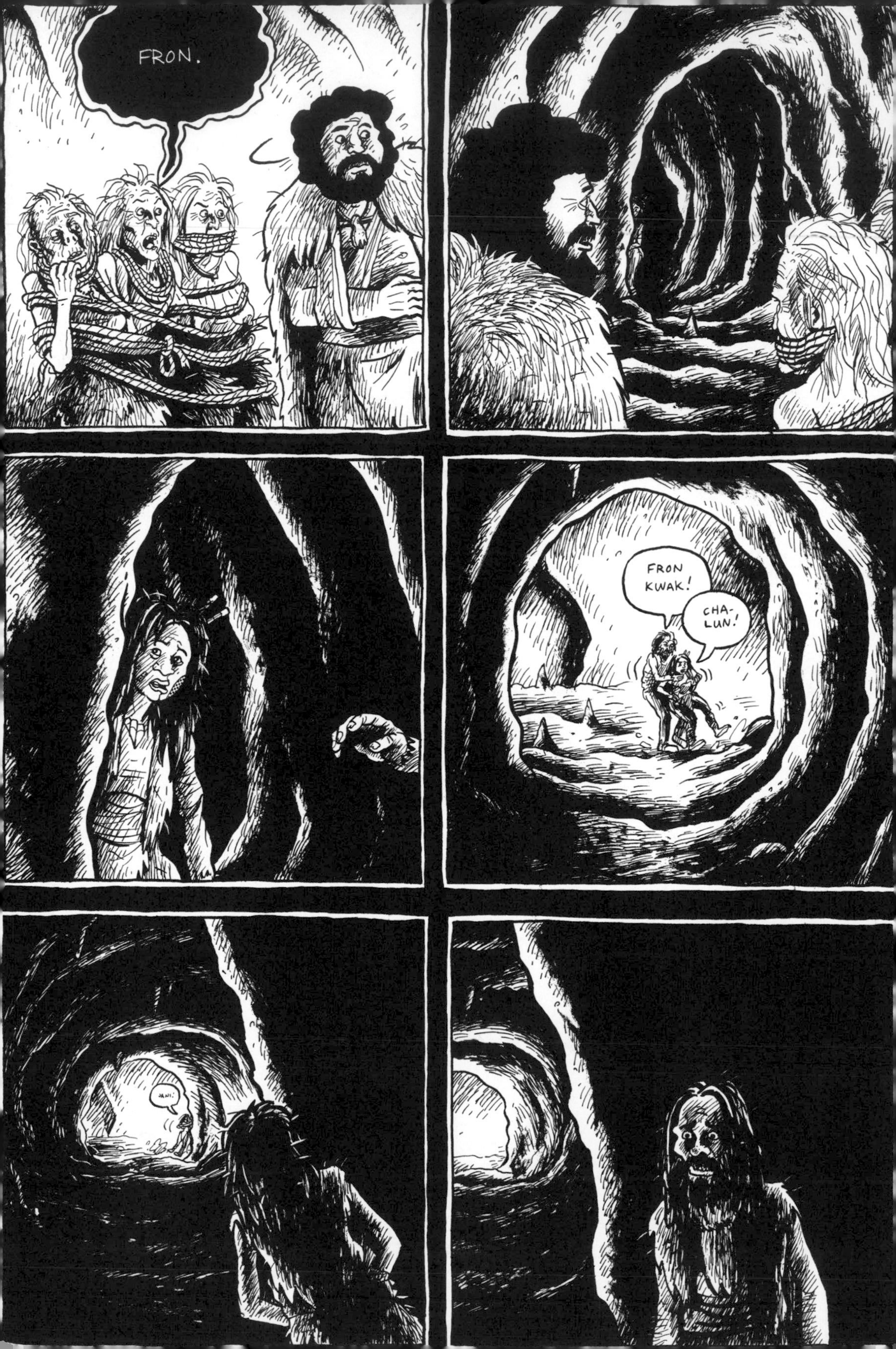
FRON.
FRON KWAK!
CHA-LUN!
JANI!

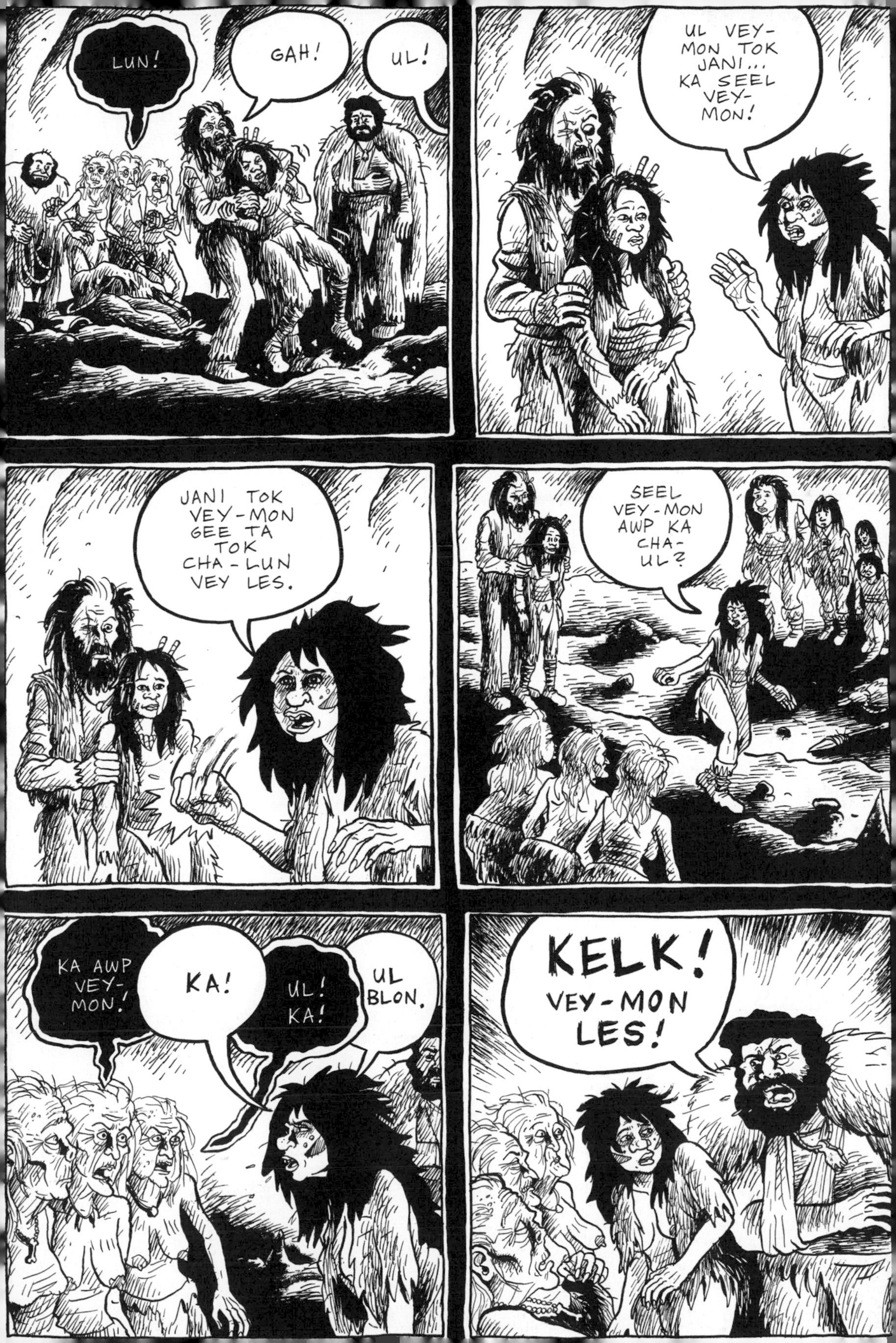
LUN!
GAH!
UL!
UL VEY-MON TOK JANI... KA SEEL VEY-MON!
JANI TOK VEY-MON GEE TA TOK CHA-LUN VEY LES.
SEEL VEY-MON AWP KA CHA-UL?
KA AWP VEY-MON!
KA!
UL! KA!
UL BLON.
KELK! VEY-MON LES!

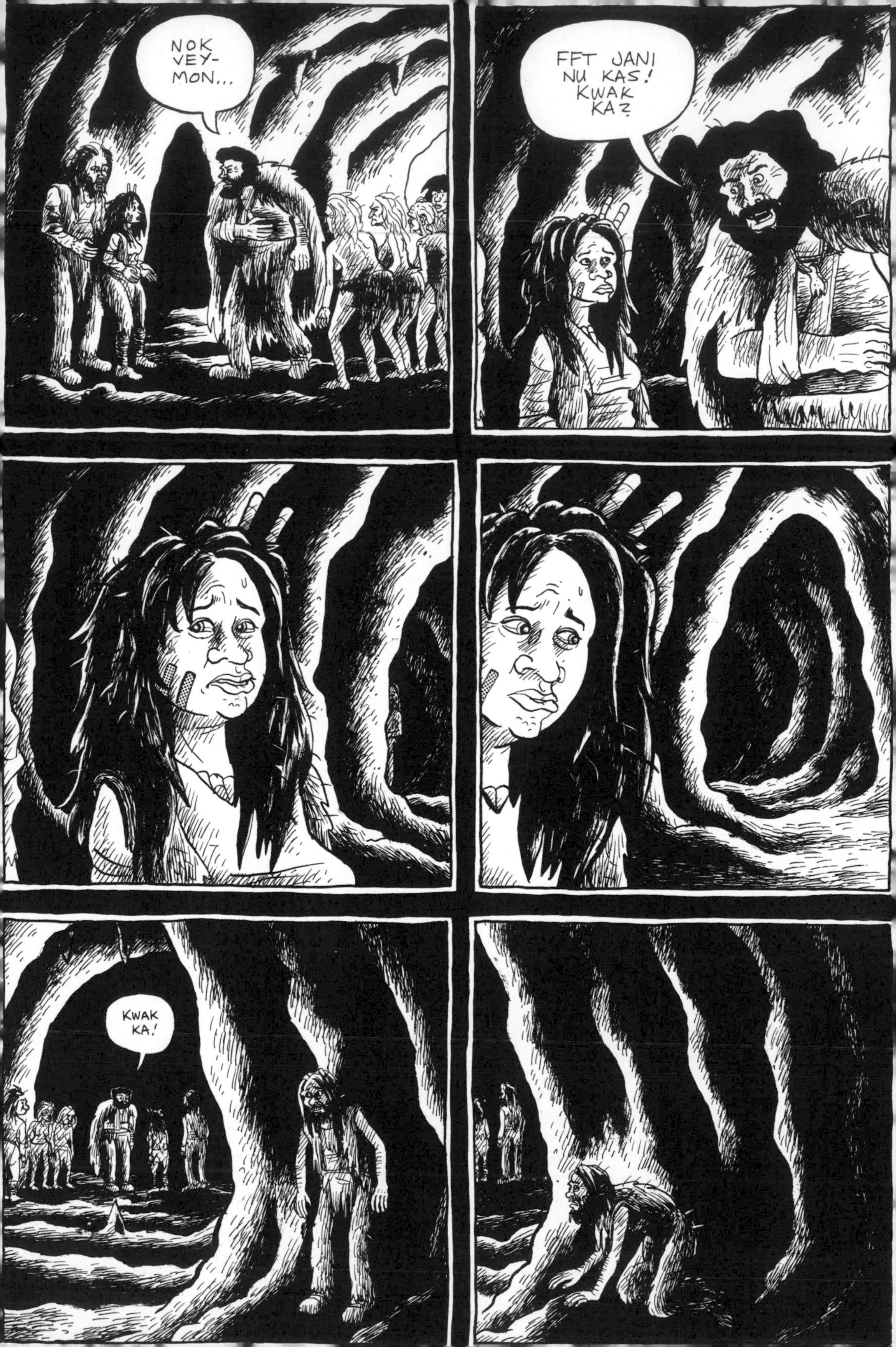
NOK VEY-MON...
FFT JANI NU KAS! KWAK KA?
KWAK KA!

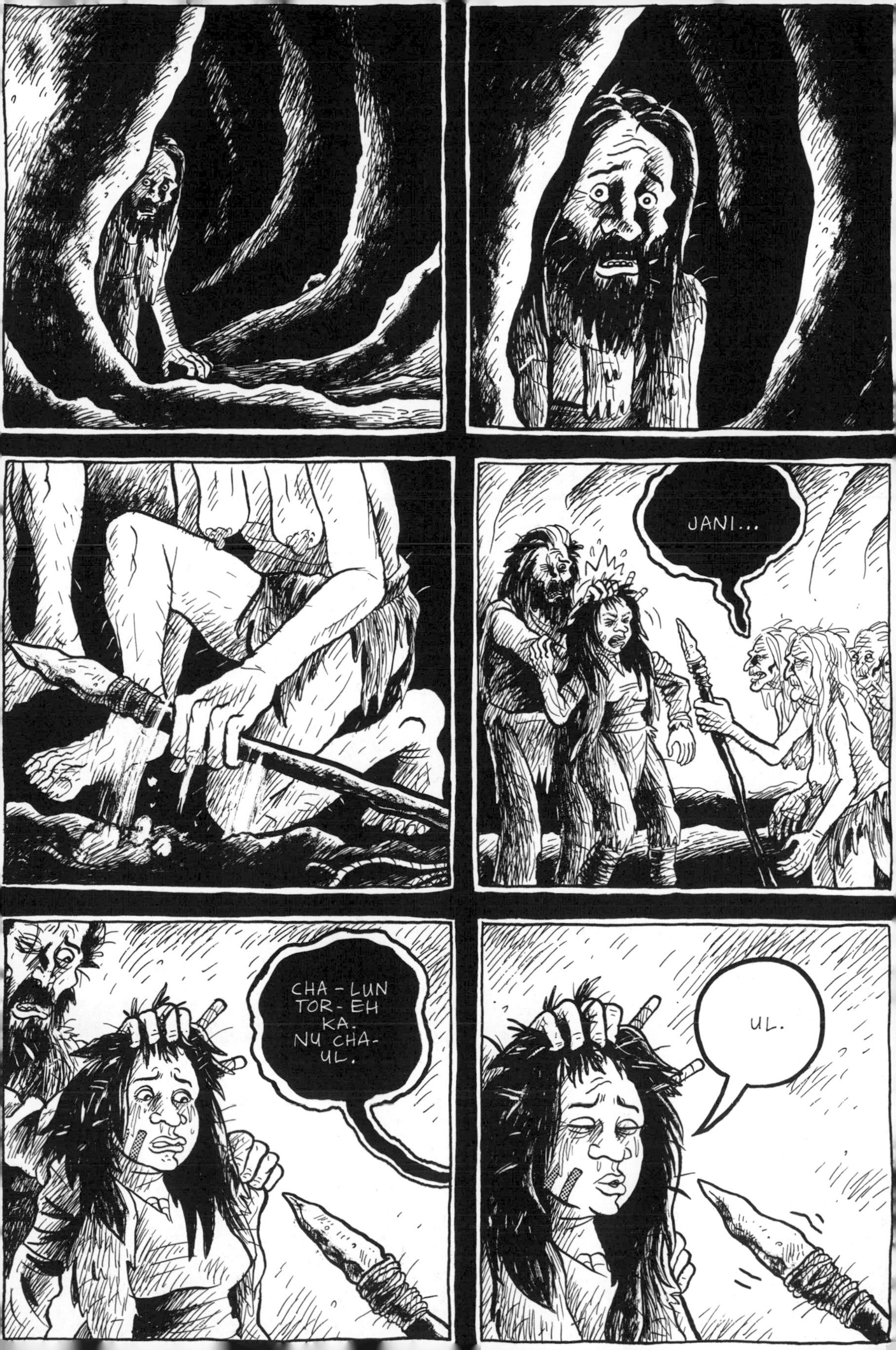
JANI...
CHA-LUN TOR-EH KA. NU CHA-UL.
UL.

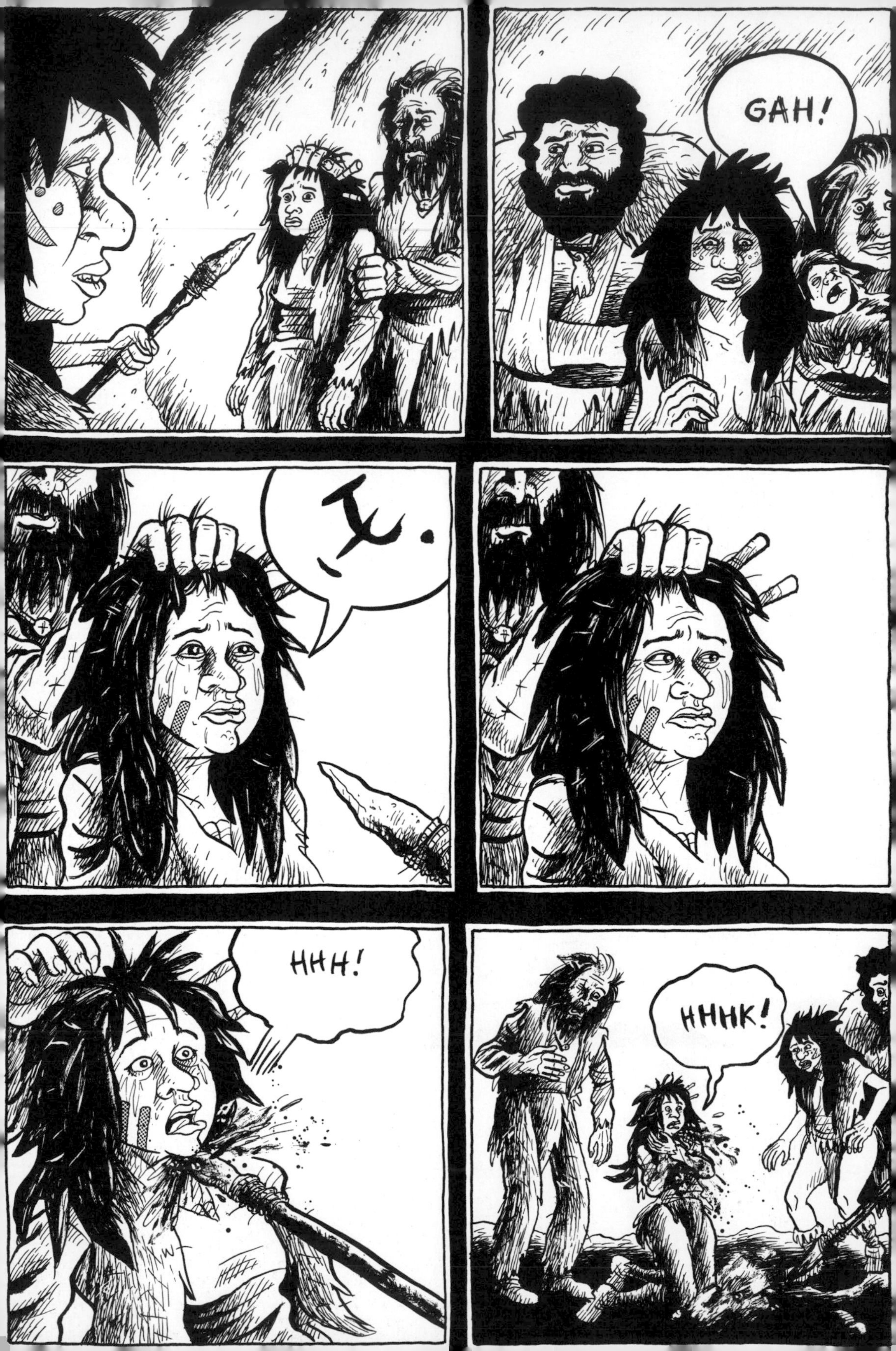
GAH!
HHH!
HHHK!

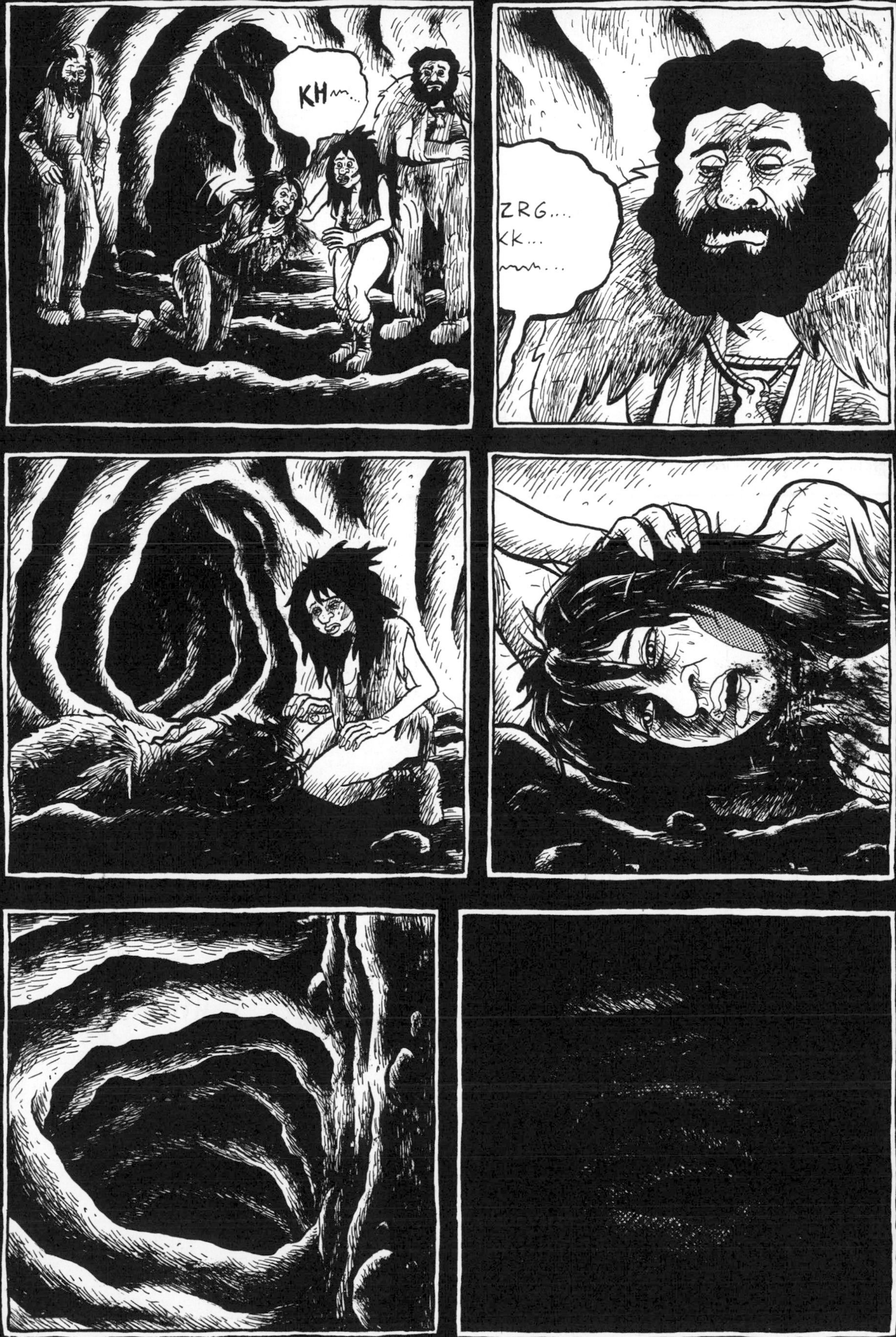
KH~...
ZRG...
KK...
~~...

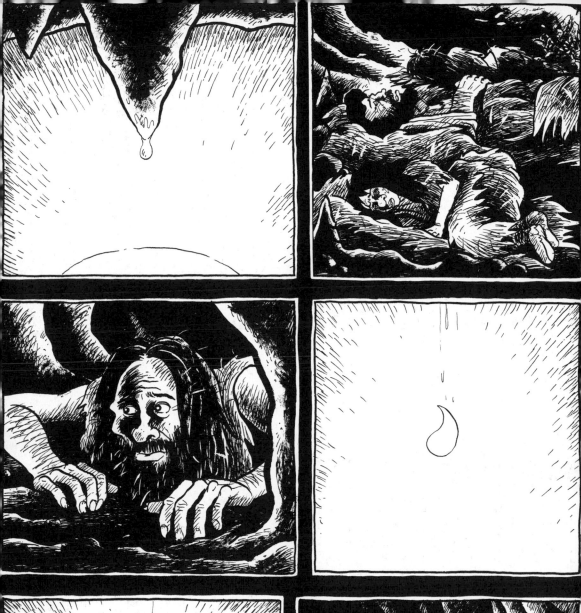

DOYT!

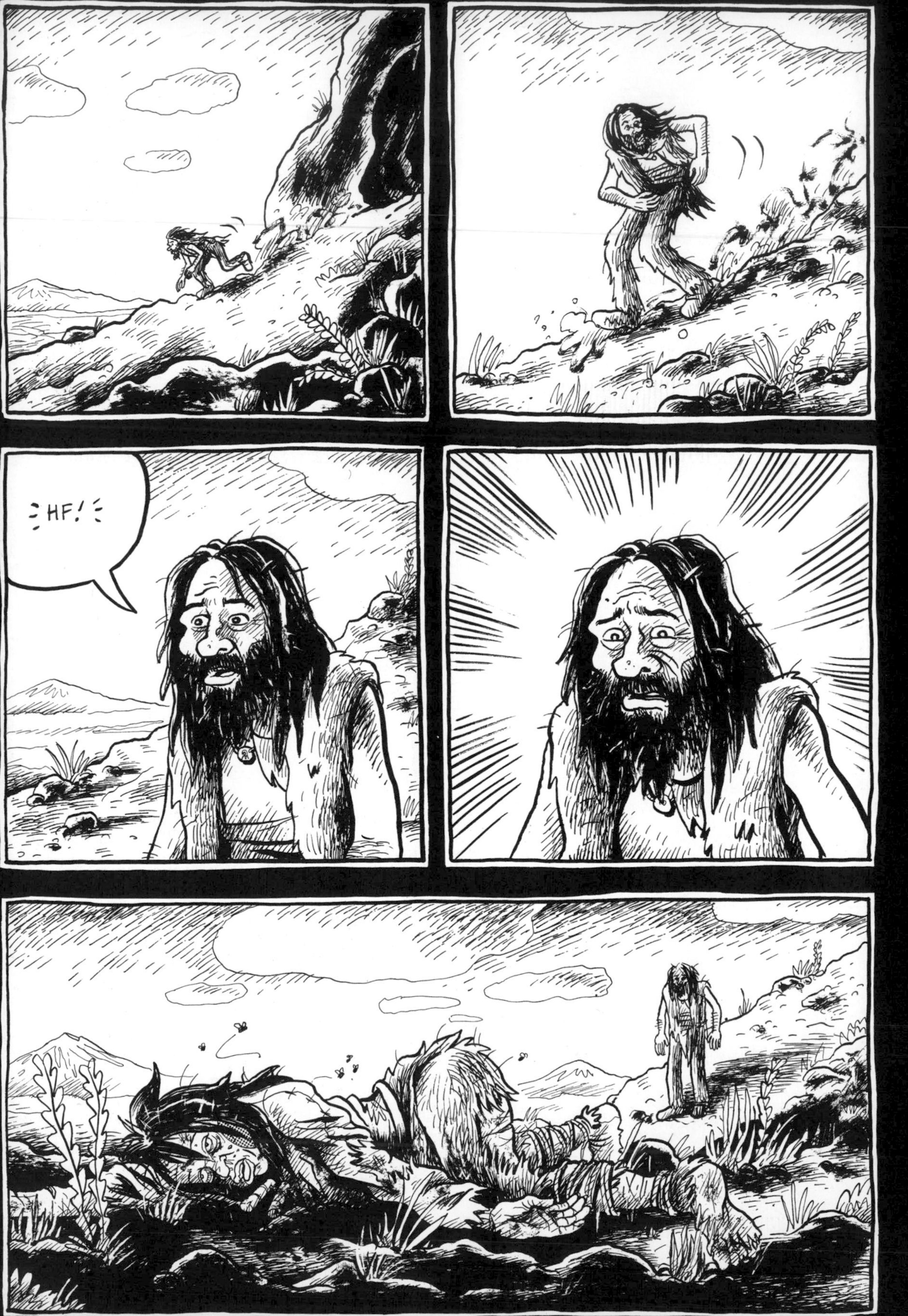
HF!

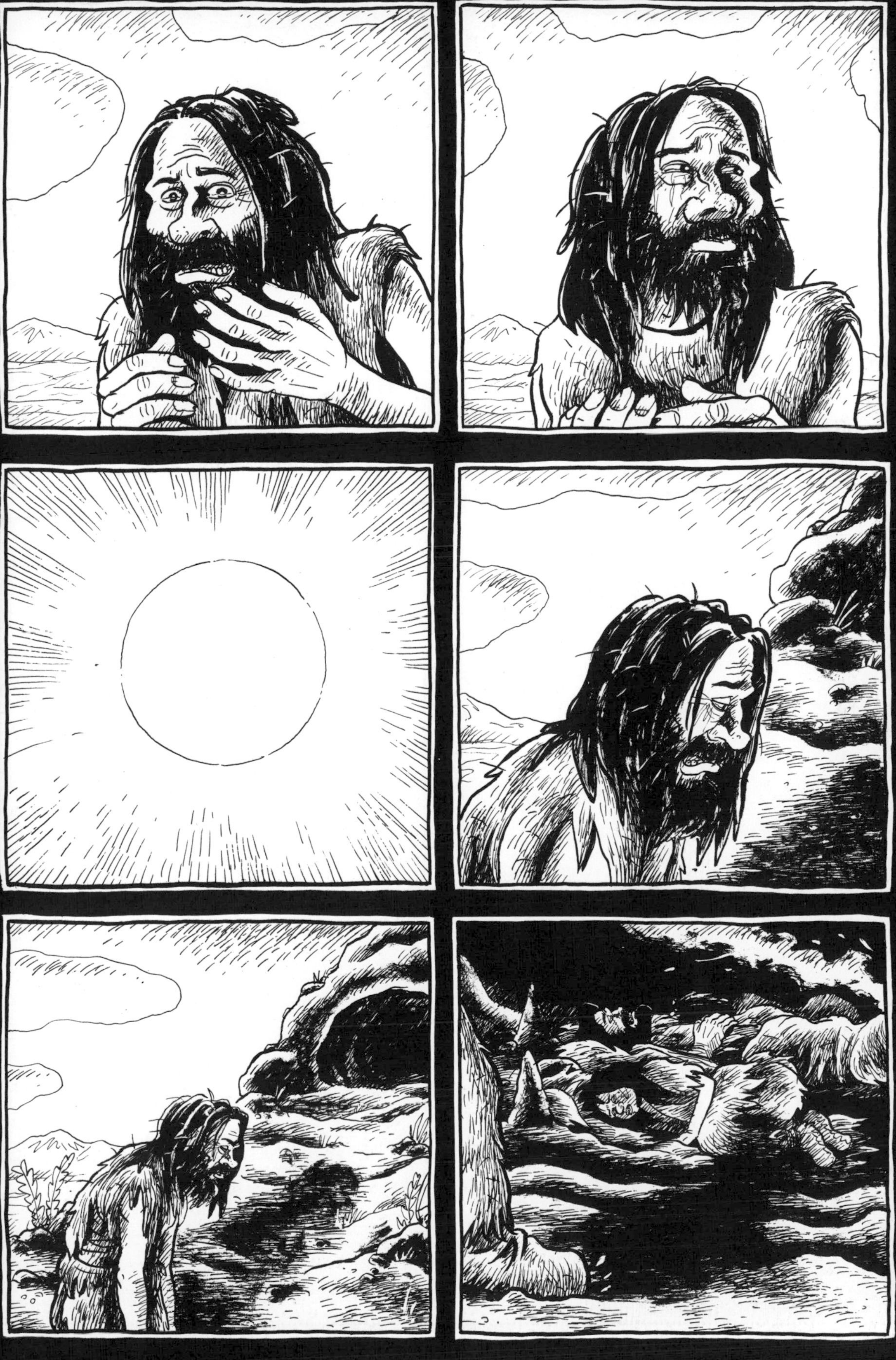

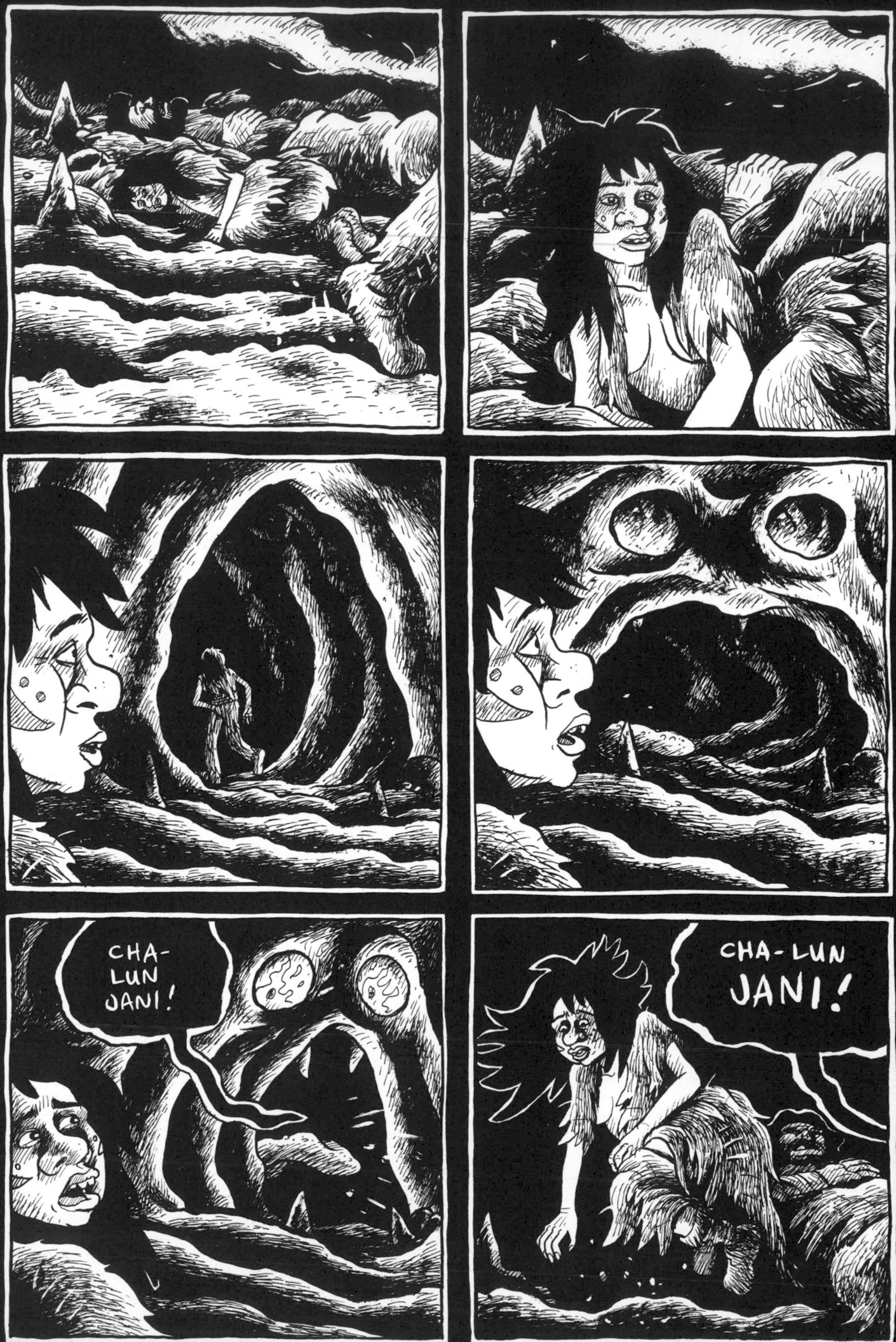
CHA-LUN JANI!
CHA-LUN JANI!

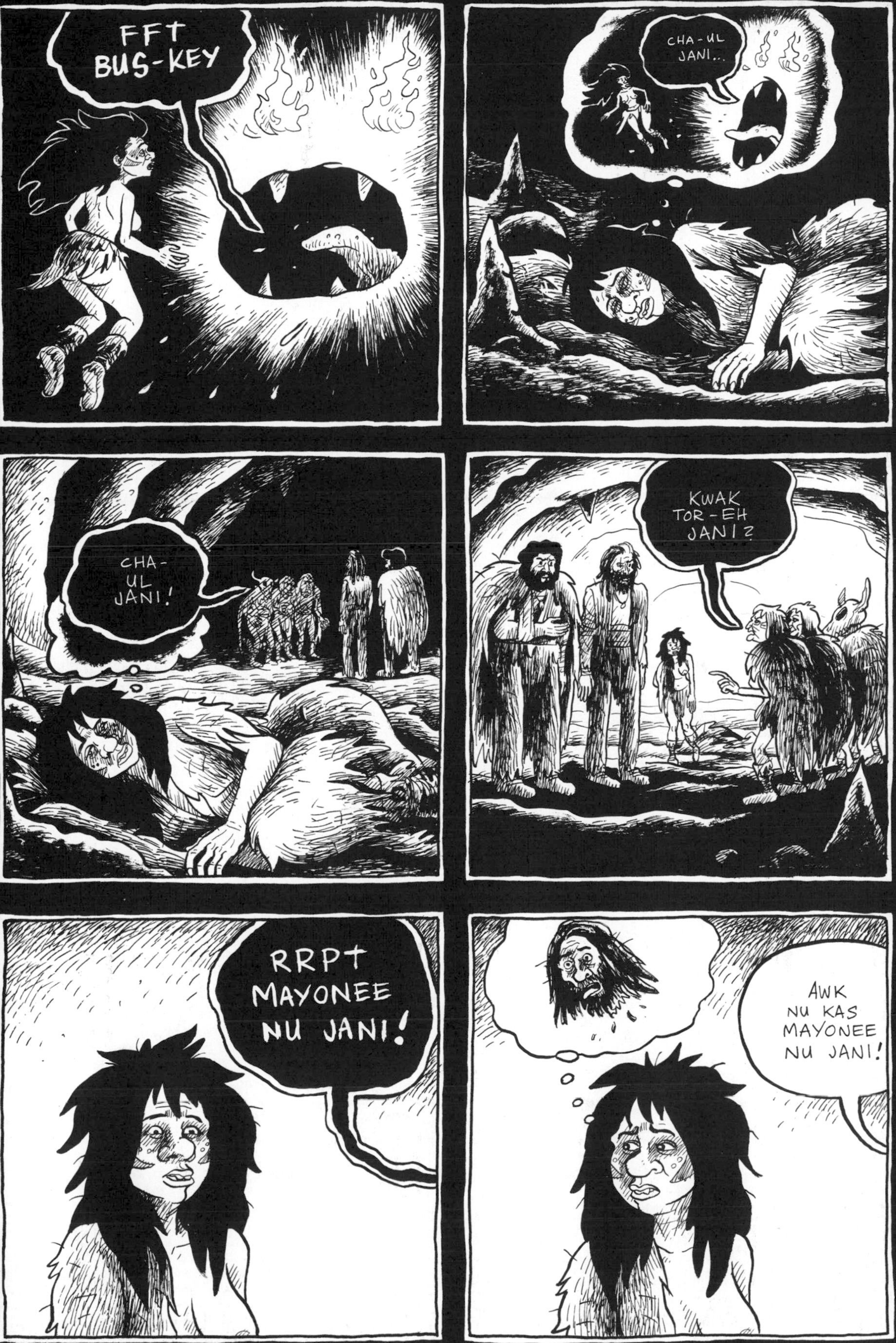
FFT BUS-KEY
CHA-UL JANI..
CHA-UL JANI!
KWAK TOR-EH JANI?
RRPT MAYONEE NU JANI!
AWK NU KAS MAYONEE NU JANI!

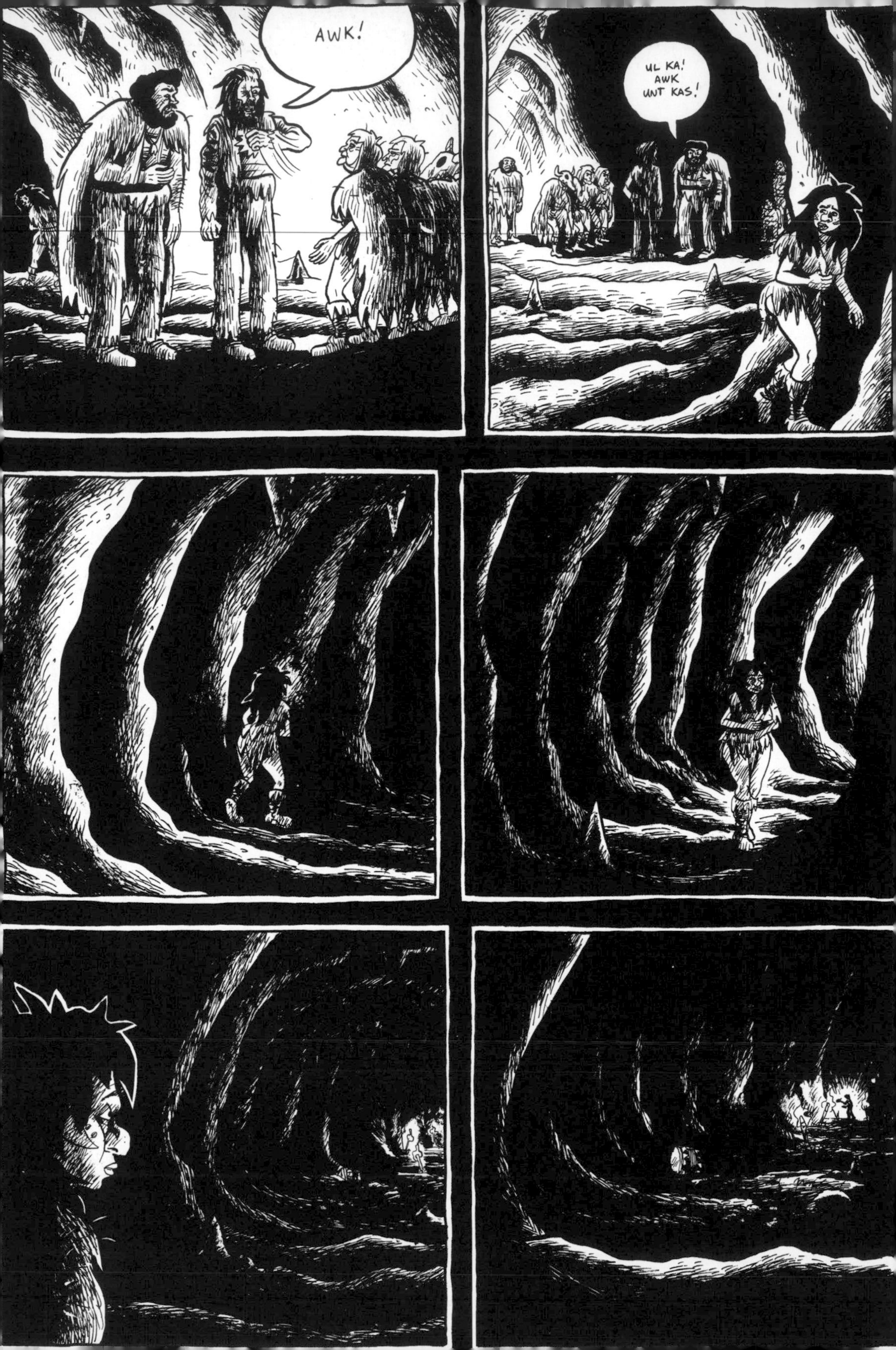
AWK!
UL KA! AWK UNT KAS!

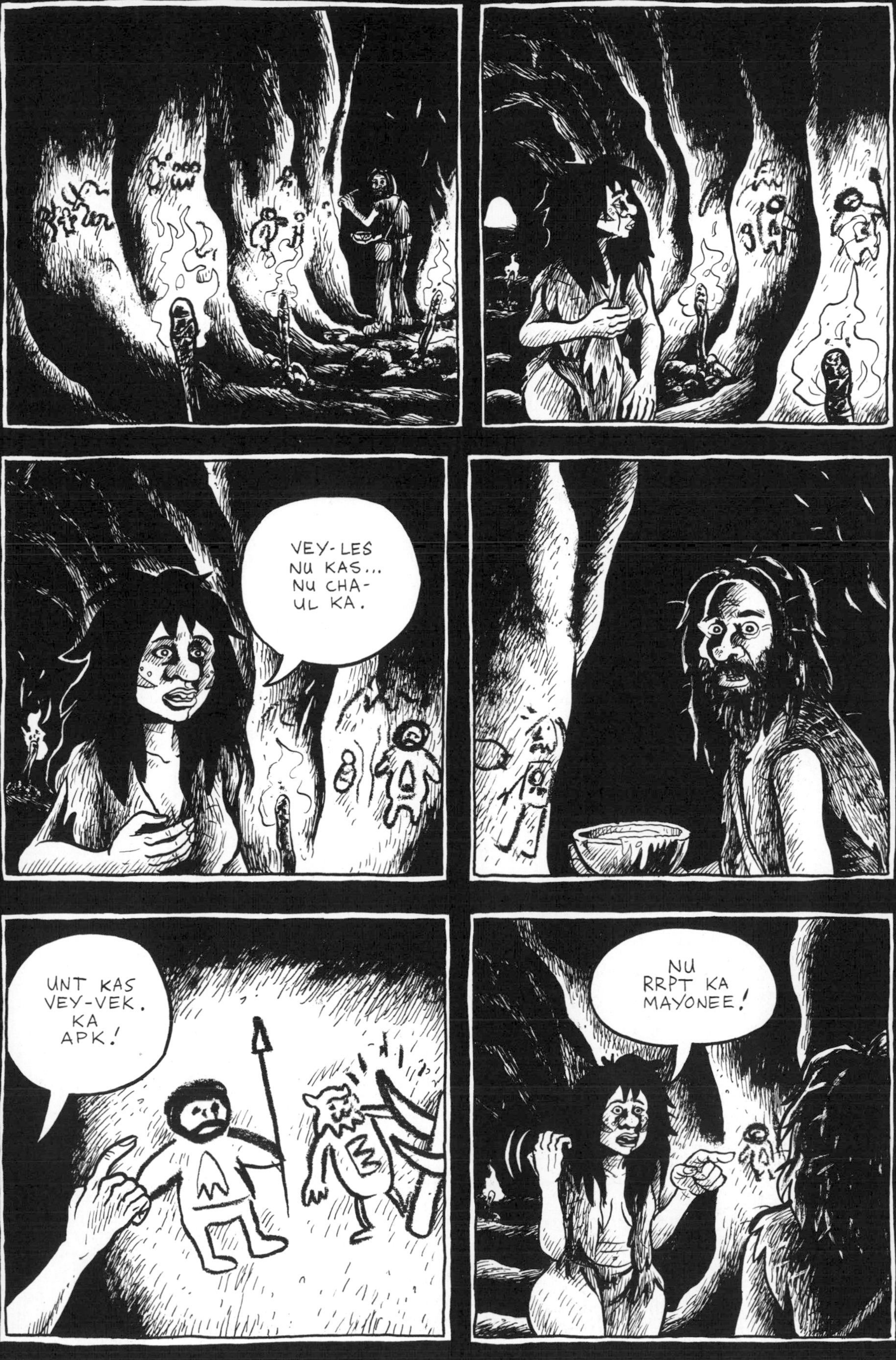
VEY-LES NU KAS... NU CHA-UL KA.
UNT KAS VEY-VEK. KA APK!
NU RRPT KA MAYONEE!

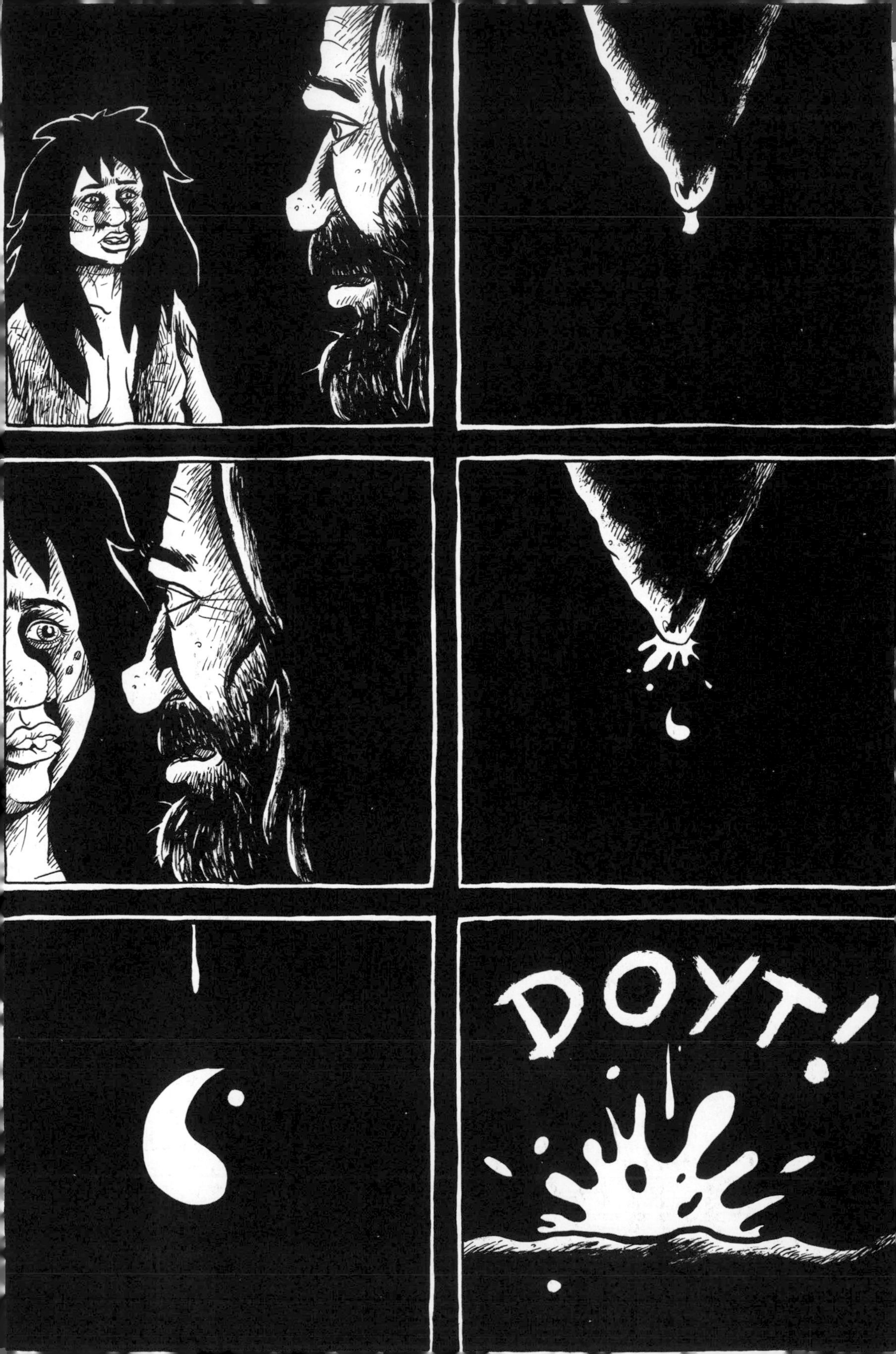
DOYT!

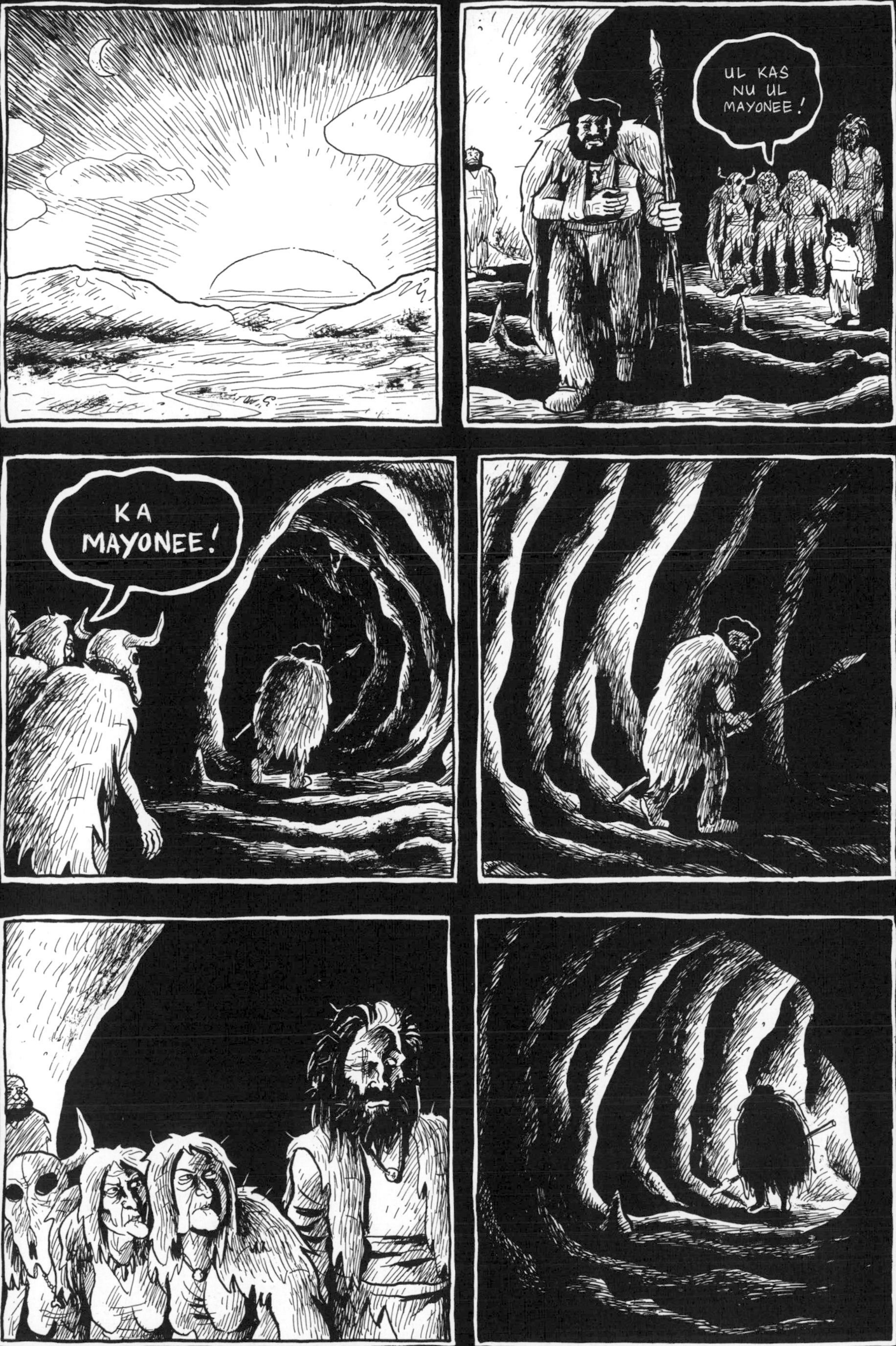
UL KAS NU UL MAYONEE!
KA MAYONEE!

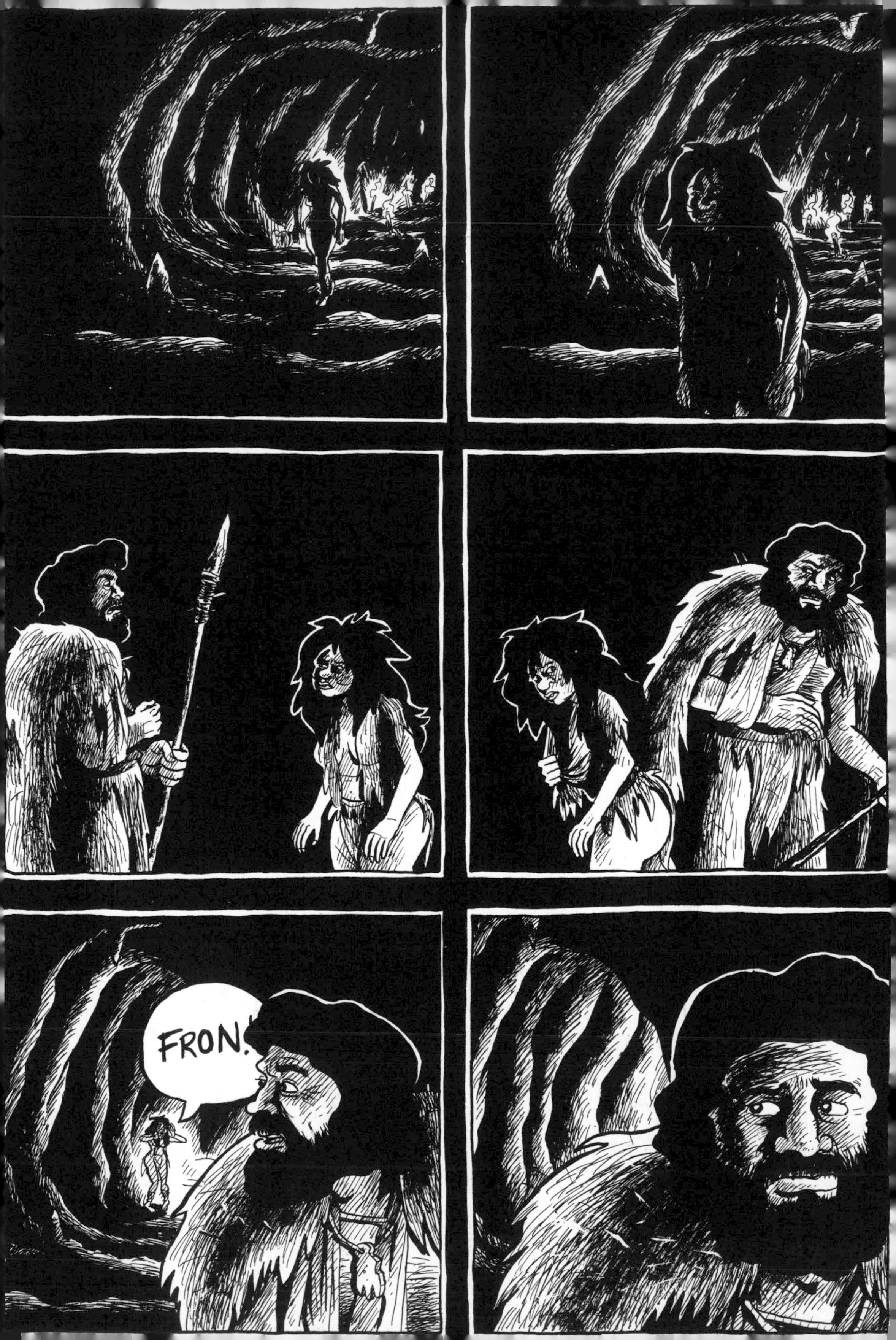
FRON!

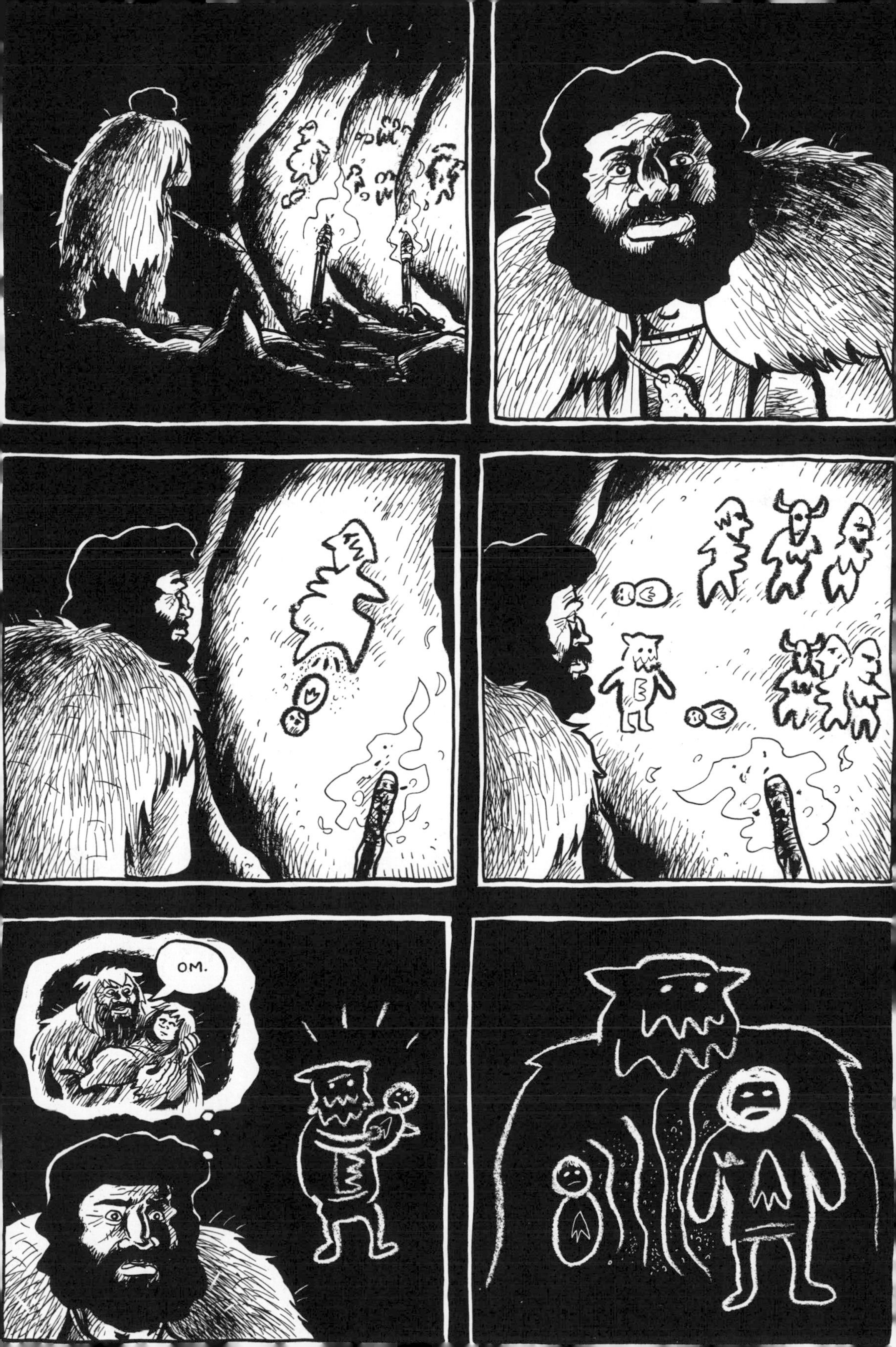
OM.

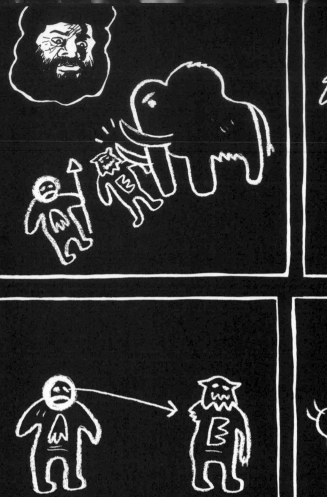

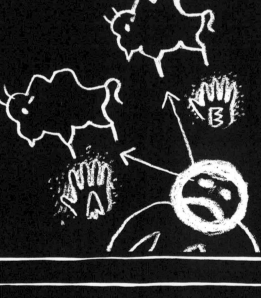

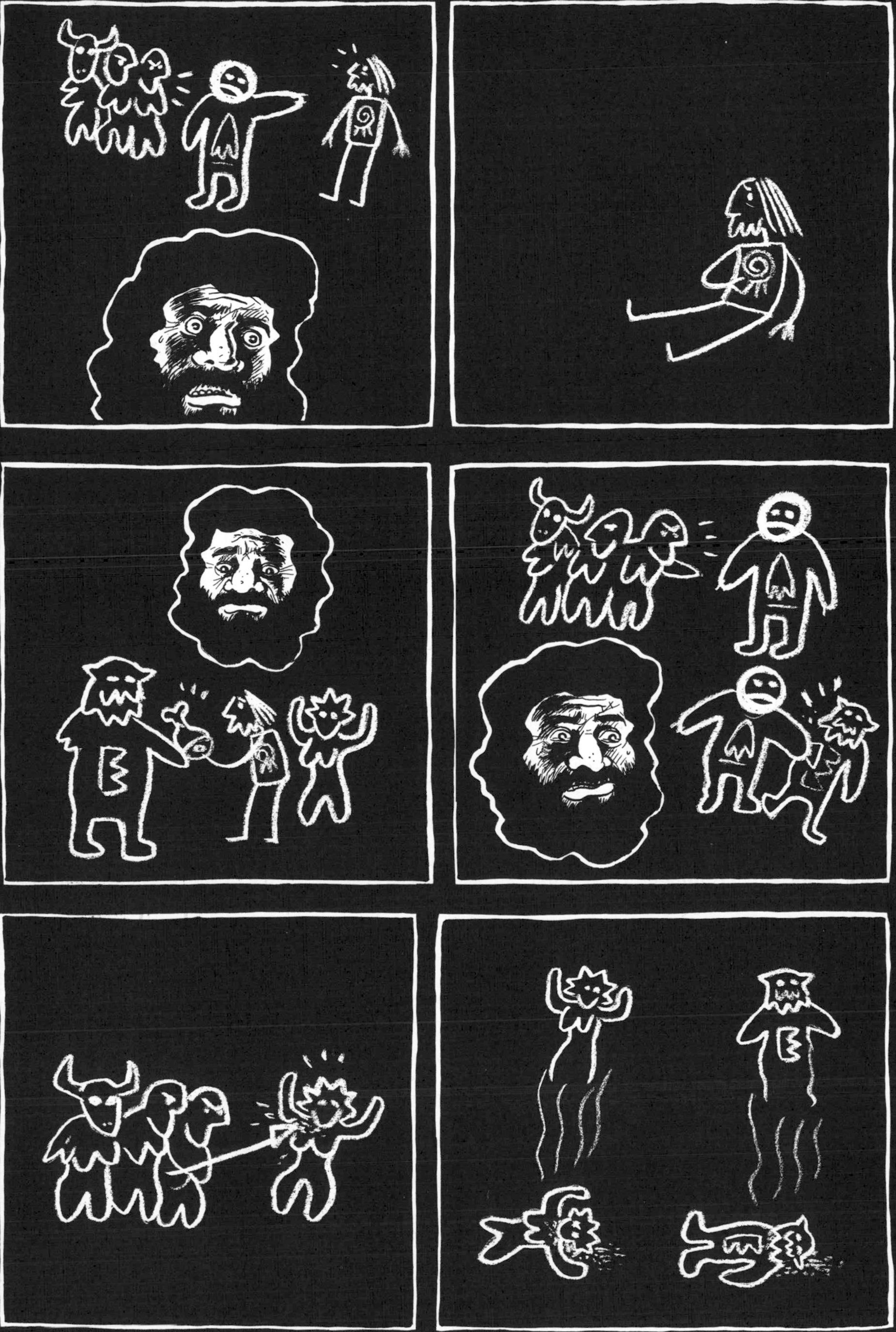

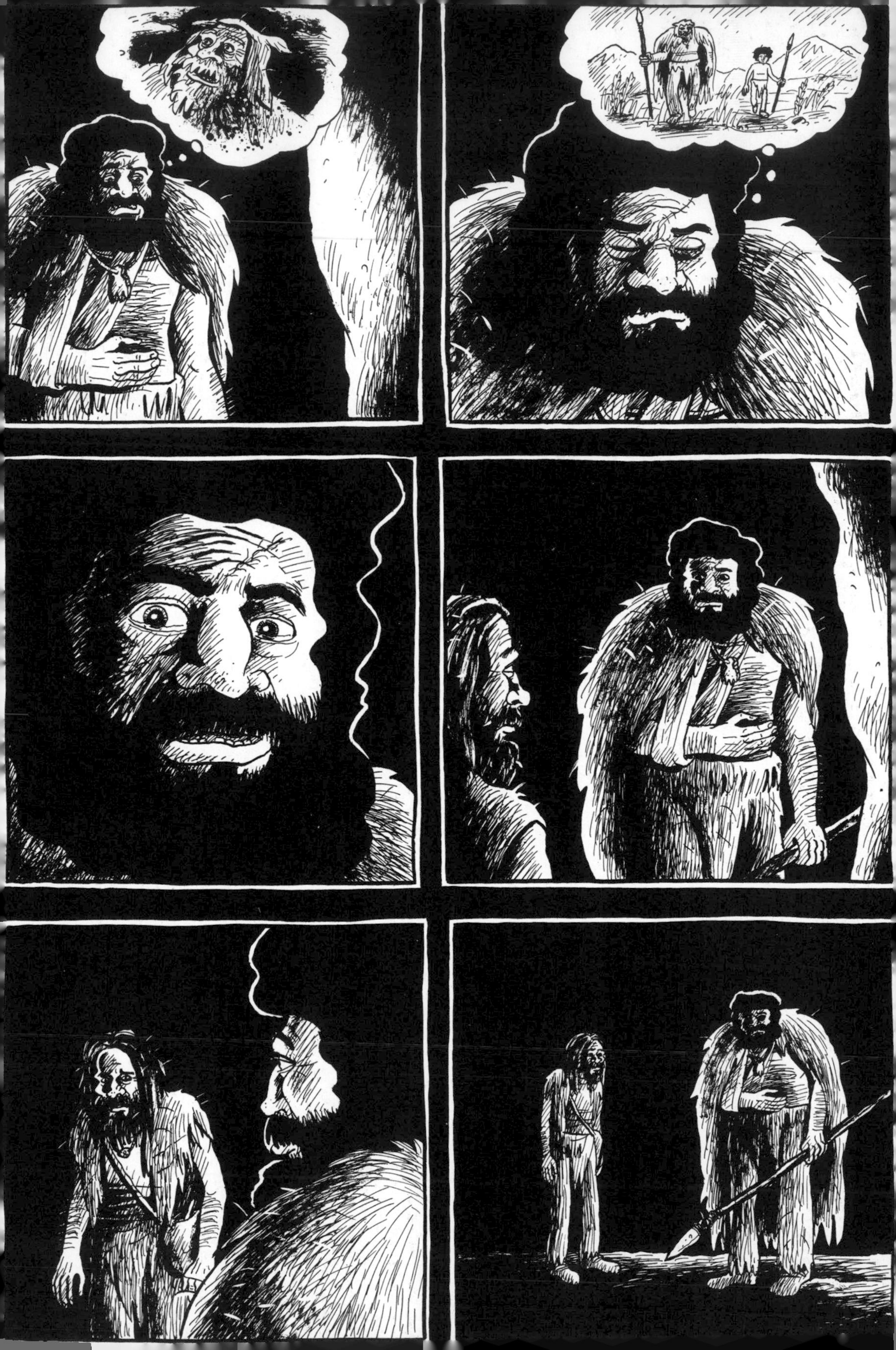

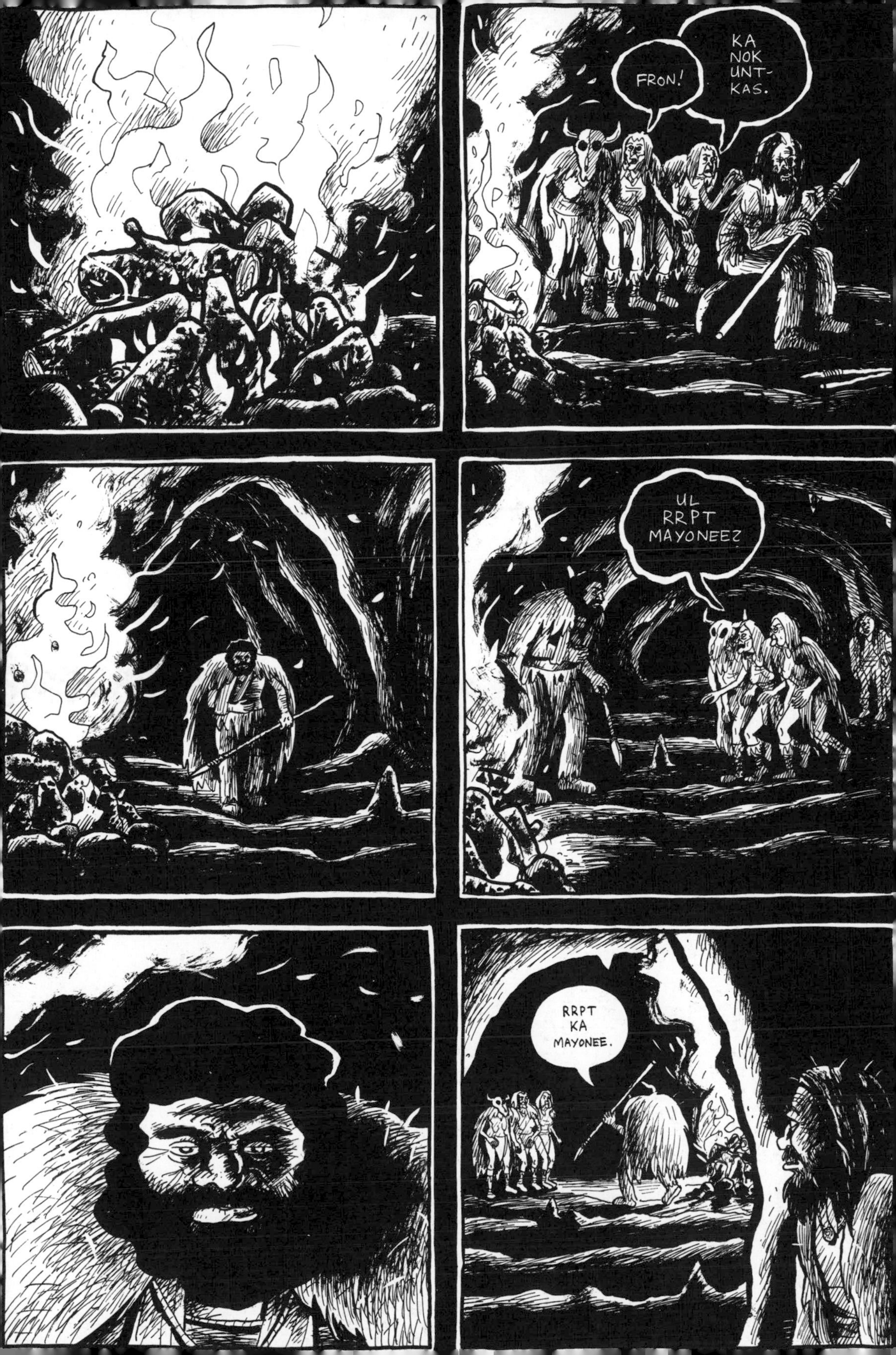
FRON!
KA NOK UNT-KAS.
UL RRPT MAYONEEZ
RRPT KA MAYONEE.

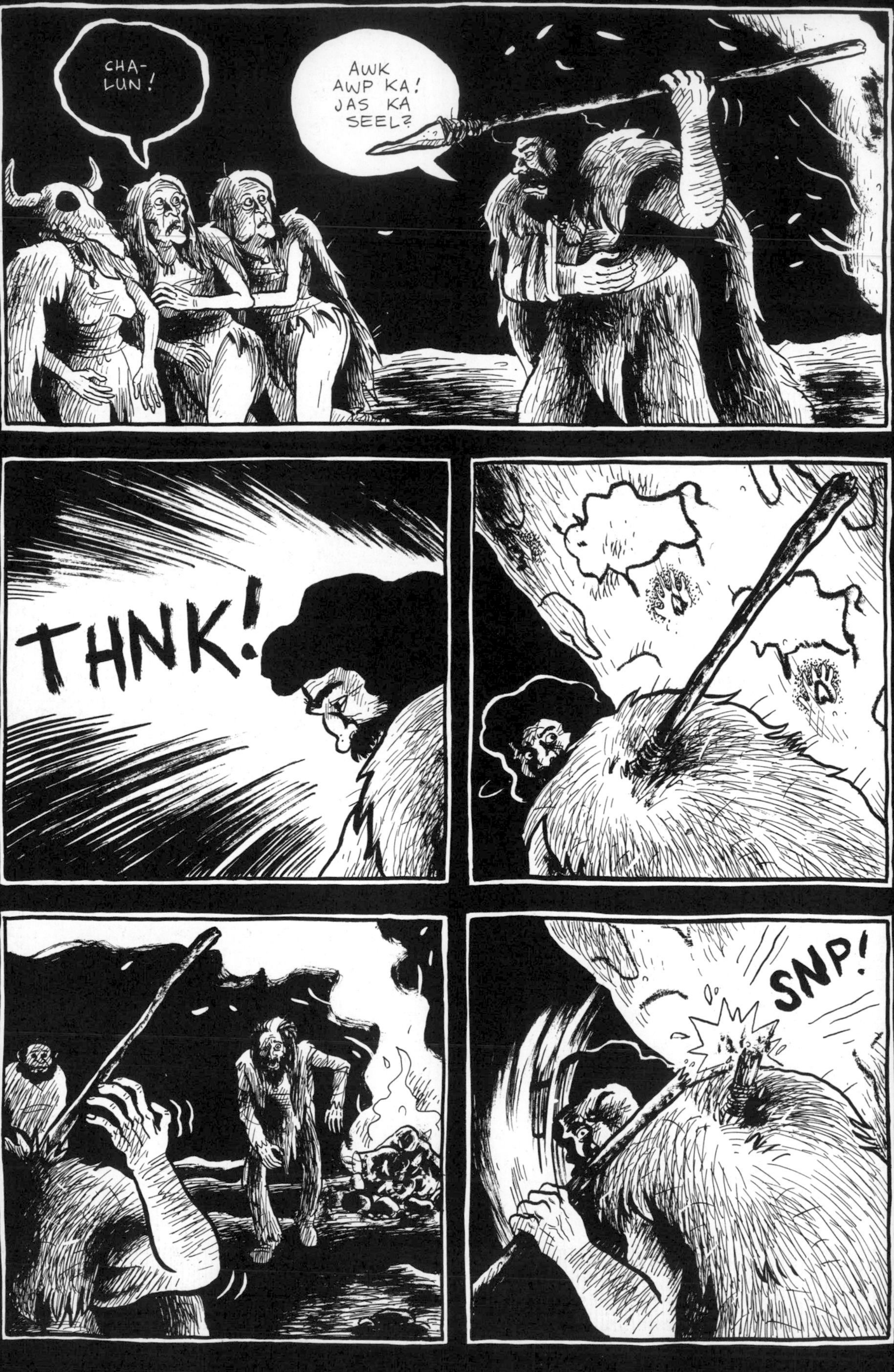
CHA-
LUN!
AWK
AWP KA!
JAS KA
SEEL?
THNK!
SNP!

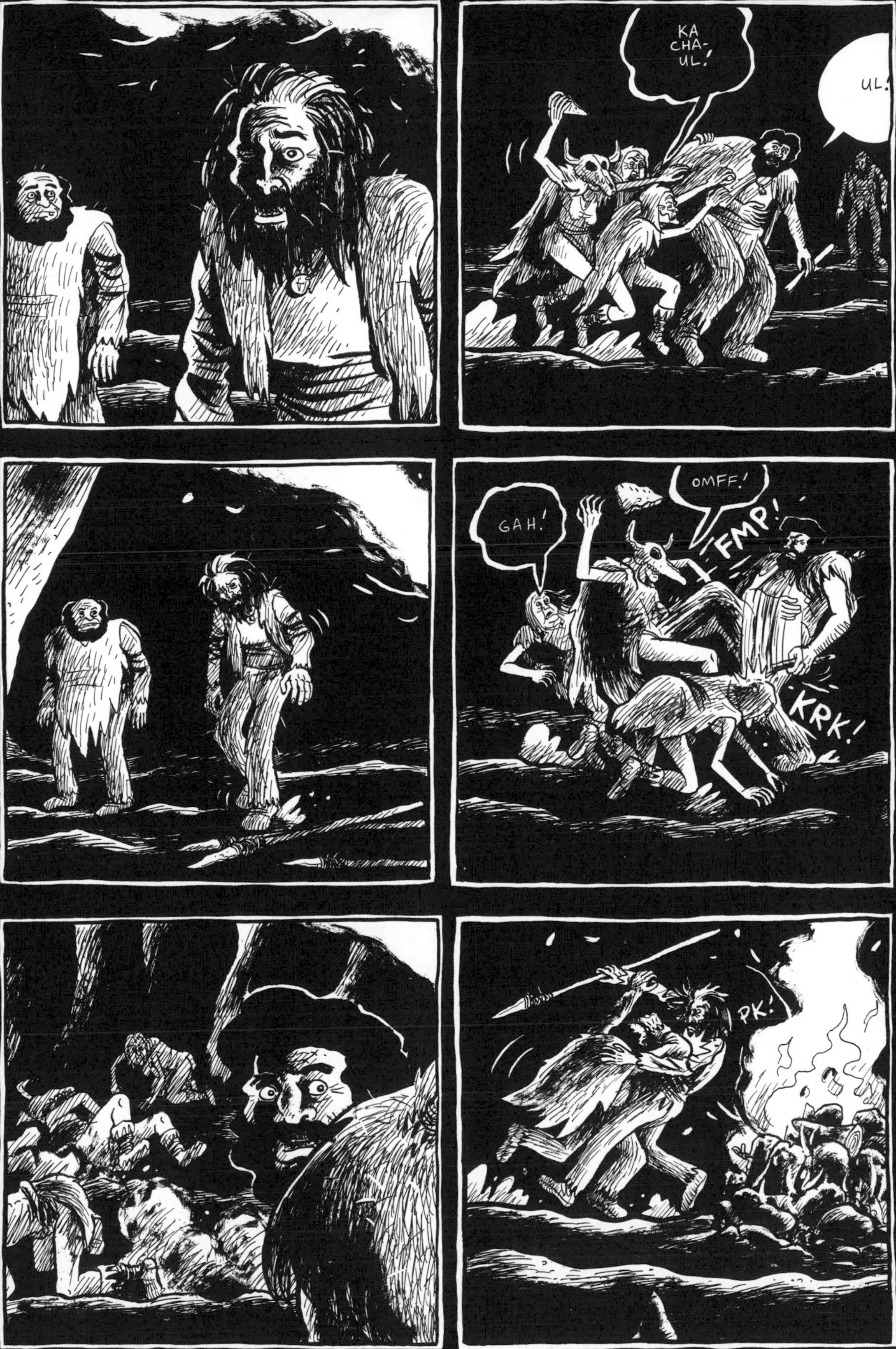
KA CHA-UL!
UL!
GAH!
OMFF!
FMP!
KRK!
PK!

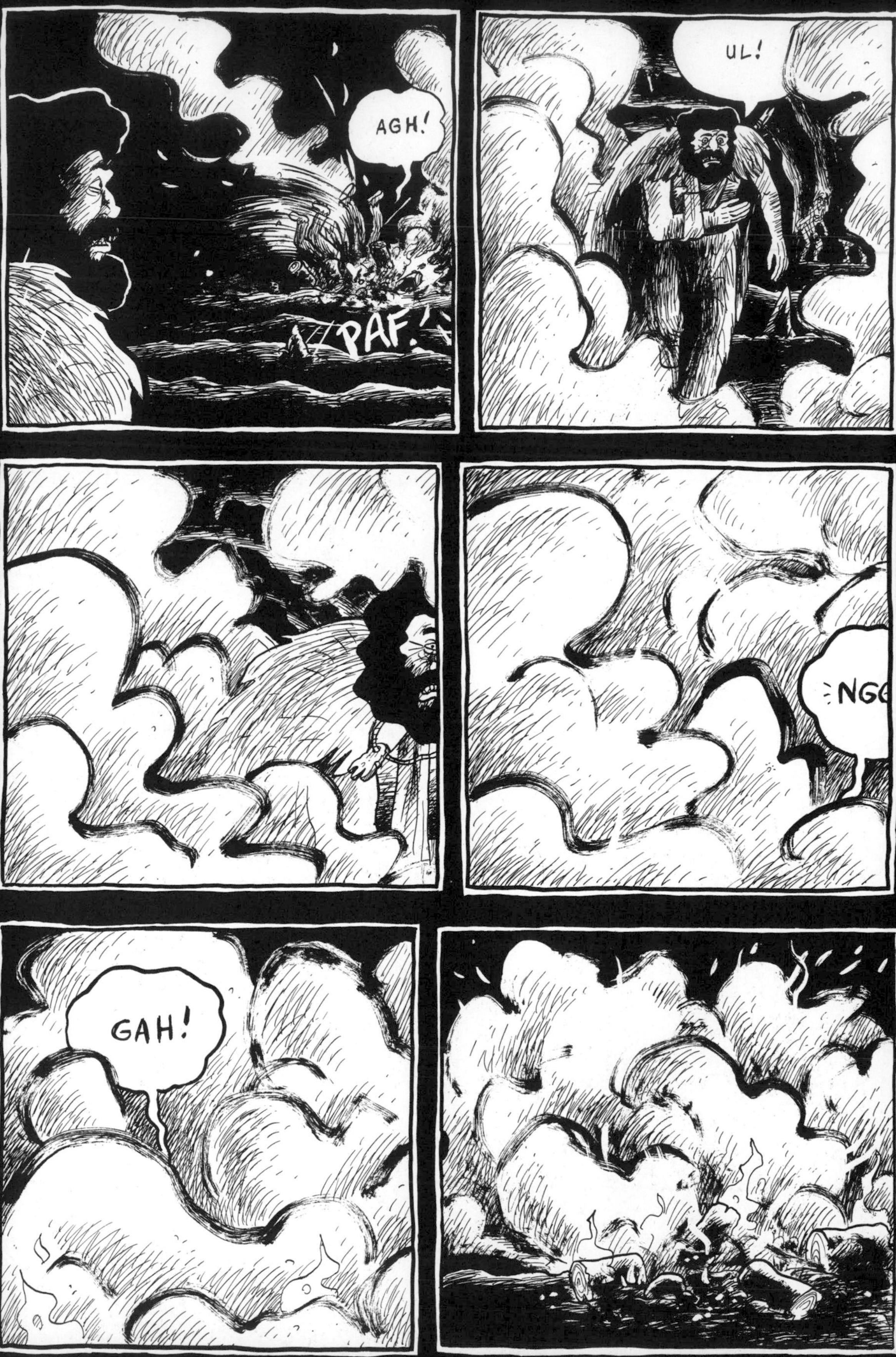
AGH!
PAF!
UL!
NGG
GAH!

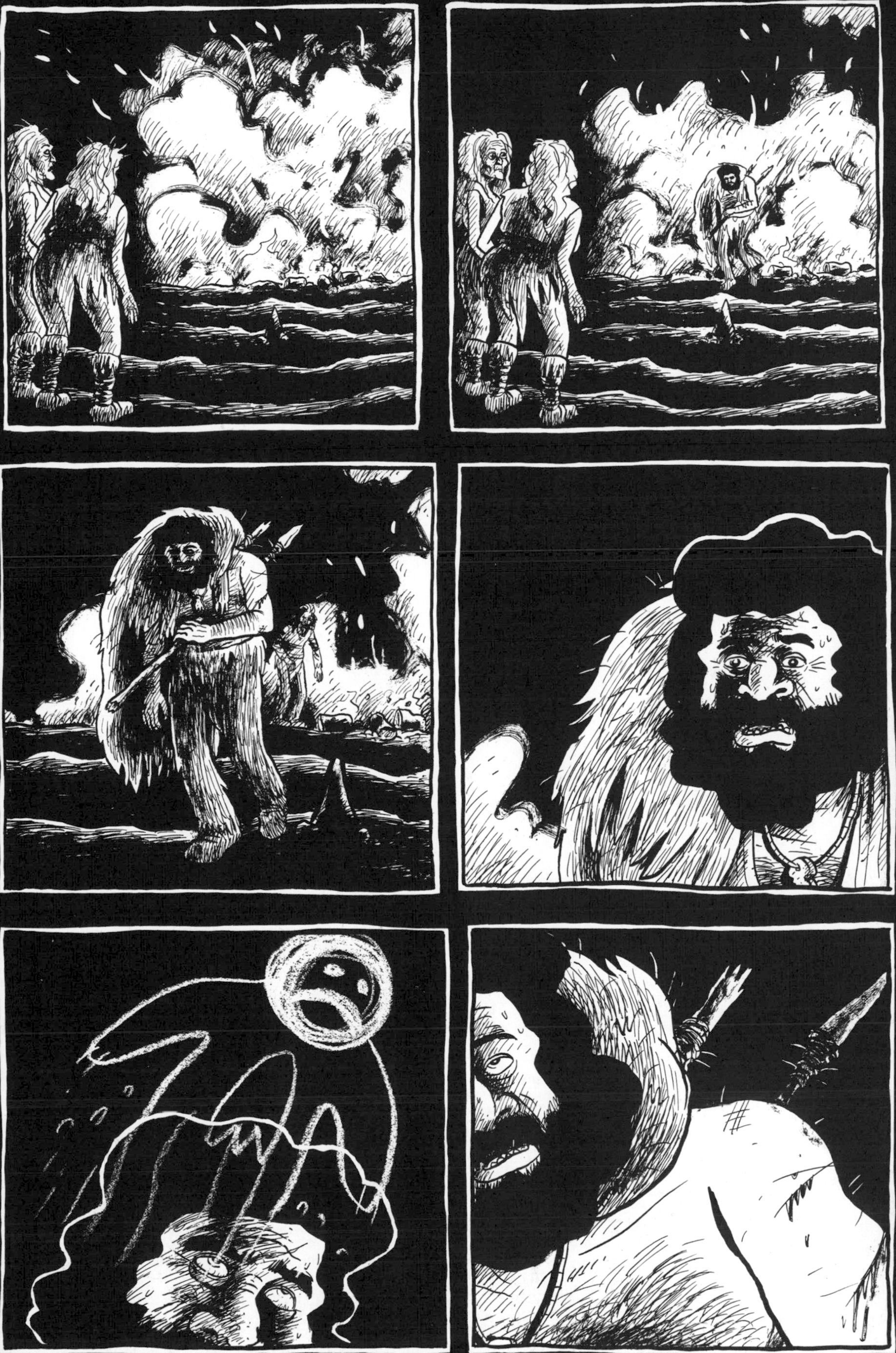

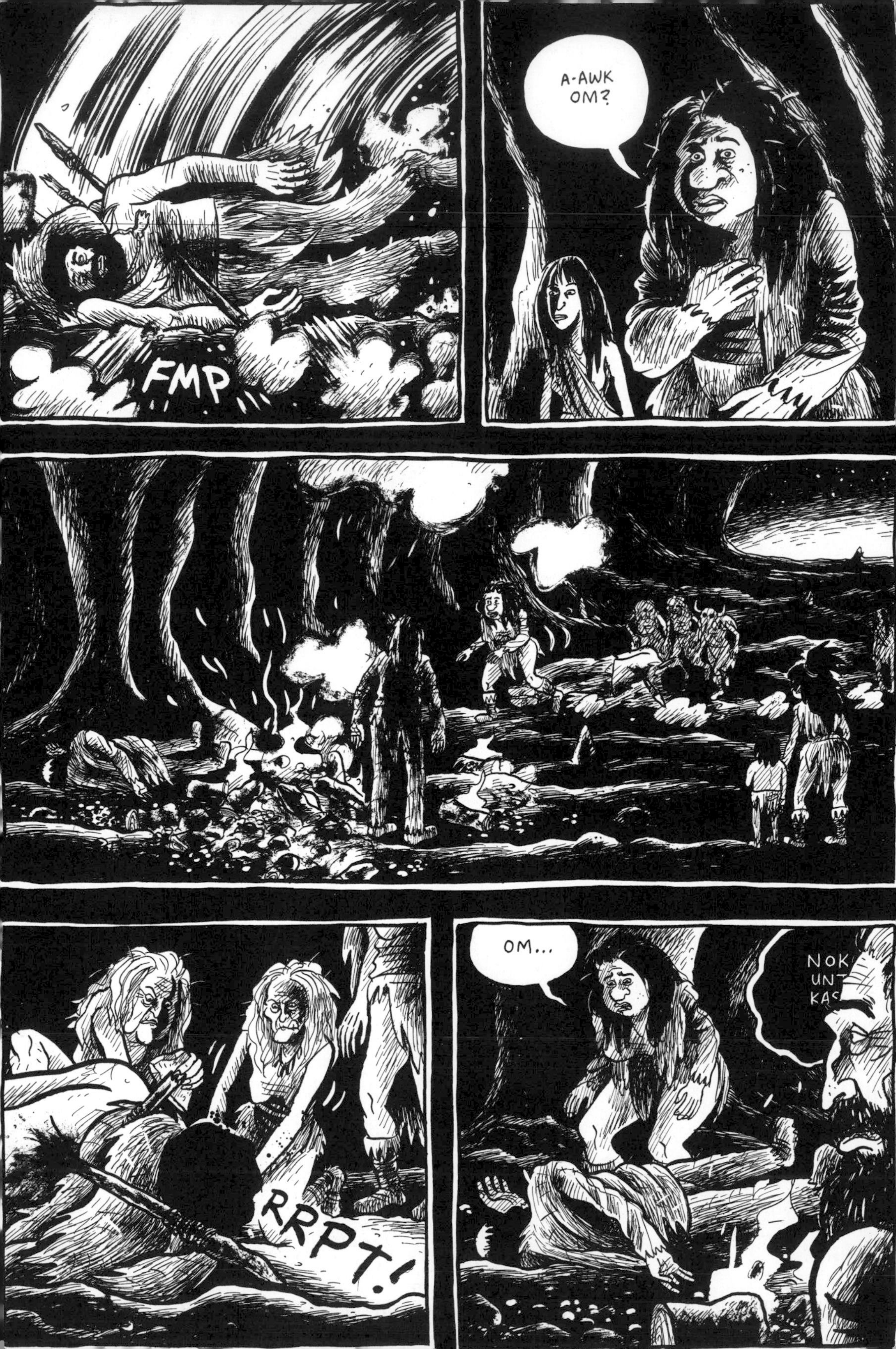
FMP
A-AWK OM?
OM...
NOK UNT KAS
RRPT!

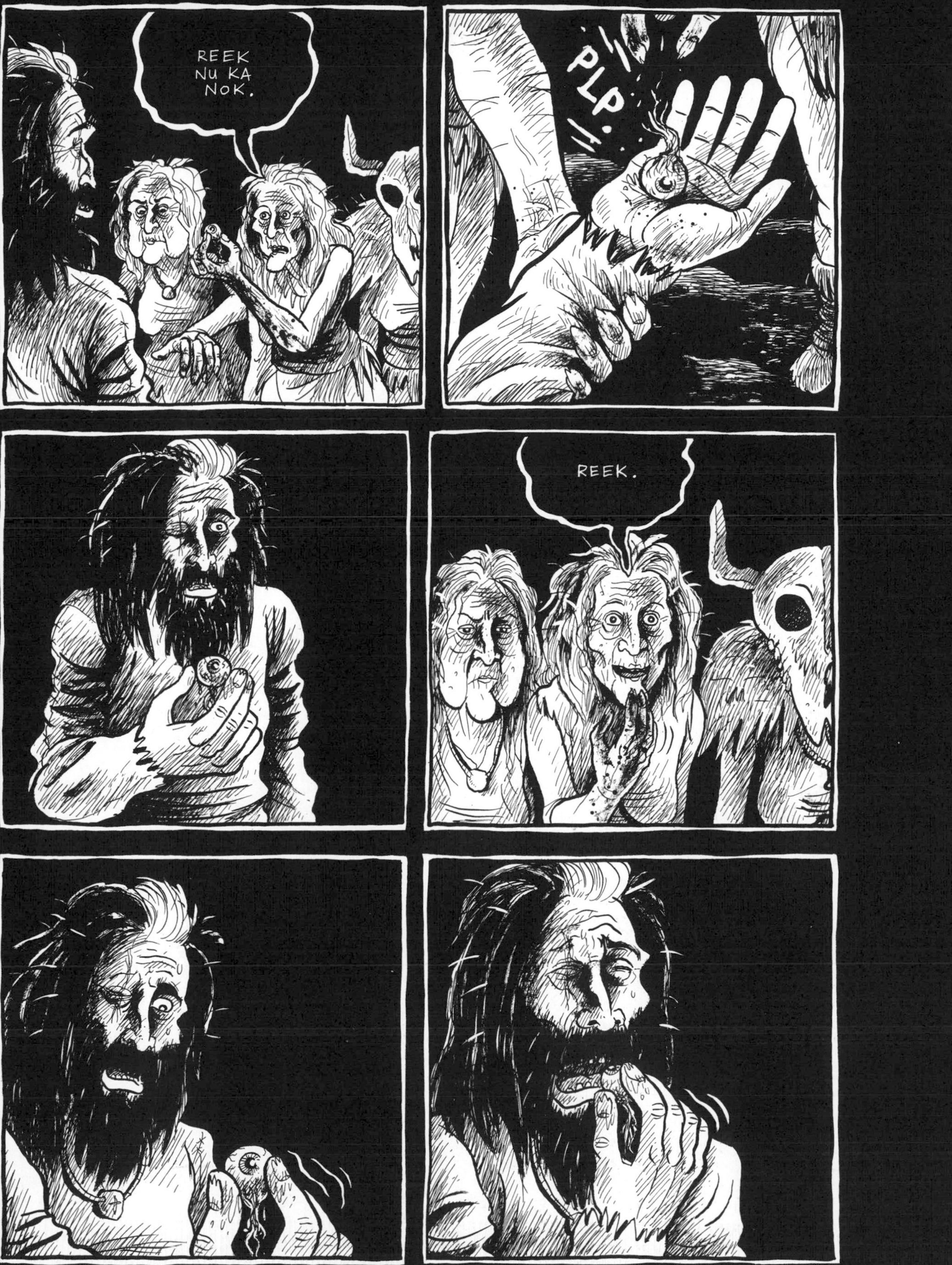
REEK NU KA NOK.
PLP.
REEK.

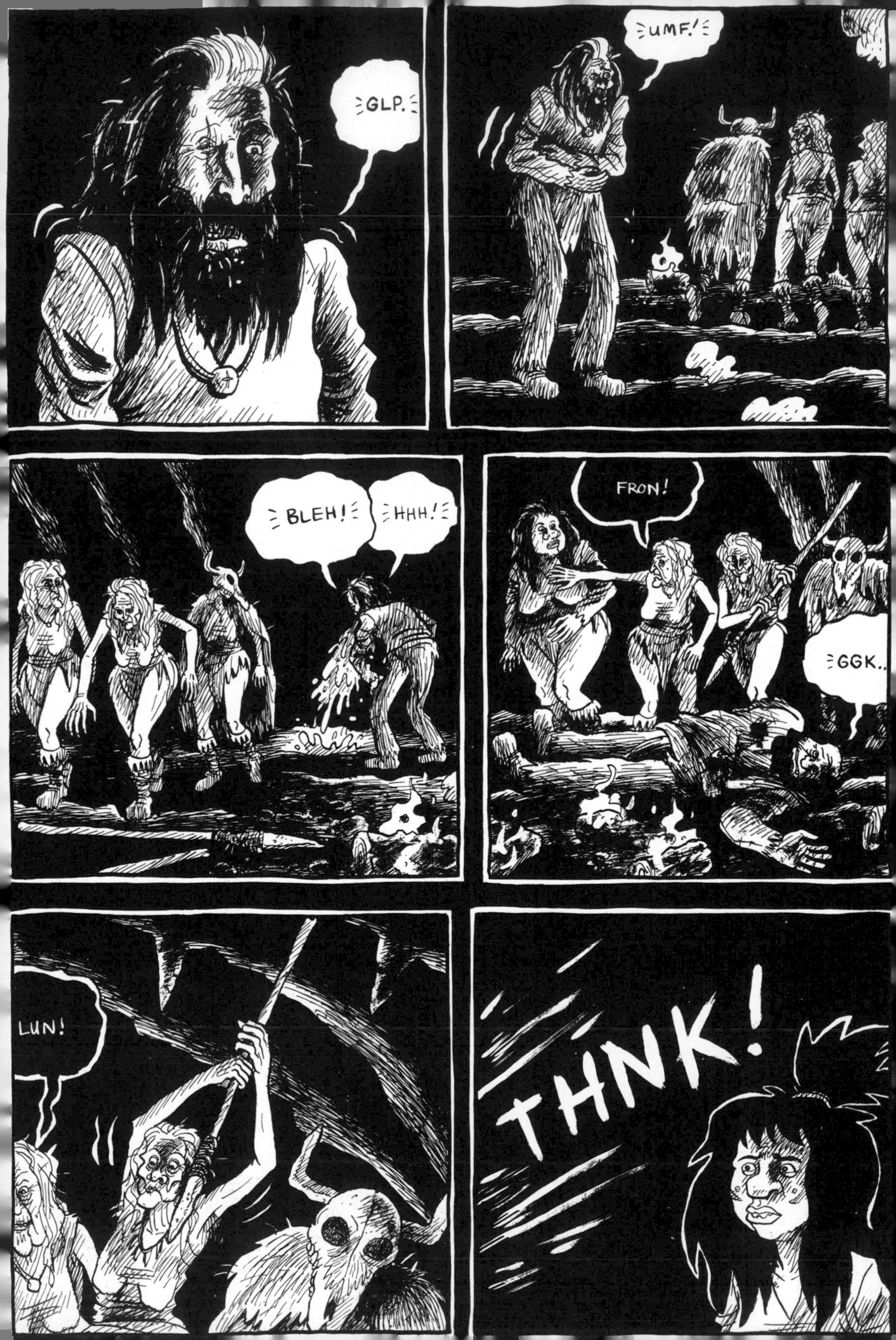
GLP.
UMF!
BLEH!
HHH!
FRON!
GGK...
LUN!
THNK!

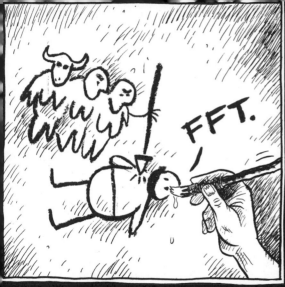

FFT.

TOR-EH...

TOR-EH
TOK
RRPT...

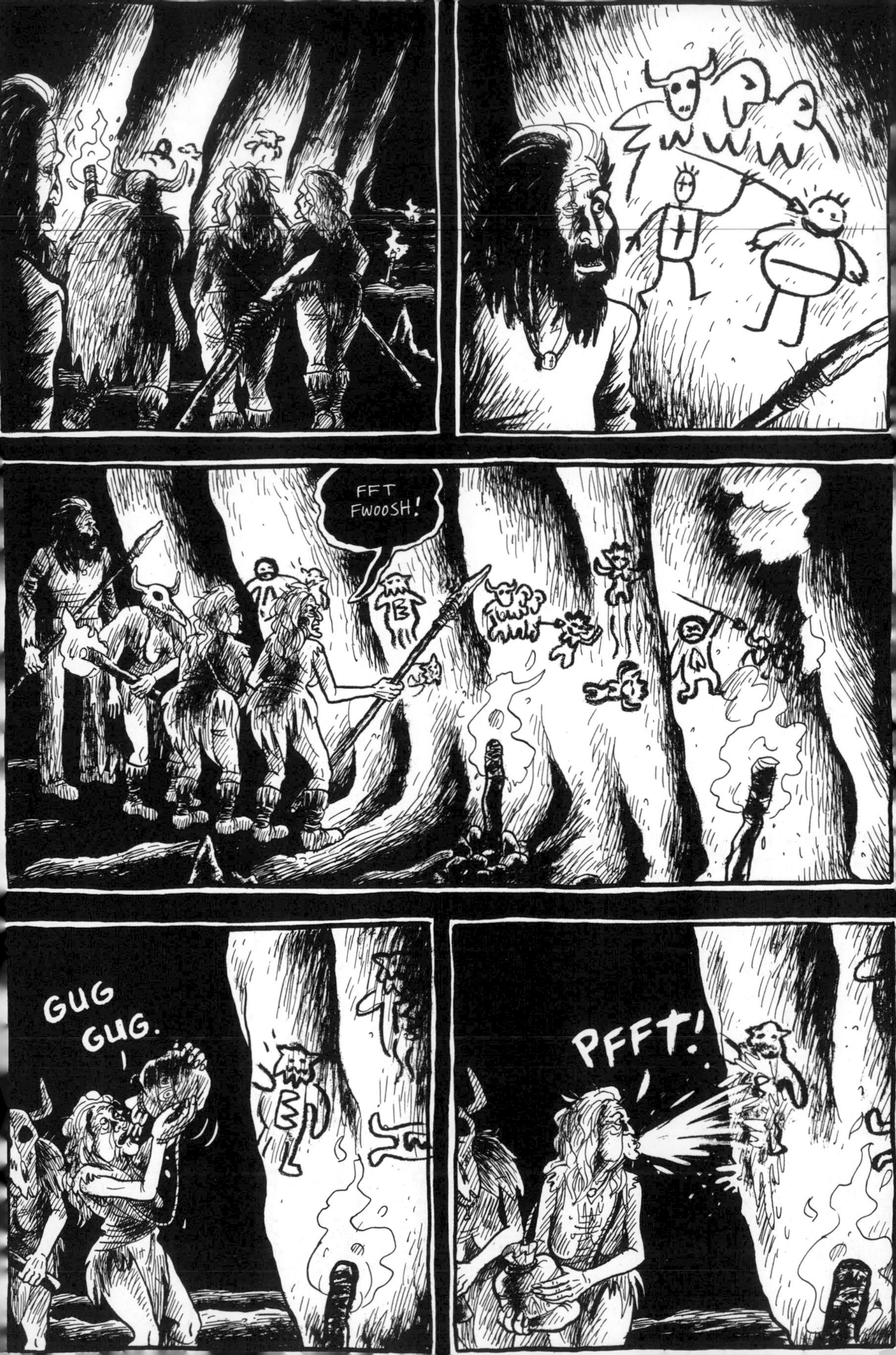
FFT
FWOOSH!
GUG
GUG.
PFFT!

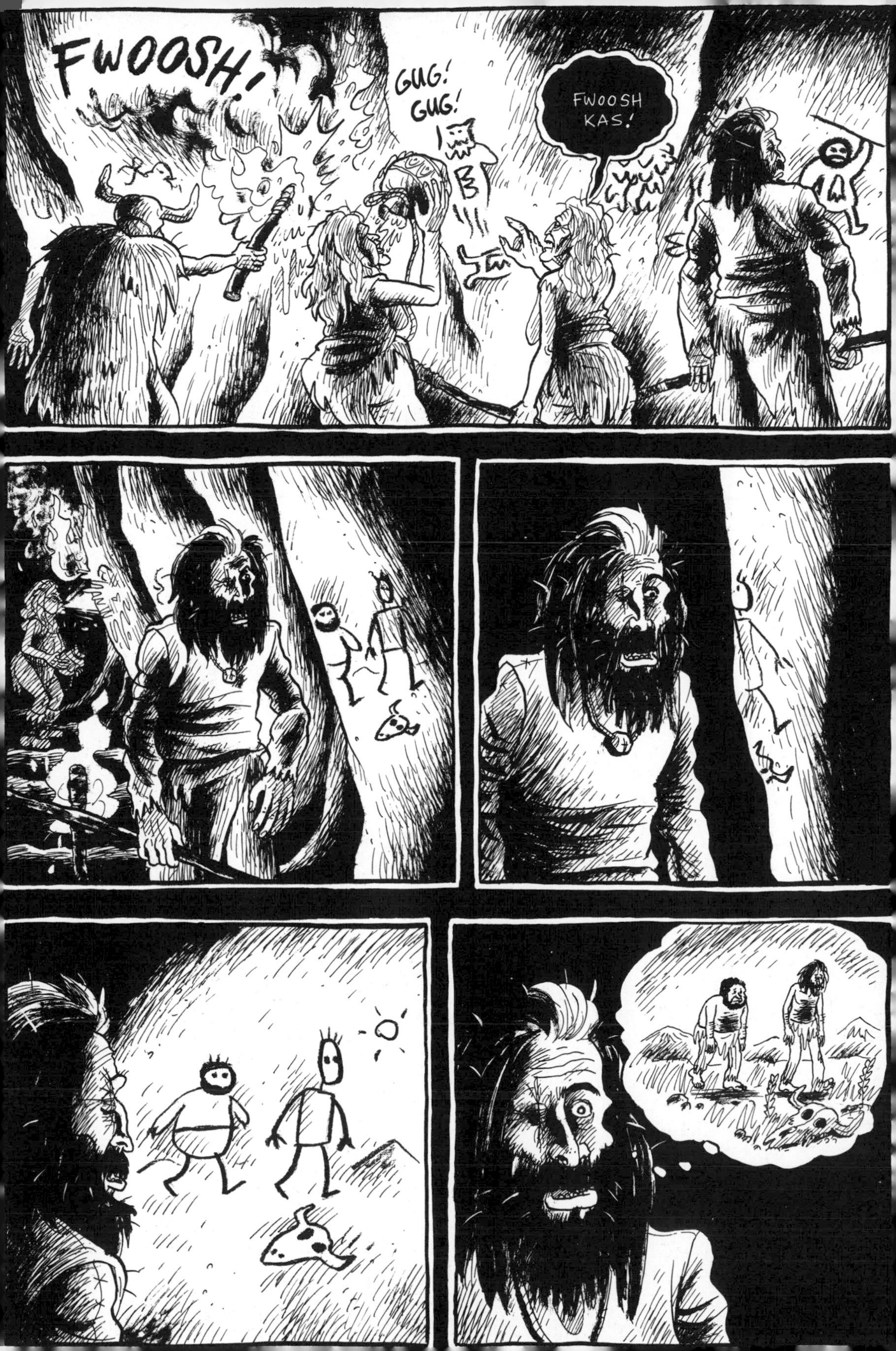
FWOOSH!
GUG! GUG!
FWOOSH KAS!

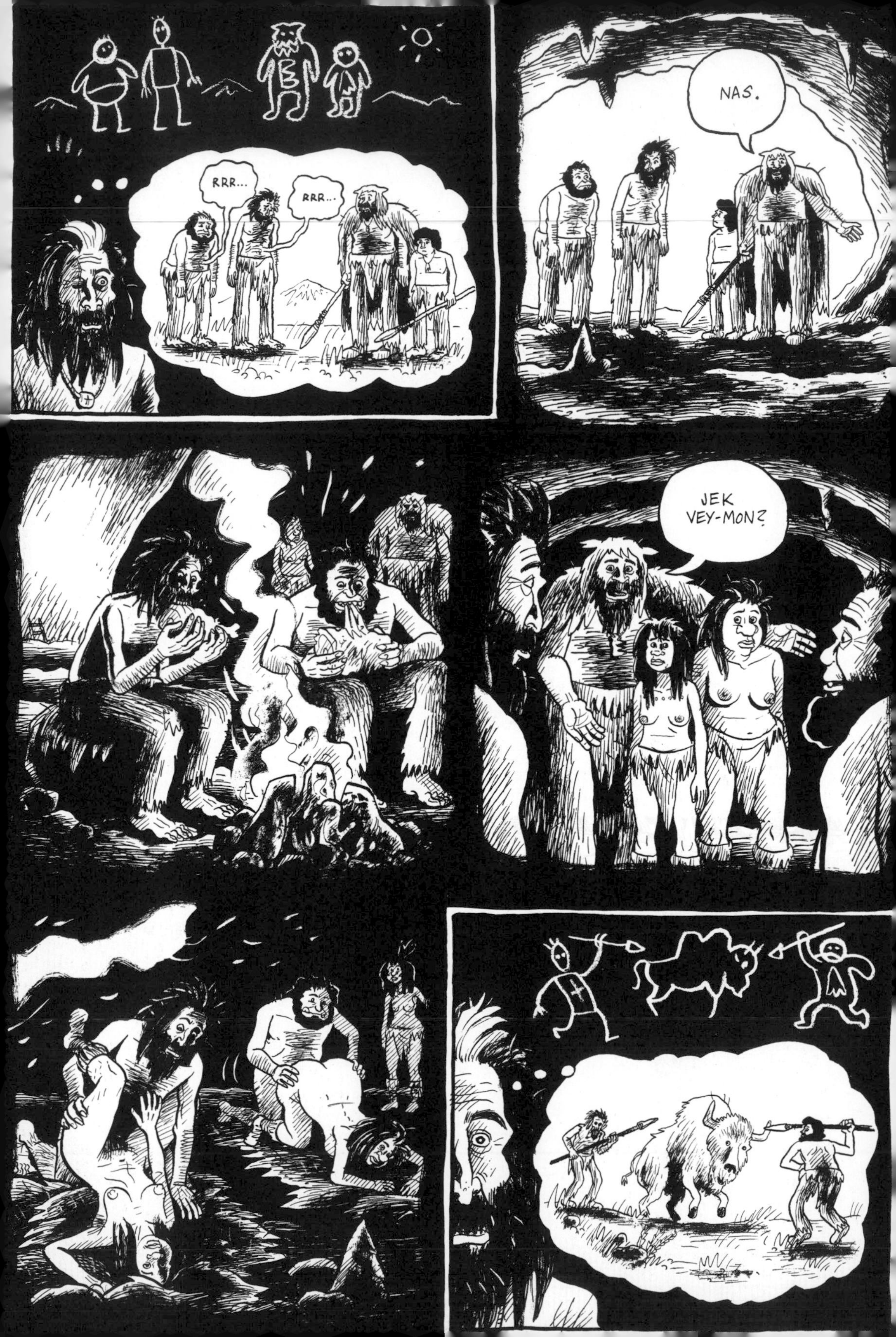
RRR...
RRR...
NAS.
JEK
VEY-MON?

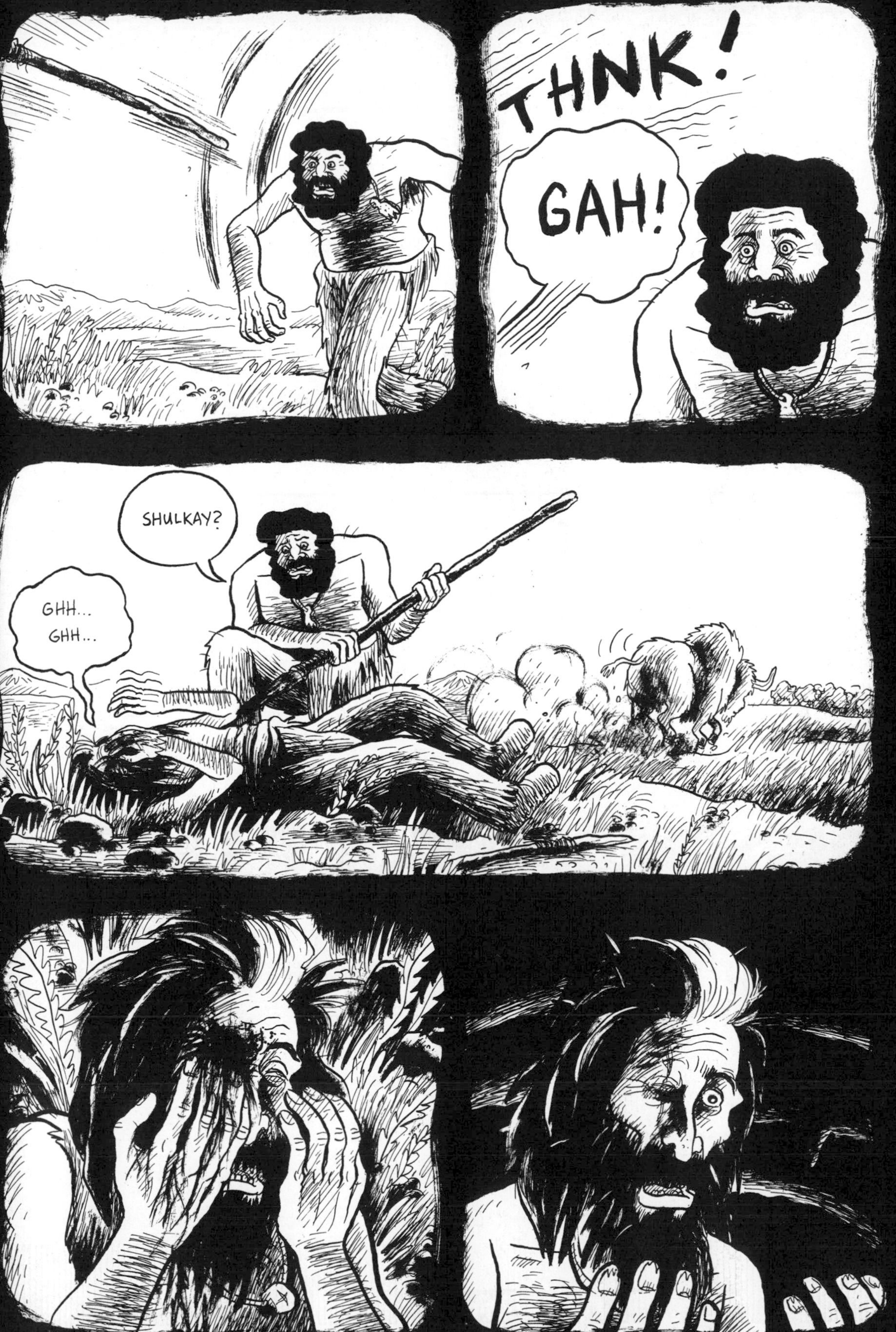
THNK!
GAH!
SHULKAY?
GHH...
GHH...

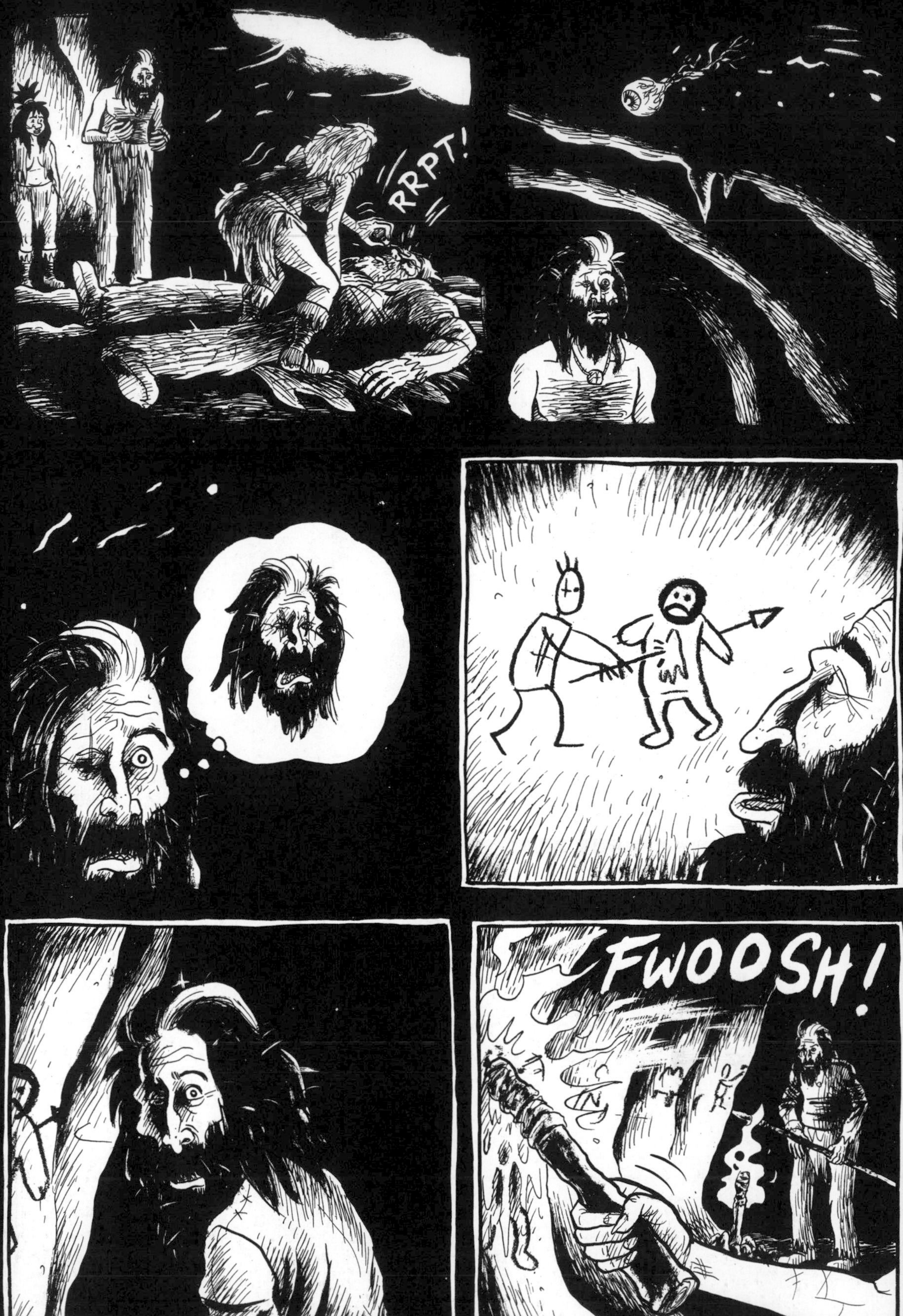
RRPT!
FWOOSH!

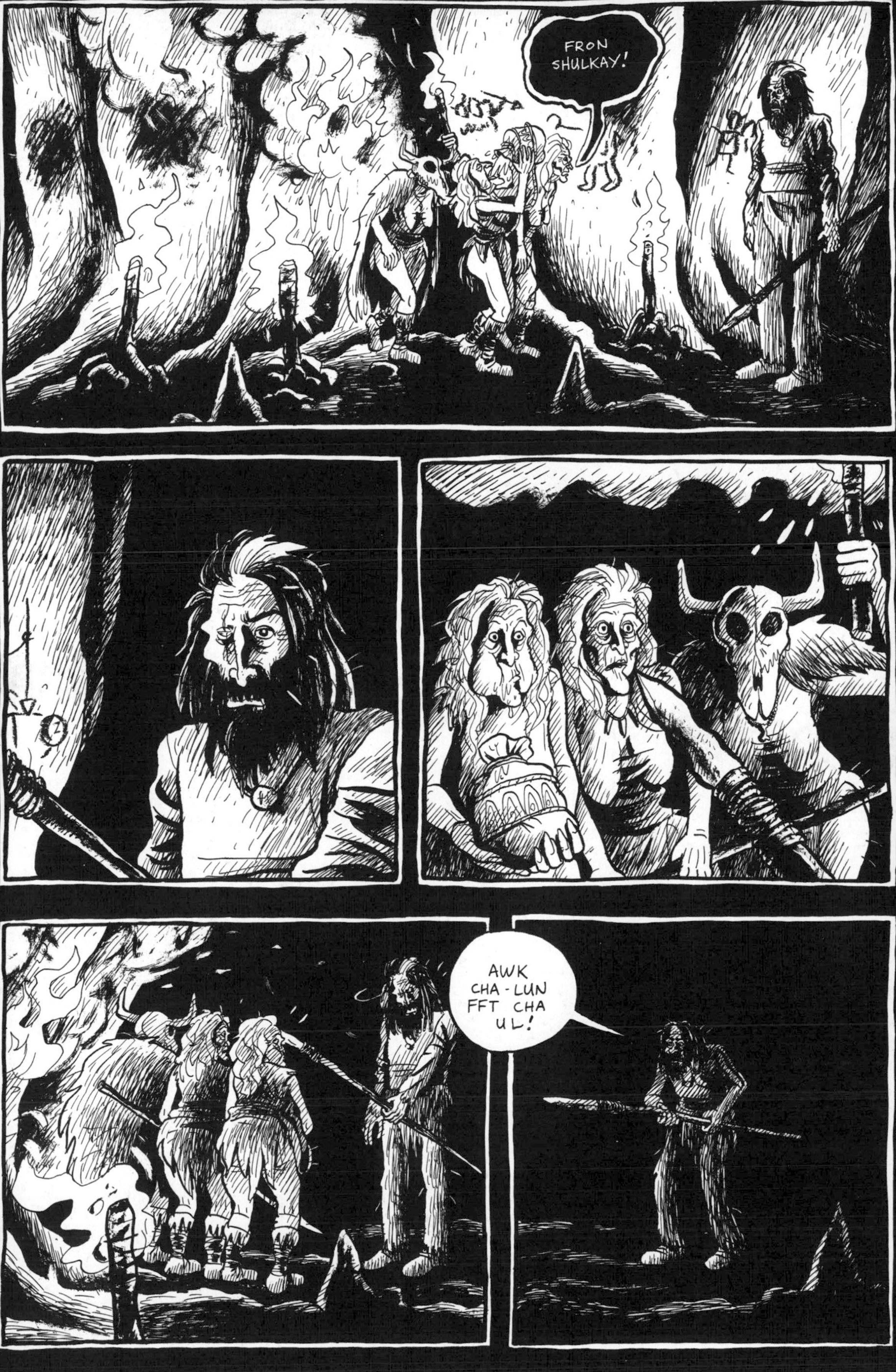
FRON SHULKAY!
AWK CHA-LUN FFT CHA UL!

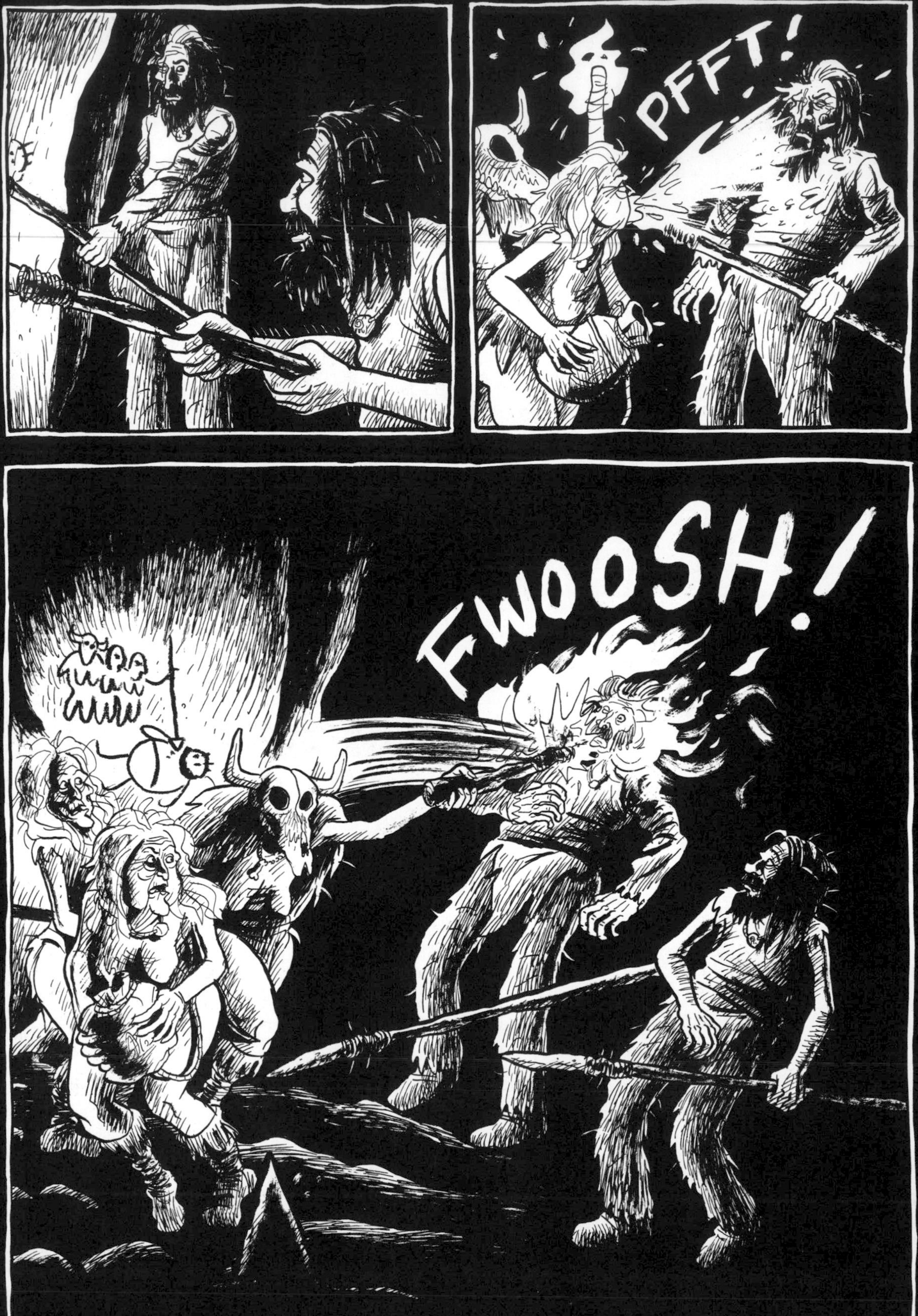
PFFT!
FWOOSH!

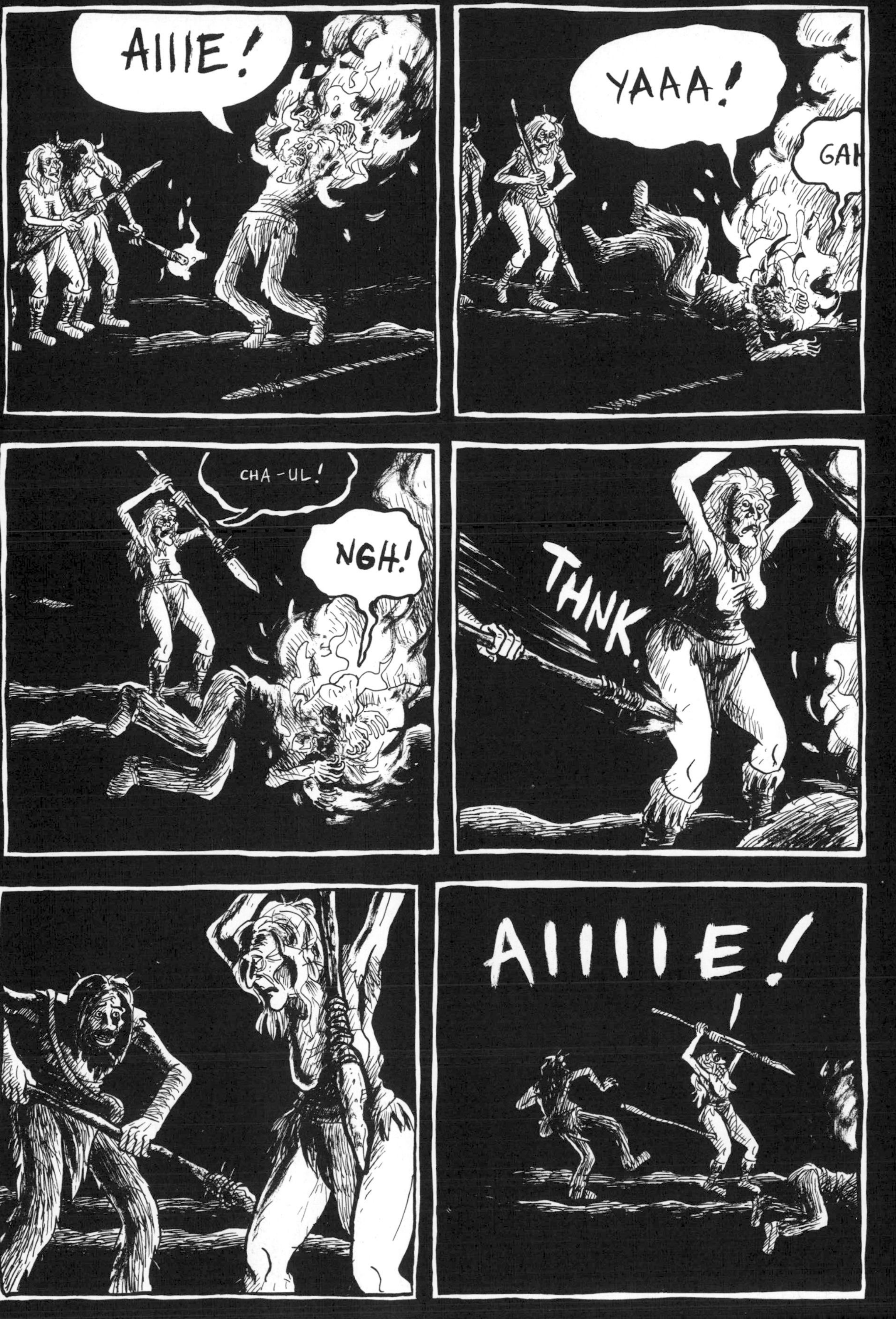
AIIIE!
YAAA!
GAH
CHA-UL!
NGH!
THNK.
AIIIIE!

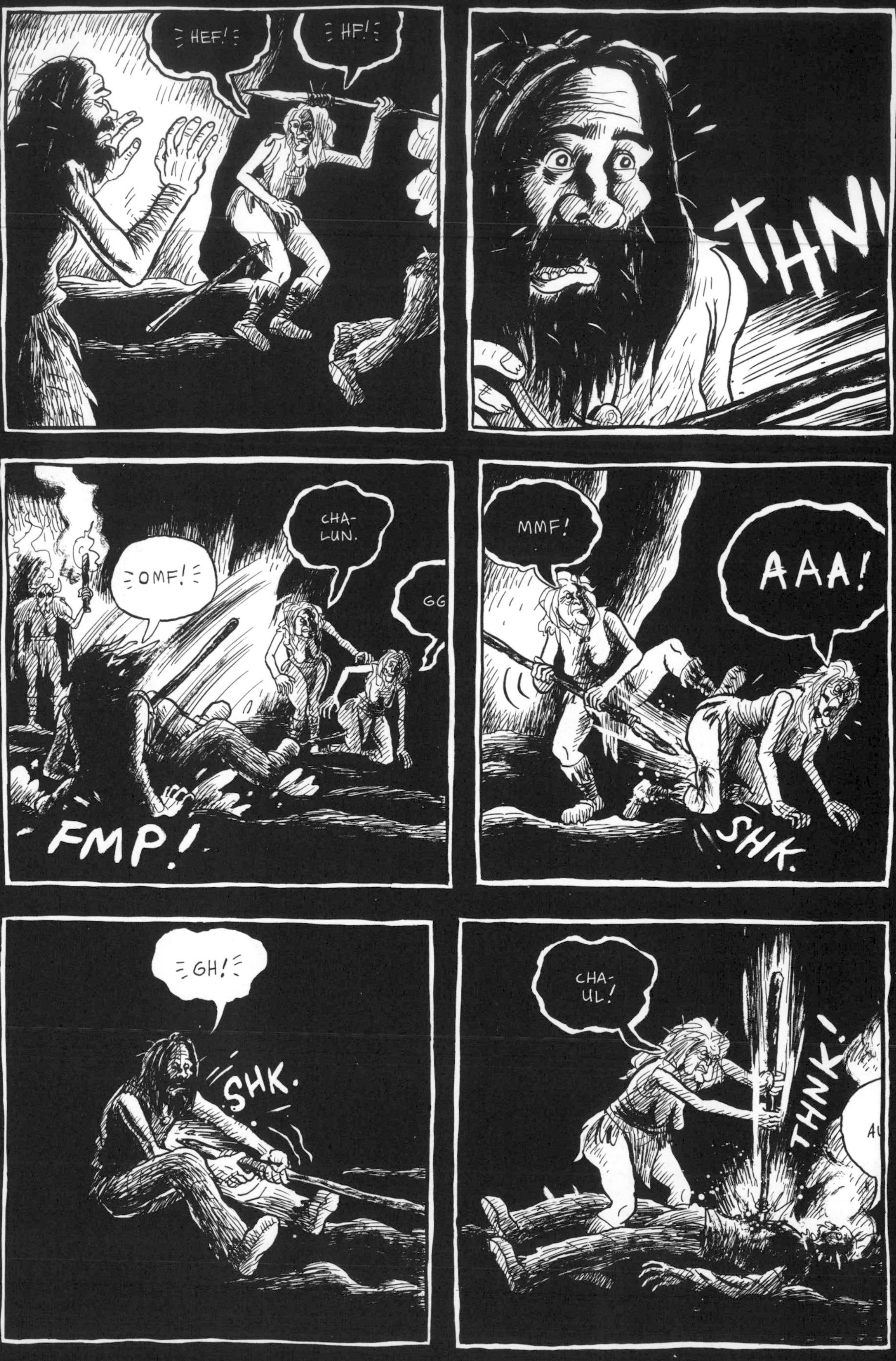

HEF!
HF!
THN
CHA-LUN.
OMF!
GG
FMP!
MMF!
AAA!
SHK.
GH!
SHK.
CHA-UL!
THNK!

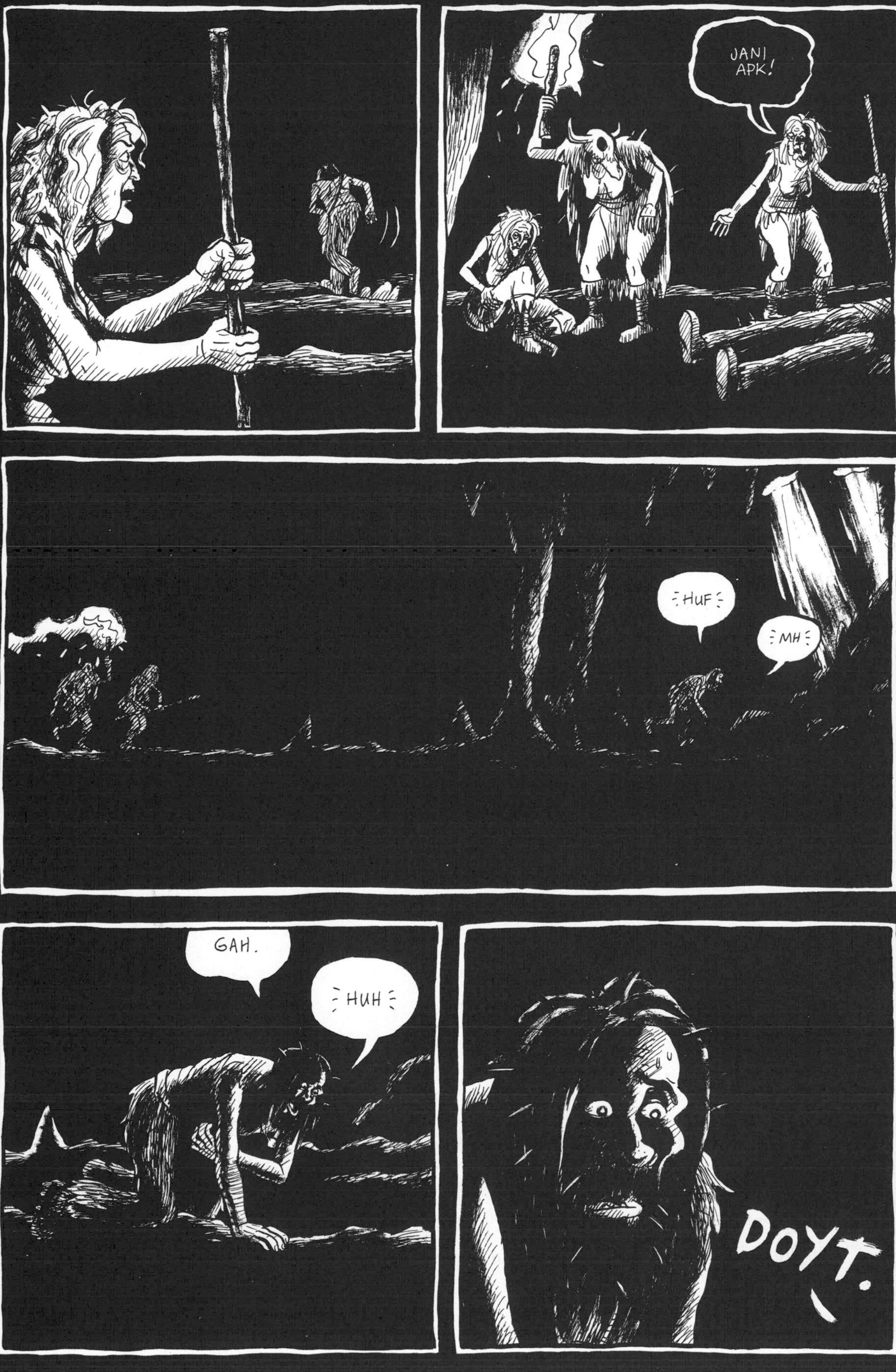
JANI APK!
HUF
MH
GAH.
HUH
DOYT.

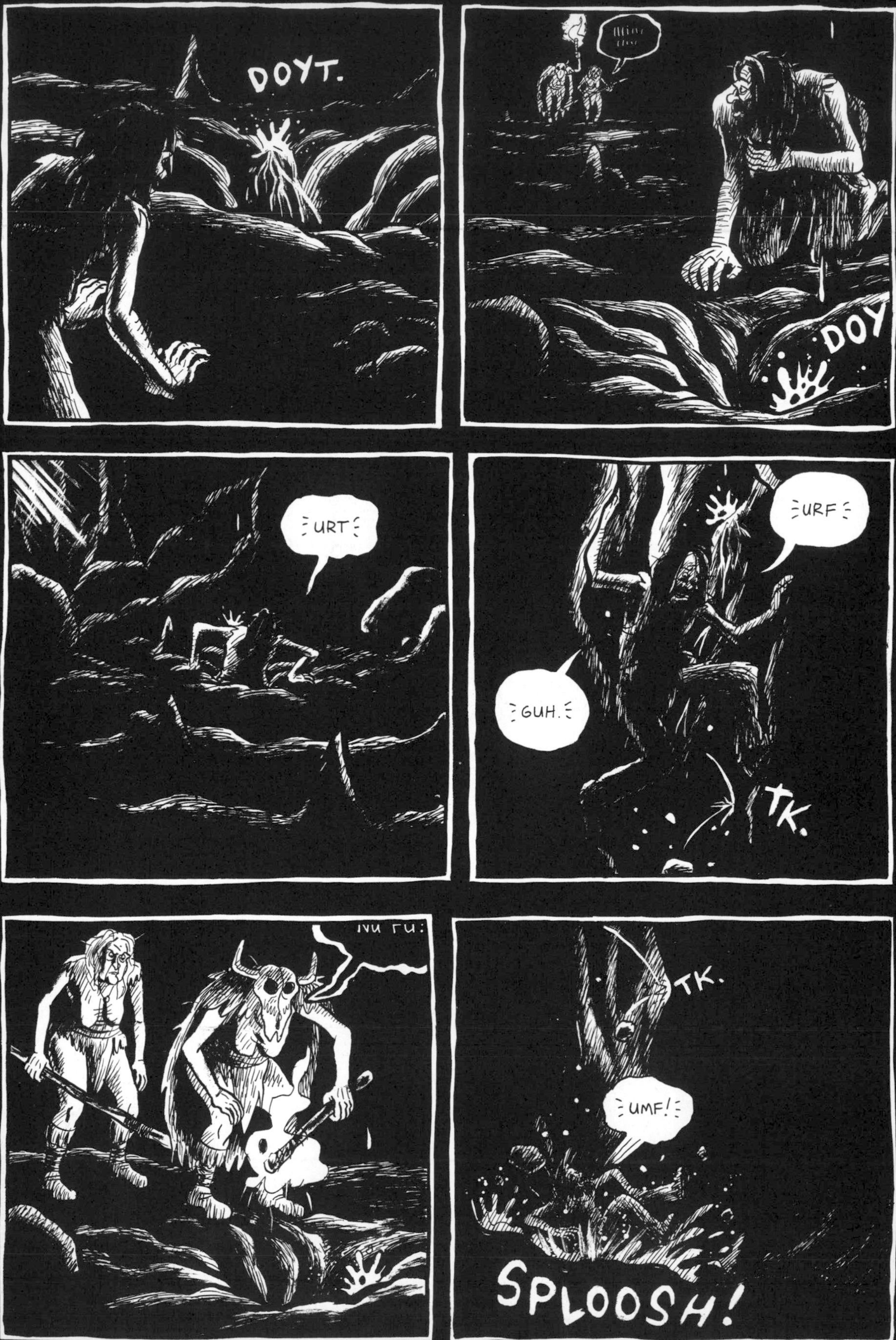
DOYT.
DOY
URT
URF
GUH.
TK.
TK.
UMF!
SPLOOSH!

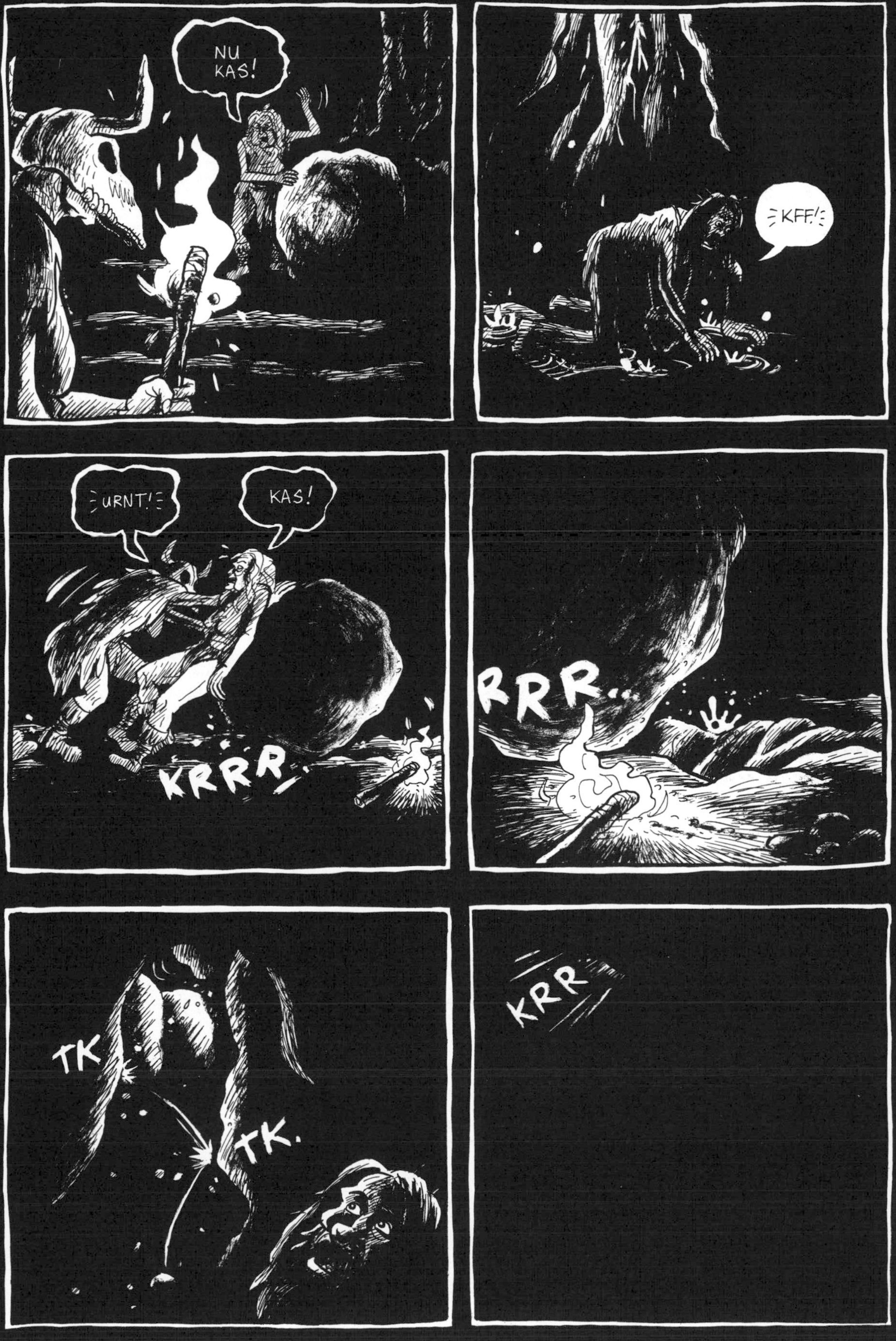
NU KAS!
KFF!
URNT!
KAS!
KRRR
RRR..
TK
TK.
KRR

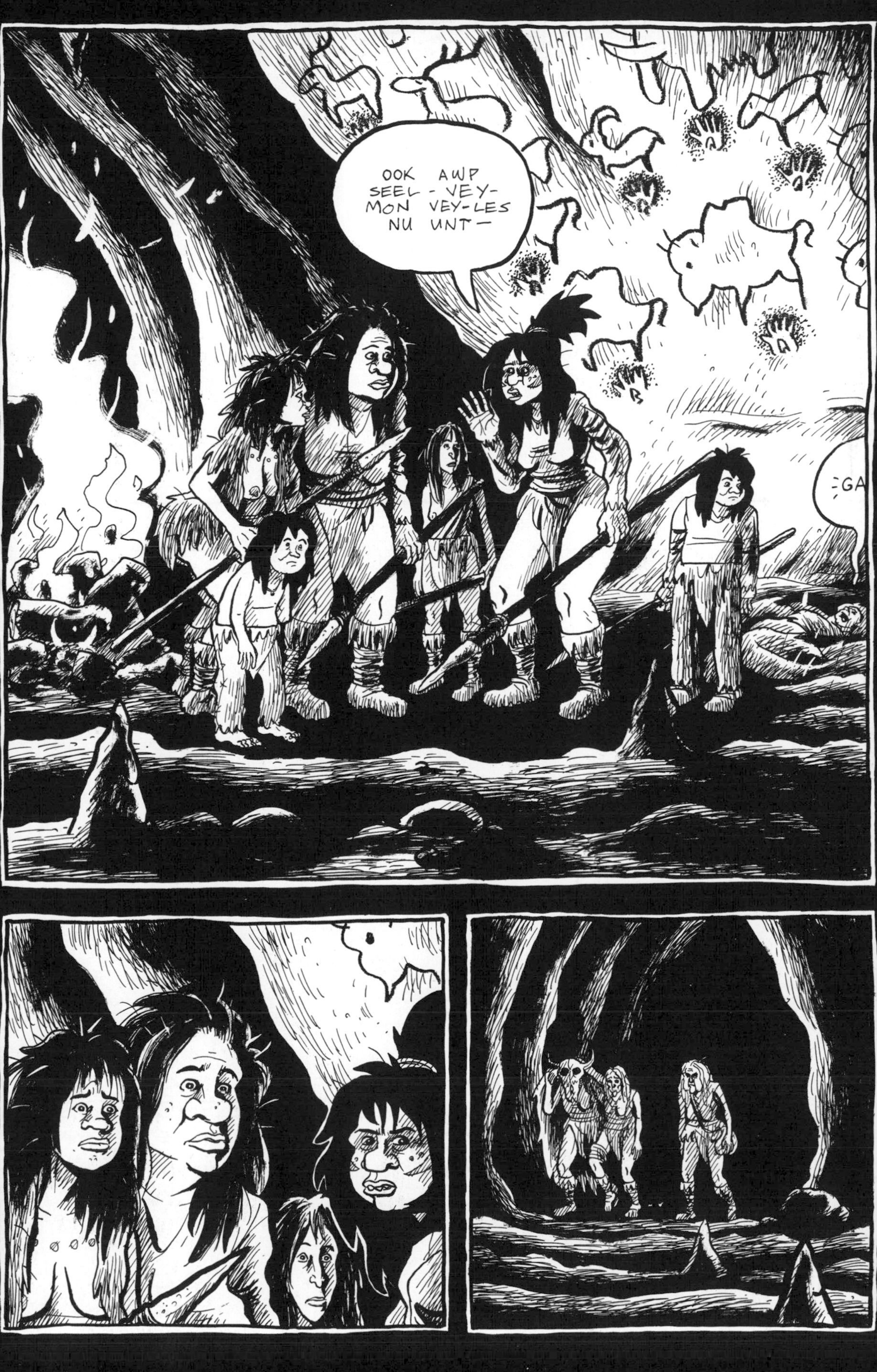
OOK AWP SEEL-VEY-MON VEY-LES NU UNT—
GA

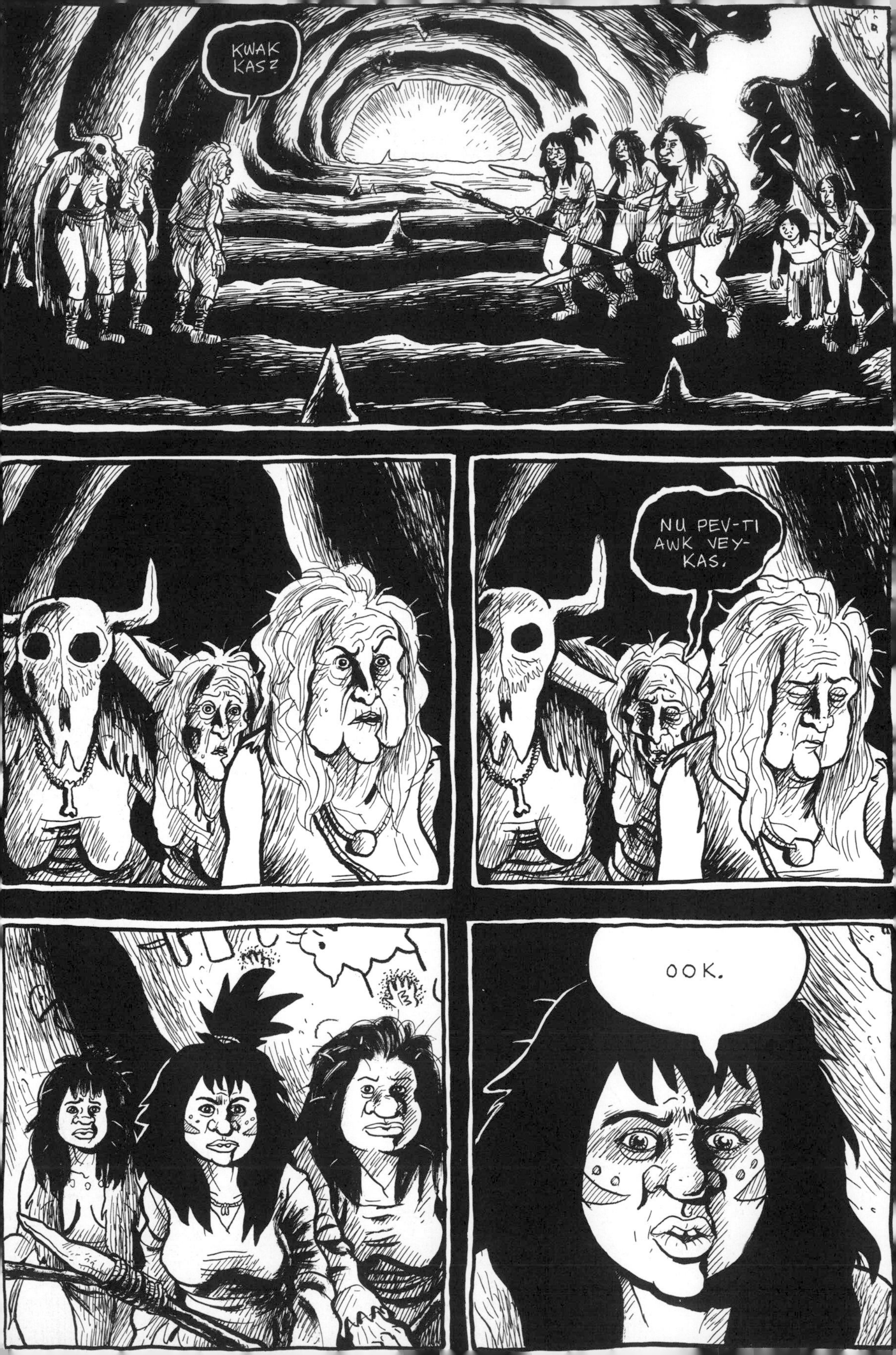
KWAK KAS?
NU PEV-TI AWK VEY-KAS.
OOK.

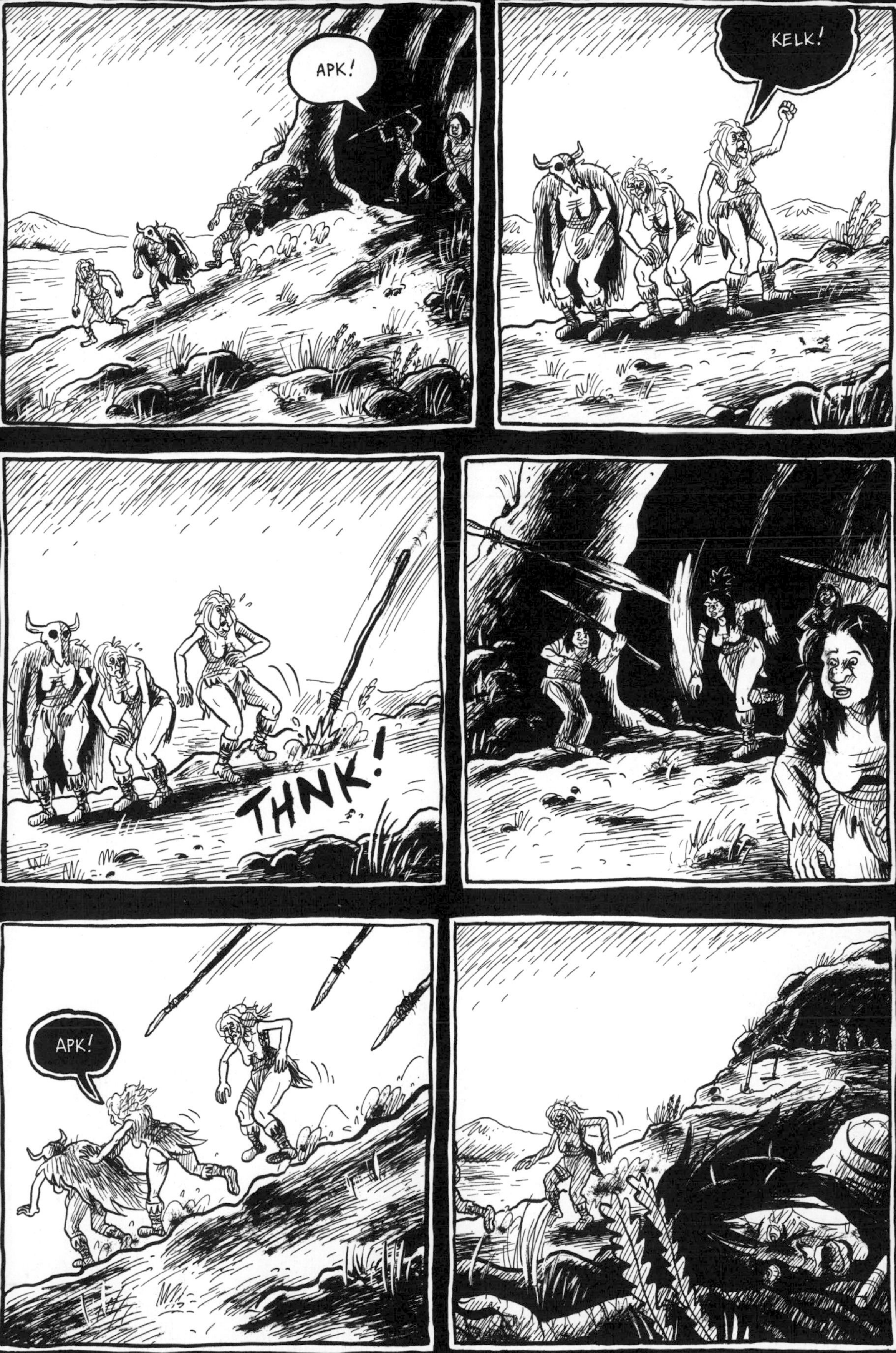
APK!
KELK!
THNK!
APK!

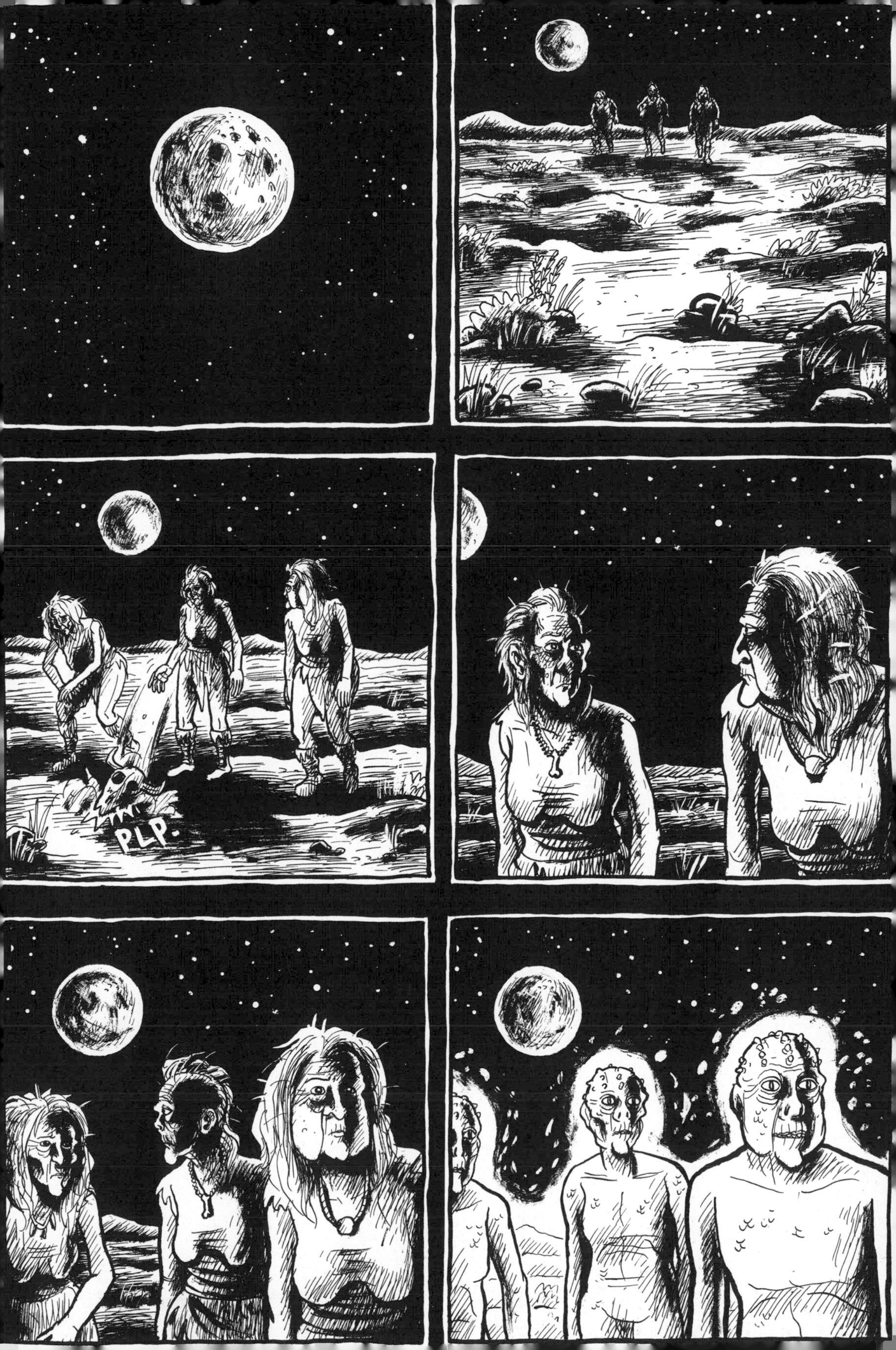
PLP.

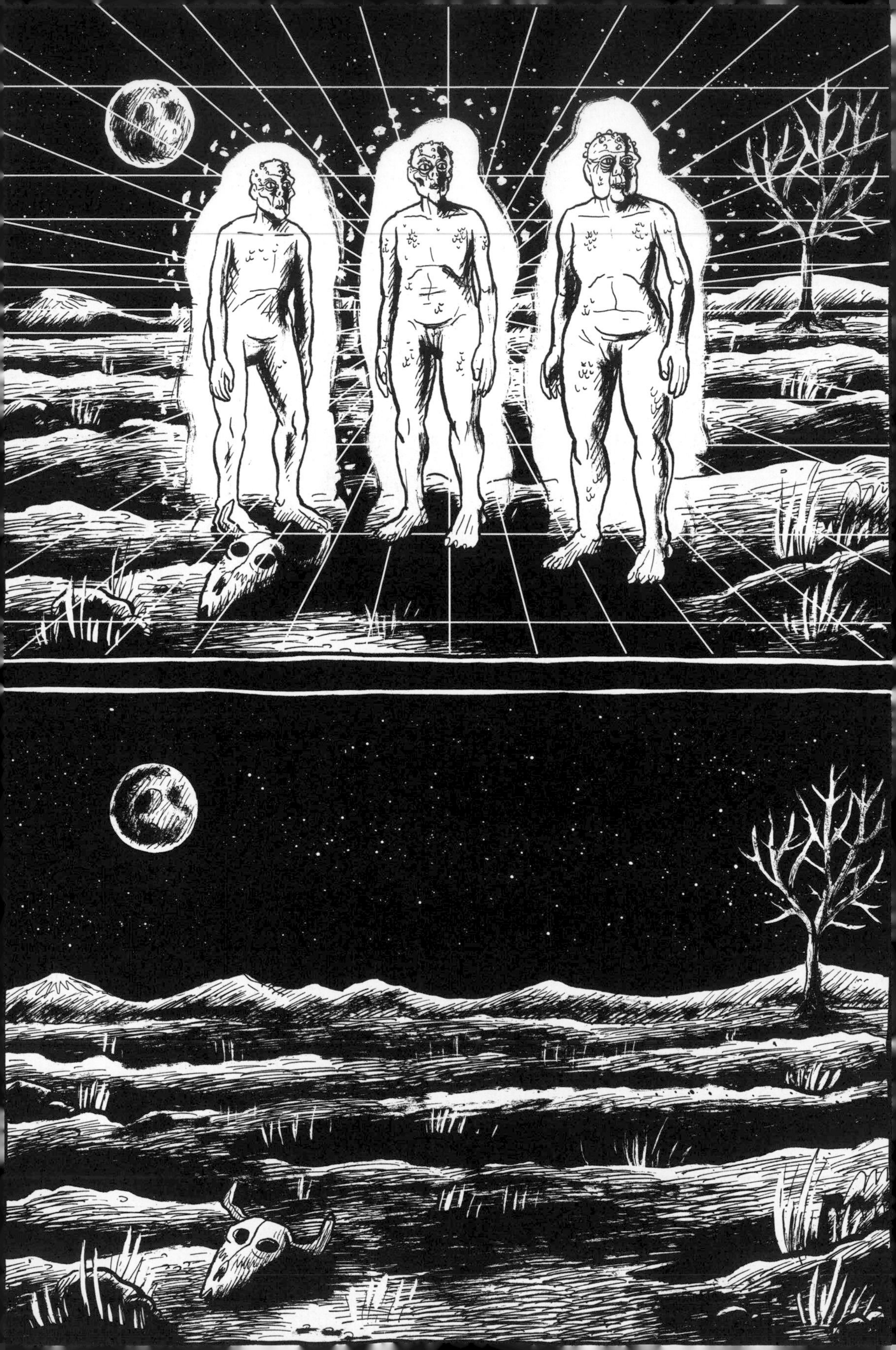

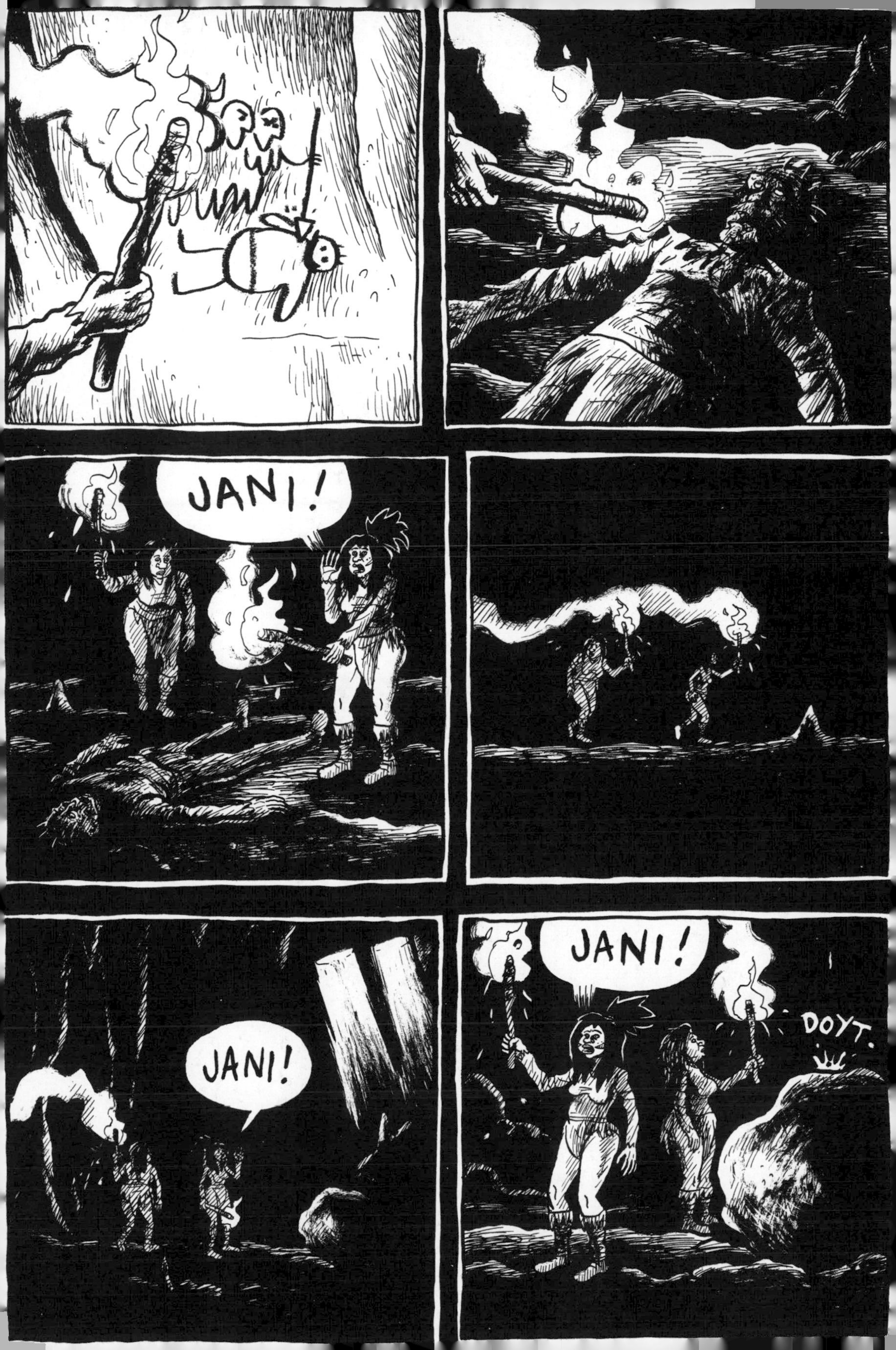
JANI!
JANI!
JANI!
DOYT.

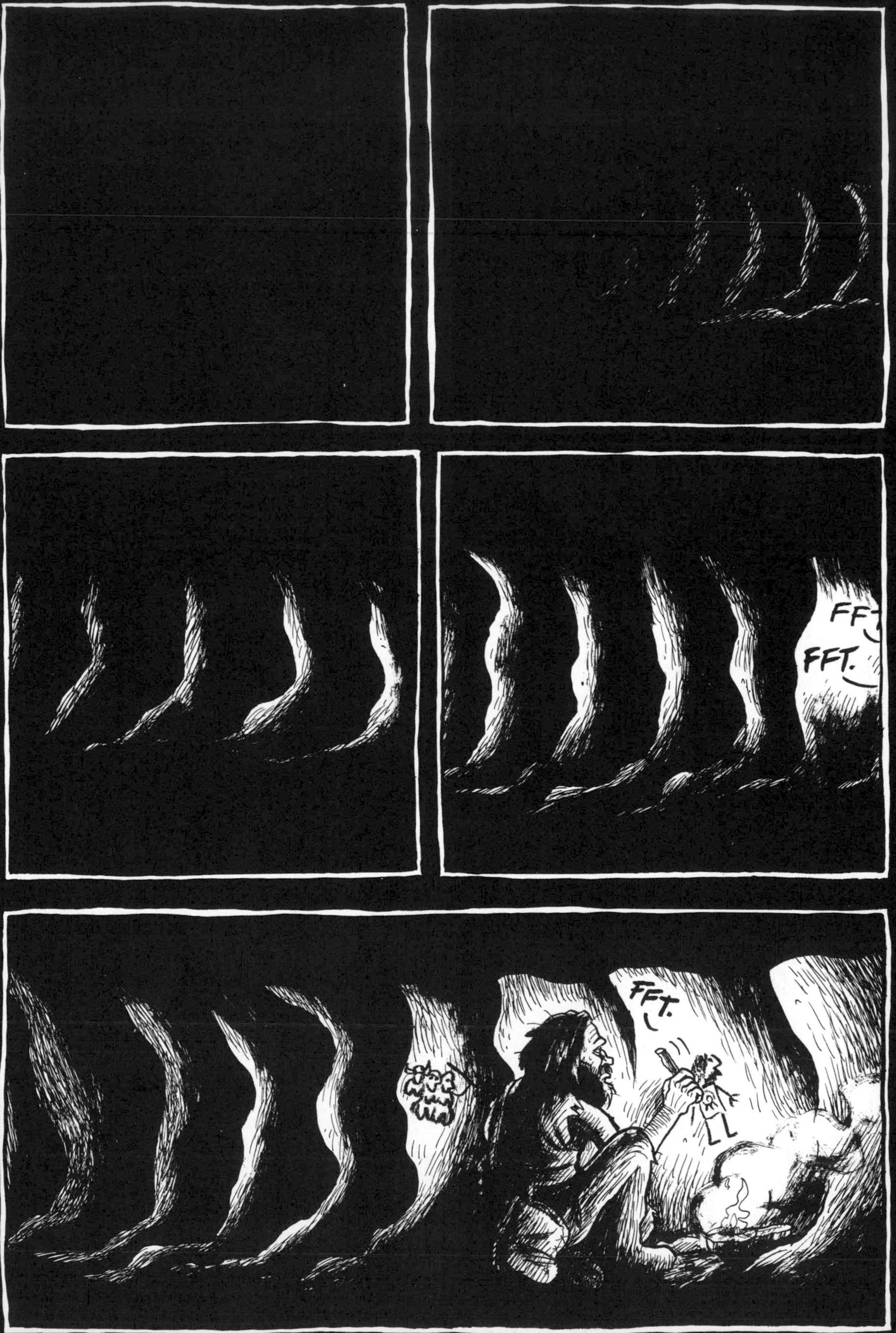
FFT.
FFT.
FFT.

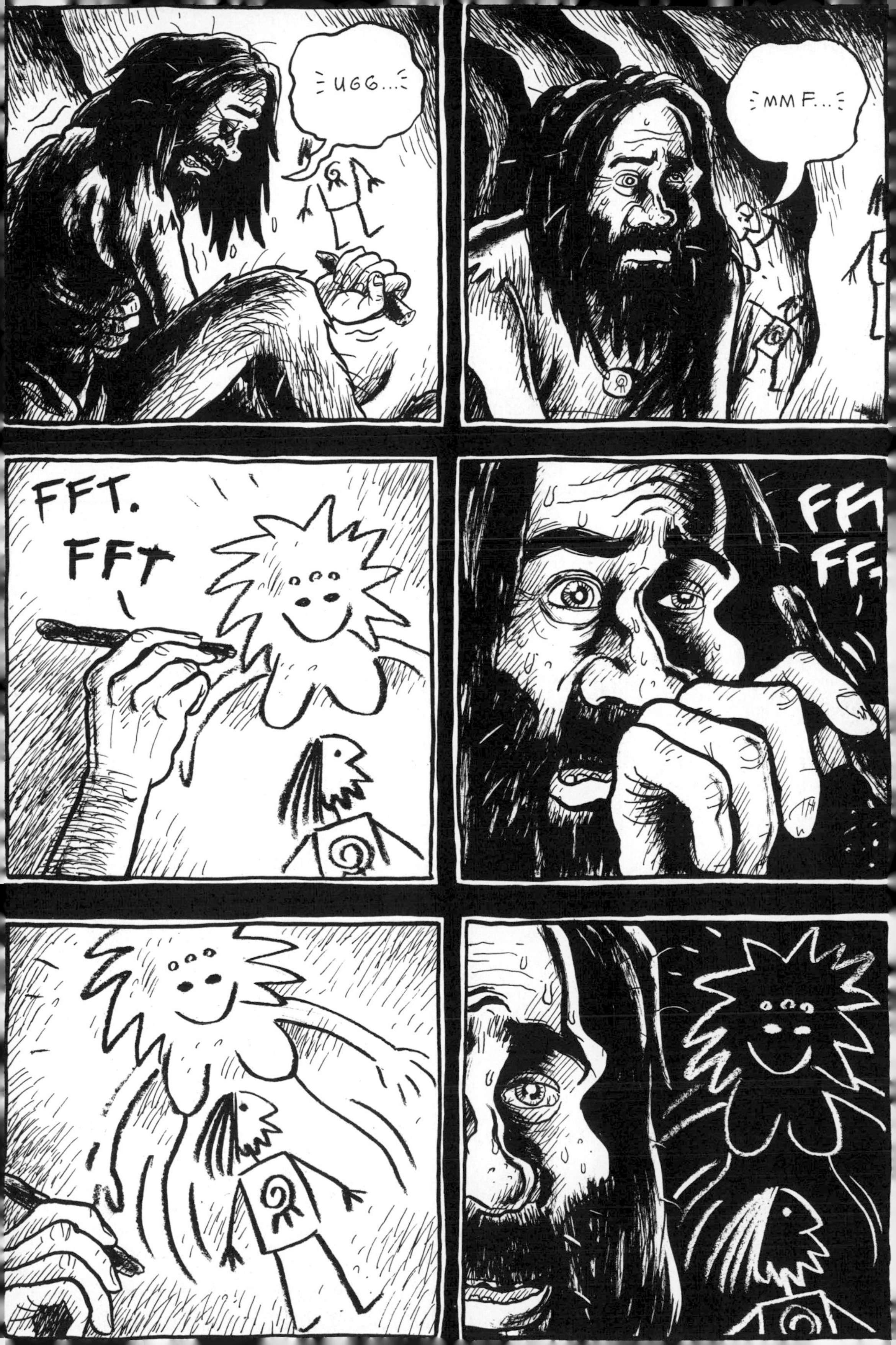
UGG...
MMF...
FFT.
FFT

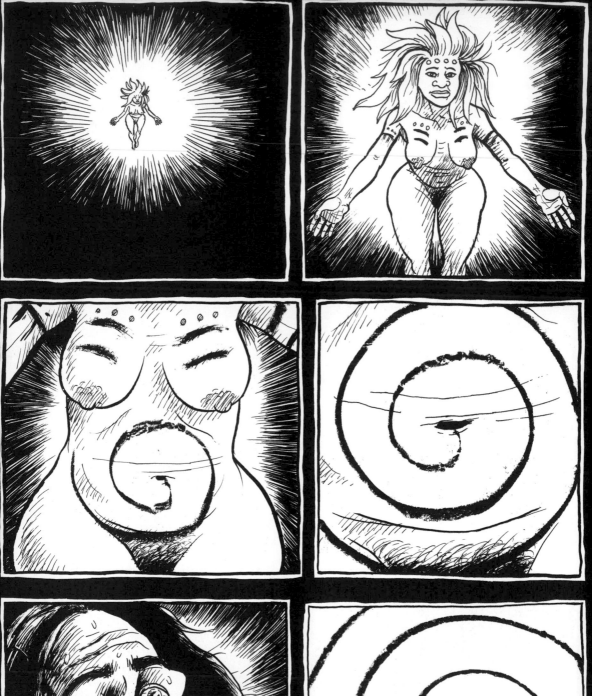

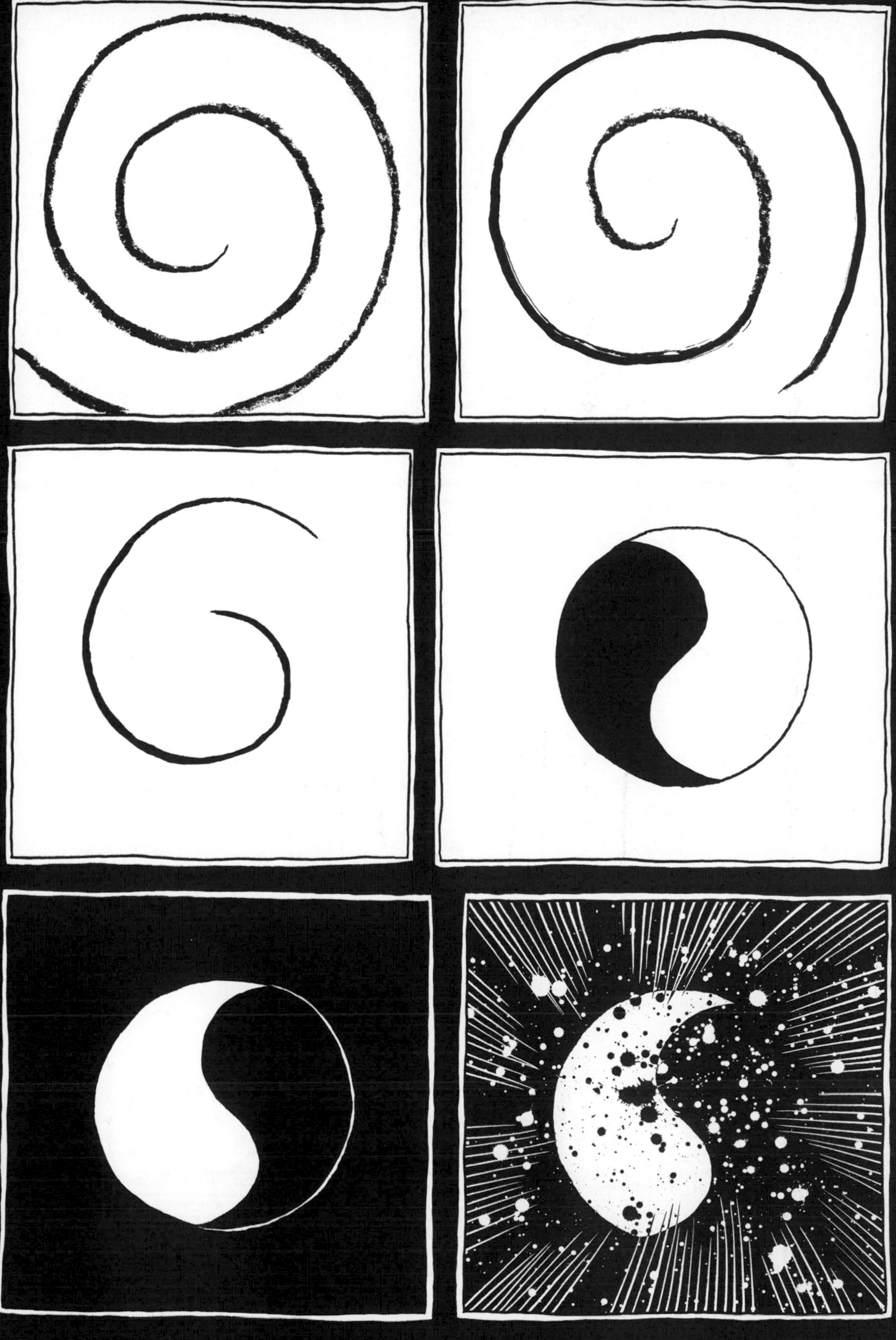

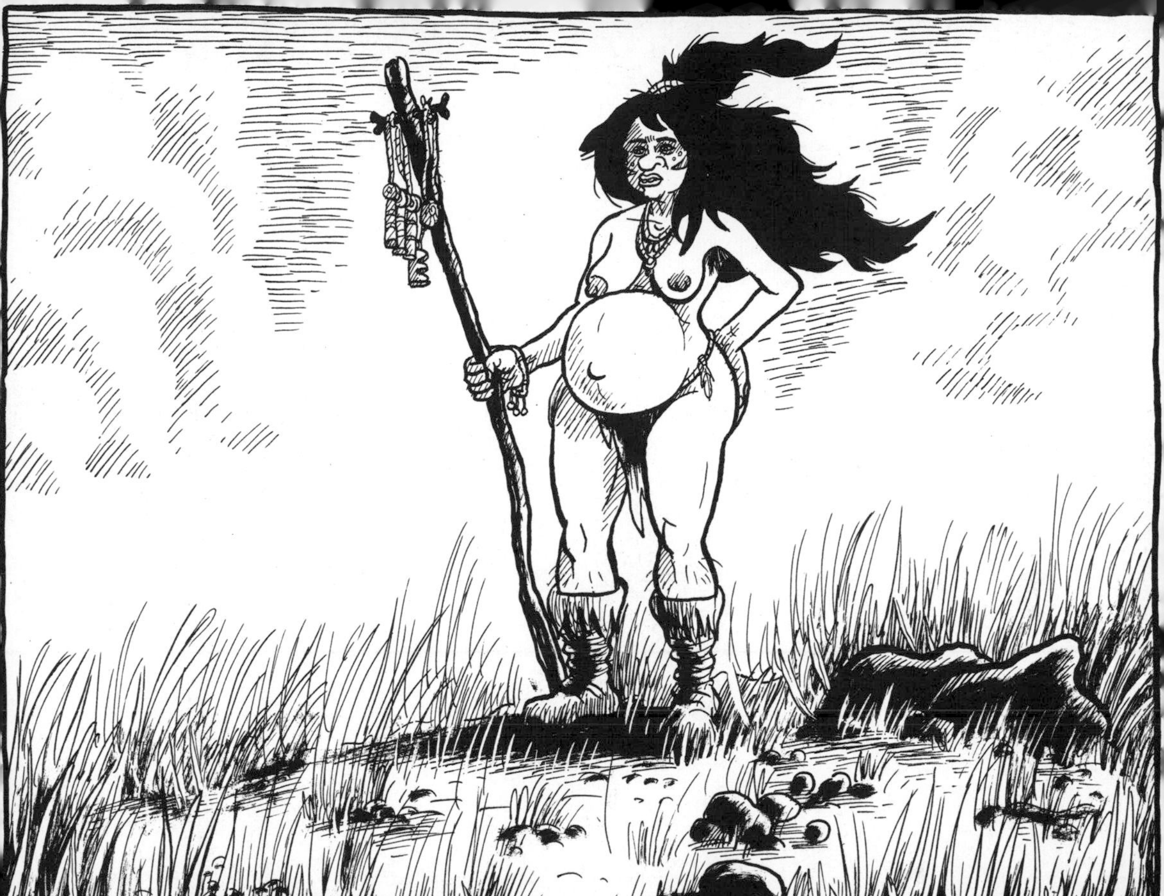
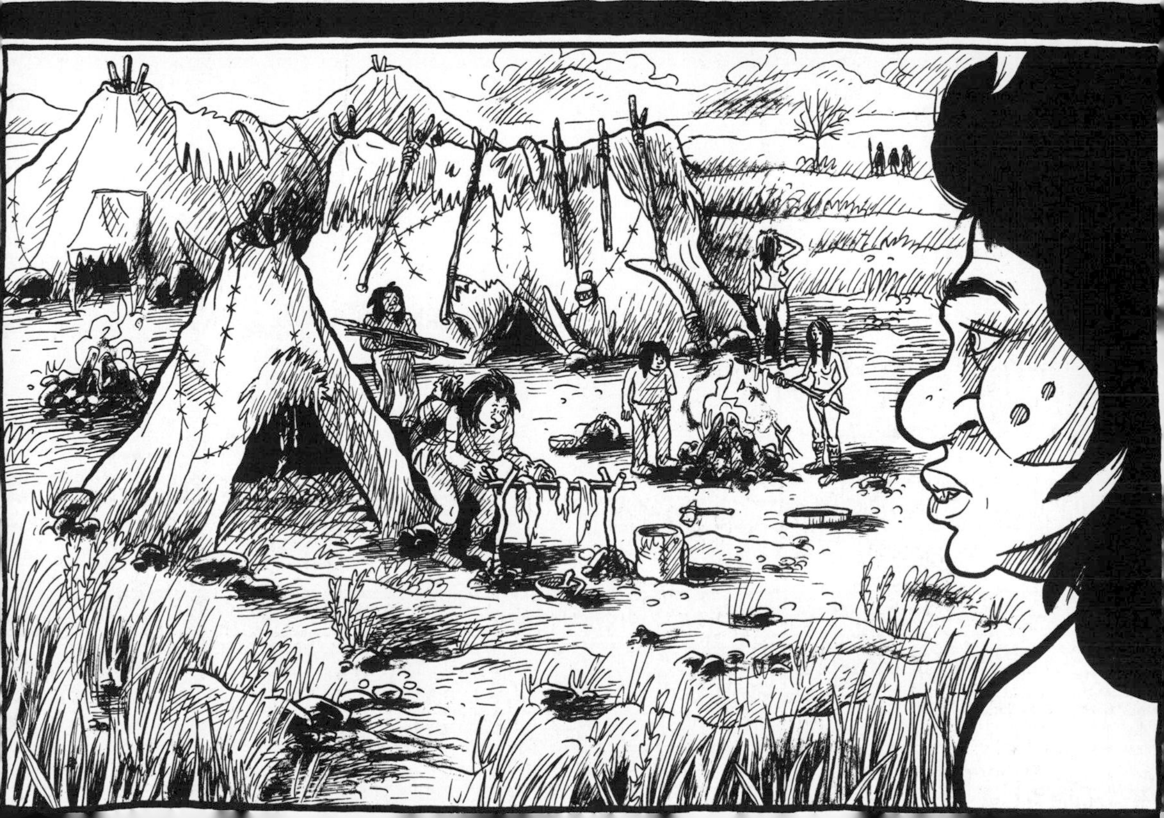

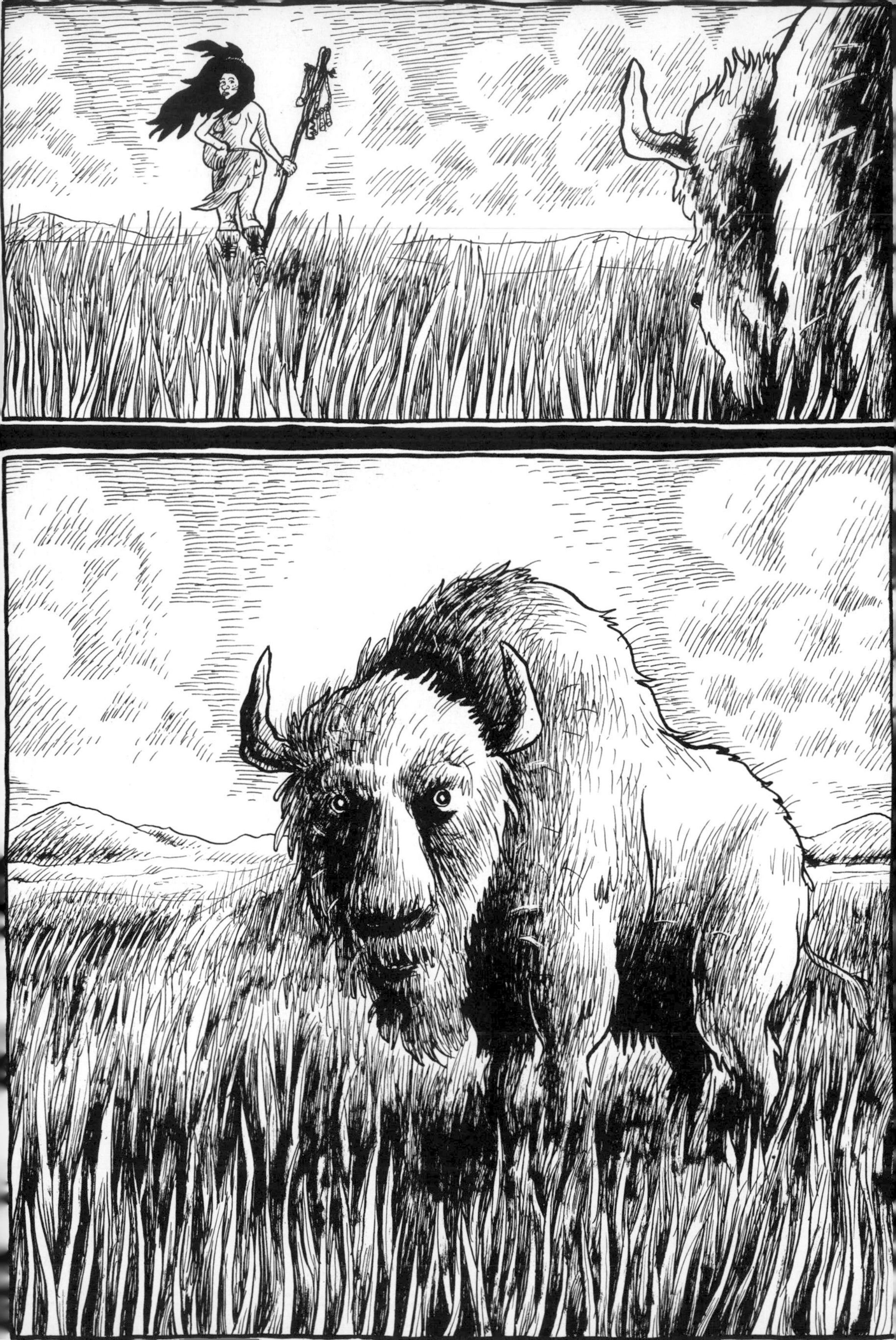

GENEALOGY

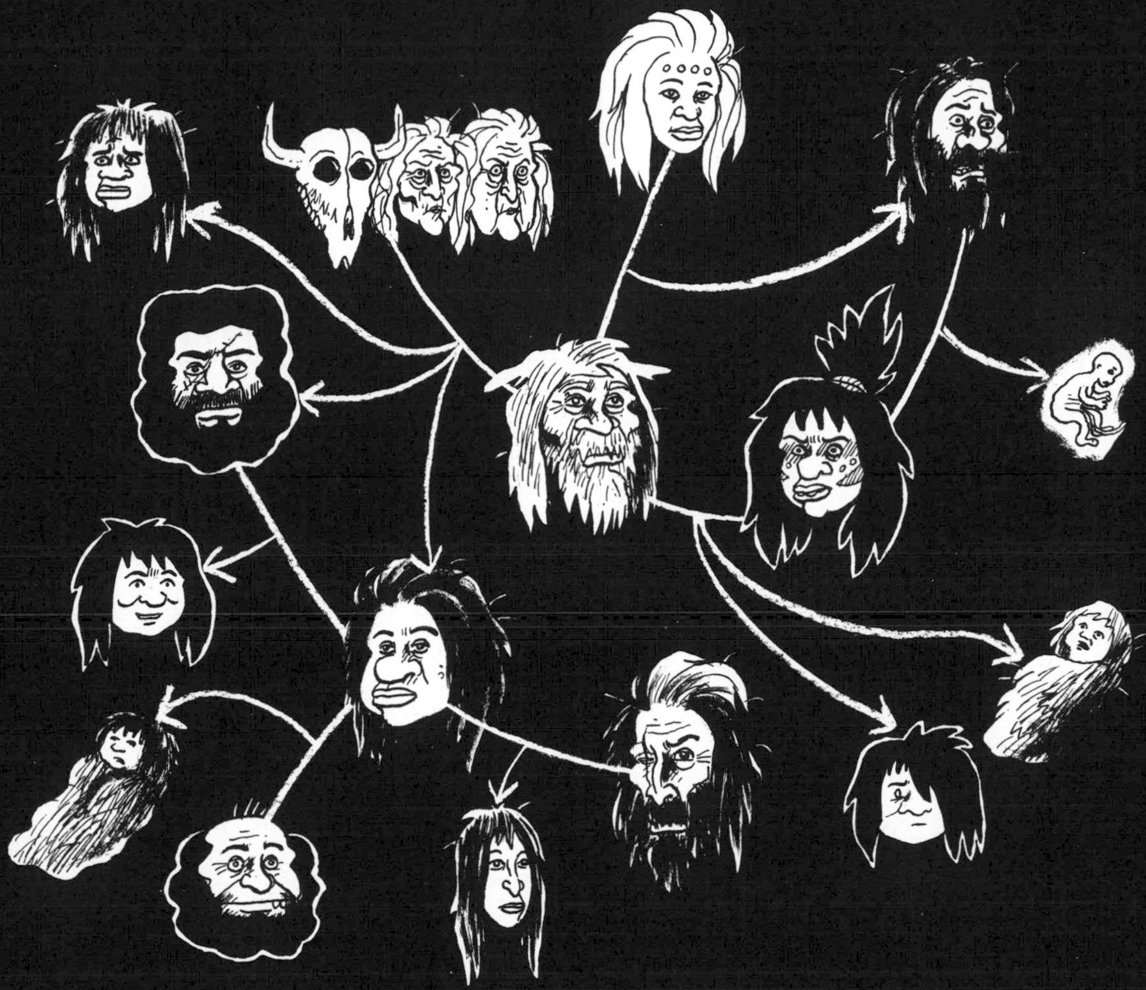

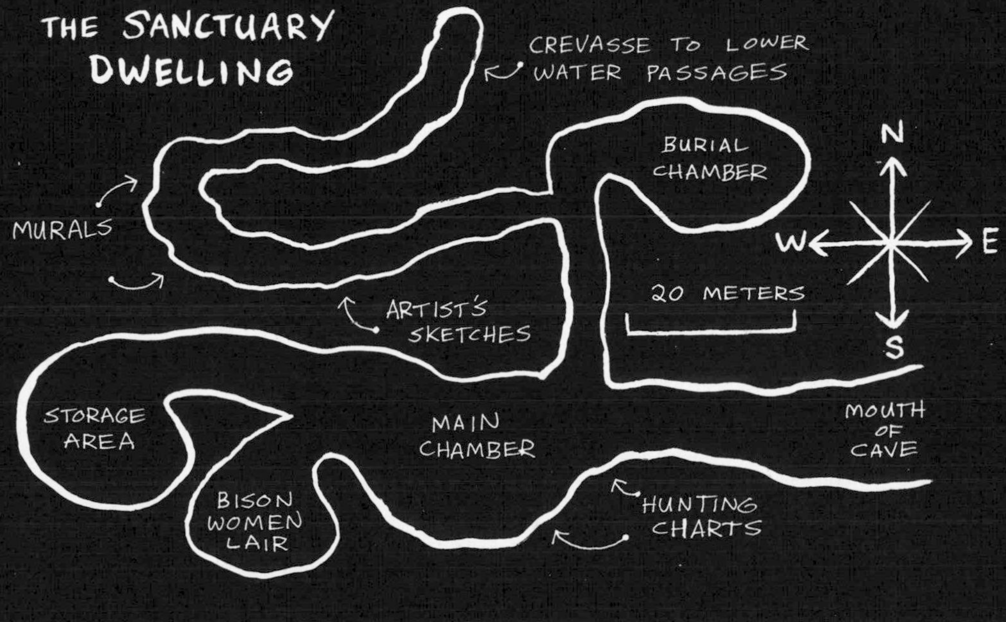
THE SANCTUARY DWELLING
CREVASSE TO LOWER WATER PASSAGES
BURIAL CHAMBER
N
W
E
S
MURALS
20 METERS
ARTIST'S SKETCHES
STORAGE AREA
MAIN CHAMBER
MOUTH OF CAVE
BISON WOMEN LAIR
HUNTING CHARTS

(SOMEWHERE IN EUROPE CIRCA 30,000 B.C....)

NATE NEAL WAS
BORN ON DECEMBER
NINTH, 1978 IN
SAGINAW, MICHIGAN
U.S.A. HE LIVES IN
BROOKLYN, NEW YORK.

THIS IS HIS FIRST
GRAPHIC NOVEL.

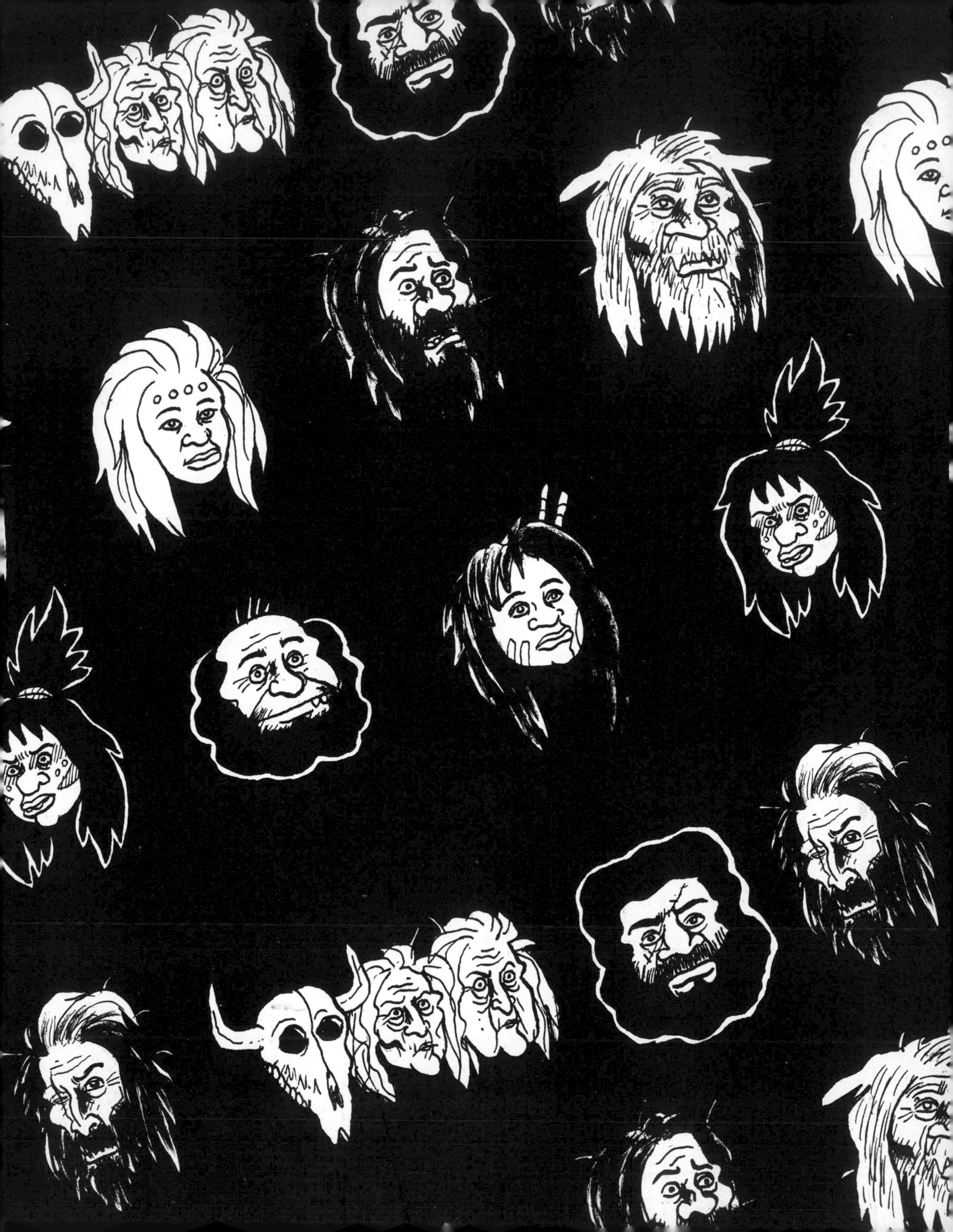